SCHOOL

General Editors: David Hop

THE SCHOOL, THE COMMUNITY AND LIFELONG LEARNING

THE SCHOOL, THE COMMUNITY AND LIFELONG LEARNING

Judith D. Chapman

and

David N. Aspin

CASSELL

London and Washington

Cassell

Wellington House
125 Strand
London WC2R 0BB

PO Box 605
Herndon
VA 20172

First published 1997

British Library Cataloguing-in-Publication Data
A catalogue record for this book is available from the British Library

ISBN 0–304–33282–8 (hardback)
     0–304–33285–2 (paperback)

Typeset by York House Typographic Ltd, London
Printed and bound in Great Britain by Redwood Books, Trowbridge, Wiltshire

This book is dedicated to Emma, Zoë, Martin, Tim and Peta –
our lifelong learners of the future.

Contents

Contents

Series Editors' Foreword

We are delighted that Judith Chapman and David Aspin's *The School, the Community and Lifelong Learning* is part of the Cassell School Development series. If ever there was one single issue that encapsulates the mission for school development, it is lifelong learning. The aspiration for school development is not just the achievement of students, but also their acquisition of a range of learning strategies that equip them for life beyond school. The success of a school should not be measured solely in terms of test scores and exam results, but should also involve the students' ability to emulate generations of lifelong learners. Although a worthy endeavour, this bold goal is, as Chapman and Aspin point out, not easily achieved. That is why their focus on community in both the title and the substance of the book is so important. Our own experience and research suggest that school development, and the increasing of levels of student achievement and learning, cannot be achieved without strategic and substantive community involvement. The crucial nexus in this is, as the authors point out, the dialectic between the school and the community.

Judith Chapman and David Aspin are well equipped to carry out the task of making these links, and establish the argument, review the research and policy context, and point to ways forward. As lifelong learners themselves, their enthusiasm for their subject shines through the book. In addition to this, they have been centrally involved in national and international studies of lifelong learning. This is particularly true of their work for the Organisation for Economic Cooperation and Development, and in that regard we are delighted that Malcolm Skilbeck has contributed a Preface to the book. *The School, the Community and Lifelong Learning* is an important work. It is comprehensive, incisive and passionate. In producing this book Judith Chapman and David Aspin have eloquently addressed issues at the core of school development.

David Hopkins
David Reynolds

Preface

For those who have had the good fortune of a sound basic education, acquiring the love of learning in childhood and youth, there has never been any question that education is lifelong. Such an education is basic precisely because it provides foundations and enduring stimulation of a lifetime's quest. A basic education depends upon a mastery of the tools of expression, communication and inquiry which goes well beyond the so-called 'basics' of popular belief – the 3 Rs. The foundation of lifelong learning must also include a challenging and engaging introduction to methods for acquiring, testing and using a range of different kinds of knowledge and practice and various ways of manipulating ideas and materials. Memorization, the practice of skills and the demonstration of competence in testing situations are a fundamental part of this but, when elevated into primary objectives and set at levels which many students cannot or will not master, they serve not as an entrée into the vestibule of learning but as doors shut hard against it.

As David Aspin and Judith Chapman point out, successful achievement of the extraordinarily ambitious aims of the lifelong learning movement requires that all children make a successful start. We still fall far short of this, despite universal provision of schooling and many forms of support for early childhood development. Formal schooling cannot be everything but the school certainly plays a key role in making or breaking the learning chain that we are seeking to extend from infancy to old age. Moreover, while parents, family, neighbours, peer groups and community all have roles to play, it is only the school, in our secular societies, which is a universal institution, constituting, for all its limitations, a formidable structure of experience, requirement, opportunity and challenge, whether for better or worse. By worse is meant the role the school does sometimes play in inhibiting learning and registering a sense of failure in children. This, at least, can be changed if we have the will to do so.

While the universal, compulsory school has proved its worth in the relatively short history of its existence, too many imperfections remain. Arguably the greatest is the school's failure, or apparent inability, to engage all children and youth in successful, fulfilling learning, learning that serves as a dynamo for currents that continue throughout life. The question to address is whether the school can continue to offer itself as the institution in society which will prepare all children and youth for a lifetime of learning. In answering positively, the authors of this book discuss the many changes that are needed not least in the public image and standing of the teaching profession.

With the active engagement of the community – and that is an essential condition – the school can reasonably maintain its mission of effective universal education. But to do so it must be prepared to undertake quite dramatic forms of self-appraisal and renewal. Just what this might entail has been the subject of intensive inquiry and debate, as is evident from the wide range of sources which David Aspin and Judith Chapman have consulted. They have drawn not only upon studies and reports of the intergovernmental organizations, but also upon the scholarly literature in the construction of a sustained argument for school reform and renewal.

After a bold, but in the event faltering, start several decades ago, the movement of lifelong learning for all is once again gathering momentum. In earlier times, the case as presented has been mainly educational – the development of persons; and social – the creation and recreation of communities. To these is now added an array of economic arguments in a context of gathering global competitiveness. Taken together, the arguments are compelling but the issue is deeper still. Never before in human history has it been so widely accepted that the worth and value of every human being is not a matter of declared rights, religious or moral affirmations – usually abridged in practice – but is a matter of practical policies for the conscious, deliberate, continuing educational development of the person and the community. The realization or achievement of this means a transformation of culture and the mobilization of the many different resources which have educational potential. It is thus not merely a matter of education responding to economic forces or to declared national priorities, necessary as these are. Strenuous, wide-ranging efforts continue to be required to build the educative society, which also functions as a productive, efficient economy yielding the means needed to live the good life.

The authors of this book recognize the need for profound changes in education but are not tempted to submerge the school beneath a tidal wave of technology-driven work and home-based autonomous learning. Such forms of learning have their place but they are no substitute for the careful nurturing of the propensity to learn and the structuring of experience – namely schooling – which the young will continue to require if the foundations are to be well laid. This book is an invitation to explore the challenges now falling upon the school as it assumes responsibility for its pivotal task in lifelong learning. To the timid and the backward-looking, it will appear unsettling or may seem far removed from the domestic affairs of the classroom. To those concerned about the future of the school and open to debate about the role of schooling in its relation to the directions society might be taking, the authors have posed many questions. Not content with questions, however, and drawing extensively on the frontiers of policy analysis and conceptual thinking, they have mapped the territory and drawn attention to the decisions which are now needed if the claims of lifelong learning are to become effective engines of policy and are to pervade the manifold practices of schooling.

Malcolm Skilbeck
30 December 1996

Acknowledgements

This book would not have been possible without the support and co-operation of:

- Bernadette Taylor, who assisted in the analysis of the implications of lifelong learning for principals, teachers and members of the school community;

- Lee Dale and Les Dale, who assisted in the collection of data on the changing relationships between school and community, funded by the Australian Research Council;

- Joan Addinsall and Peta Odgers, who assisted in the review of the literature;

- Heather Phillips and Robyn Wilson, who provided invaluable secretarial assistance;

- Members of the education profession and the broader education community in Australia, who generously shared their views on lifelong learning and the changing relationships in schooling;

- Members of the secretariat of Organisation for Economic Co-operation and Development (OECD): Abrar Hasan, Albert Tuijnman and Alan Wagner, who contributed significantly to the conceptualization of the work.

To each of the above we are sincerely grateful.

Sections of the book have been developed from our contribution to the OECD report *Realising a Lifelong Approach to Learning for All: A Review of OECD Work 1990–95* (Chapman and Aspin, 1995).

Judith Chapman and David Aspin

Part I

The Concern and the Concept

Chapter 1

The International Concern for Lifelong Learning

The provision of lifelong learning is by its very nature highly complex and multifaceted. In this book we have chosen to concentrate on one aspect of lifelong learning: the strengthening of the foundations of lifelong learning – providing young people with a good start to their lifelong learning through the agencies of school and community.

Although there has been a considerable increase in participation and completion rates of schooling during the past decade, many young people still leave school without the requisite qualifications, knowledge or skills for employment, and without the love of learning and the motivation to learn that is essential for further learning throughout the rest of their lives. These deficiencies have been identified as factors in the rise of unemployment among certain sections of our population, in dysfunctional social activities, and in limited lifelong learning opportunities for sizeable parts of the community. Provision of a broad-based, effective and equitable system of schooling at primary and secondary level, which establishes a strong foundation on which all young people are able to build, is now widely regarded as being essential for each individual's personal development and fulfilment and for an economically competitive, socially just and democratic society (OECD, Press Release, Paris, 17 January 1996).

In countries across the world there is concern about the capacity of schools and education systems to change, adapt and to provide an appropriate foundation for lifelong learning. In a context in which a multitude of factors is shaping the schools of tomorrow it is timely to review the ways in which schools are organized, the nature of curriculum content and modes of delivery, the design and location of places for learning, and the integration of new information technologies into the overall educational enterprise. In such an environment we are forced to evaluate and reassess the role of schools in our society, to reconsider relationships between schools, parents, business and commerce, and constituencies in culture and the arts, and to reconceptualize new roles and functions for educating institutions. Not least of these is the notion of *schools as community learning centres* offering a range of learning opportunities to all members of a learning society.

In the light of these considerations the objectives of this book are:

1 To identify major issues pertaining to a lifelong approach to learning and to identify how the concept of lifelong learning might be operationalized in ways that give a more concrete and specific orientation to the ideal of high quality education and training for all.

2 To lay out the problems which might be encountered in the implementation of lifelong learning, particularly during the years of compulsory schooling, and to identify new directions in policy and practice.

3 To identify the range and nature of the relationships subsisting between schools, government agencies of all kinds, and all the various interested constituencies in the community, as they seek to achieve the objectives of lifelong learning for all.

THE INTERNATIONAL CONTEXT

The topic of lifelong learning has assumed immense importance in the discourse and policies of a number of bodies and agencies across the international arena. An increasing number of countries and governments have concluded that a lifelong approach to learning should be instituted and deployed as one of the main lines of attack on some of the major problems needing to be addressed as we approach the turn of the twentieth into the twenty-first century. The deliberations of OECD, UNESCO, the European Parliament and the Nordic Council of Ministers reveal a commitment to policies of learning across the life-span, which are meant to be proactive and prophylactic. Today continued access to education and training for all a country's citizens is seen as an investment in the future, a precondition for economic advance, democracy, social cohesion and personal growth.

MAKING LIFELONG LEARNING A REALITY FOR ALL: THE COMMITMENT ACROSS OECD COUNTRIES

The Current Concern

In January 1996 education ministers from across OECD countries met to consider how learning must be adapted to the evolving needs of an increasingly global and information-based economy. Their theme was: 'Making Lifelong Learning a Reality for All'. The focus of their meeting was directed at the ways in which education could be made to be a lifelong process, with learning being provided in schools, the workplace and many other settings. Recognizing that the implementation of lifelong learning involves many other parts of government and society, the education ministers from the OECD member countries were concerned to identify ways of developing policies that would foster 'learning societies' based on the acceptance of a new philosophy of education, with new roles and responsibilities assigned to those within and beyond the world of schools, universities and other traditional providers of learning.

Member countries were agreed on the overall challenge: to make lifelong learning a reality for all people by realizing possibilities for learning to continue throughout people's lives – from education in early childhood to learning in retirement. By reviewing targets and options, ministers sought to define new directions for education policy, in which opportunities for learning could be created for people of all ages, not merely by public education authorities but also by all those who have an interest in lifelong learning, pursuing a common strategy. There was widespread agreement that a new focus for education and training policies is needed, to develop capacities to exploit the opportunities offered by the extension, growth and increasing flexibility of the global knowledge and information economy. At the same time as seeking to capitalize upon these economic opportunities, ministers were concerned to promote, through education, social goals that were, in their view, equally important: social inclusiveness, democratic participation, and individual growth and fulfilment for all citizens.

In their attempt to determine how the concept of lifelong learning could be given practical shape, the ministers identified and concentrated on three particular aspects of education and training systems:

- Ensuring that the foundations for lifelong learning enable all learners to obtain the academic and vocational qualifications they need for work and further learning;

- Improving the transitions and pathways between education and work, the transition from school to work and higher education, and the nature and extent of learning opportunities for adults;

- Reconceptualizing the roles and responsibilities of all partners – including governments and learners themselves – in implementing and financing lifelong learning.

At the conclusion of their deliberations the chair of the meeting, the Honourable Simon Crean, the then Australian Minister of Employment, Education and Training, issued the following statement (OECD, Press Release, Paris, 17 January 1996):

We are all convinced of the crucial importance of learning throughout life for enriching personal lives, fostering economic growth and maintaining social cohesion and we have agreed on strategies to implement it. OECD societies have made great strides during the 1990s, but now we need to find more effective ways of offering everyone of our citizens such an opportunity. The target may be ambitious, but we cannot afford not to work towards it.

OECD ministers jointly committed themselves to taking action which they were confident would usher in a new era of lifelong learning for all. Such action included:

- Strengthening the foundations for learning throughout life, by improving access to early childhood education, particularly for disadvantaged children, revitalizing schools and supporting the growth of other formal and non-formal learning arrangements;

- Promoting coherent links between learning and work, by establishing pathways and bridges that will facilitate more flexible movement between education, training and work, aimed in particular at smoothing the initial transition between the two, and by improving the mechanisms for assessing and recognizing the skills and competences of individuals – whether they are acquired through formal or non-formal learning;

- Rethinking the roles and responsibilities of all partners – including governments – who provide opportunities for learning;
- Creating incentives for individuals, employers and those who provide education and training to invest in lifelong learning and to deliver value for money.

The goals of future economic prosperity, social and political cohesion, and the achievement of genuinely democratic societies with full participation all depended, the ministers concluded, on a well-educated population. Governments of OECD member countries committed themselves to seeking to establish an environment that encourages individuals to take greater responsibility for their own and their children's learning and to promoting real commitment by all partners – including the co-operation of different government ministries – to implement coherent, equitable and cost-effective programmes that will cover the needs of all for high quality learning across the lifespan.

A Link with the Past

Promoting lifelong learning in societies that are becoming dominated by information and knowledge has been a recurring theme in OECD policy discussions for a number of years.

In 1990 when the Education Committee of the OECD met at ministerial level to review education and training policies and their interaction with the economy and society more broadly, their overall theme was 'High Quality Education and Training for All'. The emphasis on 'quality' underlined the key role that learning plays in sustaining economic, social, cultural and political well-being. The emphasis on learning 'for all' recognized that education is a presupposition of and a prerequisite for effective and equitable participation in society.

At the ministerial meeting in 1990 ministers identified the following eleven aims and orientations in education and training as common across OECD countries (OECD, 1992, p. 33).

1 A high quality start to lifelong learning – the crucial role of initial education and training

It was agreed that all young people should have access to opportunities for education and training – both general and vocational – that could provide a solid foundation and preparation for adult and working life. Effective schooling should build upon the highly influential pre-school years and should lay the foundation and offer incentives for continued lifelong learning in all post-compulsory and post-secondary educational settings. Effectiveness in educational outcomes was seen to be strengthened in and through close partnership with parents, the local community, the employment sector, other public and private agencies and various community, social and cultural institutions.

2 Quality and access in a lifelong perspective

Quality provision was seen to be as much a feature of vocational programmes, higher education, enterprise training, and adult education, as of schooling. The diverse approaches to, and modes and deliveries of, quality outcomes in different programmes and settings were seen as arising from and constituting a comprehensive array of opportunities to meet the multitude of learning needs of all people. It was argued that quality provision must be extensive and diverse and access to it widened. Ministers agreed that the growing and more diverse demands on the non-schooling sector call for continuing review of its structures, funding and performance.

3 Education 'for all' and the priority for the educationally under-served

To extend the benefits of education to all was deemed to be as important for educating people to meet the demands of the economy as it is for achieving the social goals of increasing social inclusiveness and educational equity. 'Education for all' entails targeting the provision of education and training to all those capable of benefiting from it; this includes providing for the needs of the different groups of under-served students – those with disabilities; minority groups; the socially deprived; adults threatened by unemployment and the already jobless; women returning to employment; and inhabitants of rural or isolated communities. It was agreed that a universal problem found to occur throughout all countries is that those with low initial education attainment levels tend not to be those who are returning to organized learning – participation by adults in further education activities throughout the lifespan continues to be dominated by the already educated. In the provision of education 'for all' measures need to be taken to encourage and enable all people actively to learn throughout their lives.

4 Overcoming illiteracy

The continued existence of illiteracy, whether defined in the traditional sense or in a new sense generated by scientific or technological change, was deemed to be unacceptable. A minimum measure of the success of schools should be that all students have mastered such a degree of the various forms of literacy as permits them to participate effectively in society and the economy. Post-compulsory and continuing education as well as the employment sector were seen as having a responsibility to ensure that literacy skills are maintained and improved.

5 The need for coherence and focus in educational provision to avoid curriculum overload

The increasingly rapid growth of knowledge, the broadening range of the clientele and the diverse responsibilities of education, in all its various institutional forms, highlighted the need for curriculum reform. However, it was argued that to avoid the dangers of epistemic incoherence and curriculum overload, the special tasks and missions of each level of the education and training sectors should be clarified. This would incorporate a review of what should be included in the foundations of initial education and training and what should be postponed to subsequent further, higher, and recurrent education and training provision.

6 Improving the quality and attractiveness of teaching in education and training

The presence and activity of expert, well-motivated, and flexible teaching staff was identified as the most vital component of high quality provision, whether in schools, vocational, further or higher education, or in other forms of organized learning. Improvements in rewards, career opportunities, initial and in-service preparation, status and prestige were identified as ways of ensuring the recruitment and retention of high quality teachers.

7 Information and data – preconditions for sound decision-making

It was agreed that information and data needed to be collected and made more readily available to assist decision-making at all levels. Well-developed information and guidance systems setting out possible career paths, qualifications and ranges of options required were seen as necessary for pupils, students, trainees, parents, the employment sector and the wider community. To this end, the potential of information and communication technologies should be further extended and exploited. As functional prerequisites of accountability and informed policy debate, ministers believed that sound comprehensive education and training statistics needed to be developed, especially in the areas of early childhood, private education, labour market and enterprise training and adult education.

8 Evaluation and assessment – identifying progress, diagnosing problems

The evaluation and assessment of students, trainees, institutions, and education systems as a whole was considered to be an integral component of policy and practice. Ministers believed it was important that procedures for student assessment should be sensitive to curricular goals and that procedures for teacher assessment should have as their foremost objective the increase of professionalism. Public forms of student assessment should provide clear information about the positive accomplishments of students that is useful to all. The employment sector in turn should play an active part in the design and updating of qualifications.

9 Research and innovation need further development

A need was identified for more R&D in education, and for this to be grounded in practice, involving staff and institutions in a constant process of diagnosis, comparison and analysis.

10 Enhancing the international dimension of education and training policies

It was agreed that increasing political, economic and cultural interdependence among countries and the mobility of skills and employment opportunities calls for close attention to be given to cross-national comparability and transfer-ability of qualifications and the possibility of access to and exchange of suitably qualified personnel.

11 Financing high quality education and training for all

Realizing high quality education and training for all was seen to depend fundamentally on adequate investment in the education and training of the young and in the recurrent education and training of adults. Ministers agreed that new approaches to the financing of education and training must be considered, in which contributions from all the different elements, sectors and agencies – public, private, national, regional and local, individual and institutional as well as the employment sector – must be taken into account.

The ministers concluded that the various challenges of the twenty-first century for the provision of high quality education and training opportunities should not be met with an excessively narrow educational approach, nor by carrying forward the spirit of 'more of the same'. Policies and programmes organized by the established education and training authorities would need to be actively co-ordinated and developed in partnership with all the other formal, non-formal and alternative sources and agencies of learning, as we move towards 'learning societies' embracing all forms of education and training and providing diverse opportunities for learning by all members of society on a lifelong basis. Of this undertaking the ministers concluded that: 'This is not solely for governments; the roles and responsibilities – for the different author-ities, the social partners, and individuals – may need to be redefined. The aim is to encourage all individuals to learn actively and continuously throughout their lives' (OECD, *High Quality Education and Training for All*, 1992, p. 36).

It is important to note that, in their conclusions to their meeting in 1990, the OECD ministers of education did not suggest or even imply any relative downgrading of the education provided for children and the young in favour of an increased provision of learning opportunities for their elders. Instead they envisaged a way forward which would improve current policies and practices of initial and recurrent education and training, in ways which recognize and reinforce the special purposes and complementarities between all sectors and agencies in society concerned with the provision of high quality education and training for all.

The Situation Today

There have, of course, been a number of critical changes in the educational landscape in all OECD countries since the beginning of the 1990s. Today education and training, and the notion, value and ideals of lifelong learning, have come to be conceptualized and appraised in a very wide-ranging and sophisticated manner. This has come about as a result of our increased aware-ness of the much greater complexity and heterogeneity of the factors operating in and directing all these matters, and of our appreciation of the need for an increased breadth and depth of understanding concerning the nature, aims and purposes of education and training programmes in the current economic, social and cultural environment.

As we approach the turn of the century, policy-makers, administrators and school-based personnel have begun to grapple with the complexity of realizing lifelong education for all. They have begun to seek answers to such questions as the following:

- How can the targets of high quality education and training for all be realized through a strategy of lifelong learning that is designed to promote both social and economic goals?

- How might the realization of a lifelong approach to learning open up participation in the knowledge-based economy, promoting a high-skills, high-wage job strategy and overcoming structural barriers to economic growth and job creation?

- How might lifelong learning promote social inclusion and sustain and develop democracy? How might policy-makers devise and manage an effective education and training strategy for lifelong learning as part of a coherent and integrated approach to a wide range of policy areas that include economic, labour market and social policies?

As we approach the end of the twentieth century these are the sorts of questions and concerns which are serving as a point of departure as ministers of education from OECD member countries attempt to address the challenge of 'Realising a Lifelong Approach to Learning for All'. But these are challenges that face not only OECD countries: they face all countries in the world.

LEARNING THROUGHOUT LIFE: THE UNESCO COMMISSION ON LEARNING IN THE TWENTY-FIRST CENTURY

UNESCO has also taken the opportunity afforded by the approach of the new millennium to conduct a major inquiry into education.

The work of the UNESCO International Commission on 'Education in the Twenty-First Century' took as its starting-point a consideration of the needs of education in a context of worldwide interdependence and globalization. In this context, according to the UNESCO Commission, developing countries are feeling: 'uneasiness engendered by the indecipherable nature of the future ... combined with ever sharper awareness of the huge disparities existing in the world' (UNESCO, 1996, p. 47).

A number of major tensions were identified by the UNESCO commissioners as lying at the heart of the problems of conceptualizing and realizing goals for education and society in the twenty-first century. Such tensions include:

- the tension between the global and the local;

- the tension between the universal and the individual;

- the tension between tradition and modernity;

- the tension between long-term and short-term considerations;

- the tension between the need for competition and concern for equality of opportunity;
- the tension between the expansion of knowledge and human beings' capacity to assimilate it;
- the tension between the spiritual and the material.

Of particular concern to the Commission was:

> the major danger of a gulf opening up between a minority of people who are capable of finding their way successfully about this new world that is coming into being and the majority who feel that they are at the mercy of events and have no say in the future of society, with the dangers that entails of a setback to democracy and widespread revolt.
>
> (UNESCO, 1996, p. 51)

In their report *Learning: The Treasure Within*, the commissioners focused their recommendations on the concept of learning throughout life, claiming that that concept emerges as one of the keys to education in the twenty-first century (UNESCO, 1996, p. 23). Learning throughout life, the commissioners argued:

> makes it possible to organise the various stages of education to provide for passage from one stage to another to diversify the paths through the system while enhancing the value of each. This could be a way of avoiding the invidious choice between selection by ability, which increases the number of academic failures and the risk of exclusion, and the same education for all, which can inhibit talent.
>
> (UNESCO, 1996, p. 24)

In a world in which rapid change and globalization were seen as transforming each individual's relationship with time and space, learning throughout life was seen as essential for people to retain mastery of their own destinies (UNESCO, 1996, p. 101). Four pillars were proposed as foundations of education throughout life: learning to know; learning to do; learning to live together; and learning to be. These four pillars reflect UNESCO's newer, more broadened conception of the notion of lifelong learning:

> Not only must it adapt to changes in the nature of work, but it must also constitute a continuous process of forming whole human beings – their knowledge and aptitudes, as well as the critical faculty and ability to act. It should enable people to develop awareness of themselves and their environment and encourage them to play their social role at work and in the community.
>
> (UNESCO, 1996, p. 21)

In common with the conclusions of education ministers of OECD member countries, the UNESCO commissioners' call for a commitment to lifelong learning involves no downgrading of their commitment to the right of all people to a sound basic education offered through the formal education system. The right to a basic education was firmly established as a 'passport to life' (UNESCO, 1996, p. 117) and as a means of granting access to continuing learning experiences across the life-span.

Acknowledging the accelerated pace of population growth in many developing countries, the wastage of natural resources, environmental damage, the chronic poverty and the oppression and injustice from which millions still suffer, the UNESCO commissioners concluded their deliberations with a call for a shift in the conception and functions of international aid, a closer examination of recent experiments in swapping debts for education programmes, and stronger partnerships between industrialized countries and developing countries.

In their conclusions stated in *Learning: The Treasure Within* the UNESCO commissioners reiterated and underlined the importance placed by the World Summit for Social Development held in Copenhagen in March 1995 on education and its role in dealing with poverty, unemployment and social exclusion. They also confirmed their acceptance of the Declaration adopted by the Fourth World Conference on Women (in Beijing, in 1995) on the importance of ensuring equal access by women to education; of eradicating female illiteracy; and of improving access for women to vocational training, science and technology education and continuing education.

The dissemination and implementation of the concept of learning throughout life was deemed by the Commissioners to be an *ethical imperative*, one in support of which UNESCO was prepared fully to exert its moral authority in the interests of promoting sustainable development, ensuring social cohesion, encouraging democratic participation at every level, and establishing a genuine culture of peace (UNESCO, 1996, p. 188).

THE EUROPEAN YEAR OF LIFELONG LEARNING: THE EUROPEAN PARLIAMENT AND COUNCIL OF MINISTERS

The European Parliament and Council of the European Union proclaimed 1996 the 'European Year of Lifelong Learning'.

This proclamation was set in a context in which the European Parliament viewed changes in lifestyles and in individual and collective patterns of behaviour as generating new education and training requirements. The emergence of new jobs and changes in production cycles as a result of new technologies and new configurations of work organization were considered as necessitating substantial expansion and change in the knowledge and skills required of workers. According to the European Parliament's White Paper *Growth, Competitiveness and Employment*, more than two million new jobs, linked with technological revolutions in the audiovisual sector and the information society, would be created in Europe by the year 2000. Lifelong learning thus becomes fundamental in enhancing long-term employment prospects for individuals. The White Paper on *Growth, Competitiveness and Employment* also stresses that education and training will play a crucial role in the renewal of national economic growth, the recovery of competitiveness, and the restoration of a socially acceptable level of employment.

The European ministers expressed concern over the scale of unemployment currently affecting young people and adults. This they saw would bring risks of the increase of dysfunctional social phenomena: social conflict, xenophobia, alcohol and drug-abuse, and a willingness on the part of some to resort to violence. In this context the importance of the purposes of lifelong education was affirmed:

> to develop each individual's personality, to teach values of private, social and public life as solidarity, tolerance and understanding of cultural diversity, to promote the ability of various cultural groups to communicate and to promote the involvement of all the citizens of Europe in democratic decision making.
>
> (European Parliament, 1995, p. 2)

Ministers were particularly concerned that long-term unemployment runs the risk of generating an attitude of scepticism towards education and training, that might well undermine and jeopardize people's confidence in the value of lifelong learning. The Year of Lifelong Learning was, in their view, intended not only to lay down the essential requirements and long-term objectives for measures and policies for lifelong learning but to create an awareness and send important signals regarding the importance of lifelong learning, through the means of community-wide information and promotional campaigns.

European ministers pointed out that, with the increasing emphasis on education across the life-span, the promotion needed for non-school education should not be funded at the expense of broadly based initial education. To ensure that educational provision across the life-span could be adequately financed the ministers advocated an examination of fiscal and other incentives with a view to securing investment by businesses and private individuals particularly in continuing education for the development of lifelong learning opportunities for adults.

Stress was placed on the importance of the Year of Lifelong Learning providing an opportunity for social partners to explore areas of mutual interest and to develop collective arrangements for investment, the exchange of ideas and the dissemination of good practice.

The objectives of the European Parliament in establishing the European Year of Lifelong Learning included:

- To make the European public aware of the importance of lifelong learning as a key factor in the personal development of individuals and in their participation in the democratic decision-making processes.

- To foster better co-operation at all levels between education and training structures and the business community.

- To contribute to European competitiveness and to an employment-intensive economic growth by promoting awareness amongst the social partners of the importance of creating opportunities for lifelong learning to meet the challenges of economic and social change.

- To emphasize the importance of providing access to lifelong learning and appropriate accredited systems for all regardless of difference in sex, age, ability, ethnic, economic and social background with a view to ending the waste of talent, combating social exclusion, giving girls and women a wider choice of occupations and eliminating regional disparities.

- To encourage parents and education authorities to shoulder their responsibility for the education and training of children and young people in a context of lifelong learning.

Fundamental to the European Parliament's establishment of 1996 as the European Year of Lifelong Learning was a belief in the fundamental importance of education and training for the construction of a Europe which is economically competitive and socially anchored in solidarity and in the encouragement of individual fulfilment. The continuing adaptation of education and training systems was seen as of major strategic importance to Europe at a time when its economic competitiveness and social model had come to be based on knowledge and know-how (European Parliament, 1995).

LIFELONG LEARNING FOR ALL: THE NORDIC COUNCIL OF MINISTERS

Perhaps some of the most enlightened thinking on the matter of lifelong learning has found expression in the report of a Think Tank established by the Nordic Council of Ministers and published in 1995 under the title *The Golden Riches in the Grass*.

The Nordic Council of Ministers' consideration of education arose from a concern to meet their countries' and region's various economic and political needs while developing and safeguarding their social values in the face of intense global competition and an element of uncertainty extending to ethics and norms:

> Lifelong learning for all constitutes a vital challenge for the growth and development of Nordic society ... Lifelong learning for all can perhaps ... become the Nordic region's most effective response to the changes which pose a threat to our competitiveness, our welfare societies and many of our democratic values. It can give us a competitive edge ... and serve as a model for the world beyond our border.
>
> (Nordic Council of Ministers, 1995, p. 13)

The Nordic Council of Ministers have a strong position regarding the type of development that they deem suitable for the information society and the Nordic model of democracy. This position has clear implications for any approach to lifelong learning:

> the ability to maintain the competitive edge of our firms and to keep abreast of developments, growth in assets and renewal on the open, international market is a *prior requirement* for the survival of the Nordic welfare societies. A necessary condition, but not the *sufficient* or adequate condition ... We must steer the development of the information society away from its inherent risks: technocratic dehumanisation and the divided society.
>
> (Nordic Council of Ministers, 1995, p. 17)

The implications of this for the Nordic approach to lifelong learning are clearly articulated as uniting the instrumental approach to life qualifications with the existential (Nordic Council of Ministers, 1995, p. 22). The key signal, it is maintained, is that people should be 'ready for action'. Learning is not conceived of as consisting solely of the acquisition of the knowledge and skills required to adapt to and cope with change. Lifelong learning must provide people with the resources that enable them to participate in the changes, developing personal resources so that each person is able to be involved in change and mould the pattern of development – at the work-place, in society and at the personal level.

The recommendations contained within *The Golden Riches in the Grass* call for added measures of both techno-scientific knowledge and more general knowledge in the arts/humanities to be included in any curriculum for lifelong learning designed to achieve favourable socio-economic conditions and balanced growth. In addition the recommendations call for a more self-steered, experience-based approach to learning, particularly among adult learners.

In their deliberations, the Nordic Council of Ministers addressed directly the question of whether there are gains to be made from opting for more schooling rather than unemployment. In response they took the position that more education, training and personal development for all will lead to increased and improved opportunities for the unemployed and less risk of polarization and social marginalization. The 'underconsumption' of people's capacity for work, it was argued, posed the greatest threat to the social balance:

> All citizens must be given an opportunity for all-round development –
> every day. Without a clear picture of the pattern of one's own life, one
> becomes a prisoner of one's repressed feelings or specialised technical
> knowledge ... If we lack self reliance and self respect, then we lack the
> basis for knowing and appreciating others. This means that we lack the
> foundations of a balanced society.
>
> (Nordic Council of Ministers, 1995, p. 89)

The Nordic Council draw their conclusions from and place confidence in people's capacity to exert influence on the future. The potential of the techno-logical revolution, they argue, will not lead to jobs and growth unless it is matched by higher levels of competence:

> Growth is no longer based on cheaper goods and services. Today
> economists are discussing a new theory of growth, where economic
> growth is based on people's ability constantly to produce thoughts and
> ideas which are rapidly transmitted to every part of the world. These
> thoughts and ideas stimulate further efforts and development. Economic
> growth is becoming a learning process. The more complex and
> knowledge intensive production is, the more motivation and creativity
> are demanded of all employees, if high quality criteria are to be met.
> This means that competence is the key to meeting the demands and
> challenges of the future ... We need a conscious strategy throughout the
> Nordic region if we are to become capable of harvesting the riches of 'the

golden tables mid the grass', turning knowledge and competence into a platform for growth.

(Nordic Council of Ministers, 1995, p. 106)

CONCLUSION

Perusal of the above reveals a number of themes running through the work of international agencies: the emergence of an awareness of the importance of the notions of the knowledge economy and the learning society; an acceptance of the need for a new philosophy of education and training, with institutions of all kinds – formal and informal, traditional and alternative, public and private – having new roles and responsibilities for learning; the necessity of ensuring that the foundations for lifelong learning are set in place for all citizens during the compulsory years of schooling; the need to promote a multiple and coherent set of links, pathways and articulations between schooling, work, further education and other agencies offering opportunities for learning across the life-span; the importance of governments providing incentives for individuals, employers, and the range of social partners with a commitment to learning, to invest in lifelong learning; and the need to ensure that emphasis upon lifelong learning does not reinforce existing patterns of privilege and widen the existing gap between the advantaged and the disadvantaged, simply on the basis of access to education.

It is clear that there is widespread agreement about the need and justification for the institution, continuation or confirmation of policies of lifelong learning for all. As a reading of the documents emerging from the deliberations of international agencies and national governments reveals, however, whilst there is on the part of many governments and government authorities a sincere commitment to the ideal of 'lifelong learning', there is much less clarity and uniformity about the ways in which the term itself is understood. Differences of opinion over the meaning and remit of the term become manifest, not merely in the justificatory arguments employed for it, but also in the policies developed for its implementation. Where the commitments of governments to the ideal of lifelong learning will very likely involve the expenditure of substantial amounts of public funds, it is obviously important that such expenditures should be supported with the clearest possible understanding and agreement as to what is being done in the name of the public interest and in the realization of the aim of lifelong learning for all.

In the next chapter we attempt to chart the logical geography of the concept of lifelong learning and to offer some clarification of the various conceptions, interpretations and justificatory arguments that have been put forward for it, as a basis for laying down our approach to the consideration of what we see as the main topics, issues and problems to which policies of lifelong learning may provide some answers.

Chapter 2

Lifelong Learning for All: Concept and Conceptions

The idea of 'lifelong learning for all', and an affirmation of the need for a continuing generation and distribution of knowledge, skills and competences throughout a country's population, has become an important focus for policy-makers in many countries today. The attention that is being paid to this notion is a function of governments' belief that their policies for education and training will have a considerable impact on economic competitiveness and labour market performance and on what they regard as fundamental social, political and cultural objectives.

Factors such as the changing nature and patterns of employment, the changing structure of the family and the nature of family relationships, population and demographic change, labour force participation rates, changing types of jobs and their availability, changes in work-place skills and competences, technological change, and globalization – these have all been observed as matters of considerable moment, with wide-ranging implications for education.

In view of the significance attached to such phenomena many governments have developed and issued a number of education and training imperatives that go above and beyond the possibilities of their being addressed simply within the confines and time-scales of traditional patterns of learning, and education and training provision. It is in the context of large-scale economic and social change that work undertaken by many governments has underlined the need for all a country's citizens to have access to and engage in lifelong learning.

This is not to say, however, that there has been little previous attack on this problem. On the contrary, international agencies such as OECD and UNESCO have been engaged in the analysis and discussion of the idea of 'lifelong learning' for many years. The concept of 'recurrent education', for example, as a proposed *entitlement* that would give adults as well as young people the opportunities for personal fulfilment and professional improvement, that result from further learning, figured large in the activities of the OECD and UNESCO during the 1970s. That concern has not disappeared. More recently, however, the notion of 'lifelong learning' has taken on a far more complex and protean character, especially in policy discussions.

In seeking to become clear about what might be meant by the idea of 'lifelong learning for all', and what might be some of the justifications for current government emphasis upon it, those of an enquiring and critical turn of mind might think it worthwhile to pose some preliminary questions. These could well include such queries as the following (cf. Chapman and Aspin, 1995b):

- What is meant by 'lifelong learning' for all?

- How has this concept changed since earlier proposals for the introduction of *'education permanente'* and recurrent education in the early 1970s?

- What are the values implicit in the idea of lifelong learning?

- Why is 'lifelong learning for all' being advocated as a strategy for addressing larger social and economic problems currently besetting many countries around the world?

- Why has lifelong learning been advocated as an element of a high-skills, high-wage jobs strategy, and how does this fit in with the larger visions that governments and educational agencies and services might have about future needs for and developments in economic, educational and social policy generally?

- What are the objectives which lifelong learning should serve?

- Why have many governments argued for a 'lifelong learning' approach in the past and why is this notion not yet a fully developed reality?

- How can the more multifaceted notion of 'lifelong learning for all' be conceptualized in such a way that policy can be developed in a more coherent and integrated manner, in order to achieve the larger vision that has been clearly implicit in government discussions on this matter?

These are some of the questions which will guide our discussion in this chapter.

THE CONCEPT OF 'LIFELONG LEARNING' FOR ALL

Although the term 'lifelong learning' is used in a wide variety of contexts and has a wide currency, its meaning is often unclear. It is perhaps for that reason that its operationalization and implementation is not widely practised or achieved and such application as it has had is to be found primarily on a piecemeal basis.

Indeed Gelpi, one of the early writers on the topic (Gelpi, 1984), bemoaned the lack of conceptual clarity and argued that there was a need for a clear definition of the topic. The problem, he maintained, was that, while one could be reasonably clear about the meaning and applicability of such terms as 'vocational education', 'technical education' and 'nurse education', no such clarity subsisted in the case of terms with much less specific points of application, such as 'lifelong education', particularly when a range of other apparently similar terms – *'education permanente'*, 'further education', 'continuing education' – were often used interchangeably with it and with each other.

Others have maintained that there is no use in applying the term 'lifelong education', claiming that such a term seeks to generalize the reference of the notion of 'education' to such a wide set of parameters as virtually to empty it of all meaning. Still others have acted as though the term 'lifelong education' were simply another way of alluding to those educational endeavours and opportunities that were offered after the end of formal schooling and thus was interchangeable and synonymous with terms that had wider currency, such as 'adult education', 'careers education' or 'recurrent education' (Stock, 1979).

Yet another group will remark that, while there may be enough examples around in the history of educational philosophy of such key ideas as 'liberal education' or 'moral education' to offer discussants a reasonably firm point of purchase, there is so little said about 'lifelong education' in the educational literature and discourse generally that there is almost nothing on which we can get a grip in our attempts to give a clear account of those elements that we may discern as being cardinal to or indicative of its meaning and application.

Bagnall highlights the various differences in approaches when he notes (Bagnall, 1990) that at least four main functions for the notion of 'lifelong education' have been assigned in the literature:

- the preparation of individuals *for* the management of their adult lives (J.P. White, 1982);

- the distribution of education *throughout* an individual's life-span (Kulich, 1982);

- the educative function *of* the whole of one's life experience (Peña-Borrero, 1984); and

- the identification of education *with* the whole of life (Lengrand, 1979).

Furthermore, Bagnall identifies another interpretation as constituting what he calls 'the Programme of Lifelong Education':

> that particular programmatic use of the term which has been developed through and in association with the UNESCO Lifelong Education Unit, and which Cropley (1979a:105) terms the 'maximalist position'. This position is that which sees lifelong education as involving a fundamental transformation of society, so that the whole society becomes a learning resource for each individual.
>
> (Bagnall, 1990, p. 1).

As we approach the turn of the century, policy-makers are grappling with the concept of lifelong learning to underpin education and training provision. At this point, then, we might usefully examine from the discourse already available some examples of the different forms and focuses of thinking on this topic and offer some suggestions as to a way forward.

LIFELONG LEARNING: SOME ELEMENTS

Education for Employability and National Economic Growth

One approach to conceptualizing lifelong learning lays it down that lifelong learning is concerned with the promotion of skills and competences necessary for the development of general capabilities and specific performance in given tasks. Skills and competences developed through programmes of lifelong learning, on this approach, will have a bearing on questions of how workers perform in their tackling of precise job responsibilities and tasks and how well they can adapt their general and particular knowledge and competences to new tasks. On this analysis a more highly educated and skilled workforce will contribute to a more advanced and competitive economy.

From an economic perspective, the OECD *Jobs Study* (1994) has enlightened us as to the ways in which aspects of economic policy might impinge upon, affect and facilitate the realization of the goal of lifelong learning for all. The effects of policies relevant to setting appropriate macro-economic policy, enhancing the creation and diffusion of technological know-how, increasing work-time flexibility, encouraging entrepreneurship, increasing wage and labour-cost flexibility, reforming employment security provisions, expanding and enhancing active labour market policies, facilitating international co-operation, and improving labour-force skills and competences, have all been identified as ways in which governments may realize the ideal of lifelong learning for all.

The authors of the OECD *Jobs Study* maintain that '[a]daptation is fundamental to progress in a world of new technologies, globalization, and national and international competitiveness' (OECD, *Jobs Study*, 1994, p. 7). The ability of economies to adapt to change, they argue, can be deployed and developed only with people possessed of a sound and appropriate set of capacities, competences and knowledge. This requires engagement in and benefit from involvement in a programme of active educational endeavour throughout people's lives:

> The new generation now entering work can perhaps expect six or more job changes in a working life, meaning that part of that education will have to take the form of 'Learning how to learn' throughout the learning lifetime. Workers will have to acquire and later re-acquire skills through training ... Many people will need help to fit the requirements of high skill jobs. But some will be unable to meet those requirements and will be unemployed or take low skill, low wage jobs. The commitment to support them will be a valuable investment towards a forward moving and cohesive society. As OECD economies progress it will become all the more important to hone the support policies and mechanisms so that they provide effective help to those who most need it.
>
> (OECD, *Jobs Study*, 1994, p. 37)

Across OECD member countries, ministers agree that extending and upgrading workers' skills and competences must be a lifelong process, if their countries' economies are to foster the creation and expansion of high-skill, high-wage job opportunities. Such an undertaking will require a major shift in policy in some countries, and sustained and continuing development of existing policies in others. Particular emphasis needs to be placed on major problem areas including: the quality of initial education; the transition from school to work; investment in work-related skills, especially for the least qualified workers; and the financing of lifelong learning provision:

Lifelong learning must become a central element in a high skills, high wage jobs strategy. This involves dismantling barriers at all levels of education and training and a sharing of the cost burden of lifelong learning between the individual, business and the public purse.

(OECD, *Jobs Study*, 1994, p. 37)

Smethurst (1995) argues strongly for the need to invest in education in this way. In his view it is important to use all possible forms of economic argument to demonstrate that both the public and the private, the individual and the social, good can be increased substantially if we place investing in education at the highest point in our order of policy priorities:

We should indeed seek to deploy the economic arguments which can show high returns from investment in some types of education. If we do not, someone else will use techniques of a basically similar kind to show that a minor motorway improvement will result in a huge return and the money will be used for that instead.

(Smethurst, 1995, p. 44)

The point is clear: if we do not frame and implement policies that will direct resources and support to all kinds of educational initiative, then the funds that might have been employed in education will end up being diverted to other, less educationally relevant areas of public expenditure.

But there is much more of moment to be derived from the necessity of lifelong learning for all than merely its economic imperatives. As Smethurst continues:

What does not come out of the statistics is that, in order to succeed in life, in the world, in history, you need not just academic skill but personality, independence of mind, and autonomy of spirit.

This view, and its underpinning of value, is in accord with the initiatives currently being developed by many countries widely across the world. For, as the advice of OECD ministers of education in 1996 has made clear, those things that would best equip their citizens for life in the twenty-first century were the prime features of what has come to be called 'the knowledge economy': not merely a wide-ranging and thorough basis of knowledge content but a plethora of cognitive competences: the ability to communicate in speech and writing; numeracy and computer literacy; the ability to do research and to 'learn how to learn'; the skills of team-building and co-operation; interpersonal skills; and the ability to judge and discriminate, evaluate and create anew.

Governments clearly believe that strategies to promote these skills, extend understanding and implement these goals need to be developed and put into place now. The aim of the policies from which such strategies are to be developed is to seek to bring about change in each of the main levels and in the principal sectors of educational provision, at the same time as providing for an integrated, multifaceted approach – and above all, one to which reference may be made and access utilized throughout the lives of all citizens in their countries.

Lifelong Education and Personal Growth

The economic justification for lifelong learning has been shown to be highly dependent upon two prior assumptions: one, that 'lifelong education' is *instrumental for* and *anterior to* some more ultimate goal; and secondly, that the goal of lifelong learning is highly job-related and economic-policy-dependent. This approach, as we have seen from discussions at OECD, UNESCO, the European Parliament and the Nordic Council of Ministers, has now been rejected as presenting too narrow and limited an understanding of the nature, aims and purpose of 'lifelong education'.

Another approach to the idea and value of lifelong learning is predicated upon different assumptions. Instead of 'lifelong learning' being seen as instrumental to the achievement of an extrinsic goal, 'education' is seen equally as an intrinsically valuable activity, something that is good in and for itself. Here the aim would be to enable those engaging in lifelong education not so much to arrive at a new place but 'to travel with a different view' (Peters, 1965) and in that way to travel with a qualitatively better, richer and more elevated perspective from which to view the world. Indeed, as Bailey points out (Bailey, 1988, p. 123), an argument can be made that human beings have a positive duty to themselves to seek that kind of improvement. The basis for such an argument is provided by Kant (see Kant cited in Bailey, 1988, p. 123):

> It is a duty of man to himself to cultivate his natural powers (of the spirit, of the mind and of the body) as means to all kinds of possible ends. Man owes it to himself (an intelligence) not to let his natural predispositions and capacities (which his reason can use some day) remain unused, and not to leave them, as it were, to rust.

The point here is that those engaging in educational activities would be enriched by having their view of the world and capacity for rational choice continually expanded and transformed by the increasing varieties of educational experience and cognitive achievements that lifelong learning would offer them. The power and importance of that kind of rational choosing as the outcome of education is as foreshadowed by Kant (Kant cited in Bailey, 1988, p. 123):

> Which of these natural perfections may be preferable and in what proportions in comparison with one another, it may be man's duty to himself to make them his aim, are matters left to one's own rational reflection upon his desire for a certain mode of life, and his evaluation of the powers requisite for it.

A possible benefit of informed and rational reflection on and choice among such a range of experiences and achievements would be an increase in people's capacity for the more varied and heterogenous types and styles of cognitive activities and judgment with which they are able to approach the problems, topics and issues that beset them. The capacity to frame solutions for such problems or to engage in informed reflection upon such issues is an outgrowth of education's commitment to an expansion of the range of people's cognitive capacities and the diverse modes of experiencing the world that education brings them. This kind of additional benefit is contingent upon the prior assumption that education is to be seen as *an end-in-itself*, and not merely as an expedient towards the reaching of other ends.

This notion has been taken very seriously by community groups, which have articulated and promoted other versions, styles and patterns of lifelong learning. Thus, in addition to the provision of lifelong opportunities available through more traditional institutions and agencies, there is a growing trend towards opportunities being offered for lifelong learning by the creation and expansion of a wide range of community initiatives.

In some countries, for example, the emergence of Universities of the Third Age for people over the age of 55 has offered enormous advances in knowledge, skill and understanding to persons, in ways that have proved life-transforming for them, and that have succeeded in increasing the levels of competence, well-being and wisdom in the communities in which such persons reside and, in some cases, have enabled employers and commercial undertakings to take advantage of these re-educated men and women, with all the resources of knowledge, understanding and humane attributes that they already possess. Similar opportunities are provided by such distance learning institutions as Open Universities, informal community learning networks and study circles, and opportunities for learning and educational experiences provided by SAGA-type tourism and travel agencies, all of which are seen as parts of the whole range of community educational endeavours and as having valuable educational outcomes in the opportunities for continuing personal develop-ment and enrichment that they offer.

This version of the community as an agency and forum for lifelong learning reaches its full flowering in the realization that, for those engaging in lifelong learning, there is continually being made available and expanded a rich range of additional options, from which they may construct a satisfying and enriching pattern of activities and life-enhancing choices for themselves (cf. J.P. White, 1982). For all people, lifelong learning conceived of in this way offers the opportunity to bring up to date their knowledge of and enjoyment in activities which they had either long since laid aside or had always wanted to do but were previously not able to; to try their hand at activities and pursuits that they had previously imagined were outside their available time or competence; or to work consciously at extending their intellectual horizons by seeking to understand and internalize some of the more significant cognitive advances of recent times, that have done so much to affect and transform their worlds.

Some might consider this argument to be highly individualistic, concen-trating on the view that lifelong learning is something that is only presented to and engaged in by people individually. But this is to mistake the potential for collective endeavour and a growth in the sense of community offered by such experiences: anyone who has observed at first hand the sense of shared excite-ment and accelerated advance exhibited by classes studying foreign languages or creative writing in a University of the Third Age group cannot fail to be aware of the way in which a sense of community involvement is extended and deepened by undertakings of collective educational activity and growth.

This is not to suggest, however, that lifelong learning, seen from this perspective, is an activity that is restricted to those who have passed the age when education in formal or institutional settings has ceased. For it is clear that the expansion of cognitive repertoire and the increasing of skills and competences is an undertaking that can – and indeed, on either argument, must – continue throughout one's life, as an essential part of one's growth and development as a human being and as a citizen in a participative democracy, and as a productive and efficiently operating agent in a process of economic change and advance. On this argument, both individual and community welfare is protected and promoted by the organization of such activities and the resources to support them, and by their being made available to the widest possible range of constituencies. Smethurst (1995) puts this well:

> Is education a public or a private good? The answer is, neither: it is both. There is some education which is overwhelmingly a public good in that its benefits accrue very widely, to society at large as well as to the individual. Equally there is some education which, while benefiting society, confers overwhelming benefits on the individual learner. But much of education sits annoyingly between these two extremes, leading us, correctly, to want to influence the amount and type of it supplied and demanded, because society has an interest in the outcome, but also to note that it confers benefits on the individual above those societal benefits.

And it is this kind of argument that leads to the view that lifelong education is most decidedly a public good, for the benefit and welfare of everyone in society, rather than being the preserve of a few.

Lifelong Learning: A Prerequisite for Participation in Democracy

Those who argue that lifelong education is a public good see the availability of educational opportunities *over the whole of people's life-span* as a prerequisite for informed and effective participation by all citizens in a democratic society (cf. Grace, 1994; McLaughlin, 1994; Smethurst, 1995). The same may be said of such services as health, welfare, law and order, and housing, all of which, with education, constitute the infrastructure upon which individuals may hope to construct, realize and work out their own versions of a life of quality in a society that is mutually supportive, inclusive and just, and so provide the necessary preconditions for active life in a participative democracy.

It is upon the notion of education as a public good that 'free and compulsory' education for all was first made available in many countries. And in the modern world, in circumstances of so many and such complex changes, demands and difficulties – economic, social and cultural – the proponents of lifelong education for a socially inclusive and democratic society, also claim lifelong education as a public good (cf. Nordic Council of Ministers, 1995).

Certainly no one would suggest for a moment that education, like other 'public goods' such as health and welfare services, requires no further financial investment from individuals and other sources; all such community services have to be supported financially and in myriad other ways. But these services are vital and indispensable to the nature, quality and operation of the democratic society in which we all live and as citizens have a share.

The point of this argument is that individuals can develop as autonomous agents capable of fully participating in society only if they are sufficiently informed, prepared and predisposed; if they are healthy and well-fed; if they have the minimal domestic conditions for perpetuating existence; and if they can engage in communication with others they recognize as equals in having the same autonomy as they are aware of developing in themselves, and with whom they can join in discussion, consideration and planning of mutually beneficial modes of action. On this view, the whole of our society has a direct interest in securing, providing and safeguarding those conditions and services presupposed by and required for our participation in democratic life. These conditions are provided, at least in part, by the contributions that all of us who shall benefit from them regard it as being in our mutual interest to make to the common wealth via a publicly funded exchequer.

Those who conceive of lifelong learning in connection with the maintenance of a socially inclusive and democratic society are making a point about the nature of the world as they perceive it – as a complex conjunction of aggregations of individual human beings. As Aristotle maintained, 'Man is by nature an animal that lives in groups'; we do not live, indeed we could not start our existence or survive, if we lived alone on desert islands. Personal freedom and individual choice is only possible as an outgrowth of the knowledge and values that other members of society have opened up to us. In this way we have been given some intimation of what choices are available to us and we can begin to understand what taking advice, and the calculation of its consequences might mean. For most of us this intimation is first made through our educational experiences, both formal and informal, compulsorily prescribed by others or voluntarily chosen by us, as being in our own interests and those of our community.

Ratz puts this well in a discussion of what he calls the duties of autonomy (Ratz, cited in Bailey 1988, p. 124):

> There is more one can do to help another person have an autonomous life than to stand off and refrain from coercing and manipulating him. There are two further categories of autonomy-based duties towards another person. One is to help in creating the inner capacities required for the conduct of an autonomous life. Some of these concern cognitive capacities, such as the power to absorb, remember and use information, reasoning abilities, and the like. Others concern one's emotional and imaginative make-up. Still others concern health and physical abilities and skills ... The third type of autonomy-based duty towards another concerns the creation of an adequate range of options for him to choose from.

It is a paradox of our existence that our autonomy requires the work of other persons. It is given to us and increased by our education; and that requires the learning of language and the transmission of knowledge. Both of these are ongoing social activities and public enterprises in which at least two people must engage in an interaction predicated upon the assumption of the mutual tolerance and regard that is only embodied in the institutions of society. Without the one, there cannot be the other; and without that key institution called education, there can be neither. For autonomy is the flower that grows out of seeds planted and tended by heteronomous hands. For Ratz this point carries a correlative moral implication: on this argument we have a moral obligation, as Bailey puts it, 'to develop and maintain our own autonomy and the autonomy of others' (Bailey, 1988, p. 124). And, as is clear from the argument, this obligation is one that we bear throughout the whole of our lives.

All this, at rock bottom, is what taxes are for – and those of us with different levels of resources contribute to the exchequer differentially. It is this contribution that grants us licence to access those good things that society wishes to be available for enjoyment by all its members. The notion of that contribution brings out the mutual beneficence and interdependence of our economic arrangements for funding and running our society and providing appropriate levels and kinds of service for the benefit of all its constituents throughout their lives – including those who, because of history, handicap, weakness or sheer misfortune, may not be able to contribute much to society at the moment but still need its support. This makes society and its various institutions, especially educating institutions, the very places in which individuals can further develop their pattern of preferred life-options, thus increasing their autonomy, and in which all sections of the community co-operate mutually for the benefit of the societal whole.

The concept of education as a 'public good' and the responsibility we all share for the mutual benefit of all members of society is fundamental to this version of the need for 'lifelong learning for all'. R.H. Tawney (Tawney, 1938) held firmly to the belief that engagement in adult education was a necessary prerequisite to and continuing part of engagement in the obligations of participation in democracy and the institutions of a democratic state. Ensuring for all future citizens their liberation from ignorance and potential servitude and exploitation is secured by guaranteeing them access to all the major forms and fields of human knowledge, understanding and communication in a high quality, wide-ranging and dynamic curriculum in a variety of institutions devoted to the education of the present and future electorate.

Such a curriculum provides people with one of the principal means of personal empowerment, emancipated understanding and making informed choices in exercising the duties and responsibilities of a citizen in a participative or representative democracy, particularly one in which, as is the case with Australia, the franchise is universal and compulsory. Indeed, as Powell argued (Powell, 1970; see also Cohen, 1981), the notion of 'education for democracy' provides us with a justification for compulsory education in a democracy; and commitment to that idea generates a dynamic curriculum and whole programme of activities for all educating institutions in a democratic state (see Strike, 1982; Wringe, 1984).

THREE ELEMENTS IN LIFELONG LEARNING: HOW THEY INTERACT AND FUSE

We realize, of course, that none of these aims and undertakings for lifelong learning can really be separated from the other: all three elements interact and cross-fertilize each other. A more competent and highly skilled agent in the workforce has more of an interest in and responsibility for contributing to the improvement of institutions and their point in a set of democratic political arrangements; both are in turn enhanced by the affective satisfaction experienced and achieved by those who have expanded their life-horizons in cognitive content and skills in complex forms of intellectual operation on which, upon reflection, they now prefer to spend their time.

There is a complex interplay between all three, that makes education for a more highly skilled workforce at the same time an education for better democracy and a more rewarding life. That is why the whole notion and value of 'lifelong learning for all' might be usefully seen as a complex and multifaceted process, that begins in pre-school, is carried on through compulsory and post-compulsory periods of formal education and training, and is continued throughout life, through provision of such learning experiences, activities and enjoyment in the home, in the work-place, in universities and colleges, and in other educational, social and cultural agencies, institutions and settings – both formal and informal – within the community.

In respect to the development of policy, this approach, this triadic emphasis, requires a far greater, more coherent and consistent, better co-ordinated and integrated, more multifaceted approach to learning and to realizing a 'lifelong learning' approach for all than has hitherto been the case.

The central elements in what we have described as the triadic nature of lifelong learning –

- for economic progress and development;

- for personal development and fulfilment; and

- for social inclusiveness and democratic understanding and activity

– are now seen as fundamental to bringing about a more democratic polity and set of social institutions, in which the principles and ideals of social inclusiveness, justice and equity are present, practised and promoted; an economy which is strong, adaptable and competitive; and a richer range of provision of those activities on which individual members of society are able to choose to spend their time and energy, for the personal rewards and satisfactions that they confer. To bring this about nothing less than a substantial reappraisal of the provision, resourcing and goals of education and training, and a major reorientation of its direction towards the concept and value of the idea of 'the learning society' will be required. Therein lies the major challenge for governments, policy-makers and educators as they grapple with ways of conceptualizing lifelong learning and realizing the aim of 'lifelong learning for all'.

EXPLORING ALTERNATIVE APPROACHES TO CONCEPTUALIZING LIFELONG LEARNING

There have been a number of attempts at conceptualizing 'lifelong learning' in the past. In the remainder of this chapter we shall review some of the more robust versions of the concept, set out the main lines of the conceptions of education articulated in them, show in what ways those conceptions might be partial, deficient or fallacious, and then go on to suggest an alternative. Our analysis begins with a scrutiny of the notion that an agreed 'essential' definition of 'lifelong education' can be achieved, moves on to the search for such a definition, and then embarks on an examination of two of the most widely held views of 'lifelong education': one that is termed the 'maximalist' position; and the other that sees lifelong learning as an extension of the deliberate and planned interventions characteristic of 'education proper'. Operating from a post-empiricist standpoint, we argue that such searches are misconceived and rest on a false view of the nature of science and of concepts, challenging the essentialism of the definitional approach and the claims to objectivity of the 'liberal education extended' account of lifelong education, and rejecting the relativism of the maximalist position. In their place we proffer a pragmatic, problem-solving approach.

The Vain Quest for Definitions

There is an important point to be made when one is considering the positions that have been taken in the past in respect to the concept of lifelong learning and the arguments that have been put forward between various proponents of these positions. It seems clear that differences in and between various versions of 'lifelong education' are functions, not only of particular educational, moral or political commitments, but also of a particular meta-theory at work in the philosophy of lifelong education.

In some versions of the term and in various attempts to produce a clear account of it, we may discern the presence and operation of a particular preconception. In many writers' work on lifelong education, there seems to be an implicit acceptance of the notion that it is indeed possible to arrive at some uniform descriptive definition of the term 'lifelong education' which all could then accept and take as a kind of *primum datum*; and that, if there were not, then there ought to be. The common postulate shared by many writers – particularly the earlier ones – seems to be that unambiguous agreement on the meaning and applicability of the term is conceivable, possible and attainable. In this tacit assumption we see evidence that these writers on lifelong education are evidently operating according to the logic and dictates of the empiricist position (cf. Cropley, 1979; Dave, 1975; Gelpi, 1985; Lengrand, 1975, 1979; Richmond, 1979; and Stock, 1979).

The main feature typically observable in the work of such writers is the holding of notions of definition that may be properly described as 'essentialist'. This is the notion that it is possible, and indeed philosophically proper, for participants in discussion about any such term in educational discourse to employ the methods of etymological derivation, dictionary definition, or the sharp-cutting tools of conceptual analysis (looking for those cases that all can agree to be 'central' or 'peripheral' to allowable utterance employing the terms in question), in order to arrive at some kind of agreement about the separately 'necessary' and conjointly 'sufficient' conditions that will underpin and define the direction of discourse employing this term.

That this presumption and *modus operandi* encapsulate a mistaken view of meaning and intelligibility has been common coinage for some time now (cf. Aspin, 1996a, 1996b). It has been subjected to the formidable elenchus of the criticisms advanced against it by such powerful antilocutors as Popper, Wittgenstein and Quine, to say nothing of more modern writers such as Rorty (1979) or Bernstein (1983). As a result of this critique we may now, we think, accept their point that this particular view can be called seriously into question if not decisively refuted. Instead of falling into the fallacy of seeking to achieve clarity about or understanding of the 'essential', 'basic' or 'central' meaning of the term 'lifelong education' according to such rubrics, then, we may start on the search for other expedients.

The view of the legitimacy of the quest for 'essential' definitions was held in an earlier era where students of education accepted the academic tenability and conformed to the dictates of the empiricist paradigm, tending only to engage in activities of conceptual analysis, pursuing philosophical inquiries and developing and applying research designs and instruments exclusively based upon it. However, researchers in education and the social sciences of a more modern cast of thought have now moved towards an approach based on advances in epistemology and methodology, that arise from post-empiricist work in philosophy and the philosophy of science, such as that of Popper (1943, 1949, 1960 and 1972), Lakatos (1976, 1978) and Quine (1951, 1953, 1974).

This work has made it possible to move beyond the hard-line demand for a so-called 'value-free' objectivity, typical of former empiricist approaches, to the attempt to clarify philosophical understandings, to engage in research and to articulate accounts, develop analyses, and produce tentative conclusions, that are quite as complex, heterogenous and multiform as the corpus of material upon which they are based and towards the elucidation of which they may be applied.

Over against the views of empiricists and positivists, we prefer to maintain that the number and range of human activities, the difficulty and complexity of objects of philosophical interest, the range and modes of their interplay, and the ways in which they are subject to various kinds of forces and pressures – not all of which are readily analysable in clear and unambiguous definitional terms – make many of them unamenable to academic inquiry understood in terms of the traditional empiricist mode. For this reason we believe that a different approach to and a wider conspectus of the number and type of the possible modes of philosophical inquiry – particularly in educational matters – is required, if we are to give a more comprehensive and flexible account of the nature, scope and purposes of philosophy of education and the point of its application to the increasingly important idea of 'lifelong education'.

In opposition to the thesis of empiricism, we may note that the main burden of the counter-arguments has been to show that there is no such distinction as that supposed to subsist between philosophy and empirical science, fact and value, or, come to that, between policy analysis and policy formation. For Quine, Popper and many others, all language and all inquiries are inescapably and *ab initio* theory-laden, far from value-free, and a mixture of both descriptive and normative elements. Indeed, says Kovesi (1967), in all discourse and inquiry, there is an unbroken continuum, at one end of which lies 'fact' and at the other end of which lies 'value'. Description, for such thinkers, is a way of evaluating reality; evaluation is a way of describing states of affairs.

Such arguments are used powerfully by such post-empiricist thinkers in education as Evers and Lakomski (1991) to develop a new approach to the elucidation of problems in educational discourse and policy. On this view all our talk on these matters is conceived of as being in itself a 'theory', embodying a complex 'web of belief' (cf. Quine and Ullian, 1970), shot through differentially with descriptive and evaluative elements, according to the contexts and purposes of which our theories of education, policy and administration are brought to bear and applied in our world.

For such reasons there is now widely held to be a need, in philosophical activities devoted to a thorough-going, intellectually responsible inquiry into such matters as lifelong education, to fuse description–evaluation, fact–value, quantitative–qualitative methods in new forms of inquiry, that are valuable both for the researcher and the policy-maker in educational matters. Such an approach would involve both groups in a common enterprise – what Lakatos (1976, 1978) might have seen as a 'progressive research programme' – of seeking to gain understanding and promote policy generation about lifelong education. On this account future work in the philosophy of education would be well advised to consider the adoption of approaches of this kind (cf. Wain, 1993a).

In this enterprise, we do not attempt to reduce everything to some absolute foundations of 'fact' and 'value', 'theory' and 'practice', or 'policy' and 'implementation', in the (vain) attempt to educe some 'analyses' of concepts and theories, that can be completely 'correct' or 'true'; or to produce some fundamental matters of indisputable research 'findings', about the objectivity and existence of which there can be no dispute. As against this notion we might tentatively advance the view that what is important when we endeavour to identify the nature, aims and purposes of all kinds of educating institutions, activities and processes – formal and informal, fixed-term and lifelong – and to promote excellence, effectiveness and quality in them, is *to adopt some such pragmatic method as the following*:

- to seek to understand the questions, the problems, the categories and the criteria with which researchers, policy-makers and practitioners in the field of lifelong learning are currently concerned and are working.

- To identify the theories with which researchers, policy-makers and practitioners are operating.

- To seek to understand the causes of success or failure in the conception and application of such theories, policies and practices, as a necessary prelude to attenuating or eliminating dysfunctions and establishing or ameliorating structures and procedures that would contribute towards improvement.

It is by looking at the various attempts that have been made to give form, content and direction to the idea of 'lifelong education' that we may begin to develop and articulate theories that will bear application to the problems that those who place so much emphasis upon the idea of 'lifelong education' are seeking to address and to solve. Of course, we cannot assume that all these problems are the same or even similar: different countries, different educational systems, different agencies of education will be taken up with some similar but many different problems. Such differences will not only be those of degree of complexity or difficulty; the problems will also be different in kind. This is something which anyone attempting to give some account of 'lifelong education' will rapidly become uncomfortably aware of.

One does not need to look far for the reason for this. Like 'art', 'religion', and 'democracy', 'education' (and a fortiori 'lifelong education') is an example of what W.B. Gallie (1956, 1964) called an 'essentially contested concept' (cf. Hartnett and Naish, 1976). To think that one can find an 'essential', 'basic' or uncontestable definition of 'lifelong education' is to embark a search for a chimera.

Rather than engaging in a futile search for the real meaning or an uncontested definition of lifelong education, we would suggest that the best one can do is to follow Wittgenstein's advice (Wittgenstein, 1953, 1968) and 'look at the use' of this term in the discourse of those who employ it. This post-empiricist approach will enable us to note the increasing frequency and growing importance of the idea of 'lifelong education' in international discussions of educational policy, planning and administration at the present time. We may then look carefully at the wide range of examples of the ways the topic appears in the discourse of education professionals and members of the broader community at the current time and see if we can discern any 'family resemblances' that may help us to move intelligently from the scrutiny of one set of uses to another.

The Maximalist Position

The post-empiricist approach to understanding the various types and shades of meaning given to 'lifelong education' in educationists' talk sits well, on the surface at least, with the position adopted towards lifelong learning by Kenneth Wain, one of the main writers on the philosophy of lifelong education in recent times (Wain, 1984, 1985a and b, 1987, 1993a and 1993b). Wain accepts the point, by now widely agreed among philosophers of education, that, for good philosophical reasons, no one absolute and clearly agreed definition of 'education' can be found. He finds proof of this in the numerous accounts of activities or programmes falling under the heading of lifelong education. Some of these are synonymous, some overlapping, some contiguous, some quite distinct, some divergent, some conflicting, some opposing.

But Wain has another explanation for this. His rejection of essentialism and absolutism and of the kind of normative conceptual analysis practised by proponents of liberal education such as Peters, Hirst and White (cf. Harris, 1979, chapter 1) lead him to look to another account of differences in understanding and intelligibility. He finds this in Kuhnian paradigm theory (Kuhn, 1973) whereby the intelligibility and normative force of a number of different theories or programmes of lifelong education are explained as functions of different paradigms.

The paradigm from which Wain develops his own account thus makes of educational theory what some people have called a 'site of contestation': 'an area of competing programmes adherence to which constitutes the basis of agreement or disagreement between philosophers and educationalists who support one or the other' (Wain, 1987, p. 29). In Wain's view, such different theories of lifelong education are not only incommensurable with but are also competing with and against each other for acceptance, support and implementation. The resolution of these conflicts and the attempt to secure some sort of inter-paradigm intelligibility can only be achieved by reference to a 'touchstone' of rationality. 'Touchstone' in this sense suggests an area of inter-paradigm agreement, constituted not only by appropriate algorithms of coherence, logic and semantics, but also by areas of common interest, problems and potential agreement.

Reference to 'touchstone' indicates that Wain has adopted a Lakatosian approach (cf. Lakatos, 1976, 1978) to the question of the multiplicity, variety and difference between theories of lifelong education. He says as much:

> the idea of using Lakatos' model to describe an 'education programme' came from reading Harris (1979) ... I regard the concept of education as one which is both contestable and liable to different interpretations ... the decision as to which interpretation is the best one depends on nothing extrinsic to the power of the 'programme' each concept translates into ... There is nothing that lies beyond the programme ... that can be appealed to to decide between competing interpretations of the concept. This view implies ... a plurality of competing interpretations of education ... that instead of one 'education' there are several 'educations' ... that the world of educational theory should be permanently regarded as one of competing interpretations of what education should mean, competing ... for the allegiance or commitment of practitioners and policy-makers.
>
> (Wain, 1993a, p. 60)

Wain adopts, as his preferred version of the 'progressive research programme' of lifelong education, the 'maximalist notion' incorporated in the UNESCO 'programme' (cf. Chapter 1). He uses this maximalist notion as the various writers on and proponents of this term (cf. Cropley, Dave, Gelpi, Lengrand, Suchodolski, in Wain, 1987) have used it:

> 'lifelong education' stands for a programme to reconceptualise education totally according to the principle that education is a lifelong process ... for a complete overhaul of our way of thinking about education, for a new philosophy of education and ... for a *programme of action* (Faure,

1972; Lengrand, 1975; Dave, 1976; Cropley, 1979) . . . as the 'master concept' for all educational planning, policy-making, and practice . . . Their ambition was that the word education would eventually become synonymous with lifelong education in people's minds . . . (today's) world . . . requires a lifelong education which is a 'constant reorganising or reconstructing of experience' (Dewey, 1966:76).

(Wain, 1993a, pp. 58–9)

Wain claims that Dewey, with his emphasis upon education as 'conceived as a continuous process of "reorganisation and readjustment" of experience and the pragmatic concerns of lifelong education' (Wain, 1993a, pp. 58–9), is the intellectual forebear of the UNESCO programme and of the maximalist position. He points out the large-scale social implications of this conception of lifelong education:

Dewey's declaration that 'to learn from life itself and to make the conditions of life such that all will learn in the process of living' (Dewey, 1966:51) lays the seed for the movement's conception of the 'learning society' . . . one which is participatory, democratic and bent towards realising humane educational practice.

(Wain, 1993a, pp. 59, 62)

According to Wain this does *not* mean that the whole of one's life is to be taken as educational. It is not the case that all activities we engage in, all the experiences we have, all the growth that occurs is, in and of itself, the education we receive. If it did, there would be nothing to distinguish between 'life' and 'education', between maturational and developmental growth *simpliciter* and 'growth' as a species of lifelong educatedness. Furthermore, Wain is at pains to argue that Dewey's concept of 'growth' did not mean that all our life's experiences are educational; he distinguishes these from those that are educationally relevant (Wain, 1987, pp. 170–1). This, Wain maintains, gives us a principle of discrimination and choice between experiences. In order to make the necessary demarcation of what experience is to be regarded as educationally relevant in this way Wain brings in Dewey's criterion of learning as *directed* growth:

Dewey . . . is interested in learning as 'that reconstruction or reorganisation of experience which adds to the meaning of experience, and which increases ability to direct the course of subsequent experience' (Dewey, 1966:76), to be distinguished from learning 'as preparation for a remote future, as unfolding, as external formation, and as recapitulation of the past' (Dewey, 1966:80) and include informal learning.

(Wain, 1993a, p. 65)

Dewey . . . does not forego adopting operational criteria to distinguish what learning is technically 'educative' from what is not . . . Making experience subject to criteria . . . effectively means bringing it under the control of the learner, researcher, or educator . . . the learning context signifies for Dewey 'a specially selected environment, the selection being made on the basis of materials and method specifically promoting

growth in the desired direction' (Dewey, 1966:38) ... Dewey ... specified
that *educational* growth should involve the direction of experience in
certain ways.

(Wain, 1993a, ibid.)

This, argues Wain, should absolve Dewey from any charge of 'having proposed
an anarchic definition of education as growth'.

Wain also points out the importance of the notion of direction and conscious
ordering in the reconstruction and reorganization of experience in desired
directions as the manifestation of a concern on the part of the proponents of the
maximalist position to show that educators are leaders of the 'learning society':
'The programme's proposal that lifelong education ... should be institution-
alised in a "learning society" clearly shows that ... it wants to make education
more central to society, not deprive people of the right to it' (Wain, 1993a, p. 67).
And Wain expands upon what a 'maximalist' conception of a 'learning society'
might mean:

> There is no 'model' learning society, there are different forms a learning
> society could take, just as there are different forms the lifelong
> education programme could take. What distinguishes one learning
> society from the other is precisely the kind of programme it
> institutionalises within its particular socio-cultural and political
> context. The political characteristics of the movement's learning society
> are ... democratic ... a shared, pluralistic and participatory 'form of life'
> in Dewey's sense.
>
> This means reassessing the role of the school and of childhood
> learning ... and prioritising adult learning on the same level. A
> fundamental strategy with regard to the latter is to sensitise social
> institutions, the family, the church, political party, trade union, place of
> employment, etc., to their educational potential ... with respect to their
> members. To encourage these institutions to regard themselves as
> potential educative agencies for their members and for the wider
> society.
>
> (Wain, 1993a, p. 68)

The learning society is one that is exceedingly self-conscious about
education in its total sense; that is conscious of the educational
relevance and potential of its own institutions and of the general social
environment that is its way of life, and is determined to maximise its
resources in these respects, to the maximum.

(Wain, 1987, pp. 202–3)

A better summation of the 'maximalist' position could hardly be found.

An Opposing View: Lifelong Education as Education 'Proper' – The Extension of 'Liberal' Education

The maximalist position is, however, severely criticized and firmly rejected by
Richard Bagnall (1990). He argues against the relativism clearly apparent in

the adoption of Kuhn's account of incommensurable and competing paradigms as an explanation for the different versions of lifelong education, many of them at odds with each other, and implicit in the idea of 'research programmes' proposed by Wain as a way of bringing them all within the same purview. Insofar as the idea of 'research programme' has any applicability to or utility for seeking to get clear about 'lifelong education', Bagnall maintains that this particular approach is 'regressive' (a term he employs in preference to 'degenerating', for, so wide is the ambit of the term 'lifelong education', that he considers it to have no high point from which to decline). He also claims that the 'maximalist' view is also 'illiberal' insofar as, in Wain's version at any rate, it incorporates a species of epistemological and ethical relativism. This, he claims, encourages 'both intolerance ... and a ... lack of humility' (cf. Paterson, 1984; Trigg, 1973, pp. 135–7). In Bagnall's view, Wain's analysis of the lifelong education programme, which Wain claims is strongly relativist, is a good illustration of this point:

> Through [its] neo-Lakatosian analytical framework ... 'knowledge' and 'ideology' are viewed as being bundled into epistemically and ethically competitive and incommensurable programmes. Such a view must encourage ... protagonists to reject, wholesale, all bundles and knowledge and ideology that are perceived to be in conflict with those of one's contemporary commitments. Consistently, ... Wain reject[s] whole systems of educational thought (liberal, humanist and existentialist), in which he perceives some conflict with the tenets of the ... Programme ... One of the features of programmatic hard cores is, of course, that they are immune to modification.
>
> (Bagnall, 1990, pp. 5–6)

Bagnall returns to the four semantic interpretations of 'lifelong education' which we referred to at the beginning of this chapter. The first – 'education as a preparation *for* the rest of a person's life' – he says

> may be identified with the traditional view of schooling ... as comprising ... an educational foundation for adult life (e.g., Peters, 1966; White, 1982:132) ... such a view of education is inadequate for adult participation in modern, technologically sophisticated, liberal democratic societies ... (cf. Evans, 1985; Long, 1983; Wedermeyer, 1981).
>
> (Bagnall, 1990, p. 5)

The second – 'Lifelong education as education to be distributed *throughout* the whole of the lifespan' – remarks Bagnall,

> accords ... with the ... conception of lifelong education as 'recurrent education' (Davis, Wood and Smith, 1986; Kallen, 1979) and with the principles of 'continuing education' (Titmus, 1989; Za'rour, 1984) ... While further development of educational systems along the lines of 'recurrent' education would clearly entail major changes in educational

provision and participation, these changes at least would appear to be a constructive development of present educational provision and understanding.

(Bagnall, 1990, *ibid.*)

The third – 'lifelong education as education *from* the whole of life's experiences' – reduces, in Bagnall's view, very rapidly to the fourth view of 'lifelong education' – that 'All events in which one is consciously involved throughout one's lifespan constitute education (as process) and contribute to and are part of one's education (as outcome). Education is the process and the on-going learning product of living'. On this view there is no need to engage in careful planning, research or evaluation of programmes we pick out for educational endeavour: since education is conterminous with the whole of life's experience there is no particular reason for doing this rather than that, or for selecting one set of activities over another. This makes the notion of 'education' vacuous: there is nothing we could possibly want or need to provide for, since, on this account, everything educative is already there.

This view – a view which Wain denies either Dewey or he himself holds – Bagnall still finds being espoused in much writing on the subject of lifelong education. He believes that it should be rejected, for it fails to accord any intelligibility to the notion of 'education proper' or of formal and active as opposed to informal and unintentional learning. On Bagnall's account, education proper consists in making distinctions between knowledge and ideology, between educative learning and the simple accumulation of experience, between offering a contingent plurality of programmes and simply following one undifferentiated path of cognitive growth, between activities that are conducive to worthwhile ends and experiences that are just simply 'had', between ends that may be epistemically difficult and challenging, but are morally defensible, laudable, and commendatory for all people, and outcomes which just simply come about after undifferentiated and unselected experiences and not as a result of informed and clearly differentiated choices of various kinds.

Bagnall maintains that 'There is a desperate need for concrete educational expression to be given to many of the liberal and humanitarian ideals of lifelong education theorists such as Gelpi (Ireland, 1978)'. This is a view with which Charles Bailey would be in strong sympathy, and for reasons that have everything to do with his stress on the importance of developing, maintaining and applying the powers of rational autonomy throughout the whole of people's lives (Bailey, 1988). Bailey cites the work of Hirst (1965) and Peters (1966a) in support:

> If . . . Hirst claims that a genuinely liberal education must involve the development of rational mind . . . then it is difficult to see why this should be a process that terminates at 16 or 18 . . . Hirst's well-known transcendental justificatory argument . . . does bear on individuals asking questions like: How should I live? How ought I to develop myself? Persons asking these kinds of questions would clearly be adults rather than children.

Similarly ... Peters' ... conception of education as involving worthwhile developments in knowledge and understanding is clearly not something that is in any essential way limited to schooling ... there is the clear implication that the rational person will have a duty, or at least might reasonably want, to continue their liberal education throughout life.

(Bailey, 1988, pp. 124–5)

There is every reason, on this account, for seeing education as a series of deliberate undertakings to choose some activities rather than others and to make them available as programmes in educational settings, on grounds that they will introduce individuals to a range of activities and experiences that will enable then to make informed judgments about the options open to them, to choose rationally between them, and consciously to accept the consequences and obligations that may arise from them. On this account it is not the case that the undifferentiated flow of life itself will guide us to make such judgments and choices; the presuppositions of human autonomy and community render it a matter of necessity for the enterprise of education to be a conscious, deliberate and discriminating series of distinctions, values and decisions. These will ensure that education proper must be based on some more deliberate, objective and interpersonal ground than those accretions of experience that come about as mere increments of growth. And that ground is provided, on these arguments, by the presupposition of individual autonomy and the moral obligations towards other autonomous agents constituting the human community and their welfare and progress, that arise from it.

Faults and Virtues of Contrasting Views

The consequences of adopting the arguments of Kant and Ratz as articulated by the authors cited above bear substantially on the idea of lifelong education and of the role of educators as leaders of a learning community. Those arguments carry considerable implications regarding the necessity of committing oneself to the correlative educational imperative of planning and seeking educational opportunities, activities and experiences and making them available for ourselves and others throughout our lives. It would be a pity therefore if we were distracted from taking the moral commendations implicit in and arising from those arguments by pausing too long over such differences between protagonists of lifelong education as those outlined above. For, after all, we can find faults and virtues on both sides.

In the case of the maximalist position outlined by Wain, for example, we can find much that is noteworthy and commendable. Wain's proposal for making 'lifelong education' a 'progressive research programme' as Lakatos conceived it is worthy of the most serious academic and professional consideration. His emphasis on the importance of and the need for a move towards inclusiveness and lack of limitation in educational provision gives point and direction to the idea of a 'learning society'. Further, his notion that lifelong education subsumes both formal and informal models of learning, and places the main burden of the control and direction on learners themselves, accords

37

well with most recent developments arising from research into meta-cognition and student-centred learning.

Wain's position does have its problems, however. The notion of internal coherence as a criterion of progressiveness in a research programme is open to all the criticisms which anti-relativists have deployed against it. Again, Wain's statements on the status of ideologies are a clear rejection of transcendental arguments but his appeal to 'touchstone' as somehow enabling inter-paradigm comparisons to be made and understood suggests that Wain's account of theory does, after all, presuppose some extra- or supra-paradigm criteria of intelligibility and corrigibility. He cannot have it both ways. Then again, as Bailey trenchantly shows, Wain has problems with his concept of 'relevance' as constituting one criterion of progressiveness. As Bailey comments:

> Saying that a particular programme must satisfy criteria of relevance to historical, social and technological circumstances is saying very little. What requires justifying is why we are being asked to respond to those particular circumstances in one way rather than in other, equally relevant, different ways.
>
> (Bailey, 1988, p. 122)

Finally, one might have some reservations about the almost totalitarian character of the position envisaged by advocates of the maximalist programme. Not only might some critical comment be made on the unitary character and personification of 'Society' evident in Wain's summary statement set out above – how can a learning society be 'conscious of' and sensitive to the educational potential of all its institutions and individuals? – but one might also be justified in sensing in the views of the proponents of that idea a vision and a sense of mission that detractors might describe as Utopian and Popperian critics might characterize as millenarian and almost totalitarian. Certainly the way in which Wain describes the views of the 'Movement' might seem to expose them to the elenchus advanced against such thinking in Popper's discussion of such matters in his *Conjectures and Refutations* (1989) and *The Poverty of Historicism* (1960). These considerations should caution us against a too ready acceptance of maximalist rubrics for the idea of lifelong education as Wain adumbrates it.

On their side, Bagnall and Bailey have properly drawn attention to some important questions to be asked of those advocating programmes of lifelong education. It is good that they have underlined the need for concepts of lifelong education to be analysed in such a way that they make clear the underlying value-judgments at work in them. It is good too that they make it clear that education, however we conceive it, is not something to which artificial barriers can be drawn and that, properly conceived, it is an enterprise that lasts over the whole of a lifetime. Perhaps, however, they have committed themselves too much, within the empiricist and 'essentialist' approach of Peters and Hirst, to the pre-eminent importance they both assign to the idea of active discrimination in a formal institutional sense. As Wain rightly remarks, they give too little attention and scope to the idea and functioning of informal education, and too much to the place of the idea of particular conceptions of liberal education in debates about the meaning and content of lifelong education programmes.

A great deal has been written in criticism of that view of liberal education and its justification (see Langford, 1973; Harris, 1979; and Evers and Walker, 1983 for references to the plethora of criticisms against the Peters-Hirst view of liberal education, the use of transcendental arguments, and the status and activity of analytic philosophy of education generally). The apparent espousal by Bagnall and Bailey of a similar view of the concept of lifelong education – though they do say many wise things about it – should perhaps caution us against a too ready acceptance of their rejection of arguments based on 'relevance' and 'coherence' and of their plea for lifelong education to be seen as a species of liberal education generally.

A SUGGESTED WAY FORWARD

Rather than getting bogged down in this debate, we should like to suggest a different expedient. We believe that Bagnall's and Bailey's adherence to a conception of philosophy of education that is both empiricist and normative can no longer sustain the weight of all the critical arguments marshalled against it. At the same time we are quite clear that the relativism urged by Wain may be reduced finally to the kind of incorrigible solipsism into which all such arguments ultimately fall, if they are not, that is, to seek to make some tacit appeal to some kind of overarching criteria of intelligibility and adjudication and thus either fall into contradiction or betray an underlying predilection for transcendental arguments.

As against these positions, there is, we believe, something to be said for trying a different expedient. There is, we think, not much point in attempting to achieve some kind of resolution between the different accounts of the term, especially when we accept the view that there can be as many different conceptions of the concept of lifelong education as there are philosophers to put them forward and communities willing to put their own versions of lifelong education programmes into effect. Rather than participating in an exercise of interpretation that might in the end prove self-defeating or inconclusive, it might, in our view, be better to look, not so much at the various interpretations and accounts of lifelong education, but rather more at the circumstances in which various theories and policies of lifelong education have been articulated, developed and applied.

In other words, we are suggesting, an objective referent may be found: it lies in the problems to the settlement of which lifelong education programmes are addressed. There is, we believe, more point in looking at the difficulties, issues and predicaments, the attempted solution of which different policies of lifelong learning have been conceived to tackle. In that way we might attempt to see how, why, and in response to what pressures and quandaries the various versions of lifelong education have been developed or are in play and can be seen to be at work in the attention educational policy-makers devote to them, before attempting to assess how far those policies and practices have succeeded in addressing the problems that policy-makers are attempting to solve.

One resolution that might be suggested, then, is to take a pragmatic look at the problems that policy-makers are addressing when urging that learning be lifelong and open to and engaged in by all people. This will help us accept that, just as there is a myriad of such problems, some of them unique to particular countries, educational systems or institutions, some much more general and widespread, so there will be a large difference, not only in kind but also in degree of complexity and sophistication, in the type and scale of the solutions proffered to them. There will be small- and large-scale differences too in the particular terms of significance in those solutions, the tests for efficacy, the standards of success, and the criteria and arguments that make certain approaches more fruitful than others, for the particular times and circumstances in which they are brought to bear and applied.

Examples of such problems may be speedily and readily found, though our examination of them is likely to start closer to home rather than further away. Clearly the main versions of lifelong education delineated above may be associated with attempts to respond by educational means to problems of a very large-scale and widespread international presence. These are:

- the need for countries to have an economy sufficiently flexible, adaptable and forward-looking to enable it to feed its citizens and give them a reasonable quality of life;

- the need for people to be made aware of the rights and duties open to them in the most widely preferred modern form of government, to be shown how to act in accordance with those rights and duties, and to become committed to the preservation and promotion of that particular form of political arrangement and set of political, social and community institutions; and finally

- the desirability of individuals having an informed awareness of a range of options of activities from which they can construct and continually reconstruct satisfying and personally uplifting patterns of life for themselves.

All of these require educational address. That is particularly necessary if we are to alleviate or, we might hope, eliminate the occurrence of such distressing phenomena as domestic violence, child-abuse or teenage suicide, incidents of which are constantly reported in the media. And these are only a few dysfunctional phenomena. In his *Re-Inventing Australia* the social analyst Hugh Mackay (Mackay, 1993) suggested a list of other causes of social tension and individual disorientation and disaffection, all of which are posing increasingly large problems for our communities:

- radical changes in the structure of some traditional institutions such as marriage;

- the agonizing reappraisal of their world experienced by many men;

- the dynamic changes in modes and structures of employment and non-employment with which we are all now familiar;

- the move towards a cashless society;

- tensions brought about by recent patterns of immigration;

- the alienation of the young from the political process (to which we might add: public suspicion and reservation about the institutions of law and order);

- changes in our approach to questions of health, trade unionism, the information society, science and technology, the environment, manners, politeness and the norms and conventions of communication and social intercourse

– the list goes on and on.

So rapid and dynamic have the changes in the demands and opportunities, difficulties and openings attending all these problems been that it is clear that people need, as a matter of survival as well as for the sake of individual and community enrichment, to be encouraged to keep on engaging in 'the reorganization and reconstruction' of all their learning experiences in order constantly to be reorientating their lives in directions they see as being in their own and in their communities' welfare and best interests.

Movements in that direction are already there to be noted. We may observe with great interest some of the developments that have already come about, and look at the progress that some lifelong education programmes have been making – and at some of the outcomes at which they have been aiming. Bagnall comments approvingly (1990, pp. 4–5) on some of the observable outcomes of programmes that might be gathered loosely under the rubric of 'lifelong learning':

> One may note here, for example, developments in learner participative involvement in educational planning, implementation and evaluation (Knowles and Associates, 1984), the removal of unnecessary and inequitable barriers of access to educational opportunities (Commission on Non-Traditional Study, 1973), and the development of distance education programmes (Holmberg, 1986). The same may be said of those developments which are of a more theoretical nature, but which have practical implications, such as the flourishing of research into adult learning and teaching (Knox, 1977), the breaking down of the rigid distinctions between education, work and vocation (Vermilye, 1977), and the recognition of self-education and its study.

Wain puts the same point more simply (Wain, 1993b, p. 88). He refers to Cropley's contention (1979, p. 101) that 'there is an identifiable "philosophy" of lifelong education and this is loosely humanitarian and humanistic in nature'. Its main tenets are that education should:

- involve learners as actors in their own learning rather than as passive recipients;

- foster the capacity to play the role just mentioned;

- lead to democratization of society; and

- improve the quality of life of men and women.

We might, then, with greater interest, observe some of the recent innovations in the approaches towards learning and teaching methods being advocated and employed in educational institutions of all kinds, formal and informal, traditional and alternative. We could find much that would provoke serious reflection about the ways in which established patterns of educating people are being transformed by the technologies they are employing. These are bidding fair to knock down the conventional concepts of school, college and university as we have known them.

Smethurst puts this well:

> We have to think in terms of designing compulsory education – what I would call initial education – so people learn how to learn and how to want to learn. Initial education must look to the need for people to continue learning during their lives and to acquire the habits ... which lead to learning. The notion that education is a painless process is misleading. Post-initial education must be designed to make it easy for people to enter and move about in without being made to feel small or failures. We need continuous encouragement through a series of relatively small steps people can take and feel good about having achieved, although we must beware of patronising adult students by telling them they are doing well when they are not. I am also worried that recent changes in the funding of adult education are constructing a system where ladders only go upwards. The ideal system would look more like a complicated climbing-frame where people are able to go up and across and down a bit, depending on what courses suit them at particular times.
>
> (Smethurst, 1995, p. 43)

If we do this we may come to a growing awareness of the increasingly wide range and remit of the institutions, agencies and locations in which educational opportunities are offered to potential recipients in their area of influence and operation. Some of these are being provided by firms in the work-place and elsewhere, as for example in the French classes and trips to France provided by Ford in Dagenham UK for its workers; we may look at the 'day-long' opportunities provided for educands of all ages and at all stages of development in such close-knit communities as Sutton-in-Ashfield in their Sutton Centre; or we may think of sports clubs in Australia; of unions and professional organizations in Western Europe; of crèches, clinics and health centres; of arts and cultural centres, art galleries and museums; ethnic welfare centres; churches, and so on. The list could be extended almost indefinitely. Each of these institutions is, in its own different way, helping its own constituency, customers, clients and congregation to acquire additional resources, advice and support for facing the challenge of change in the exigencies of their daily lives, to enjoy themselves while doing so, and to feel a sense of success in personal achievement.

There is no shortage of problems, issues and questions which individual countries, institutions and individuals have to address in attempting to work out what will be most conducive to their individual and communal welfare, how they should act, what choices they need to make, in which directions they should try to shape their futures, and for what reasons, as matters of ongoing educational endeavour and self-discerning and deliberate concern. Because their facing the kinds of problems instanced above will enable them consciously and purposefully to work out ways in which they might bring about an improvement in their own lives and those of all members of their community and how they may hand this on to their successors in coming generations. And that, in the eyes of Mary Warnock (Warnock, 1978), is the purpose of all education.

A PRAGMATIC APPROACH TO REALIZING LIFELONG LEARNING FOR ALL

The criteria for determining improvement and advance in their respective accounts, policies and undertakings of lifelong education will require philosophers, researchers, educators and policy-makers to attend to the interplay of both function and form with respect to the purposes of the institution in which they are all interested and – albeit in different ways and for different purposes – actively engaged. This area of common ground in which agreed interests are enmeshed provides both sets of researchers with a 'criterion' and a standard against which the success or failure – the progression or degeneration of their ongoing research programmes or policy initiatives – can be measured.

This area of engagement – what we have elsewhere called 'enmeshment' (Aspin and Chapman, 1994) – is where the activities of philosophers, educators, researchers and policy-makers coincide. Their common interests provide the area of overlap that Lakatos called the 'touchstone' area (Lakatos, 1976; cf. Evers and Walker, 1983), against which the theories of one and the policy enterprises of the other – and indeed of all other workers in the field – may be tested. It is this that we may call the new 'science' of educational philosophy, policy construction, and educational management – and it is to the application, extension, elaboration and refinement of this new scientific way of looking at and dealing with the problems of philosophy and education that we believe that those concerned with lifelong learning may now be well advised to consider turning.

Perhaps the most plausible account of the way in which this approach may best work is to be found in the Quinean notion that knowledge in matters of educational policy, curriculum construction and the management and administration of schools and school systems is, like any other cognitive enterprise, a complex web of belief, made up of different elements that interweave and form, in their separate parts, a coherent whole (cf. Quine and Ullian, 1970). Conceived of in this way educational discourse and policy analysis and construction is thus like any science – an unending quest to comprehend clearly the theories with which we are working, to compare them with the theoretical efforts and productions of others faced with similar problems, to subject them to positive criticism, and to attempt to improve them and make them fit for their educational purpose: the advancement of efficiency and excellence in all forms of educating institutions, for the benefit of all individuals, for society and for our nations.

The analogy which is most helpful, and the one that is frequently employed by Quine, is that of Otto Neurath (Neurath, 1932). This is that the theory we work out in our educational endeavours is like a boat crossing the sea. Because of the continuing stresses and strains upon it, the craft that is our best theory has to be continually repaired and rebuilt even as it crosses the ocean, while it is still on the move, so to speak – and in a way that will, while still giving overall coherence to the whole, make for a vessel that, at the end of the enterprise of theory-building, is fairly radically different from the 'theoretical vessel' upon which the journey began. For human beings, that 'end' comes when they die: it is part of the human cognitive condition that we are *always* rebuilding our theories. It is the end of our lives that marks the end of theory-change.

What is critical to this enterprise of theory or vessel building and repairing – the pragmatic criteria with which we work – will be the need to look continuously at all plans, theories and forms of cognitive transport, drawn up both by ourselves and others, in an attempt to see how well they manage to fulfil their function of conveying their passengers and their intellectual *impedimenta* across what might be seen as a further example of Don Cupitt's as yet uncharted 'sea of faith' (Cupitt, 1985). This will be the criterion of success in any cognitive endeavour: has our thinking efficiently fulfilled its function and secured the end towards which it was striving? This will be achieved by subjecting our theories, beliefs, policies and solutions to critical scrutiny, appraisal and comparison. This will enable us to assess their functional utility, fecundity and felicity in meeting the challenges of the problem situations in which we have devised and applied them.

This then is the nature of our enterprise. Neither logical empiricism, positivism, nor ordinary language analysis will serve as single or 'would-be' comprehensive theories to account for all the phenomena constituting the bases and interstices of our subject of the soundness and comprehensiveness of our educational policies or the effectiveness of our provision of lifelong education. What we need to adopt, rather, is a pragmatic 'evolutionary epistemology', an approach that goes, as Richard Bernstein (1983) puts it, 'beyond objectivism and relativism' and enhances and facilitates discriminatory theory construction and comparison and so makes our own theories meet for application, modification and repair at every stage of our intellectual journey.

Perhaps the best model for us in this inquiry is to adopt a pragmatic approach as one of our principal modes of operation in the examination and attempted solution of one of the more serious problems facing education today: what we ought to do about the various challenges posed for us by the need for our policies of education to be 'lifelong'. To conceive of our enterprise as an activity of problem-solving is to propose, in the best Popperian tradition, that, in our desire to solve the problems that face us, we should be concerned to proffer our solutions on the basis that they are put up as tentative hypotheses to be, if possible, knocked down. We should seek widely after all possible sources of criticism and potential refutation and, if we find one powerful enough to falsify our proposed solutions, then, from whatever quarter it might have come, we should be open-minded enough to admit it and treat it on its merits not only as a source of criticism and further clarification but, in the novelty of its contribution, as an imaginative essay in the attempt to provide answers, solutions and best provisional theories for application to the difficulties that beset us on the road to finding policies that will best address the imperatives of the need for learning to be lifelong.

CONCLUSION

Given many governments' concerns for the multifaceted character of lifelong learning and its relationship to a broader and more diverse set of goals, it may well be that, in setting the agenda for education for the next century, a more comprehensive analysis of all the various dimensions and features of the nature, aims and purposes of policies for 'realizing a lifelong approach to learning for all' will have to be tackled, and a more wide-ranging set of justifications addressing the differences in those aims and purposes will have to be more clearly articulated and provided. In this way policies pertaining to lifelong learning endeavours are more likely to be developed and articulated, not merely with respect to providing arguments to vindicate a country's concern for its economic self-sufficiency, but also with respect to reinforcing its appreciation of the need for a multiplicity of initiatives, that will increase the emancipation and participation of all citizens in its various social institutions, political arrangements and culture.

For the time being, however, we suggest that the triadic notion of lifelong learning that we have put forward and the pragmatic approach with which we are working will be sufficient to tackle the questions with which so many governments, authorities and agencies are currently preoccupied.

We believe that we have already provided some answers in response to the question: to what problems are proposals for lifelong learning deemed to provide solutions? We hope to have made it clear that governments in many countries are now concerned to increase their economic potential, to make their political and social arrangements more equitable, just and inclusive, and to offer a greater range of avenues for self-improvement and personal development to all their citizens – because in the interplay of all these three they believe that the welfare and felicity of all their individual and community constituencies may best be secured and extended. They hold that the most effective means of bringing this about is by getting all citizens to be ready to engage in education and training throughout their lives.

In the following chapters we try to identify other important questions, show how governments and other agencies are embarking on the endeavour of developing answers to them, attempt to assess the likely success of such policies against pragmatic criteria, and draw any implicative conclusions for educational action. This, we hope, will be sufficient to generate a range of suggestions for policy and a set of agenda for implementation in such attempts in the future.

Part II

The Policy Context

Chapter 3

Understanding the Policy Context: Socio-economic Trends and Challenges to Education

On any interpretation or approach, lifelong learning for all, and the generation and distribution of knowledge, skills and competences, is an important focus for policy-makers because of their simultaneous impact on economic and labour market performance and fundamental social, political and cultural objectives. In this chapter we shall explore the reasons why a coherent lifelong learning approach is being advocated as a strategy for addressing larger social and economic problems besetting countries around the world. We shall analyse the implications for education and training of recent developments and trends in economy and society. Some justifications for lifelong learning will be reviewed and the deficiencies and barriers in conceptualization and implementation will be identified.

A number of questions will guide our considerations:

- Why is there a need for policy-makers to reorientate education and training policies in the direction of lifelong learning?

- What have been the important trends and developments that are creating a global knowledge economy? What is the readiness of education and training systems to meet these challenges?

- What is the social impact of recent economic trends and developments, including their impact on: fragmentation and polarization in society; disparities between rich and poor; trends in leisure and productive time spent in activities other than paid employment? What are the dimensions of social exclusion in the knowledge economy? What is the value of a lifelong approach in relation to the perceived weaknesses in current provision, particularly in respect of social inclusiveness?

- What are the principal economic, social and technological developments that can be expected to have an impact on education over the next ten years and in what ways do these reinforce the arguments for a lifelong learning approach?

- How can education be reconceptualized and relationships reframed in a way that recognizes the complex interactions between education and training and the wider economic, social and cultural environment?

LIFELONG LEARNING SEEN WITHIN THE CONTEXT OF ECONOMIC AND SOCIAL CHANGE

Throughout the world a number of trends in the economy and society have developed, that have highlighted the need to adopt a 'lifelong' approach towards education, training and learning in the knowledge-based economy of the late twentieth century. The economic factors that have become clear include such matters as the changing nature and patterns of employment, population and demographic change, labour-force participation rates, changing types of jobs and their availability, changes in work-place skills and competences, technological change, and globalization. The changes in society that have become clear include such factors as changing family structures and relationships; an ageing population; the increasing incidence of the numbers of children and youth defined as 'at risk'; and the increase in discretionary and non-work-related time. These economic and social factors have all led to the setting up of a series of economic and social imperatives needing to be addressed via a country's policies for education and training. Such imperatives, however, are above and beyond the possibilities of being addressed simply within the confines and time-scales of traditional patterns of learning, and education and training provision.

It is in this context of large-scale economic and social change that work undertaken by many governments has underlined the need for all a country's citizens to have access to opportunities for, and continuing freedom to engage in, programmes of lifelong learning.

CHANGES IN ECONOMY

The Knowledge Economy

The demand for people to exercise their capabilities to acquire further knowledge and learn new skills has always played an important role in society and economy. Today, however, the mode of production and the distribution of knowledge has changed so radically that it is considered: 'legitimate to speak of a new historical era – the knowledge-based economy or the information society – where the economy is more strongly and more directly rooted in the production, distribution and use of knowledge than ever before' (Foray and Lundvall, 1996, p. 12).

While the provision of widespread access to opportunities to increase knowledge, skills and competencies is now seen by many governments as a key element in economic growth, one of the striking facts about the knowledge-based economy is its impact on the structure of employment, unemployment and social cohesion (Fitoussi and Luna, 1996, p. 327).

Fitoussi and Luna (1996) identify two theories that have been put forward for the edification of governments seeking to capitalize upon continuing advance and development in the knowledge economy. The first theory assigns a pre-eminent role to the market. The second, which is informed by growth theory, recognizes two factors in the growth process: education as human capital accumulation; and the institutional structure of the economy.

In contrast to the first theory identified, which relies solely on the market, the second involves some government intervention and public investment in such assets as human capital, infrastructure and R&D. As an example of such intervention, this second approach would involve direct intervention on the part of government to counter inegalitarian wage distribution and to encourage lifelong learning by such means as subsidizing employers who accept the proffered subsidy as a resource from which to raise the educational level of their workers. Fitoussi and Luna highlight the differences between these two theories:

> If, according to the dominant concept (the market approach), there is a trade off between competitiveness and social cohesion, this second approach stresses, on the contrary, the complementarity that links the two goals. Hence, competitiveness should encourage social cohesion which, in turn, improves productivity and competitiveness. Growth is the objective; energies and resources should be devoted to this aim rather than to conflicts over market shares or national income distribution. Thus, the amount of social contribution that employers are forced to pay is not really an issue; what matters is how this money is administered. The correct use of these resources is obtained through investment aiming at increasing productivity via new physical infrastructures and the preservation of social cohesion.
>
> (Fitoussi and Luna, 1996, p. 333)

Fitoussi and Luna argue strongly in favour of the complementarity between social cohesion and growth. Clearly the theory which governments adopt and the strategy they pursue will have wide-ranging implications for our economies, our societies and the opportunities available to all people for lifelong learning.

Unemployment

The present unemployment problem in many countries is a matter of very serious concern with wide-ranging implications for education and training. High unemployment creates insecurity and resistance to organizational and technological change. The rise in youth unemployment means that many young people are losing, or never even gaining, appropriate job-related skills and competencies, and hence failing to secure for themselves the goal of employability. Groups in society that have never before faced unemployment, such as mid- and late-career white collar workers, are losing jobs, with all the personal and societal costs that occasions and implies. Long-term unemployment lowers self-esteem, and has the potential to impact adversely on health, interpersonal relationships and social and community structures, leading at its most extreme to such individually and socially dysfunctional phenomena as crime and substance abuse (OECD, *Jobs Study*, 1994, p. 41).

As Killeen (in Coleman and Warren-Adamson, 1992, p. 200) points out, the immediate impact of unemployment on young people is a loss of income. More than this, however: in the absence of family or state support, there is not only a greater likelihood of young people falling into poverty but a greater likelihood of problems in personal well-being and mental health.

The basic policy message of the *Jobs Study* report is unambiguous:

> High unemployment should be addressed not by seeking to slow the pace of change, but rather by restoring economies' and societies' capacity to adapt to it. But this must be done in ways that do not abandon the objectives of OECD societies. Rather social objectives must be met in new more carefully designed ways that do not have past unintended and undesirable side effects ... The challenge is twofold: to look across the full range of policies that have been in place over the last forty years to see where and to what extent, each may have contributed to ossifying the capacity of economies and the will of societies to adapt; and then to consider how to remove those disincentives without harming the degree of social protection that it is each society's wish to provide.
>
> (OECD, *Jobs Study*, 1994, p. 30)

During the 1950s and 1960s the total number of unemployed in OECD countries averaged below 10 million. From 1972 to 1982 this number tripled. The subsequent prolonged economic expansion reduced unemployment to 25 million in 1990 but since then the number and percentage of unemployed in the potential workforce have risen sharply. Unemployment of 35 million in 1995, representing 8.5 per cent of the OECD labour force, is now widely agreed to constitute an unacceptably high level of wastage of potentially productive human resources.

In most countries young people experience a much higher rate of unemployment than do adults. The few exceptions to this generalization are found in those countries with a traditionally strong apprenticeship system, notably Austria and Germany. This indicates the extent to which education training policies and strategies can have a positive impact on levels of employment, sustainable economic growth and a climate conducive to individual opportunity.

The dysfunctional economic and social effects of unemployment not only originate in people's becoming unemployed but are exacerbated by people's remaining so for extended periods of time. Across many countries there are considerable differences in the relationship of percentage amount of long-term unemployment to total employment. In the European community in 1992 more than 40 per cent of the unemployed had been out of work for twelve months, compared with 15 per cent in Japan and 11 per cent in North America. The incidence of long-term employment also differs considerably with age. In almost all countries workers aged 55 and over are most at risk of experiencing long-term unemployment.

The impact of such factors on the nature, direction and chances of success of programmes of 'lifelong learning' deserves the most serious attention and consideration. The long-term unemployed need opportunities to upgrade and/or change the employable and job-related skills and competencies they possess, but they also need access to lifelong education programmes of other kinds, that will offer them access to a range of interesting and life-enhancing activities, and that will assist or enable them to reconstruct satisfying and potentially enriching patterns of new life-choices for themselves, in case the availability of employment opportunities remains restricted.

Population trends

At the present time in nearly all OECD member countries both the population and the labour force are ageing; at the same time in many countries unemployment is increasing, as the availability of salary-earning opportunities in an increasingly highly skilled, service-related and technologically driven employment environment is decreasing. These two trends are likely to accelerate over the next two decades. Clearly these phenomena have considerable implications for policies and the planning of programmes of education and training, particularly insofar as these pertain to the type, content and accessibility of programmes offered throughout people's lifetimes.

Changes in patterns of migration internationally have also affected patterns of labour supply and availability. The highest rate of workforce growth due to migration has been in European Free Trade Association (EFTA) and European Community (EC) countries; in Oceania the relative contribution of net migration to population growth has also increased, though much less so than in EFTA and EC countries. In North America by contrast there has been little change in patterns of migration into the workforce. Net migration in Japan has been insignificant over the last two decades.

To date there has been only a relatively small amount of research done into the relationship between international migration and further education and training, and of both with the labour market. With the increasing globalization of economic productivity and development, and the increasing mobility of workers with high levels of skills and competencies, together with the increased portability and applicability of high-level employment-related knowledge, the time is right for serious attention to be paid to the need for co-ordinated and interconnected programmes of further education and training.

Labour-force participation rates

Rates revealing the total percentage of the population participating in the labour force show that in Japan (74 per cent) and the EC countries (67 per cent), such percentage participation has changed little over the past thirty years. In EFTA, Oceania, and North America, by contrast, participation rates have grown significantly to 75 per cent. In most countries participation rates generally have been rising for women and falling for men, bringing the percentage proportions of men and women participating in the workforce closer. Participation rates for younger people generally declined during the 1980s. The average educational attainment of the labour force has continued to rise throughout OECD member countries, with the arrival of successive waves of new, more qualified, labour market entrants and the retirements or withdrawal of the less qualified workers (OECD, *Jobs Study*, 1994).

The increasing participation of women in the workforce has had its own impact on demand for further education and training programmes and provision, with the need to consider making appropriate adjustments called for in catering for the particular personal, familial and life-cycle needs of women entrants to the labour force.

Jobs

Across all western countries jobs have been disappearing in agriculture. The availability of employment in traditional and/or heavy industry has also decreased, at the same time as there has been a continuing rise in employment in the 'sunrise' and service sectors, including finance, insurance, tourism, hospitality, social, community and personal services. During the 1980s there has been a significant growth in the number of people who are self-employed and who are in part-time employment. Clearly these changes in the type and pattern of employment-related activities have enormous implications for the style and pattern of courses and programmes offered in compulsory, post-compulsory and further education and training agencies and institutions.

Technological Change

Technological change alters the nature of jobs but, contrary to some claims, technological progress has not accelerated to the point where it has resulted in 'technological unemployment'. The larger countries, with their strong domestic markets, have had the highest share of employment in high technology manufacturing, though growth has also occurred in Japan, Australia, Finland and Norway. This requires a continuing commitment to the training, education and production of a workforce made up of highly technologically literate and skilled men and women. The existence of a technologically literate population also means that in the planning and provision of further education and training *and* lifelong learning programmes, much more use can be made of all the devices and techniques of the information technology revolution, deliverable not only in formal and institutional settings but also informally and in the home.

Wages

The question of wages and remuneration plays a significant part in any discussion of the consequences of employment and unemployment, and the implications for further education and training. The process of wage determination is strongly influenced by labour-market pressures, social perceptions, legislation, and industrial relations requirements and legislation, all of which affect the determination of rewards for labour, the settlement of real wages and the evolution of wage differentials (OECD, *Jobs Study*, 1994).

Across the OECD member countries, for example, the share of wages as a proportion of national income has generally been declining in recent years, and the concomitant rise in profits has much enhanced the climate for business investment. At the same time as the overall share of wages in national income fell, however, there was a considerable shift in the proportion of wages earned in respect of the emoluments paid to unskilled and highly skilled workers. All countries have experienced a shift in demand away from unskilled jobs towards more highly skilled jobs and more highly skilled workers are thus receiving a higher proportion of the share of wages paid. The willingness of workers to accept low-paid jobs depends in part on the relative generosity of unemployment benefits. Unemployment benefits relative to wage earnings are generally higher in Europe than in other countries.

The implications for education and training of these trends and differentiating processes are obvious and manifold. Programmes of compulsory and post-compulsory education must reflect and seek to address the requirements flowing from and generated by these realities, particularly insofar as they have an impact on people's life chances and their preparation for frequent job changes, periods of unemployment and increased longevity. For the unskilled the implications of the trends referred to above will be especially acute.

All this highlights the need for a multifaceted approach to policy development, incorporating serious and detailed appraisal and considerations of the relationship between economic policy, education and social welfare services.

Globalization

Globalization is replacing internationalization as the key characteristic of the world market (Rasmussen, OECD, *Employment and Growth in the Knowledge-Based Economy*, 1996, p. 7). The increasing globalization of all aspects of the productive and exchange processes – products, personnel, processes, raw materials – is recognized as exercising a growing influence on national economies and international co-operation and development. The international investment boom at the end of the 1980s increased the importance of the roles played by foreign affiliates and the great multinational corporations in most economies. International collaboration among firms increased, especially in manufacturing, R&D-intensive, and assembly industries.

As Tuijnman points out (OECD, *Literacy, Economy and Society*, 1995, p. 21), the reintegration of Central and Eastern European countries into the world economy has upset the economic status quo. While new forms of co-operation across borders have emerged, competition for investment capital has intensified. Some countries, firms and individuals are well positioned to compete successfully for investment capital; others have difficulties in capitalizing on the opportunities that globalization brings. While the emerging global economy is characterized by increased flows of information and financial capital, these tend to decrease the traditional hold of governments and social partners over specific policy domains.

In respect to global competition, analyses of international trade in goods suggest that there has been a small negative effect on demand for unskilled labour in OECD countries, as a result of trade with low-wage, non-OECD countries, but from the perspective of national economies overall, this has been offset by the emergence of low-wage countries as growing markets for exports from OECD member countries. In practice, most of the economic competition among OECD countries comes about as a result of competition between OECD countries themselves. Trade between these countries usually involves trade within sectors, even within individual firms, involving the exchange of similar products with similar skill and labour content. This has led to the rise and fall of activities and the relocation of production within and between countries and regions resulting in the disappearance of many jobs, together with the creation of many new ones.

The authors of the OECD *Jobs Study* conclude: 'the perceived importance and complexity of globalization suggest the need for further work to quantify the effects of trade, investment and other element of globalization on employment skills and earnings' (OECD, *Jobs Study*, 1994, p. 28).

The implications of globalization for education and training also warrant considerable further investigation. For what this factor in economic development, and phenomena resulting from it, portends is the need for a very extensive range of education and training programmes to be made available across countries, yet working on an integrated, properly co-ordinated and interconnected basis. Not only must many of the courses offered have similar aims, content and applicability, but also many of the examination credits and terminal qualifications must have interchangeability and acceptance.

CHANGES IN SOCIETY

Changes in Family Structure and Family Relationships

The last two decades have seen substantial changes in family structures and family relationships. In the UK, for example, Coles (1995, p. 59) reports that the number of single-parent households has more than doubled from 570,000 in 1971 to 1,270,000 in 1991; since the 1960s there has been a fourfold increase in the number of divorces, and almost a fivefold increase in the number of single (never married) parents. There is thus a growing likelihood of a sizeable proportion of young people living in families that will experience divorce and of children being brought up by single parents and/or joining reconstituted families. In the UK, Coles cites research (Coles, 1995, p. 64) which suggests that young people who have experienced the separation or divorce of their parents appear to have a reduced chance of obtaining school qualifications, an increased chance of being unemployed at 18 years of age (Kuh and Maclean, 1990; Maclean and Wadsworth, 1988) and are less likely to get a university qualification (Elliott and Richards, 1991).

Changes in family structure and relationships are occurring contemporaneously with an increase in an ageing population. The convergence of changing family relationships and changing demographic trends poses considerable problems for society and economy. There are fewer active people in paid employment to support an increasing number of elderly people, and fewer traditional families to offer the comfort, support and mutual solidarity that were provided to elderly people in the past. Of particular concern are the relationship between poverty and the changing nature of the family, and the danger of a widening gap between those people who have access to resources (including financial, educational and family resources), enabling them to cultivate a rewarding life, and those who do not.

There is considerable concern that the changing nature of the family and the increasing individualism which has emerged from these changes (Lutz, 1994, p. 103) may run the risk of eroding social cohesion and fragmenting our society, unless new social patterns and relationships are created and new ways of relating positively to each other are considered, created and maintained:

> There will be more ways of living together – several parents sharing the education of their children, working partly at home, partly outside the home and partly not at all, developing small enterprises together, cooperating in a neighbourhood network, developing new social services ... a constellation of family, neighbourhood, friendship, professional and public networks, services and systems.
>
> (Lutz, 1994, p. 104)

Educating people in a way that will enable them to forge satisfying inter-personal relationships and relate to a society integrated in new ways is a major challenge for lifelong learning.

Children and Youth at Risk

Children and youth defined as being 'at risk' are generally deemed to be those pupils who are unsuccessful in reaching the necessary standards in school, often drop out and fail to make the necessary transitions to adult life. As a result they fail to become fully integrated into normally accepted patterns of social responsibility, particularly with regard to work and family life. A number of factors have been found to be associated with young people at risk: poverty; family issues (including transience, child-abuse, inadequate housing); poor knowledge of the majority language; and community factors (including lack of community support; non-availability of leisure activities; and lack of political resources). 'At risk' behaviour manifests itself at the school level in low attainment, low satisfaction and self-esteem, truancy, school refusal, behaviour problems and drop-out. At the societal level, 'at risk' behaviour manifests itself in various levels of marginality such as substance-abuse and use of drugs, early pregnancy, crime, and an inability to integrate into work and unemployment (Evans, 1995).

Poverty dramatically increases the likelihood of young people being placed 'at risk'. Huston reports that in the USA the proportion of children living in poverty increased substantially during the 1980s and remains high today. In 1985, for example, 20 per cent of all children in the USA lived in families with incomes below the official poverty line; 41 per cent of all black children and 37 per cent of all Hispanic children lived in poverty (Huston, 1994, p. 2).

Duncan (in Huston, 1994) has identified three main factors for the increase in child poverty in the USA: changes in family structure, especially the increase in 'mothers only' families; changes in the labour market associated with unemployment and low wages; and reductions in state support. Unemployment is the most common reason for a sudden loss of income level in men; divorce is the most common reason among women. Duncan shows that family income has effects on children's long-term attainments and their physical and mental health. And, as Klerman (in Huston, 1994) points out, the health problems of poor children have long-range effects on their cognitive, social and emotional development.

Children and young people experiencing such disadvantage can begin to redress the balance of disadvantage in their favour by access to a strong foundation of learning, and by undertaking programmes or courses of study provided by institutions offering a range of avenues into continuing education and training.

Research also appears to show the cumulative effect of disadvantage and the need in our educational programmes for young people to develop an awareness of the risks to them of early pregnancy, substance-abuse, and the use of drugs. We need to provide opportunities to enable such young people to recognize the benefits available to them by taking up opportunities for various forms of personal development, the productive use of discretionary time, and the availability of various forms of community counselling, advice and support. All these things are likely to increase and enhance the sense of personal efficacy that young people feel when confronted with the numerous challenges with which modern life faces them.

Social Exclusion and the Underclass

High levels of unemployment and underemployment, with all the associated insecurity and non-standard patterns of work, the changing structure and relationships of the family, with an increase in single-parent families and increased poverty among women and young children, have challenged traditional patterns of social organization. In this environment a new social category has emerged – the residual category of the 'underclass', a class of people who are perceived as living outside society's norms and values and who are separated not only from the more affluent in our community but also from the traditional working classes and others on low income. The idea of 'an underclass' is associated with the notion of social exclusion, be it cultural or structural in nature. In the eyes of some members of society the idea of 'underclass' has connotations of a dangerous class of undeserving poor:

> The term itself suggests a group which is in some sense outside of mainstream society, but there is disagreement about the nature and scope of their exclusion. One position argues that welfare dependency has encouraged the breakup of the nuclear family household and socialisation into a counterculture which devalues work and encourages dependency and/or criminality. The other position emphasises the failure of the economy to provide sufficient secure employment to meet demand. The former sees the source of exclusion as lying in the attitudes of the underclass; the latter sees it as lying in the structured inequality which disadvantages particular groups in society.
>
> (Morris, 1994, p. 81)

Clearly there are two different theories of the 'underclass' in operation. Of these Coles (1995, p. 201) argues that the first analysis of social exclusion and 'the underclass' offers no real policy agenda, apart from castigation of the vulnerable; the second analysis, however, provides a positive policy agenda especially for young people. This includes the identification of their welfare needs, rights and interests during the periods of the three main transitions of youth: from education to the labour market; from living with families to attaining some measure of welfare independence from them; and from leaving home to living independently. The demands of each of these transitions have wide-ranging implications for lifelong learning.

To begin with, it is vitally important that all young people have the requisite education and training, that will offer them access to a full range of life choices and make them fit for independence, through employability, and the development of a sense of self-worth and a capacity for sound interpersonal relationships. This will necessitate a reassessment of the traditional school curriculum, especially in respect of education for personal development and well-being; a renewed commitment to overcoming the sense of 'failure' experienced by sizeable numbers of our children in schools; and proper career counselling, guidance and support, especially for those students who may be in danger of 'dropping out'.

It is particularly important that the needs of young people with disabilities or special needs are addressed by employing a co-ordinated approach to the provision of education and training opportunities and indeed to welfare more broadly. This should include the assessment and provision of education and training, work and social security, health and social support.

Life-chances and Literacy

Literacy has an effect on people's capacity to adapt to economic and social change, to participate actively in political processes, and to avail themselves of lifelong learning opportunities. A literate population is now recognized as a major factor in the ability of governments, communities and individuals to realize the benefits of economic development, globalization, and the diffusion of information technologies, while safeguarding cherished values of social inclusiveness and personal autonomy: 'The central importance of the human factor in securing an adequate foundation for economic growth, personal development and social and cultural revitalization underscores the imperative of cultivating a highly literate population' (Tuijnman, in OECD, *Literacy, Economy and Society*, 1995, p. 23).

Whilst economic and occupational changes are opening up new opportunities for literate and skilled workers, those with low levels of literacy are finding it increasingly difficult to adapt to the new demands, thereby facing increased risks of social alienation and economic exclusion:

> The distribution of literacy in a population is a good predictor of the magnitude of differences between social groups. Literacy is therefore an essential element in any strategy for promoting social cohesion. An instrumental view of literacy, focussed on economic objectives only, is therefore untenable.
>
> (Tuijnman, in OECD, *Literacy, Economy and Society*, 1995, p. 23)

In response to an international concern regarding the level and distribution of literacy, the International Adult Literacy Survey was conducted in 1994 in Canada, Germany, the Netherlands, Poland, Sweden, Switzerland and the USA. Defining literacy as 'using printed and written information to function in society, to achieve one's goals and to develop one's knowledge and potential' (OECD, *Literacy, Economy and Society*, 1995, p. 14), the survey found (p. 115):

- Important differences in literacy exist across and within nations and these are large enough to matter both socially and economically.

- Literacy skill deficits affect large proportions of the entire adult population, not just marginalized groups.

- Literacy is strongly correlated with life-chances, especially in regard to employment stability, the incidence of unemployment and income. As the structural adjustment that is reducing the prospects of adults with low levels of literacy is incomplete, it is reasonable to predict that those with low levels of literacy will have fewer opportunities in the future.

- Literacy skills are maintained and strengthened through regular use. Formal education provides the raw material for adult literacy, but literacy practices will need to be established within organizations of all kinds to ensure that literacy is sustained and developed over a lifetime.

It is clear from the findings of the International Adult Literacy Survey that government interventions, through their policies of education and training, can have a positive long-term impact on literacy levels. In the current context, however, there is a need to move beyond traditional conceptions of literacy. Notions of literacy are evolving, expanding and becoming more complex, and their impact on and implications for government policy in respect to education and training are broadening considerably.

Foray and Lundvall (1996, p. 19) have highlighted the distinction that might be made, in the growth of the knowledge economy, between four different kinds of knowledge. As we approach the twenty-first century, each of these forms of knowledge has important implications for literacy:

- *Know what*, which refers to knowledge about facts and information which can be mastered by reading books, attending lectures, accessing data bases.

- *Know why*, which refers to scientific knowledge of principles and laws in nature, in the human mind and society which can also be mastered by reading, attending lectures, accessing data bases.

- *Know how*, which refers to skills and the capability to do something and which is usually mastered through practical experience, especially in apprenticeship relationships with significant others.

- *Know who*, which refers to a different mix of skills normally acquired through social practice in professional and collegial environments accessed through networks and relationships.

The ability to read and write and to be able to communicate and profit from the gaining of such knowledge continues to be important in the knowledge-based economy. Increasingly, however, knowledge and cognitive competence is being developed co-operatively, interactively through information technology, and shared within subgroups, individuals and technological networks of all kinds. In this new learning context, computer literacy and the ability to communicate through computerized network facilities have joined with literacy, as traditionally defined, as key determinants in facilitating people's life-chances (Foray and Lundvall, 1996, p. 29).

Awareness of the relationship between literacy, broadly defined, and life-chances clearly has a number of implications for lifelong learning. It is becoming increasingly clear that computer literacy has now to be seen, not merely as an addition to the skills of literacy more traditionally conceived, but in some sense as subsuming them in its educational remit and global communication possibilities. Ability to operate the personal computer and to take advantage of all the opportunities and services offered by interactive communication technology will clearly be a major factor in the ability of the individual to cope with the exigencies of life in the modern communication society and to take advantage of all the additional goods it has to offer. The implications of these needs for lifelong education are obvious.

Non-Work-Related Activities and Extended Discretionary Time

Unemployment, underemployment, technological progress, increasing prosperity and a shift towards post-materialist values indicate the emergence of a new relationship between work and non-work-related activities in people's lives (Lenk, 1994; Stevens and Michalski, 1994).

Unemployment creates a situation in which a sizeable proportion of the population will spend extended periods of time in non-voluntary, non-work-related activities. At the same time as sections of the population will have non-voluntary, non-work time imposed upon them through unemployment, however, there is a strong likelihood that sections of the community will voluntarily increase their non-work-related, discretionary time. In the future it is conceivable that many wage earners will become increasingly willing to consider working fewer hours or retiring at a younger age. In Europe there has been a decline in the number of average working hours from 3000 hours per individual per annum a century ago, to around 1700 hours today. This trend is likely to be continued with increasing prosperity. In the USA, per capita disposable personal income is predicted to increase by one-quarter in real terms between 1990 and 2005, in Japan real growth of disposable household incomes between 1990 and 2010 is projected to be in the order of 30 per cent. Increases of a similar magnitude are expected for many European countries (OECD, *Societies in Transition*, 1994, p. 14).

The results of national and international public opinion polls indicate significant shifts in people's attitudes to work, away from materialistic values such as economic and physical security towards post-materialist values such as self-development, self-fulfilment and aesthetic and intellectual orientations (OECD, *Societies in Transition*, 1994, p. 14). The results of the 1990 Allensbach study in Germany revealed, for example (Lenk, 1994, p. 81), that the perception of life as a task and a duty had diminished over the last four decades, whereas the perception of life as pleasure had increased considerably. This attitude was particularly evident in the under-30s age group and sections of the older population, revealing a generational cleavage or 'scissors effect' in life orientation.

As Stevens and Michalski (1994, p. 15) note:

> Rising prosperity, together with the widely observed shift in attitudes to work, opens up a range of opportunities in the search for some of the most pressing work and society related problems that OECD countries will face in years to come. The combination creates most favourable conditions for a broad based reconsideration of the potential of working time reductions and work sharing. The two factors hold out the promise of broader acceptance within society of unrenumerated activities, and offer the prospect of both work and leisure becoming accepted and respected sources of self development and self fulfilment.

In this context governments are considering voluntary flexible arrangements which offer a diversity of options for reducing working time, such as various forms of leave (educational, parental, sabbatical leave), and the introduction of monthly and annual working hours. The justification for such strategies is social as well as economic:

> One indispensable guideline in contemplating the future of work and society from a social-philosophical point of view is to develop and foster the idea of a socially just and comprehensive division and distribution of labour – in other words to provide all people willing to work with at least a chance to obtain work. This could well imply reductions in overtime work, the shortening of working time, and (in particular) the promotion of job sharing.
>
> (Lenk, 1994, p. 90)

Such strategies are complemented by technology-driven options for organizing working time flexibility which enable more people to work from home and which blur the distinction between work and discretionary time. These changes are being considered in conjunction with other changes designed to bring about flexibility in living and working conditions, such as a loosening of regulations governing work practices, the extension of shopping hours, and so on.

Such developments necessitate a shift in community attitudes, particularly in respect to the role of work in achieving social status, the value attached to unremunerated, socially productive community work and the recognition given to educational, recreational and creative activities.

However, Stevens and Michalski (1994, p. 17) have pointed out that:

... this projection of a 'leisure society' is not without its problems. Continuation of present·trends in a number of countries would ensure a very uneven distribution of capacity to exercise leisure activities in two respects: 1) some population groups have more discretionary time than others; and 2) the diversity of available leisure options in particular the pursuit of cultural activities correlates strongly with the level of education. Generally speaking, active people in the 20–50 age bracket constitute a group whose discretionary time is being squeezed between rising workloads on the one hand and studies on the other (women are often under additional strain due to family and household responsibilities). They stand in sharp contrast to those in the population who, because of unemployment, underemployment, disability or early retirement find themselves with a lot of free time but not necessarily the means to translate that into self development and self fulfilment on the basis of leisure activities.

The increase in discretionary time and in non-work-related activities has a number of implications for the provision of education and lifelong learning. For example, the teaching of creative and relational skills will be an inherent part of preparing and sustaining people in their pursuit of quality leisure activities and the constructive use of free time. Opening up the opportunity for appreciation and engagement in sports and outdoor pursuits, the theatre, music, art, literature and culture must thus constitute an important part of any curriculum for lifelong learning.

Educational programmes can provide the basis for active personal involvement, personal and authentic achievement and access to a range of socially meaningful and productive activities, that, as Lenk (1994, p. 90) points out, 'can engender a particularly satisfying, humane way of life, namely caring for the young, elderly or disabled, engaging in voluntary activities'. The inclusion in the school curriculum and school programmes of opportunities for learning to engage in and become committed to such caring concerns will do much to widen people's range of access to a choice of life-fulfilling and enhancing activities, and to contribute to community involvement and social cohesion. For this to come about, however, attitudes towards achievement and career success as fundamental conditions of 'value', self-esteem, social status and meaning in people's lives will need to be reassessed and the culture, reward systems and values operating within educational institutions will need to change and expand accordingly.

IMPLICATIONS OF SOCIAL AND ECONOMIC TRENDS FOR LIFELONG LEARNING

We have seen how changes in the economy and in society have enormously altered the landscape in which policies for education and training have to be considered. The demands of the knowledge economy, unemployment, labour-force participation, demographic change, the changing nature of jobs, technological advance, wage distribution, and globalization have all impacted upon countries' and individuals' capacities to achieve and sustain economic advance and growth. At the same time changes in society, associated with changes in family structure and family relationships, an increasingly ageing populace, the increase of numbers of children and young people 'at risk', the emergence of new social categories, have increased the dangers of social exclusion and diminished the possibilities for personal fulfilment and satisfying patterns of life-option for sizeable proportions of our population.

The policy challenge for governments is to provide for economic advance at the same time as ensuring that all its citizens are able both to participate in that process and to take benefit from it; for without contributions from all its citizens – from all its potential pool of talent – the chances of a country's achieving economic stability and social cohesion are likely to be significantly impaired. As we approach the twenty-first century many governments are addressing this challenge through policies associated with the realization of lifelong learning for all.

THE OVERALL POLICY CHALLENGE: REALIZING LIFELONG LEARNING FOR ALL

The OECD *Jobs Study* (1994) currently provides perhaps the most powerful analysis of the forces bringing about the pressure for policy change. The planning and implementation of policies designed for setting appropriate macro-economic policy, enhancing the creation and diffusion of technological know-how, increasing work-time flexibility, encouraging entrepreneurship, increasing wage and labour-cost flexibility, reforming employment security provisions, expanding and enhancing active labour-market policies, facilitating international co-operation, and improving labour-force skills and competences – all of these have been identified by the OECD *Jobs Study* as ways in which governments might realize the ideal of lifelong learning for all.

The authors of the OECD *Jobs Study* maintain that '[a]daptation is fundamental to progress in a world of new technologies, globalization, and national and international competitiveness' (OECD, *Jobs Study*, 1994, p. 7). The ability of economies to adapt to change can only be developed with people possessed of a sound and appropriate set of capacities, competencies and knowledge. This requires engagement in and benefit from involvement in a programme of active educational endeavour throughout people's lives:

> Many people will need help to fit the requirements of high skill jobs. But some will be unable to meet those requirements and will be unemployed or take low skill, low wage jobs. The commitment to support them will be a valuable investment towards a forward moving and cohesive society. As OECD economies progress it will become all the more important to hone the support policies and mechanisms so that they provide effective help to those who most need it.
>
> (OECD, *Jobs Study*, 1994, p. 37)

Policy recommendations for changes in these areas must, the authors of the study contend, be built on a social consensus and be considered in the light of their potential to solve unemployment or improve the quality of employment, by elevating people and jobs to the world of the future. Attempting to slow the pace of change is not, in the view of these analysts, the appropriate approach to meeting the challenges which now face many countries:

> ... But governments cannot meet the challenge alone. A high degree of social consensus will be needed to move forward with the necessary changes. Businesses, trade unions and workers need to be innovative to develop new products, processes, and ways of working that will create new jobs and help to shape skills to fit with the jobs of the future ... The most successful economies will be those which plough back some of the gains from change into accelerating the process by helping them to adapt.
>
> (OECD, *Jobs Study*, 1994, p. 7)

One aspect of the response to the employment problem is seen by the authors of the OECD *Jobs Study* (1994, p. 33) to reside in creating more jobs. Although it is impossible to predict what these jobs might be, they are likely to share some basic characteristics:

- New jobs are likely to appear in the service sector; some will be new types of jobs; others will be activities that formerly were performed within manufacturing enterprises but are now subcontracted.

- New jobs will be generated by the private sector.

- New jobs, particularly in tradable goods industries, will increasingly have high-knowledge requirements in firms that have a strong capacity to innovate and use technology effectively.

- Many new jobs are also likely to be low-productivity, low-wage jobs, particularly in the non-tradables sector.

The authors of the study recommend that efforts to improve the capacity of economies to create new job opportunities should focus on a number of strategies. Among these strategies are many which will have a direct impact on the need for alteration and expansion in policies for education and training and for the realization of governments' aspirations for lifelong learning for all (OECD, *Jobs Study*, 1994, pp. 43–9). Such strategies as are recommended by the authors of the study include:

1 Setting appropriate macro-economic policy

Macro-economic policy should be set in such ways and forms that it will encourage growth. An economy's ability to create viable jobs will be enhanced when a greater synergy is created between macro-economic policy and structural policy.

A supportive macro-economic environment is seen to include:

- sound public finances, so that the public sector financing does not impinge adversely on investment: lowering the public sector borrowing requirement automatically releases more money into the economy;

- inflation that is kept under control, so that companies and workers are not held back by uncertainty associated with distorted price signals;

- aggregate demand that is managed, so that growth is neither too rapid, risking inflation, nor too slow, with the risk of deflation and economic stagnation.

Clearly this has major implications for education and training policies. The need and desire to move forward to a situation in which there are more effective opportunities for further education and learning will only become realizable in a climate in which there are sound economic policies in place and where there exist opportunities for sound investment in policies needed to bring this advance about. The need for partnerships among traditional education and training providers and agencies, business and industry, and worker unions and trade associations, will only be addressed in an environment of sound economic management.

2 Enhancing the creation and diffusion of technological know-how and promoting the development and use of technology

Advance in technology generally destroys lower-wage, lower-productivity jobs, while it creates jobs that are more productive, high-skill and better-paid. The absorption and profitable utilization of new technologies is usually possible only after major organizational change and relearning. This involves adapting education and training systems to a more technologically driven world, together with the encouragement of learning for enterprises as well as individuals (OECD, *Jobs Study*, 1994, pp. 33, 34).

There is also an educational element involved in the attempt to reduce the gap between the standards observable in the utilization of technology and models of organizational and managerial best practice, that merit emulation, and the methods of applying technology currently in place in the existing work-place practices of very many organizations and firms. This has a number of implications for lifelong learning, not only in respect to the creation, communication and diffusion of technical skills and competencies among persons entering employment, but also in respect to the education of senior and middle-level management and existing staff performing operations in increasingly technically sophisticated organizations.

3 Increasing work-time flexibility

Traditional patterns in the setting and organization of work and working time remain enshrined in legislation and collective agreements and these prove powerfully recalcitrant to change. In this way such traditional practices and conceptions of the organization of work-time hinder labour market flexibility, and indirectly, thereby, job creation and opportunities for lifelong learning.

Less rigid and more flexible arrangements for daily, weekly, annual and lifetime working hours could better meet the entrepreneurial requirements of firms and organizations, while at the same time responding better to worker needs, aspirations and life-patterns.

One great attraction of greater flexibility in the setting of work-time is its potential to integrate working time with new patterns of lifelong learning. More flexible working arrangements would also facilitate greater participation in the workforce by women. More flexibility in working time could also lead to more flexibility in the very concept of and arrangements for 'retirement', thereby retaining the contributions of highly trained and knowledgeable workers, to the optimum profit of the organization and the preferred involvement of individuals in a continuing function of contribution that acknowledges and enhances their sense of individual worth.

4 Encouraging entrepreneurship and an entrepreneurial climate

Entrepreneurship will be facilitated by policies that will remove red tape, regulations and controls that discourage new and expanding ventures. But dynamic entrepreneurship thrives when there is a highly trained and flexible workforce and easy access to the graduates, work and research programmes of universities and centres of technological expertise and research. Programmes to foster entrepreneurship and small business development need to be an integral part of local development policies, particularly as they relate to education and training. This is particularly important now that, in some countries, a considerable proportion of national economic growth is coming about as a function of the expanding activities of small enterprising and innovative firms and businesses.

Past evidence suggests, however, that small businesses have not always invested greatly in further education and training. Policies need to be developed that will provide incentives for small businesses to engage in or provide the requisite amount and extent of education and training for their workers. In addition, enhancing the capacities of future workers to engage in enterprising and innovative activities needs to be an essential component of compulsory and post-compulsory education and training programmes.

5 Increasing wage and labour cost flexibility and reforming employment security provisions

Increasing wage and labour cost flexibility is likely to have the effect of creating more employment opportunities. However, the means by which governments seek to achieve their objectives in wage and labour cost flexibility must keep abreast of changing economic and employment circumstances, and be sensitive to social and equity concerns. The private sector, for example, would be likely to create more jobs if there were fewer constraints on hiring and firing, but there may be good social arguments for keeping some current employment regulations in place. Reform in this matter may require fundamental redesign of employment and industrial relations policies, together with the making of necessary changes in institutional practices and attitudes, especially in the field of taxation and collective and individual enterprise bargaining, while at the same time taking into account the possible impact of such changes on social policy and equity matters.

One aspect of the policy response to this issue has considerable implications for lifelong learning. Employment protection legislation, along with job guarantees negotiated by collective bargaining, can bring considerable benefits. Employment security through long-term contracts can encourage investment in on-the-job training that would normally be hindered by high labour turnover.

6 Expanding and enhancing active labour market policies

Active and effective labour market policies are needed to improve access to the labour market and jobs, and develop job-related skills. Countries which reject a widening of wage dispersions as a means of increasing employment will have to rely particularly heavily on active and effective labour markets, and the planning and implementation of appropriate, effective and inclusive education and training policies. Active policies can strengthen the links between the growth of aggregate demand, job creation and the supply of qualified labour. Higher public spending on active labour market measures may lead to wage moderation by strengthening the ability of the long-term unemployed and first-time job seekers to compete effectively for jobs.

As an illustration, the authors of the OECD *Jobs Study* (1994) report that a typical OECD country spends 2–3 per cent of its GDP on labour market policies (including unemployment benefits); but there has been little progress in shifting these sizeable resources from passive policies, such as granting unemployment benefits, to active measures called for in active labour market planning, creating new jobs, and providing appropriate and effective education and training opportunities, especially for those who in the past have made up the numbers of the educationally under-served. There is considerable scope for the development, articulation and implementation of more effective education and training policies through careful programme design, implementation and monitoring.

An effective public employment service (PES) has been regarded by some countries as a key element in such active planning and policy measures. This involves integrating job placement and payment of unemployment benefits with access to active programmes of further education and training. The availability and utilization of places and opportunities in training or job creation programmes can serve as a work test for benefit claimants.

Careful targeting is another important aspect of such programmes. Broad and generalist education and training programmes for the unemployed have not proved to be effective, either in the economic or in the individual and social senses. All the key actors at the local level – employers, trade unions, educational institutions and local government – need to be involved in designing and implementing training programmes, carefully targeted and relevant to local economic and social needs. In general, young people and the long-term unemployed have been found to be the best targets for such policies and programmes.

Other active measures have been identified (OECD, *Jobs Study*, 1994):

- maintaining supply side measures such as training for the unemployed during cyclical downswings;

- targeting and diversifying training programmes for the unemployed, based on a thorough assessment of labour market needs;

- allowing the labour market authorities to buy and sell training places for the unemployed in the private training market. They should also have the possibility of supplying training courses directly in order to increase flexibility and target efficiency in difficult to place groups;

- involving employers in the design and execution of training programmes for the unemployed at the local and community level;

- targeting job creation measures to workers for whom joblessness is particularly harmful for future prospects, e.g. unemployed youth or workers whose bargaining power is relatively weak, such as all long-term unemployed.

Tax benefit systems are another strategy of particular relevance to attempts to overcome the 'poverty trap', whereby low-wage earners lose benefits as their earnings rise, thereby leaving little incentive for people in part-time or low-paid work to increase their hours of work or to invest in training that would increase their chances of getting higher-paid jobs. Eliminating the 'poverty trap' might involve measures to integrate tax and benefit systems through a negative income tax or income tax credit scheme.

7 Facilitating international co-operation

Governments now face and must operate in a climate of the much greater international interdependence of their economies. They need to think realistically and globally, so that national policies fit in with and take into account the broader international context. The OECD *Jobs Study* (1994, p. 40) identifies six areas of international connectedness to be taken into account in governmental shaping of their economic and employment policies:

- macro-economic policy;

- multilateral trade rules;

- foreign direct investment;

- taxes;

- international migration;

- science and technology.

To date there has been little consideration of how these matters impact on the provision of lifelong learning, when viewed from the perspective of international connectedness and the need for international co-operation.

8 Improving labour-force skills and competencies

Across the world governments are stressing the need to upgrade the skills and competencies of their populations. But effective reforms are difficult to implement because of the number, range and diverse interests of the different actors, agencies and institutions involved. Moreover, for maximum effective change to come about, both the lead-in time and the time of most effective output of such policies can be considerable.

Governments agree that extending and upgrading workers' skills and competencies must be a lifelong process if their countries' economies are to foster the creation and expansion of high-skill, high-wage job opportunities. But governments also agree that education and training policies should be directed not only at furthering these economic and employment goals but, just as importantly, at achieving other fundamental social and cultural objectives.

Such an undertaking will require a major shift in policy in some countries, and sustained and continuing development of existing policies in others. Particular emphasis needs to be placed on major problem areas including: the quality of initial education; the transition from school to work; and investment in work-related skills, especially for the least qualified workers:

> Lifelong learning must become a central element in a high skills, high wage jobs strategy. This involves dismantling barriers at all levels of education and training and a sharing of the cost burden of lifelong learning between the individual, business and the public purse.
>
> (OECD, *Jobs Study*, 1994, p. 37)

Strategies to implement these goals will need to be developed, the aim of which will be to seek to bring about change in each of the main levels and in the principal sectors of provision, at the same time as providing for an integrated, multifaceted approach. As a starting-point the authors of the OECD *Jobs Study* (1994) recommend:

(a) *Pre-school and early childhood*. Development programmes should be designed to establish a sound basis for subsequent learning, especially for children from disadvantaged backgrounds. Such pre-schooling should encompass education and socialization as well as child-care.

(b) *Primary and secondary schooling*. There is a need to reduce early school-leaving and improve student performance through a wide range of reforms, including more diversified curricula and learning methods; more scope for parents to choose schools for their children; more active involvement of parents; better incentives for motivating teachers; and more opportunities for their professional development. Curriculum and teaching methods need to be reviewed, particularly to consider the needs of underachievers and to provide the necessary support and continuity from pre-school through to entry into the labour market.

(c) *Transition from school to work*. Apprenticeship and work-based learning must develop in synchronicity with changing and evolving demands for labour and as new jobs demand multiskilled labour with general competencies. School to work transition can be improved by:

- promoting industry–education partnerships to support new forms of apprenticeship-style training and to ensure that education remains relevant to labour market needs;

- creating, at the national level, frameworks of standards for assessment, recognition and certification to encourage young people to invest in skills and facilitate their mobility;

- setting the training wage or allowance sufficiently low relative to the average wage in the occupation sector in order to induce firms to supply a sufficient volume of training places;

- preparing students better in post-secondary education by providing effective career guidance and by ensuring that the overall balance is achieved between the more traditional academic studies and technical and advanced vocational studies.

(d) *Post-secondary education and training.* A better balance needs to be achieved between academic studies and technical and advanced vocational studies. Both should prepare and stimulate students for enterprising and innovative activities.

(e) *On-the-job training for adults.* Currently individual firms are discouraged from investing in their workforces, by the constraints of directing their operations largely towards short-term profit-maximization objectives. One solution to this shortfall would be to implement a training levy or grant scheme to stimulate enterprises to undertake more skill development and a system of training credits for adult workers which permits them to acquire new skills at certified training establishments or firms. Some countries have adopted training levies but such strategies have had mixed results, perhaps because of problems of design and implementation. Another solution would be to make more transparent the value of skills relative to other factor inputs so that firms can treat workers as long-term assets. Reforms to financial accounting and reporting practices could help to improve information on the value of training investments, as would agreement on and implementation of training standards and credentials. This would enable financial markets to account for the stock of workforce skills in a firm as part of recorded assets and in turn encourage investors to invest in firms with a proven track record in training their workforce. Another strategy would be to allow workers to alternate between work and extended periods of off-the-job training over the period of their working life (e.g. through reduction in working times that are compensated by increases in training time).

(f) *Other forms, styles or patterns of lifelong learning*. In addition to provision of lifelong opportunities available through more traditional institutions and agencies, there is a growing trend towards opportunities being offered for lifelong learning by the creation and expansion of a wide range of community initiatives. One example is the growth of institutions such as Universities of the Third Age, adult education, community centres, etc. for senior citizens which offer them opportunities for learning that add to their existing knowledge or transform the knowledge they have. Senior citizens find that access to new pursuits and pastimes increases substantially their quality of life. Such people then become additional resources for the community's cultural and educational milieux and for its commercial undertakings; employers have seen the benefits of drawing on the knowledge, skills and mature judgment such people offer and of using them to support their firms' endeavours. Once people see that their wisdom and further learning are valued, they increase their enjoyment in advancing their intellectual horizons and developing their interests by enthusiastically engaging in further learning of this kind.

JUSTIFICATION FOR A LIFELONG APPROACH TO LEARNING

The OECD *Jobs Study* (1994) has highlighted the need for a lifelong learning approach on the following grounds:

1 The relationship that is held to subsist between skills, competencies and aggregate economic performance

The importance of labour force quality as a factor in and determinant of aggregate economic growth has been strongly maintained and is widely accepted by many leading economists, for whom productivity and income levels are held to correlate highly with high levels of educational attainment and professional skills. Despite the limitations of current empirical analysis, it is reasonable to acknowledge that the skills and competencies possessed by members of the labour force are significant determinants of economic growth and productivity performance (OECD, *Jobs Study*, 1994, p. 116). There is an important caveat to be made, however: it would be incorrect to interpret the data as saying that all types of education and training have identical benefits or that across-the-board increases in educational attainment will improve growth prospects.

2 Educational attainment and the labour market performance of individuals

(a) Low earnings for the least qualified

A review of the effects of education and training on labour market experience reveals that persons with higher levels of education and training receive higher earnings; the most pronounced disparities occur between those who have completed upper secondary schooling and those who have not.

People who have not completed upper secondary school or who have not acquired vocational qualifications have markedly lower earnings and higher unemployment rates. Moreover the general conclusion of recent research concerning the influence of education and qualifications on the structure of wages has been that in some countries there has been a widening of wage differentials both across and within groups especially over the 1980s and early 1990s (OECD, *Jobs Study*, 1994, p. 116).

Workers coming into the labour market in the 1990s with no qualifications are especially disadvantaged. Those who enter the labour market with no educational qualifications are on the average the most disadvantaged – both at the start of their career and throughout it.

(b) High risk of unemployment for the least qualified
There is held to be a positive correlation between low levels of education attainment and unemployment rates. Those who have failed to complete upper secondary education or otherwise acquire suitable vocational qualifications are most at risk of becoming unemployed. The data do not imply an across-the-board upward shift in educational requirements but they do suggest a change in the relative distribution of requirements with a shift in demand away from unskilled workers – a shift that is consistent with the disappearance of jobs requiring only minimal levels of attainment. The resulting rise in the 'minimum threshold' of requirements has its most immediate and most marked effect on the least qualified. The completion of upper secondary education or vocational qualifications is especially relevant to the task of minimizing the risk of unemployment. There is a consistent pattern of high risk of unemployment for early school-leavers, that persists well into adulthood. Lifelong learning opportunities may be one way to address this cumulative disadvantage.

(c) A growing disadvantage for the less educated
The multiple disadvantage of poverty and hardship suffered by people with low educational attainment has been increasing in some countries as the jobs in which they might have been employed in the past are disappearing or are being filled by the more qualified. The evidence suggests that the relationship between low attainment and higher unemployment is becoming stronger over time, with the least educated suffering more in the 1980s than in the 1970s.

(d) The widening of the skills gap: opportunities for overcoming low educational attainment
Rather than compensating for the low levels of educational attainment of many workers when they first enter the labour market, provision of education and training in most countries is tending to widen the skills gap among workers.

Better-educated workers generally enjoy more opportunities for formal training within an organization, and this can lead to widened occupational horizons and increased earnings. Those workers who have no qualifications are considerably less likely to receive additional enterprise-based training and are less likely to take any training on their own outside the enterprise (OECD, *Jobs Study*, 1994, p. 122).

Research has consistently shown that participation in further training is associated with higher earnings – although they do not indicate exactly how much of the average rise in earnings with work experience results from training as opposed to job matching, long-term wage bargaining and other factors. Whatever the possibility of rigorously linking access to further training with earnings, it seems clear that complementarity of initial schooling and subsequent labour market training is an important component of the life-cycle returns to investment in education (OECD, *Jobs Study*, 1994, p. 125).

3 Education, skills and competencies, and their relationship to enterprise performance and improved productivity

Both the skills and competencies of workers and measures to upgrade them influence the performance of enterprises. Evidence from comparative case studies show that training and the ability of employees to function in different tasks are important determinants of the viability of high-performance work organizations. Statistical evidence isolating the role of further training in explaining productivity differences among firms is limited but supportive. The effect of education on productivity appears strongest in providing knowledge and skills that can be used at work, improving the ability of individuals to communicate and co-ordinate and better enabling them to learn new tasks and acquire new information (OECD, *Jobs Study*, 1994, p. 119).

4 The relationship between national, individual and enterprise performance

There is considerable evidence, from data emanating from both OECD and non-OECD countries, of a strong association overall between the skills and competencies of workers and the performance of national economies. There is, however, no one ideal profile of workforce qualifications, and no single relative distribution of educational attainment level that is key to better performance. Moreover, there is no one level at which increased returns are likely in all countries, with the exception of upper secondary education or its equivalent. As a result there is little evidence to indicate an across-the-board increase of educational attainment, or to support the argument that 'more' without regard to level is better (OECD, *Jobs Study*, 1994, p. 127).

Further training serves as a means for upgrading the skills and competencies of experienced workers and, when taken in conjunction with changes in other factor inputs or improved organization, contributes to improved enterprise performance, while benefiting individuals as well. But access to further education is biased, with those with the lowest level of educational attainment participating (and benefiting) least.

CONCLUSION

As is clear from the foregoing, major analyses of the current climate of change in economic and social affairs have provided a powerful rationale and justification for the realization of the idea of lifelong learning for all. Perhaps the most powerful of these analyses, the OECD *Jobs Study*, concentrates heavily on the link between the economic policies and performance of countries and the concomitant need for the continuing availability of a high quality, skilled and knowledgeable workforce.

This is, however, only one of the goals of many countries' education policies. The others – democratic engagement and personal fulfilment – are now held to be quite as important as economic goals, if the aims of social inclusiveness and personal development are to be achieved. Although the OECD *Jobs Study* makes reference to the importance of these other goals for countries' education policies, they are given nothing like the attention that economic factors and arguments receive.

Given many governments' stated concern for the multifaceted character of lifelong learning and its relationship to a broader and more diverse set of goals, it is clear that, in setting the agenda for education for the next century, governments will now have to undertake a more comprehensive analysis of all the various dimensions and features of the nature, aims and purposes of policies for 'Learning: Realising a lifelong approach for all'. They will also have to develop a more wide-ranging set of justifications addressing the differences in the aims and purposes provided by such analyses.

In this way policies pertaining to lifelong learning endeavours are more likely to be developed and articulated, not merely with respect to providing arguments to vindicate a country's concern for its economic self-sufficiency, but also in reinforcing its appreciation of the need for a multiplicity of initiatives, that will increase the emancipation and participation of all citizens in its various social institutions, political arrangements and culture.

Without the more far-reaching and wide-ranging analyses of the changes that are occurring in society and their impact upon social cohesion and opportunities for increasing personal growth and life-chances, the danger is that policies pertaining to lifelong education will be dominated by an instrumentalist/economic approach. There is more to the life of a society, a community and an individual than economic concerns. It is hoped that governments will attend to analyses that address those dimensions of current change that relate to the challenges of increasing democratic participation, social inclusion and enhancing the quality of life of individual members of society.

In this chapter we hope to have pointed to some of the emerging themes in contemporary literature on social change, that have direct implications for education and that must be attended to if governments' rhetoric regarding lifelong learning is to have force and plausibility and be translated into lasting effect for all members of society.

Chapter 4

Establishing a Basis for Lifelong Learning: Curriculum, Teaching and Learning

The motive to provide all members of society with access to lifelong learning can only be realized if all people are able and willing to engage in learning. People's capacity and willingness to learn throughout their lives depends to a considerable extent on whether they draw positive experience from their period of initial education. A prime prerequisite for lifelong learning for all is that schools and other institutions for initial education and training offer environments in which students experience a sense of self-worth, a sense of excitement and challenge in learning, and a sense of success and lasting achievement in making their learning gains. If all young people are obliged to undergo a sustained period of compulsory education, society must ensure it offers them the best possible opportunities to learn, in programmes and by processes that conform to the foregoing criteria. Systematically failing or rejecting learners is a sure way of diminishing the motivations of students and frustrating the work of governments to provide the necessary prerequisites for the learning society and ultimately the knowledge economy.

The second prerequisite for lifelong learning is to ensure all students in formal and compulsory learning environments master a relevant range and high quality groundwork of knowledge and skills, that will prepare them effectively for the world of work, for the domain of sound interpersonal relations, and for the life of the creative imagination (Warnock, 1978). All these will be established in the initial stages of education and later on by programmes of further learning. However, while there is agreement on the importance of a solid and secure basis of knowledge and skills for lifelong learning, there is no agreement on the essential elements of this foundation. Moreover, there is no clearly conceptualized notion of the relationship between the different levels of education and training provision, the types of knowledge and skill required at each level, and the ways in which these fit into a coherent and integrated approach to lifelong learning for all.

There is the further important point that a shift to a lifelong learning approach is likely to make new and larger demands on the education service and the teaching profession. The task of preparing the service and the profession for facing and meeting these demands has widespread and large-scale implications for policy-makers, for teacher education providers, and for professional and industrial organizations concerned with the education service, the training imperative, and the teaching profession.

In this chapter we shall consider the implications for the curriculum, teaching, learning and the education profession of a lifelong approach to learning for all. A number of questions have guided our discussion:

- How can schools create an environment conducive to a lifelong learning approach?

- What are the elements of a relevant and high quality foundation of essential knowledge and skills, that all young people should acquire and all members of society should possess as a basis for lifelong learning?

- How should students acquire such a foundation? What should be the content? Should the foundation be common to all?

- To what extent do such foundations compete with or complement the acquisition of specific, job-related skills and knowledge on the one hand and general knowledge on the other?

- How can trade-offs between excellence and exclusion, and between consolidation and expansion be better balanced, and which skills and knowledge acquired at one stage or in one setting provide the best basis for learning at other stages and in other settings?

- What are the best means to enable and encourage individuals to acquire and develop the foundations, and to what extent are these consistent with current provision and current teaching and learning strategies?

- Is there a need for a complete overhaul of current curricula and methods of teaching and learning to bring about a concrete realization of lifelong learning for all?

- What are the implications of all the foregoing for the teaching profession? What incentives might be needed to change attitudes and upgrade skills?

GOALS, VALUES, CURRICULUM AND LEARNING

In seeking to redefine curriculum, teaching and learning, many governments locate the reform effort in a broad social and economic context. Yet while acknowledging that the goals that are crucial to the enterprise of reform in curriculum, teaching and learning must connect with the exigencies of the economic and social context, we should recognize that many countries, in their provision of educational services and institutions, are not formulating educational goals solely in response to the thrust of major economic and social forces and demands; each country is also making its own statement about values more broadly conceived. Many of these goals will embody values above and beyond the merely economic and social. Very many members of the community would desire to see, for example, an increased presence in the curriculum of educating institutions of moral and interpersonal values such as consideration of others' interests, respect for other people, tolerance of different points of view, intercultural understanding, personal sensitivity, individual autonomy, social responsibility, cultural imagination and creativity.

In the various schemes of curriculum, approved modes of teaching and learning, and styles of organization that they construct for their education and training services, each country is revealing its commitment to a set or system of values. Each country defines its value stance by what it includes and what it omits in its curriculum frameworks and guidelines and in its selection and provision of particular learning experiences for members of its community.

In formulating the goals for its education and training systems, therefore, each country's government will be seeking to address a number of questions, the answers to which all relate, directly or indirectly, to their concern for the protection, promotion and securing of certain values. Among such questions, some of the key ones include:

- What shall be the goals of a country's education and training system, its educating and training institutions and schools?

- What shall be the curriculum that is held to be most conducive to the attainment of those goals?

- Who shall decide the nature and composition of that curriculum?

- Who makes that selection, on what basis, and how shall it be composed? How might integration and coherence, continuity and stability in curriculum, teaching and learning, particularly with respect to wider value concerns, be achieved?

- How should we ensure goal statements remain relevant and effective?

- How do we ensure values implicit in goals statements find expression in curriculum, teaching and learning and in classroom practice?

- And, most importantly, how do we make sure that discourse about such values means that they remain open to criticism, review and change?

The evidence collected as part of OECD activity on *The Effectiveness of Schooling and of Educational Resource Management* (OECD, 1994) suggests that significant differences subsist between countries and individual states in their approach to the design and implementation of educational reform, as a set or package of measures conceived as appropriate to address questions such as the above. But no matter what the approach to the process of change, no one can doubt the overriding importance attached in all current reform efforts across most countries to three key matters:

1 the nature and purposes of the goals of education and training;

2 the body of knowledge and skills that shall be constructed to help those goals be achieved;

3 the quality of the teaching and learning process, their impacts and outcomes.

In planning and arranging for quality lifelong learning for all, governments have recognized that questions concerning the nature and number of the goals of education and training, and the curriculum appropriate to deliver them, transcends the immediate and limited character, constituency and remit of the local educating institution. Across many countries there is perceived to be a need, in the framing of educational goals and curricula, for a broad social partnership to be forged between a range of community 'stakeholders'. Such a partnership will then be able to take account of widely held goals, of a range of educational and social needs and interests, and to relate them to educational and training objectives more generally. In this way governments will seek to take action to secure the transmission of particular values, attitudes and beliefs, and to put in a larger context the educational point and purpose of all those teaching and learning activities and experiences provided in a country's educating and training institutions, to which value can be attached and for which teachers and resources must be furnished.

At the present time a widespread stocktaking is taking place on these and other related questions: does it matter, for instance, if, at the national level, legislation enacts requirements as to those subjects to be covered in the curriculum? How do such enactments determine delivery? Are there inflexibilities of institutional structure or function that inhibit change? How can the infrastructure support and not impede what happens at the local level? If legislation sets in place the objectives and goals to be achieved in specific subjects or learning areas, does this interfere with professionals' rights, not merely in respect of appropriate teaching methods and curriculum, but also in respect of their properly qualified view of what constitutes and counts as the subject itself? Is there any danger that the promulgation and imposition from the centre of national statements of goals and curriculum frameworks, schemes and guidelines might overtly or covertly condition and shape the nature of curriculum subjects, in such a way that the very epistemology of a subject can become distorted from what the professionals believe it is or should be? From which dominant intellectual traditions and cultural values shall the curriculum selection be made, and on what grounds?

CONCEPTIONS OF KNOWLEDGE AND THE SELECTION OF CURRICULUM CONTENT
Three Approaches to Curriculum Construction

As part of facing the challenge of laying down an appropriate and solid groundwork for lifelong learning for all, there needs to be a re-examination, a reappraisal and a reconceptualization of the ways in which, and the bases from which, it is proposed to construct a curriculum suitable for addressing and delivering the educational and learning imperatives emanating from adoption of the concept of lifelong learning for all. It will be illuminating and helpful at this point to cite instances of some of the bases upon which various curricula have been developed and articulated for programmes of education and training, and the goals to which those programmes are held to lead (Chapman and Aspin, 1993; Aspin and Chapman with Wilkinson, 1994).

We might make a start by observing that a concern in many settings is to link education to economic advance. Recent education reforms and efforts at curriculum determination suggest that the goals of education are seen primarily in instrumental terms: education is seen less as an activity worthwhile in its own right, and more as being of value insofar as it leads to other ends. The function of education and training is thus seen primarily as providing personnel to run the economic engine of the state – to give it a leading edge of economic competitiveness in the world's economic market-place.

There is also, however, another current of thinking which holds that the prime function of education is to induct people into all those traditions, experiences and cultures that constitute both the identity and the value of being human in today's world, and that will thereby enable the graduates of educating institutions to become bearers of that culture, those traditions and values, and cope with the demands of living in that world. Proponents of this view hold that learners are therefore 'entitled' to be given access to all the great and good 'that is known and thought in the world' (Matthew Arnold) in the ascent of humankind, and that form the starting-points for all future endeavours, particularly those that will stand individuals in good stead when they come to face the exigencies of daily life. These curriculum 'entitlements' can be concentrated into a number of areas of experience, culture and value, entry into and learning in which provide the building-blocks for a life in society that will enable a person to enjoy civilization and culture in all their multifarious forms, and to cope with the demands and predicaments of the modern world.

Yet a third approach considers the definition of educational goals that transcend immediate economic, political or social concerns, and that stand aside from the momentary interests of particular sections, groups or pressures. Proponents of this approach regard the central undertaking of educational endeavour as lying beyond the need for vocational training, moral development and cultural awareness. For them what is important is the tenet that education is first and foremost about initiating and developing the life of the mind, and this is the purpose of 'liberal' education.

A truly liberal education is, on this view, one that gives a person access to and competence in all the various forms of intelligence, all the powers of rational thinking, without which any approach to other questions, whether those of a vocational, moral or cultural import or those which deal with the requirements of daily life in the modern world, is impossible and unintelligible. For Hirst (1973), Gardner (1983, 1987) and others, what matters is that we direct our educational attention towards developing the powers of intelligence and the rational mind. It is in and by those modes of experience and understanding that humankind has progressively structured, developed and made things meaningful over the millennia, that people are able to make sense of their experience and communicate it intelligibly to others of their kind. Such modes of intelligence and rationality are of a finite though progressively developing number, but the number of various discrete modes of understanding constitutes the totality of the rational apparatus by means of which human beings can understand and appraise the reality they share, face the dilemmas of existence, and tackle the exigencies with which the world confronts them.

These different conceptions of knowledge and goals for education will clearly generate different curricula. Instrumental education, for example, will see it as the prime necessity that the curriculum concentrates on the transmission and acquisition of those selected bodies of content and forms of cognitive skill that will be causally related to vocational competence and strong economic performance. In such a curriculum subjects such as communicative competence in one's mother tongue, mathematics, science and technology, modern foreign languages, and some knowledge of those aspects of history, geography and economics that can be specifically related to our national identity, social needs and economic competitiveness will clearly be crucial. Competence at other life- and vocationally desirable skills, such as competence in the creation of, opera- tion of and communication by modern information technologies, team management, and the organization of knowledge, research and interpersonal relations, will also be conducive towards the end of efficient and successful commercial, industrial and business production and performance.

Those who opt for an 'entitlement' curriculum will lay it down as a requirement that access to a knowledge and understanding of all the various products, artefacts and advances that have marked what Bronowski called *The Ascent of Man* (1973), and to all the great human traditions of 'critico-creative thought' (Passmore, 1967) by means of which these major cultural, social and intellectual accomplishments have been wrought, will form the main content of such a curriculum. Mathematics, science, technology, medicine, the arts, reli- gion, history and philosophy will constitute the core of those subjects where the store of cultural traditions, cognitive excellences and a community's identity can be discerned and concentrated and in which human potential for future development might begin to be realized.

For the third group, what matters is that, either by the skills of cognitive psychology or epistemological and philosophical analysis, those modes of intelli- gence and ways of knowing that constitute the totality of human rationality at its present stage of development be identified and defined; and that then, in some shape or form and at some time or other, students in our educating institutions be given induction into them and practice in their application and deployment. Such ways of thinking as the mathematical, the scientific, the philosophical, the historical, the moral, the religious, the aesthetic and artistic, perhaps even that of interpersonal understanding, will all function as building- blocks upon which the edifice of human intelligence and rationality can be constructed. Using these forms of intelligence and awareness, students will be able to enlarge the number of ways in which they can actually have experience and cognition of their shared world, understand and address the issues and problems arising from their situation in the world, and the needs and concerns they have in it; for without such primary modes of rationality, experience and intelligence, no such address or engagement would be possible. Initiation into *at least* these modes of awareness, experience and appraisal, such thinkers will argue, must be the primary curriculum prerequisite.

Common Elements in such Curricula – and a Criticism

At this point it will be clear that such positions as those delineated above have some features in common. One is that, in the quest for educational goals, there will always be some *foundations* that have to be provided, which function as the basic building-blocks for the construction of curricula and the articulation of appropriate teaching and learning activities and processes. The second is that those foundations will be *separable and discrete*: the central concepts, operating procedures, tests for truth claims, and criteria for evaluating success, for instance, will be different as between say, mathematics, morals and the arts, and it is these varying characteristics that require us to provide a differentiated and heterogenous curriculum. What is agreed among proponents of such approaches is that there *are* different forms of cognition and intelligence: what has to be done, in curriculum terms, is to differentiate them according to various categorial criteria and conceptual schemata, defend what they are, and show, in educational terms, what they are for. Yet a third feature is the clear implication that, in some way or other, knowledge is *hierarchically structured and arranged*: there are some forms of knowledge and experience that are prior to and presupposed by others, and the study and acquisition of these must come first in any form of education, before any approach can be made to those other forms of knowing, that rest upon and presuppose mastery in those basic constituents of human rationality.

It should be pointed out, however, that these premises have been under considerable challenge for many years. There is now a substantial body of literature containing critiques by theorists who claim that the holding and promulgating of views of the curriculum such as those described above should be seen as little more than the expression of contentious theories of intelligence and meta-cognition, or controversial philosophies of knowledge (cf. Evers and Walker, 1983; Hindess, 1972; Kleinig, 1973; Phillips, 1971; and Watt, 1975).

Clearly, considerations of values, theories of knowledge, and the need to take into account factors relating to current economic and social change must be key elements in the planning and formulation of appropriate curricula for educational institutions in the future. But it would be right and proper to require that constructors of curricula should be entirely comfortable with the models of knowledge and of learning embodied in the curricula they aim their educational institutions to deliver. Recent work in epistemology and cognitive science suggests that, despite their widespread acceptance, the theories set out above have no uncontested rightness about them. As we face the challenge of providing lifelong education for all, there is clearly a need for curriculum planners to reconsider the epistemological bases for curriculum choice, and to consider anew the range of alternatives now proffered for curriculum planning and construction.

The Construction of Curricula: A Post-Empiricist Approach

Among the alternatives generated in recent years, post-empiricist philosophies of knowledge suggest the giving up altogether of the ideas of foundationalist epistemology, coercive demarcations between areas of knowledge, and the postulate of a hierarchy operating among those areas, and the adopting of a stance of caution towards those curriculum theories deriving from them. Curriculum philosophy, seen in this newer light, is *not* an activity of conceptual clarification; rather it is an activity of theory construction, correction and contention, engaged in for the purpose of providing *temporary best solutions to problems*, the lack of a solution to which is otherwise threatening to human well-being and social harmony.

Curriculum building and planning, from this perspective, is devoted to the framing of answers to problems, the examination and criticism of the hypotheses proposed as answers to those problems, and to the tentative trying-out and application of those theories that have hitherto resisted falsification.

It is thus not a priori preconceptions as to the logical structure of knowledge itself, nor a set of judgments and prescriptions relating to those desirable cognitive activities and cultural values that, according to *this* perspective, must determine the pattern of curriculum planning. Rather it is *problems* that provide a set of agenda for curriculum action. Using this framework one could easily construct a 'Dewey-type' curriculum comprising an intellectual attack on a range of pressing concerns and present-day perplexities.

As examples of some of those problems we might point, for instance, to such matters as the following:

1 The common concern of many countries to enhance the literacy of their citizens.

2 The need of many countries to acquire the requisite skills and competences to enable its citizens to operate in a world where the amount of available productive work is decreasing, where service industries of all kinds are increasingly likely to provide the main means of work, where advances in knowledge and the information technology revolution will mean that a worker will have to be prepared to change jobs four or five times in a working lifetime, where working life is likely to become shorter and shorter, and where – notwithstanding the increasing scarcity of salaried employment – many persons will also enjoy increasing longevity.

3 The question of interpersonal relations, in a time when the incidence of phenomena such as domestic violence and child-abuse shows no sign of decreasing, when the divorce rate is already high and climbing, when suicide among young people is a phenomenon of disturbing frequency – with all the attendant dysfunctions that these bring about.

4 The problem of constructing healthy lifestyles and a regimen of risk-avoiding behaviours, when the problems of diseases of various kinds are now continuingly and in some cases increasingly recalcitrant to treatment.

5 Above all, perhaps, is the problem of how to assist human beings to acquire and retain their values of *humanity*, of sensitivity, sympathy and compassion, at a time when the emphasis upon what Habermas (1972) called technocratic rationality, upon technicization and the dominance of particular kinds of economic interest threaten us with the loss of a sense of individual worth and a loss of a sense of commitment to a set of values that will help define and enrich the

quality of relationships between ourselves and others – what we might call the problem of the need for the *humanization* of the curriculum.

The Need for a Criterion of Coherence and Continuity

It should be pointed out, however, that there is one element in such an approach that is still needed to provide a set of guidelines for steering curriculum planning. What is needed is a criterion of stability, consistency and coherence, so that educational institutions may guard against what could otherwise be a somewhat anarchical curriculum situation.

One way that curriculum planners and developers respond to this challenge may be found in the pragmatism developed and articulated by Peirce (1955) and espoused so firmly for education by Dewey, Popper and their successors up to the present day (Ackerman, 1980; Guttman, 1987; Mendus, 1988; and White, 1973). Such a criterion is provided by the idea of *'education for democracy'*.

A modern curriculum of the flexibility and dynamism described, it is argued, may be constructed and continually adapted for delivery on the basis of those various foci of knowledge, skill and value that future citizens in a participative democracy will need in order for them to be able, on a fully-informed and committed-for-action basis, to participate in the democratic processes of policy formulation, appraisal, criticism, application and assessment. Such participation will be required, as a matter of course, on any of the issues raised above and tackled as matters of overriding importance by the community. This could involve work-place literacy, or it could be the educational imperative of inhibiting such life-threatening diseases and conditions as AIDS, drugs, crimes of violence, and nuclear accident.

Generating a Curriculum for Lifelong Learning: The Place of Values

From this examination of theories of knowledge and the curriculum, currently dominating discourse in this area, it is clear that of vital importance in the undertaking of redefining the curriculum for lifelong learning for all must be the debate regarding what constitutes appropriate curriculum knowledge for a programme extending far beyond 'education' as it has been traditionally conceived. Such a debate will encompass such questions as the following:

- What counts as knowledge? How should knowledge be conceived? How should knowledge be established and certified?

- How should it be acquired and employed in a society in which knowledge itself is continuing changing and expanding?

- How shall the values of breadth of knowledge, depth of understanding, and curriculum balance be best addressed and assured?

This last question raises an issue of major concern. This relates to the important point that *values* exist, are found in and embodied across the whole curriculum. Values are not a separate domain of discourse nor definable as though they were an autonomous element in the curriculum, as being in some way a distinct subject or area on its own, with its own body of theory, cognitive content, typical activities, disciplinary procedures or criteria for success. As Peters remarked (1966a), to be a scientist is *ipso facto* to be committed to the values implicit in the procedural principles that define the nature of the subject and prescribe its appropriate activities in it. Science is not value-free: it is shot through with value elements that help structure and define it.

Thus it is plain that questions of *value* in knowledge and the curriculum are not solely restricted to subjects or areas such as the humanities, the arts and religion. Questions of value also underpin and indeed permeate the whole syllabuses of other curriculum subjects such as mathematics, science and technology. Indeed in the last-named curriculum area, as well as that of medicine, it might with reason be claimed that value questions are of prime importance.

This interplay of epistemological and axiological elements and considerations, in association with reflections drawn from the psychology of learning, the sociology and anthropology of learning institutions, and the values – individual, economic and social – attaching to and embodied in institutions of learning by the society in which they are located, will obviously occupy a central place in discussions about lifelong education, and the effective development of education and training for all in the 1990s and into the next century, and the necessary reconceptualizing and redefining of the curriculum that will have, in consequence, to take place.

In all this one clear point emerges: the curriculum is no longer seen as a solid, stable and immutable organization of existing and traditional valued knowledge to be passed on in pedagogic instructional mode, but as a set of problems to be tackled by those seeking solutions to them, engaging in the search for knowledge as a dynamic process involving large-scale and rapid epistemic change, planning, delivery and assessment.

LEARNING TO LEARN

New conceptions of knowledge are thus going to play an important part in assisting educational planners to develop and articulate schemes of curriculum appropriate to each of the phases and goals of lifelong learning. Equally important in such planning, however, will be reference to new modes and styles of learning that have been developed in recent years as a result of work in learning theory, cognitive development theory and meta-cognition.

Instead of more traditional conceptions of teaching-learning, in which learning progress was largely teacher-centred and instructive in mode, linear in progression, and didactic in character, there is now a realization that the progress of learning is not 'roughly the same' for all learners in a particular age group, and that learning does not necessarily proceed in a linear fashion. Rather it is now coming to be much more widely accepted that learning occurs most securely when students are centrally involved in controlling, directing and monitoring their own learning progress, and that a co-operative, rather than a competitive approach to learning is of immense help to groups of students in facilitating rapid gains in the acquisition of their learning and mastering difficult, complex and heterogenous forms of knowledge and skill (cf. OECD, *Learning to Think: Thinking to Learn*, 1991).

This means, for the individual, that learning has much less to do with the mere acquisition of bodies of content for replication later, and much more to do with their becoming active in acquiring and then operating the skilled techniques, rules and procedures by means of which knowledge can be acquired and one's own circle of understanding expanded.

One of the most vigorous of the currently expanding research programmes in the reconception, elaboration and refinement of modern approaches to learning is that known as 'constructivism'. This approach works so as to emphasize and give primacy of place to the learner's own engagement with, and attempt to make sense of, the phenomena which confront him or her, rather than operating on the assumption that students' learning processes must be dominated by models of teacher-centred authority and that knowledge must be heteronomously transmitted, received and reproduced. According to this view, 'knowledge cannot be conveyed: it can only be constructed'.

Thus learning must start from the individual's trying to make sense of his or her perception of phenomena; it is individuals who then, striving to make sense of their contacts with the world 'out there', will individually 'construct' their perceptions into some sort of arrangement that will make sense to and constitute meanings for them. They will construct their own world of cognition in much the same way that an architect-and-builder constructs a dwelling, an opera house or an airport. Osborne and Freyberg (1985, p. 82) put this succinctly:

> [this] view of learning with understanding focuses on the proposition that learners themselves must actively *construct* or *generate* meaning from sensory input ... No-one can do it for them ... Piaget, too, considered that knowledge is *constructed* by the individual as he or she acts on objects and people and tries to make sense of it all ... Knowledge is acquired not by the internalisation of some outside given but is constructed from within.

This all means, in sum, that among the prime prerequisites in any approach to learning for individual students will be the skills of research, inquiry, and expansion of the concepts and categories one already has, linking them together so that they become *meaningful* (i.e. that they make sense for the individual *from the inside*) and then exercising, applying, monitoring, checking, correcting and extending them further, in the actual situations in which the various skills and learnings are called for. The motto we may most appropriately employ for this endeavour is that of 'learning to learn'. R.M. Smith puts all this well:

> Learning to learn is a matter of both aptitude and personal experience, and people can typically be said to learn to learn in a relatively

haphazard manner. From in-school and out-of-school experience people constantly acquire new information and behaviours. While so engaged, they gradually develop personal learning strategies and personal knowledge about the optimum conditions for learning. Each person develops a concept of self-as-learner. The learning to learn process is understood as haphazard, because it results not so much from deliberate interventions on the part of teachers or trainers to improve learning capacity and performance, as from personal interpretations over time of learning-related experience. These interpretations often prove dysfunctional as far as becoming an active, flexible, confident learner in a variety of contexts is concerned. Hence the growing interest in the deliberate enhancement of learning capacities, dispositions, and strategies, through such means as curriculum planning, instruction and training.

(Smith, 1994, pp. 3345–9)

In providing a foundation for lifelong learning, then, governments and education systems will find it important to take into consideration the emerging research, knowledge and understanding relevant to the ways in which people learn and to the ways in which that learning can be made more rapid, effective and secure. For it is on the basis of their mastery of the skills of research, knowledge expansion and learning to learn that students will be able to recognize situations in which such skills can be applied and utilized to the acquisition, internalization and appropriate deployment of new facts, information and knowledge. For policy-makers and curriculum planners the challenge is to ensure that learning to learn ceases to be a haphazard enterprise and instead becomes an integrated, conscious and deliberate element in the content, style, structure and organization of all learning.

NEW LEARNING TECHNOLOGIES

Modern technologies offer cost-effective possibilities for learning. Technical devices and instruments, such as computers, CD-ROMs, VCRs and interactive laser video, can be used to positive and creative effect in many courses simply by changing their software. High-speed computer networks, such as the Internet, offer access to varied tools and resources. Global internetworking is expanding so rapidly that each day sees addition of new archives and computer-based tools (cf. OECD, 'The future of post-secondary education and the role of information and communication technology: a clarifying report' presented at the International Conference on 'Learning Beyond Schooling', 1994).

With the use of these new instructional technologies the old problem of the 'either access or quality' trade-off is beginning to be transcended. Learning can be enriched and extended by learners having access to basic hardware or software either directly or by network connection. Internetworking makes it technically possible to distribute academic resources for low marginal costs, often for zero costs. Young people and adults, many of them using study centres, have the potential to participate in courses of study that feature strong emphasis on project-based collaborative learning, with materials of directed instruction developed for large-scale use, supported through real-time and time-delayed communications. Time-delayed exchange by electronic mail and computer conferencing have the added advantage of enhancing access, as many types of students seem to participate more fully in learning opportunities offered in this medium than they were able to do in traditional face-to-face settings.

Until now much of this use of technology has been largely concerned with or even devoted to the reproduction of current pedagogical practice, whether lecture, experiments, discussion or other ways of presenting information. This is the standard beginning for the adaptation of any new technology – the replication of traditional approaches using new methodology. The next stage is innovation in which the newly available technology itself leads to new ways of teaching and learning or supporting the administration of education. This may be the realm of the newer interactive technologies such as networks and multimedia and the growth of distance education that links the learner with the institution by technological means. The final application of technology is the transformation of education, making it into something that is different in content, purpose and traditions. This may be the more futuristic vision of individual learners all over the globe interacting to create and share knowledge and learning (Hebenstreit, 1994, p. 101).

This vision of the future, however, should not be driven solely by technology. The agenda for future learning in general must be generated and driven forward much more by considerations of how society can exploit technology in order to provide the most effective education for a democratic, socially inclusive and economically advanced community. The newly available technology should not therefore be the sole means to drive or dictate the direction of learning gains but should be a major force and asset in the achievement of goals that are conducive to social betterment.

Hebenstreit (1994, p. 117) identifies the elements of a new agenda to integrate information technology into larger frameworks of learning at different levels:

- All students will need to become computer literate as well as normally literate and numerate: they should be able to handle current information technology at a level appropriate to their discipline or field of study and be equipped to employ it appropriately to further their cognitive development in the future. In addition to this, new means of information technology will contribute to and play a part in the methods of assessment as well as entering into and strengthening learning gains and student progress in the curriculum and pedagogy of subjects.

- Students and teaching staff will need to enjoy ready access to workstations and networks. There will be a rapid growth in the availability to staff and students of electronic information services such as the electronic availability or provision of the complete texts of books and journals. Collections of software for use in teaching, including computer-based learning and multimedia materials incorporating audio and video as well as computer-generated graphics and text, should become accessible anywhere on the network and in the educational establishment.

- New information technologies should open up and increase access to educational establishments and agencies for the development of open learning organizations or dual mode institutions. It will be important to capitalize upon the realization that educational pathways and institutions may not be rooted in time or place. They could be accessible electronically from anywhere and available at any time. Institutions could be constituted by and rendered open through a mix of physical and remote access points, thus meeting the needs of groups whose commitments and constraints in the past prevented them from having easy access to learning.

The vision of a networked society with equal access to knowledge and information, made up of communities and individuals, themselves in charge of their own learning environments; and governments, educators and the private sector working in partnership, is fundamental to the evolution and achievement of a democratic, free, economically stable and just society in the twenty-first century. But realization of this vision will require a close examination of the content, style, structure and organization of modern methods and technologies of learning, particularly in respect of the new possibilities offered by the emphasis upon student-centred and self-directed modes of progression, together with an examination of the purpose and function of educational institutions and their use of electronic technologies to meet new educational needs. In setting the agenda for education in the twenty-first century policymakers and educators will clearly need to direct their attention to an exploration of the ways in which the availability of modern information technology devices and new modes of student progress will make possible, effect and shape frameworks for curriculum content and styles of assessment in educational institutions, in ways that will enable the realization of broader social goals.

THE CONTENT, STYLE, STRUCTURE AND ORGANIZATION OF LEARNING

A relevant and high quality basis for the acquisition of further knowledge and skills will be necessary to provide the solid groundwork for effective learning throughout an individual's life, as will the practice and mastery of the skills of self-directed learning, that must clearly become the norm during the compulsory years of schooling. For both will be vital prerequisites and parts of the learning that individuals tackle subsequently, for purposes consonant with their need to engage in lifelong learning for further academic, professional, economic, social, cultural and personal purposes. Thus, given the widespread international concern for lifelong learning for all, the nature, role and function of schools in providing the groundwork for lifelong learning, and the complementarity of services provided by schools, tertiary institutions, the work-place and other agencies in the community concerned with learning, must now be reconsidered. Lifelong learning reinforces the imperative of examining anew the content, structure and organization of appropriate and necessary pathways towards the acquisition of new learnings throughout an individual's life-span, and the various modes and learning styles by which individuals can best make progress in achieving such acquisitions.

Learning in the Compulsory Years

The concept of lifelong learning places compulsory education in a new setting. As Hughes points out:

> Rather than being a unique period of schooling leading on to vocations or higher education, [compulsory education] is a phase in a lifelong process. That phase however has two key requirements: one is to provide a basis for further learning; the other is to ensure a continuing motivation for it. This may imply a greater organisational flexibility in approach than is the case with current schooling. It certainly implies a need for greater and more constructive student involvement in the planning and conduct of their education.
>
> (Hughes, 1993, p. 17)

Sir Christopher Ball (Ball, 1993, p. 2) has argued that compulsory school-ing must achieve two goals: the provision of a knowledge-base; and the provision of meta-skills of learning. But it should try to do so in a way that does not generate difficulties: problems will arise if we continually add further elements to the curriculum content of the compulsory years, for such an approach risks bringing about an information overload and can lead to con-ceptual confusion. Moreover, it risks seriously attenuating the time available for, and the available energy to be given to, the emphasis upon the mastery of learning and research skills and procedures called for in newer approaches to learning and its modes.

Increasingly now the compulsory period of schooling is to be regarded as the phase of education in which students must be provided with a general base for their cognitive and affective development and for their acquisition of the learning skills which they will need for learning throughout their life. More specific knowledge, skills and understanding can be taught and mastery in them achieved as needed later on. The case for helping students acquire a broad basis of general knowledge and skill development in the compulsory years is expressed most comprehensively in the Swedish report for the OECD, *A School for Life* (Swedish Report, 1993).

During the OECD Conference on 'The Curriculum Re-Defined', the follow-ing questions were raised as being among the prime issues that policy-makers concerned with lifelong learning and its implications for compulsory schooling must take into account:

> What might be the minimum of subject matter to be included in the

compulsory school curriculum? How should general skills such as learning to learn and learning to solve problems be built in? What might be the right mix of knowledge and skills which a school can provide? How and by what means can learners acquire this? What learning environments, in and out of school, are best suited to realise this objective? How might what is learned in a person's younger years be made more relevant to the opportunities and challenges which confront them in early adulthood and beyond?

With respect to the matters raised by some of these questions the authors of the OECD/CERI (Centre for Educational Research and Innovation) study on lifelong learning commented:

> There is general agreement that the basic elements of literacy and numeracy should be included in any school curriculum, although the means by which these subjects are taught in schools might be adapted to reflect the fact that many adults who can carry out mechanical reading or arithmetical operations are unable to apply such skills in real life situations. At school, as in adult life, learning of these subjects may be more effective if contextualized ... A harder question concerns the amount of knowledge of subjects such as history, geography, science and literature, that should be universally known in any one country – or internationally – as part of what has been called 'cultural literacy'.
> (OECD, *An Introduction to Learning: Re-Defining the Curriculum in a Life-long Perspective*, 1993, p. 4)

For some years now policy-makers and educators have been grappling with the question of the appropriate knowledge basis for compulsory schooling and considerable advance has been provided by the work of Malcolm Skilbeck on the idea of core curriculum. Skilbeck sees core curriculum as providing the conceptual and methodological tools to enable young people to continue their own learning. In this sense core curriculum is seen as an 'opening up', a leading on, and not a finishing point. Its construction will be multidimensional and will be approached from different perspectives.

In preparation for the Conference on 'The Curriculum Re-Defined', the OECD Secretariat (*The Curriculum Re-Defined: Background Document*, 1993, pp. 44–5) set out suggestions for areas of knowledge and experience and core learning processes that might be considered as forming part of the basis for the curriculum in the compulsory years of schooling. These might include:

> *Areas of knowledge and experience: for example*
> Mathematical skills and reasoning and their applications
> Social, cultural and civic studies
> Health education
> Scientific and technological ways of knowing and their social
>   applications
> Communication
> Moral reasoning and action

Core learning processes: for example
Learning and thinking techniques
Ways of organizing knowledge
Forms of expression
Interpersonal and group relations

The above is, of course, a list of desiderata. These are some suggestions as to the elements that might comprise a compulsory curriculum. Policy-makers and educators in each country will want to formulate their own list and apply it to their own needs and interests, if they decide to adopt some such list of essential elements to form part of the core of their own curriculum for compulsory years of schooling. The decisions that each country makes about the contents of such a list will be shaped and framed on the basis of the conceptions of knowledge they bring to it and the substantive values they are concerned to promote – and not all of these will be the same for different countries.

The OECD, in its work *The Curriculum Re-Defined*, recommends, however, that, in whatever way the question of a basic curriculum might be approached, some general or common principles should apply across all settings: these are the principles of *breadth, balance, relevance, focus, coherence,* and *continuity*. To this we might tentatively add another criterion, calling attention to the necessary amount of *differentiation* necessary for getting our students to appreciate and acquire some awareness of and ability to operate appropriately in the heterogeneity of the cognitive world. We should also want to underline the importance of students' acquisition, mastery and application of the full range of *learning and thinking skills* (OECD, *Learning to Think: Thinking to Learn*, 1991). For without these any notion of the applicability of the other criteria will remain unrealized.

Implicit in the foregoing is the clear presumption that all the elements in such a core curriculum shall be available to all students. In Skilbeck's view, to have access to a high quality and empowering curriculum is a necessary part of every citizen's democratic entitlement. Notions of democratic entitlement and the accompanying concerns for equity and social justice bring to the fore the issue of the educational needs of those who are disadvantaged in some way or at risk and for that reason may be hindered in keeping pace with the educational progress of their peers or taking advantage of the educational opportunities that society should, on this premise, make available to them in the compulsory years. Such a motive lies behind Hughes's remark that:

> ... the concerns of children with special educational needs and students at risk pose a sharp challenge to the sincerity of commitment to an aim such as high quality education and training for all. If the aim is accepted fully as part of a commitment to equity, as a basic requirement for membership of a democratic society, then we need to consider the organisational form and the changes in curriculum and pedagogy which will provide substance to that purpose.

(Hughes, 1993, p. 17)

Seen from the perspective of those committed to the idea and value of lifelong learning for all, the years of compulsory schooling lay a vital foundation for educational progress, economic involvement, social advance and individual fulfilment in the subsequent years. Clearly all a country's students must have access to the means of making progress in all these domains of activity and existence. What shall follow in the post-compulsory years must be decided by considerations relating to the ways and extents to which individuals wish to make further progress in any or all of these domains. The important thing about individuals' cognitive growth, development of learning skills and learning achievements during the compulsory years is that those gains must give them the equipment for making such choices and directing and monitoring such progress much more from their own efforts during the course of their lifetimes. It is the function of the curriculum in compulsory schooling to give students the tools to enable them to press their own learning forward themselves. What is important, in the post-compulsory years, is that institutions, structures and programmes shall be provided that enable them to make such progress in all the domains in question.

Learning for the World of Work

Rapid changes in the world of work, the changing nature of the goals for education and training, and the realization that most people will have a number of occupations and job-changes during the period of their working life, have resulted in a general acceptance that the 'front-end loading' approach for preparation for the world of work is no longer appropriate – if indeed it ever was. Emphasis has altered from a concentration on instrumental conceptions of vocational education as a preparation for work during the compulsory years of schooling and the years of early adulthood, towards a concept of lifelong learning that is work-related. The old dichotomies between general and vocational education, between liberal education and specific job-training, are now dying away. There is now a growing realization that, as well as highly specific job-related technical skills, the demands of the work-place make it imperative that social and interpersonal knowledge, skills and competencies be incorporated in any programme of learning for the world of work.

This kind of approach towards preparation for the world of work has implications for curriculum content, pedagogy and styles of learning, and the organization and structure of educational provision. Learners must be ready, not only to bring to bear the content knowledge and cognitive skills they have in the changed situations in which their employment movements will often engage them, but also to add new knowledge and skills and integrate them effectively with the ones they already possess. And they will have to be prepared to do this not on any regular or linear basis; changes in employment, location and interests will face them with a swiftly changing array of demands, some rapid, some less so, some planned, some unforeseen, to which a flexible and adaptable learning response will be required.

The OECD publication *Vocational Education and Training for Youth: Towards a Coherent Policy and Practice* (1994) has provided some important insights into the ways in which stronger foundations might be provided for work-related learning. In her paper 'Learning and work: the research base',

Senta Raizen explores ways of creating learning situations, that link the acquisition of cognitive skills and knowledge with real-world activities. The evidence is strong, she avers, that learning and motivation for learning are most securely mediated through activities embedded in a context that makes sense, and matter, to the learner. The paper contends that research involving analyses of individual performance have resulted in greater attention being paid to the several types of knowledge and their structure and interrelationships, that competent individuals display.

Raizen counsels that research on 'situated' learning and socially-constructed knowledge highlights the need for and importance of providing a 'real-world' context, both physical and social, for education and training intended to prepare people for the world of work. An optimal educational response melding these requirements would appear to be the creation and provision of learning environments that make task-knowledge and problem-solving procedures explicit, and that provide for feedback and tutoring by more experienced workers. Raizen advises (1994, p. 79):

- The analysis and distribution of complex tasks to allow shared performance or its simulated counterpart by less experienced and more experienced workers provides a highly effective learning situation.

- People build work-place expertise through the opportunity to participate under the tutelage and mentorship of experts in physical and intellectual tasks specific to a particular work-setting.

- Situated learning enables them to use the social, symbolic, technological and material resources provided by the work context to structure problems and problem-situations.

- The symbol manipulation and abstract thinking required in many technical jobs today are learned effectively through a combination of practice and explicit teaching in a meaningful context.

- The process of progressing from novice to expert takes time, as individuals achieve increasing levels of understanding of knowledge, procedures, strategies and social interactions relevant to their work and the sub-culture of the occupation or profession.

Drawing on the work of cognitive psychologists over the last twenty-five years, Raizen addresses the issue of domain-specific knowledge versus generalizable skills, by recognizing the important role of each. Theories of learning are being constructed to accommodate the importance of domain-specificity and yet take advantage of general heuristics, as well as meta-cognitive self-regulatory skills. Raizen reports current research as indicating that instruction must intermingle context specificity and generality, including the development of self-regulatory skills and performance control strategies.

Research on the knowledge and skills that learners bring to instruction, Raizen maintains, has provided new insight on what makes instruction effective. Instead of constructing curricula 'top-down' by encoding the knowledge of experts in suitably simplified material for onward transmission to a receiver, instruction should take into account the learner's own original ideas, stage discrepant or confirming experiences and use these to stimulate questions and encourage the generation of a range of responses, with the opportunity to apply these in various situations. Researchers concerned with the ways in which people actually move from their initial state of knowledge and skills to effective performance in work settings are uncovering the importance of learning in context. This reveals that the most effective learning takes place through 'situated' activity, using the physical environment and the tools it provides; the co-operative construction of knowledge among groups of learners engaged on a common task; and involvement in the activities of the specific work community.

The hallmarks of successful learning situations for the world of work are identified by Raizen as follows (1994, p. 97):

- Any learning experience must be meaningful and motivating for learners: they must be able to make sense of it and understand its purpose.

- Any learning experience must take into account what the learner brings to it; individuals come to any learning experience with prior knowledge and experience, which may either facilitate or impede the intended learning.

- Learning experiences should interweave domain-knowledge, problem-solving strategies appropriate to the domain, and real-world applications of both: most people learn best when declarative knowledge – 'the what' – procedural knowledge – 'the how' – and strategic knowledge – 'the when' – are integrated.

- Learners must be actively involved in their own learning, even as they are provided with models of expert performance to emulate. They need coaching and error-correction, arranged to 'fade', as they become autonomous and independent.

- Learning sequences should introduce increasing complexity, yet students should learn at any level of complexity to attend to the general nature of a task before attending to its details.

- Learning experiences should go beyond domain-specific learning, to each person's strategies for controlling their own performance – setting goals, planning, checking work and monitoring progress, and revising their courses of learning. Most important, learners need to develop strategies for acquiring additional knowledge and expertise.

- Learning experience should enculturate the learner into the community of participants in a given domain or occupation, so that the individual will come to understand the physical, conceptual, symbolic and social tools of the community and their uses.

In his paper 'Linkages: a new vision for vocational and technical education' (Papadopoulos, 1994), Papadopoulos calls for a revamped approach to vocational education and training for youth, through changes in the curriculum and in training regulation, particularly in the achievement of a better balance between what is general and what is vocational. Papadopoulos argues that the redefinition of curricula must involve dialogue with representatives of the world of work, both employers and employees, as well as with employment and training agencies. The objective would be to institutionalize the process of curriculum renegotiation, thus improving its balance and relevance, while avoiding the risk that its core, long-term educational purposes become vitiated by the need to respond to transitory or locally defined requirements.

With respect to teaching and learning, the fact that the period of basic preparation, on which subsequent job-specific skills can be built, is becoming more intense and extended, leads Papadopoulos to consider the timing of the introduction of vocationally-specific skills within the educational continuum. It appears that there is now general acceptance that the introduction of vocationally specific skills is not a function of basic schooling and, when it does become necessary or appropriate, it can be best done in conjunction with the workplace.

There is thus clearly a need for a much greater convergence of theoretical and practical elements and styles of learning throughout the educational experience of all young people. Such a convergence of the theoretical and practical, and the general and vocational, would help enhance the status of vocational and technical education, as well as giving participants greater possibilities for transition to higher education studies and other forms of further education and training. Papadopoulos calls (1994, p. 174) for a review of policies and procedures for access and admission to higher education institutions, thus building up a continuum throughout the system of lifelong learning opportunities for all categories of students.

Papadopoulos also highlights the need for a social partnership in defining and developing comprehensive policies for learning and the world of work. Such partnerships could take the form of:

- partnerships mostly of a bilateral nature between business and education, operating mainly at the local level;

- collective bargaining agreements primarily between employers and employees, but also involving a role by the state in which training is an important component;

- tripartite agreements among employers, unions and the state, under which social partners are systematically consulted and actively involved in policy-making, setting standards in education and training, and in monitoring outcomes.

In their attempts to provide an adequate foundation for the entry of an appropriately educated workforce into employment, governments have tended in the past to concentrate largely upon the compulsory years of schooling and on the immediately post-compulsory period devoted to specific preparation for the world of work as foci for their provision efforts. What we hope to have shown in the foregoing is that the nature of this foundation must undergo a radical reappraisal, in line with new epistemologies and patterns and styles of learning, as well as changes in the nature of employment and of the workforce itself. But it is clear that a 'front-end' model of effective approaches to education and training is itself hardly viable as a template upon which future patterns of provision should be defined, structured and delivered. The need for lifelong learning requires that governments accept the responsibility for providing far more than a 'foundation' for education for its citizens and accept that they must cater for all their needs and interests – economic, social and individual. For it is clear that merely providing 'foundations' for future learners and learning is not sufficient; governments and other learning agencies have a clear responsibility for funding, providing or otherwise offering access to a range of continually expanding, increasing and changing opportunities to their citizens in all aspects of their lives and in all their main concerns.

IMPLICATIONS FOR THE TEACHING PROFESSION

It is clear that, in their endeavour to establish a basis for lifelong learning for all, policy-makers will have to work in partnership with a well and appropriately trained, high quality, and committed teaching force and education profession.

The changing conceptions of knowledge and student-centred styles of learning, changing goals for education in response to pressures of social and economic change, and the increasing commitment on the part of governments to lifelong learning for all, have wide-ranging implications for educators and members of the teaching profession. The realization of a lifelong learning approach for all will be possible only with a teaching force that is also in itself committed to maximizing its own opportunities for lifelong learning.

This means a substantial change in motivation, attitude and values on the part of all members of the teaching profession. That is not to say that there will be any radical shifts in their activity away from the central conception of the teacher's role, which is that of bringing minds to birth and assisting in their formation and development. But there will be a considerable refocusing of their efforts, away from their traditional functioning and 'banking' concepts of knowledge and its transmission, and towards the idea of learners' centrality in the process of cognitive growth and its direction and the facilitation of that process, that will not see the end of formal schooling as some sort of *terminus ad quem* of all education and training, but rather reconceptualize it as a *terminus a quo* for further intellectual, professional and personal development, the apparatus for which is now at hand and the goals and orientation of which will, from then on, be controlled and driven by learners themselves.

This means that teachers' horizons will, from their understanding and acceptance of the need for that reconceptualization, require considerable expansion. For, with the arrival of the new concept of lifelong learning, schools and other centres in which learning is offered and encouraged will become places to which all members of the community repair, as and when they wish, for purposes that their employers, the state, the community or they themselves have in mind. Already we have a situation in which schools, which were formerly institutions to which attendance was restricted solely to students below the age of 18, are now accustomed to seeing adults – working parents, those without full-time paid employment, the middle-aged and senior citizens – come back to take 'secondary level' curricula, alongside young people taking them for the first time, and to prepare themselves for public examinations of all kinds relevant to their own or others' needs. Teachers are already appreciating the amount of rethinking and retraining that the presence of such varied constituencies in their classrooms calls for, both in respect to learning content and styles of progress, and also as regards their own status in the study-room and the basis of their authority.

The challenges that lie before members of the education service are therefore likely to include:

- the need to keep abreast of changing conceptions of knowledge and learning;

- the need to develop expertise in modern technologies of learning;

- the need to adapt their approaches to teaching and learning in line with the latest advances in the communication of knowledge and in information technology;

- the need to redirect their pedagogical approaches to personalized systems of instruction and learning;

- the need to accommodate in their classes the presence of learners with a wide range of ages and stages in cognitive growth and interests;

- the need to develop a different basis of authority and style of classroom management, in face of the changes in epistemology, modes of learning, and the varied composition of classes and goals of those seeking to benefit from the opportunities for learning they offer;

- the need to enter into partnerships with other providers of learning in other agencies and institutions, formal and informal, throughout the community;

- the need to enter into productive partnerships with others who have an interest in the progress of learners towards the achievement of goals that both they and all parts of their communities can value. These will include parents, churches, cultural groups, employers' and employees' associations.

Facing such demands will involve substantial changes in the pattern and provision of courses for professional training and retraining for work in the teaching service. This will also mean making sure that the motivation of teachers to cope with the demands and challenges of large-scale changes in the roles and responsibilities of members of the teaching profession is positively promoted and constantly reinforced. And that will mean in turn that, just as the nature of teachers' work is changing in these ways, so the nature of the rewards and remunerations offered to them will have to be reviewed and reassessed.

Primarily, however, those training for work in the education service will need to be helped to the realization that recent advances in conceptions of knowledge and styles of learning, as well as changes in social and personal goals, betoken a gradual disappearance of the role, function and activity of 'teaching' as traditionally conceived and a move towards a new conception of the proper activity of those who carry responsibility for the facilitation of others' learning.

Helping teacher educators and trainers, as well as teachers' associations, to bring about an understanding, acceptance and a positive embracing of these changes will prove to be among the major challenges for the future.

Chapter 5

Using Educational Goals and Standards to Enhance System Provision of Lifelong Learning

As societies move towards adopting a lifelong approach to learning there is a need to consider not only curriculum, teaching and learning provision but also the approaches to standard setting and the monitoring of achievement. We need to ask whether the goals, standards and methods of quality control now used in governing education and training systems are consistent with a lifelong approach to learning. How might standards be set that embody the newly emerging goals associated with lifelong learning for all? Where are standards needed? How can policy-makers and other stakeholders in lifelong education know whether the standards are actually being met? Where might standard setting and achievement monitoring be harmful and in what respects?

In setting and implementing standards, countries need to ensure they will be applied fairly and will meet the needs of a population with diverse learning abilities and requirements. Policy-makers need to establish how and by whom the standards might be best evaluated, whether by inspectors, by standardized assessment procedures, or by other means. Once standards are set, monitored and evaluated, policy-makers and educators need to determine the ways in which performance might be certified and signalled to the institutions of education and work. This means they will have to determine the relationship between assessed standards and qualifications and the ways in which equivalence might be judged in accordance with national and increasingly with international specifications.

In this chapter we shall attempt to evaluate the reasons and causes for the emphasis on standard setting that has been brought to the fore in recent times. International and national trends and prospects in standard setting will be reviewed, particularly as they provide insights into approaches relevant to lifelong learning. Comment will also be made on the extent to which findings about standards can be used to assist policy formation and decision-making, particularly in bringing about a strategy to promote lifelong learning for all.

A number of questions have guided our discussion:

- What are the international and national trends and prospects in standard setting and performance assessment?

- How can established goals contribute to the development of provision which fosters lifelong learning for all and what standards should encapsulate these goals?

- How should education and training standards be set, monitored and evaluated in a coherent approach to lifelong learning for all?

- Is a standard setting and monitoring strategy compatible with the goals of fostering lifelong learning for all and overcoming exclusion?

- How should learning progress be judged against standards and how can recognition of achievement best be credited and signalled to the labour market?

- How can established goals contribute to the development of provision that fosters lifelong learning for all and what standards should encapsulate those goals?

- How should education and training standards be set, monitored and evaluated in a strategy for improved quality, efficiency and effectiveness in a coherent approach to lifelong learning for all?

THE INCREASING FOCUS ON STANDARD SETTING AND PERFORMANCE ASSESSMENT

In recent years there has been an increasing focus on the need for standard setting and performance assessment. This focus has arisen and sharpened as a result of such factors as the following:

- The concern for quality in education and the pressure for more and better information about the ways in which quality in education is created, promoted, assured and evaluated.

- The perceived need for increased, centrally determined and centrally monitored quality control in more decentralized and devolved systems.

- The growing demand, locally, nationally and internationally, for accountability in a time of fiscal restraint.

- The public concern about what are perceived to be declining standards in education, at a time when the nature of the population undergoing education is expanding and changing, particularly with mass enrolment in upper secondary and higher education.

- The shortcomings of current evaluation and accountability policies, procedures and strategies, to bring about improvements in school effectiveness, the provision of post-compulsory education, and the realization of the aim to offer lifelong learning for all.

Yet another factor to be brought into consideration in explaining the increased attention to standards is the growing recognition of the importance of education in improving economic performance and international competitiveness, and the increasing realization that current approaches to education are failing to keep abreast of wider economic and social changes. As Rumberger has commented:

Of particular concern is that the use of new technologies and new forms of work organization that are being used to raise productivity are greatly increasing the skills and educational demands of work. The increased use of computers, sophisticated communication systems, workteams and other technological and other organizational innovations are claimed to require higher levels and more varied skills in the workers that are using them.

(Rumberger, 1991, p. 3)

The concern is that without substantial improvements in the provision and range of education and training countries will fall behind their competitors in the international economic market-place. Monitoring the achievement of educational systems through standard setting and through mechanisms such as educational indicators is seen as one way in which governments can obtain better, more precise and more timely information as to the comparative 'performance' of their country's education system. The increasing availability of computer technology to process data on educational performance has been seen as one way in which this need can be met.

THE NATURE AND PURPOSES OF EDUCATIONAL STANDARDS

The concerns of government, parents, teachers, students, business leaders and members of the general public have highlighted a need to reconsider the issue of standards, particularly as they pertain to the task of preparing people for the world of work, lifelong learning, improving curriculum and instruction and increasing education options, and improving student attainment and performance standards.

The majority of countries have a clearly identified set of national standards for primary and secondary education. Only in a relatively few countries (Australia, Canada and the USA) is standard setting for primary and secondary education decentralized. The focus and level of specificity of standards, however, varies across countries. While some countries focus primarily on curricular content, others specify objectives for student attainment. Curriculum standards serve a variety of purposes, although their most common use is to inform the construction of content of internal assessments and external examinations. Curriculum standards are also widely used to guide classroom instruction. Japan, the Netherlands and some states in the USA also use standards to ensure all students have equal access to quality educational opportunities (cf. Pelavin Associates, *Educational Standards in OECD Countries: A Compilation of Survey Standards*, 1993).

In primary and secondary education standards exist for all subjects in some countries, whilst in others they normally exist and apply only in the case of a limited core of subjects, such as language, mathematics, science. In some countries standards exist only in subjects that are included in post-secondary education entrance examinations. Types of standards employed fall into two categories: standards for each grade level; and standards for specified levels of education. In all countries the existing standards apply to all students, although these are generally varied to meet the needs of those with special education requirements. In most countries the standard setting process is a multistep collaborative effort, typically involving subject experts and key stakeholders in education.

Translating standards into classroom practice at primary and secondary levels usually involves the central education authority's issuing guidelines for course content, that are then adapted by local authorities, schools and teachers for use in the classroom. There is, however, some variation in the extent to which national authorities actively pursue and promote their guidelines. The extent to which a national authority specifies its standards also influences the roles of the various education bodies. In countries where the national authority translates its standards into specific curricula, the local authorities' role tends to lie in ensuring that schools adhere to national guidelines. But even in contexts where there are fixed content standards, very rarely are there standardized instructional methods, although textbooks can play a key role in the implementation of standards.

Assessment is a key component in the maintenance of standards. At primary and secondary levels the most common type of assessment is for the purpose of evaluating student achievement. In some countries assessments are conducted to evaluate system progress towards meeting established standards. The assessment of the effectiveness of individual schools or teachers in educating students is still relatively rare.

Periodic review and revision is one way to ensure that standards continue to meet student and societal needs; however, some countries have tended to differ over this matter, with a number of them having no established procedures for reviewing standards. In countries with a decentralized approach to education, procedures may vary across states or provinces. Schools are the primary reviewers in those settings where the central authorities provide only broad guidelines.

In the past policy-makers and educators have tended to undertake extensive work in the matter of establishing and measuring standards at the level of primary and secondary schooling and extensive data are now available for policy-makers on traditional practices pertaining to these matters in those phases of education. As will be shown below, however, the changing nature of economic and social demands, and the changing values and conceptions of knowledge and learning which are having an impact on educational goals, has brought to the fore new requirements in standard setting and monitoring at the primary and secondary levels, which have yet to be subject to systematic analysis.

Moreover, whilst some work has been undertaken by some countries on standard setting in the vocational area as a component of vocational education more broadly conceived, there is still a need for future inquiry in the domain of vocational education and training generally, and most particularly in the provision of education on a lifelong basis, by the range of agencies outside the traditional boundaries of educational services and institutions now involved in educational planning and provision. This is especially important given the nature and direction of the move towards a mass system of further and higher education.

ASSESSMENT OF LEARNING ACHIEVEMENT

The Failure of Traditional Assessment Techniques to Assess Newly Emerging Learning Goals

Along with changing work practices and technological advances, new knowledge and skills are emerging as important elements of education and training systems in all phases during the learning life-span, and success in them is held to be a goal for such systems. Problem-solving ability, interpersonal competencies, thinking skills and the readiness and willingness to accept change are among those cognitive and affective competencies emerging as important for all members of society.

Although these competencies are to some degree embedded in and promoted by more conventional approaches to styles of teaching and modes of learning, there is a growing realization that, until such time as performance in the key competencies called for in the response of individuals and groups to the exigencies of economic and social change can be validly assessed, they will not be given the place in educational provision that their importance in the broader economic and social environment warrants.

Broadfoot (1991) has argued that one of the difficulties of ensuring that educational provision reflects broader economic and social change is that the assessment industry is simply not keeping abreast of changing educational goals. She comments:

> Until such assessment procedures are available not only will it be impossible to produce valid judgements about the success of the educational enterprise as a whole in terms of its goals, it will also help to guarantee that certain desired educational outcomes will be neglected in the classroom. Thus the challenge facing those charged with the evaluation of education systems is to define and to find ways of measuring, indicators that adequately reflect the full range of educational goals. Not to do so will result in both the generation of inadequate information about performance and a tendency to ignore some of the problematic teaching objectives.
>
> (Broadfoot, 1991, p. 3).

Among the limitations of traditional approaches to assessment, Broadfoot points to their preoccupation with psychometric measurements, with their concentration on the easily measurable, such as the acquisition of content knowledge, and their concomitant neglect of higher level intellectual skills such as thinking and personal qualities. Broadfoot comments that the concentration of psychometricians on the criteria of differentiation and reliability has resulted in an emphasis in educating institutions generally on such measuring devices as multiple choice achievement tests, as these can be shown to have acceptable psychometric properties and, in addition, are easy to mark. Broadfoot points out, however, that there is an increasing awareness that some psychometric tests can be shown not even to achieve their stated objective of providing objective, reliable evidence of attainment. For such reasons, Broadfoot maintains, dissatisfaction with traditional testing approaches is increasing.

As causes of the growth of this dissatisfaction Broadfoot points to other factors:

- their emphasis on comparison between students rather than describing specific and changing levels of attainment;

- the frequent mismatch between curriculum and test content;

- the tendency to test in a relatively limited number of aspects of a programme of instruction;

- the assumption that students learn in a linear fashion and therefore that students must learn and be assessed on the basics before going on to more complex intellectual processes;

- the back-wash effect of assessment on instruction and the attitude students take to their work;

- their failure to reflect the most recent conceptions of knowledge, theories of learning, and most important advances in cognitive psychology;

- their failure to incorporate the new and emerging skills, competencies and qualities deemed to be important to modern societies and their social and economic advance.

To overcome these difficulties in existing approaches to assessment, Broadfoot argues, there is a need for a new theory of test design and validation – one that emphasizes individual learning rather than individual difference. She warns, however, that:

> The international interest in the generation of effective educational indicators means that there is a very real danger of invalid, shallow data and inappropriate correlations being generated in an attempt to short cut the necessary development work that still needs to take place in designing new assessment approaches ... the issues are both technical and political involving both the generation of suitable techniques and rendering these acceptable for the various social purposes that assessment fulfils.
>
> (Broadfoot, 1991, p. 27)

THE SETTING, MONITORING AND EVALUATING OF STANDARDS AS A STRATEGY FOR REALIZING LIFELONG LEARNING FOR ALL

It is clear that there need to be changes in the approaches adopted to the monitoring and evaluating of standards in education. That such changes are needed becomes clear not only from an appreciation of the deficiencies and omissions associated with reliance upon quantitative and psychometric methods of assessment, but also from an awareness of the changing nature of the goals of education, the accounts of knowledge being articulated as a result of advances in the philosophy of knowledge, particularly in the philosophy of science, and a changed attitude to our understanding of the ways in which students learn and achieve understanding. It is such new conceptualizations of learning that provide us with a clear basis for structuring new approaches to curriculum and assessment.

All this is particularly important when we come to questions of the development of such lifelong learning competencies as:

1 conceptual understanding;

2 integration and application of learning;

3 the transfer of learning to new situations in a dynamic way.

Taken together, the new conceptualizations involved will lead to the application of a whole range of approaches to the assessment of standards and goals in education over a lifelong span. Informed by the work of Broadfoot (1991, p. 26), we might point to some approaches to assessment that might be recommended as capable of achieving such broader learning goals. Such approaches are likely to be characterized by:

- their focus on actual performance;

- their comprehensive coverage of learning goals;

- their application of clear criteria as a basis for validity (widely conceived) and for transparency so that those being assessed understand the criteria being applied and can direct, control and assess their own learning appropriately, for illuminative, formative and summative purposes;

- their ability to address both domain-specific and general learning goals; both short- and long-term desired outcomes;

- their ability to combine both cognitive and conative dimensions;

- their capacity to be usable in a range of potential performance contexts (verbal, symbolic, physical and social) and to take account of idiosyncratic, unanticipated learning as well as instructional goals;

- their provision of data that are generated in a form that allows for aggregation across individuals and that are relevant for making policy decisions as well as decisions concerning instruction.

Broadfoot has provided some trenchant criticisms of existing practices of assessment, some valuable insights about new directions for development in the light of advances in epistemology and cognitive learning theory, and some powerful recommendations, that could better ensure learning activities and achievements are consistent with changing goals emerging from the changing economic and social circumstances. It is clear that concentrated attention needs to be given to ensuring that suitable modes and strategies of standard setting and assessment are devised and put into place, and that an appropriate range of activities are provided, if the aims of offering opportunities to all for lifelong learning are to be realized.

ASSESSMENT OF SYSTEM PERFORMANCE

The Emergence of Educational Indicators as a Major Orientation in Educational Decision-making

In response to the widespread concern for quality and in an attempt to meet the legitimate demands for accountability, national and international agencies have put considerable effort into investigating the utility and validity of educational indicators as a means for monitoring the performance of educational systems, as a mechanism for improving and reforming the provision of education, and as a basis for international comparability. As Cohen and Spillane explain:

> Educational indicators are seen as a way to improve education by improving decision making about education. Advocates argue that if policy-makers have better evidence on the performance of students, schools and teachers then they will be able to make better decisions about resource allocation, policy direction and the like. The belief that scientific knowledge would improve political decisions is at least as old as Saint-Simon's dream of a social science, but the recent enthusiasm for indicators suggests a renaissance of belief. The ambitions are appealing but can they be realised?
>
> (Cohen and Spillane, 1991, p. 3)

The concern regarding the validity of an 'indicators' approach has already received considerable attention. What has become clear is that 'indicators', whilst offering some assistance to policy-makers in the monitoring of educational standards across systems, have no more uncontestable self-evidence, acceptability or 'value-free' status than any other set of judgments, in which significant parts are played by the assumptions, values and preferences of the policy-makers and other stakeholders in the community.

Cohen and Spillane (1991) argue that, even if we accept the claims of objectivity, knowledge gained from indicator data is only dependently authoritative: 'whatever effect indicators have on knowledge or decisions is likely to be indirect, mediated through existing beliefs and values rather than supplanting them' (Cohen and Spillane, 1991, p. 16).

There are some other concerns regarding the status and utility of indicators as appropriate measures to evaluate educational progress and achievement. Linda Darling-Hammond, for example, in her discussion of 'Policy uses and indicators' (1991, p. 25), refers to:

- The emphasis on quantitative data in educational indicators, which often tends to override considerations of other kinds of information. This is a particular problem when the limitations of quantitative data and the appropriate inferences that can be drawn from quantitative data are not always widely understood. There is therefore a need for indicator systems to be accompanied by a concerted effort to educate users about the relevance and meanings of particular kinds of information within the educational context. Indicators should be reported along with a discussion of their meanings, limits and appropriate and inappropriate interpretations.

- The need for multiple indicators as requisites for building an accurate and comprehensive picture of a situation. Changes in a single indicator can rarely be accurately interpreted without information as to how related variables are changing. Better policy-making will come about from a greater array of information.

- The need for policies, whether using an indicator system or not, to take into consideration what motivates individual and organization change. Policy-makers and administrators are often tempted to use information from indicators to focus narrowly on first-order changes rather than looking deeper at the capacities of people within the different parts of the education systems to sustain the desired performance or produce the desired change.

- The use of indicators as a grist for further assessment and evaluation of a situation, not as a mechanical trigger for actions that may prove counterproductive. Indicators should not replace thoughtful, reflective and complex decision-making. Indicators provide pointers and signals towards improving education but should not be the sole basis upon which educational change and advance should be planned and driven.

There are deeper conceptual and epistemological issues underlying these concerns so ably articulated by Darling-Hammond. Carla Fasano (1991) has provided a powerful undergirding for these concerns by pointing to:

- The paradigm expansion which has brought to a consideration of educational indicators approaches which, although beneficial in other aspects of economic and public policy, can result in narrowness in the conceptualization of educational goals and effectiveness.

- The knowledge dilemma: given that it is impossible to obtain complete and rigorous knowledge of an entire education system, the construction of educational indicators will have to take into consideration strategies for the management of what she describes as 'non-knowledge' in education (qualities and characteristics that, as we may say, are not readily amenable to assessment conceived in traditional terms, such as increases in personal sensitivity, community commitment, or cultural empathy) as well as strategies for knowledge maximization.

Among those outcomes of education that we may regard as most important, it is clear that such 'non-knowledge' components will figure largely. Yet it is clear that, for all the expenditure of effort and resources on the assessment of advance in education, growth and progress in such areas remains unamenable to the more traditional forms of assessment. Having conducted a survey of national assessment and examination practices in fourteen countries, Binkley, Guthrie and Wyatt (1991) conclude that, although there have been many attempts to develop indicator systems at school, district, state and national levels, there has been the greatest difficulty in adequately and appropriately reporting the most important outcome of schooling – what students have learned (Binkley, Guthrie and Wyatt, 1991, p. 1).

With such cautions in mind, governments may find it helpful to consider adopting an approach to the use of indicators for the assessment of educational standards that takes advantage of their positive aspects but enables them to move away from the deficiencies and omissions they display, and thus from the criticisms that may be levelled against them. It is perhaps with some such note in mind that Cohen and Spillane (1991) proffer a number of suggestions as to how to improve the design and use of indicator systems.

With respect to the design of indicator systems, they argue that it is important that those who are designing systems of indicators are clear in the areas of educational activity upon which they wish to concentrate. They might focus on:

- educational resources;

- educational outcomes;

- relations between resources and outcomes.

The difference in focus is crucial for it affects the knowledge that is produced about education, as well as affecting the construction and operation of indicator systems. As we have already indicated, however, the problem is that the sort of data that research suggests have a greater impact on student learning, such as teachers' knowledge of their subject or tests that require more complex intellectual performances by students, are more costly and complex to devise, administer and analyse. In addition, the assessment technologies for devising and applying such instruments are not yet fully developed, articulated or in place.

Among other suggestions Cohen and Spillane include the following recommendations for an indicator system:

- it should be designed and organized as a means of reporting on status and change in education systems;

- it should monitor a range of educational resources, from the most rudimentary such as unit expenditure to the more complex such as teachers' knowledge of the subjects they teach;

- it should monitor traditional measures of educational results, such as school completion rates; and it should also monitor the best available measures of student performance.

Cohen and Spillane suggest that indicators may be part of a new portfolio for central government, enabling better oversight and the improved exercise of central influence and responsibility. The test for governments is to avoid being drawn into more central control and regulation. Cohen and Spillane highlight the point that, whatever part educational indicators turn out to play in democratic accountability, formal governance will not be the only influence at work. Various dynamic features of political and educational systems are also likely to feature in and shape the setting of standards and the uses to which indicators and other measures of assessment are put.

Indicators and Reporting to the Labour Market

Many recent reforms in education have been predicated on the need to align the performance of a country's education system more closely with the economy. As a result indicators of economic outcomes have been proposed as a better way of monitoring that alignment.

Rumberger argues (1991, p. 3) that if policy-makers are concerned with the question of whether their nations' education systems are adequately respond-ing to the needs of the economy, then they will need additional information on the economic outputs that result from education. He points out that there is a substantial body of theoretical and empirical research that suggests a direct and strong relationship between educational outputs and a wide variety of social, political and economic outcomes. For example, individuals benefit from increased levels of education by receiving higher salaries, obtaining better jobs, and having access to further education and training. There are also increased social benefits in the form of improved productivity and economic growth, and reduced demands for social welfare and social support services.

Rumberger cautions, however (1991, p. 12), that the relationship between education and economic outcomes is much more complicated than many exist-ing analyses, particularly those based on human capital theory, suggest. He points to two major limitations in the ability to assess the economic outcomes of education: first, economic outcomes are derived in the labour market and are influenced by factors of both supply and demand; but how supply and demand of educated labour interact to produce economic benefits is difficult to predict. Second, the labour market itself may work imperfectly and distort the economic benefits of education. Thus, he remarks:

> the economic outcomes most commonly attributed to education, such as employment and earnings, may provide quite imperfect and distorted information about such questions as how well the education system is meeting the needs of the economy, how much education is attributing to economic growth, and other questions that educational indicators are frequently supposed to address.
>
> (Rumberger, 1991, p. 13)

Rumberger claims that such limitations do not negate the value of trying to monitor the economic outputs of education but they suggest necessary cautions in doing so. Among the cautions emphasized by Rumberger, we find the following especially noteworthy:

- the importance of acknowledging from the outset the inherent limitations in any indicator system's capacity successfully to monitor the operation of a complex social system;

- the indicator system must be based on a robust, conceptual model of how the economic system works and how it is related to the outputs of the education system.

The challenge still remains as to how to construct a conceptual framework for developing labour market indicators of educational performance, particularly when education is more properly conceived of as a lifelong process. Rumberger suggests a tentative way forward with a conceptual model, the major components of which fall into the following categories (1991, p. 14):

1 supply-side components such as population characteristics and the education system;

2 demand-side components, which consist of economic systems;

3 labour market outcomes, which result from the interaction of the supply side and the demand side components;

4 the social and political environment which initially affects both the supply-side and demand-side components and is then affected by the outcomes of the education system and the labour market.

Working on this basis Rumberger proposes a set of indicators that could be used to measure the economic outputs associated with education:

1 the educational qualifications of the population;

2 the employment status of the population;

3 the characteristics of firms and jobs in the economy;

4 the extent of mismatch between the qualifications of the population and the characteristics of the firms and jobs;

5 the formal and informal training activities of workers;

6 work-place attitudes and behaviours;

7 earnings.

The overall conclusion of Rumberger's analysis (1991, p. 19) is that economic indicators can be useful in judging the performance of the educational system and for promoting policies that better align the education and economic systems; but Rumberger cautions that the education system performs other functions *besides* the preparation of an adequately trained workforce and that the limitations of economic indicators must always be kept in mind.

The issues of standard setting, accountability and reporting to the labour market and to other stakeholders will remain as vital components of improving the provision of education. The questions which policy-makers and educators must address include that of discovering the most appropriate ways and means of establishing and assessing standards of educational progress and achievement in all the diverse range of activities and experiences offered to participants in a country's educational systems, institutions and schools. Another vital question to be dealt with concerns the ways and means by which the breadth, depth, complexity and relevance of educational endeavour is to be determined, implemented and assessed on a lifelong basis.

STANDARD SETTING, MONITORING AND EVALUATION AS STRATEGIES FOR IMPROVING QUALITY, EFFICIENCY AND EFFECTIVENESS

In their development of agenda for standard setting, monitoring and evaluation in education and training, it will be important for policy-makers and educators to remember that it is not possible to have one single criterion of quality or effectiveness. Rather, quality is associated with and found in a number of characteristics and features in educational systems and institutions. In the quest for improved standard setting and achievement-monitoring it may be helpful, therefore, to give some tentative adumbration of the sites by which quality in an educating institution may be discerned and the characteristic features by which it might be identified. A useful guide in this endeavour is provided by the Scottish Education Office in their *Country Report* to the OECD on 'The effectiveness of schooling and of educational resource management' (1991). Extrapolating from their work on effective schooling to education and training more broadly conceived, we suggest:

- Quality in education may be judged in terms of the characteristic features exhibited by its 'graduates': what do people know and understand, what can they do, what are their values, beliefs and attitudes, that are brought about as a result of their education and training experiences?

- Secondly, quality may be judged by features of the processes and activities of the education that is believed to take place in educating institutions. How good is the planning of teaching and learning? How well are the various 'lessons' delivered? How well are the lessons learned? What is assessed and how satisfactorily? What feedback is provided to the students and how satisfactory/appropriate is it? To what extent are parents, the wider community, business, commerce and industry involved? Are continuity and progression to the next stage assured? If not, why not – and what mechanisms are available for continuing review and correction of those teaching deliveries and learning outcomes found to be deficient?

- Thirdly, quality may also be judged by the range, type, excellence and appropriateness of the resources and facilities provided. Resources include trained teachers, teaching and learning materials, accommodation, amenities and facilities, and opportunities for engaging in learning by all kinds of means, formal, informal and alternative.

- Fourthly, quality may be judged by the ways in which educating institutions and their operations are organized, administered and managed. How are learners grouped? How is teaching arranged? What is the structure, range and relevance of the curriculum? What are the institution's policies, for what purposes, and how appropriate are they? Is administration sound? Have management practices been well thought out and implemented? How adaptable and responsive to change are they? How are they evaluated and held accountable to public scrutiny and inspection?

- Finally, quality may be judged by the tone, atmosphere and ethos of the institution. Does it provide a secure, relaxed, non-threatening, supportive and purposeful atmosphere, conducive to learning and to optimizing growth and development? Are relationships based on mutual trust and respect? Is there real equality of opportunity? Are contacts with parents, industry and the wider community supported and promoted? What connections are there with external agencies that can help foster the mission of the learning institution?

Having looked at all these diverse sites with which quality might be associated, and around which a set of agenda might be framed, we might reasonably suppose that even to ask, in the search for some kind of preliminary benchmark, which, in general, is likely to be the better indicator of good quality – a set of clearly articulated and agreed procedures *or* a set of output measures (even if related to input, and the notion of *added value*) – is to run the risk of dangerous superficiality and oversimplification. The search for, the identification of and the assessment of quality is, as the above list shows, much more complex, demanding and difficult than that. We say this to underline the point that in looking for quality in education and training we cannot expect to have one single criterion by means of which we can generalize and then apply a single benchmark to the whole of the processes, activities, operations and resources of a country's education and training system and individual institutions.

Instead we believe that countries may like to note carefully that the identification, appreciation and assessment of quality in any education institution must be hedged about with all sorts of caveats. A report by the Australian Vice-Chancellors Committee (AVCC, 1992) on quality in higher education institutions makes this point very forcibly:

- Quality cannot be monitored across whole systems, or even whole institutions, without due sensitivity to the fact that data can be used in a comparative sense, only where organization units, courses, goals and missions are identical.

- Any individual judgment of quality requires very careful consideration against a range of variable factors, such as geographical location.

- Each difference introduces another variable into the quality equation, making national judgments and evaluations so difficult as to be almost impossible.

We take this last point, together with the rest, to mean that countries should be extremely cautious about assuming or inferring that what makes for quality delivery or assurance in any one institution or system can automatically be transferred and applied in any other institution or system without any further need for adaptation or adjustment. In the end, quality, its recognition and its reward, must come from concepts and criteria adopted or elaborated upon and operating within and valued by the particular educational institution, system and country.

In addressing the quality delivery and assurance agenda, then, countries may find it important to remember some critical notes of caution (Aspin and Chapman, 1994):

1 It is not logically sound to aggregate institutions or individual departments within institutions, just as it is not valid to aggregate individuals, and then talk about their quality 'in the round' or in any general sense. (To do so is to commit the fallacy of composition.)

2 It is unhelpful and uninformative to base any judgments about the quality and excellence of an institution, department or individual member of staff or student on any particular description, observation or appraisal, that has been made at one particular point in time. To do so ignores past history, future intentions and the present context and environment (internal and external). (It also commits the fallacy of isolating the object appraised from its context.) There must be some expectation of stability and continuity in the assessment of the activities and operations of the institution, staff or student whose quality we are seeking to appraise.

3 It is not helpful, in making judgments about quality, to conflate different styles or types of appraisal, assessment or evaluation. In the formation of judgments about the quality of a restaurant, for example, the purpose and style of evaluations made of it by inspectors of the Department of Health are obviously quite different from those made by the inspectors from the *Michelin Good Restaurant Guide*, and we should not confuse the two. (To do so commits the fallacy of making a 'category mistake'.)

4 Instead we do well to remember that the qualities of an institution or a department exhibit different kinds and styles of quality and excellence. For that reason the judgments relating to those different kinds must be domain-specific, or else operating at a very low level of generalizability. Judgments of quality in education and training involve a search for particular kinds of excellence. This is because quality assurance is a positive form of appraisal and involves the determination to ensure the *presence* of particular kinds of *virtue*. Quality in an education and training institution is not, like a restaurant preparing for a visit by Health Department inspectors, assured by a desire to ensure the *absence* of dysfunctional conditions. (To think it is, is to commit the fallacy of omission.)

5 The judgments of quality about which educating institutions are chiefly concerned demand peer judgments from agents of evaluation, deeply, directly and centrally involved with the nature, aims and values of education, and from members of the education profession,

who themselves exhibit those standards in their own being and work, and who are concerned for discerning and defining the ways in which the standards set by those things can prolong, extend or even create excellence in the domain in question. It is clear that the work of such people is of crucial importance in defining excellence: their work therefore needs a great deal of money, devoted to programmes of R&D of and into appropriate forms of evaluation and assessment – particularly the illuminative and formative ones.

6 In this enterprise what will be important in framing initiatives for the continuation, development and extension of the quality work an institution is doing at any one particular time – especially in teaching, learning, curriculum and professional development and management – will be the availability and sharing of advice, assistance, monitoring, collaboration and review.

7 These considerations generate a set of principles for application:

(a) In making academic and professional assessments of quality in education and training policies and institutions, we have to think about evaluation and assessment in new ways. Professionals will want to face what they do in their work and to ask themselves, and be helped to ask: what kinds of evaluation and assessment will help them to appraise what they do, in ways that will enable them to engage in activities leading to improvements in their professional practice overall. What we are after here is a process of appraisal involving future planning, the utility and validity of which may best be seen in terms of its consequences for the system and the institution, their professional teaching staff and their learners.

(b) We have to keep in mind the distinction between the different types and purposes of evaluations and appraisals. This may help to remind us that it is logically impossible to see one particular form or type of evaluation as a mere extension of the other, or as a form of appraisal that can be built on top of the other. (The fallacy of composition/conflation is committed by those who do this.)

(c) We must remember that no single form of evaluation is by itself sufficient to do the job of defining and monitoring standards as a whole: instead we have to operate with a sort of aggregate of partial and insufficient forms of judgment. This will give us an appraisal of quality that will be a summation of the application of a broad mosaic of measures, that when reflected on and used will give us some indication of the wide range of excellences in the whole domain of learning activities and practices, interests and concerns, aims and values. However, they will not give us a complete picture of, nor recipe for, 'total quality'. (To think that they can is to commit the fallacy of essentialism.)

CONCLUSION

The challenge of setting standards, developing mechanisms for monitoring, and working out strategies for evaluation for education conceived as a lifelong process has hardly yet been met. As is clear from the foregoing, the issue of quality delivery and assurance is highly complex, difficult and demanding.

It is noteworthy that recent changes and developments in the styles and procedures of evaluation and assessment have been articulated and elaborated along with, and perhaps as a function of, parallel changes in theories of knowledge and accounts of learning and cognitive growth in individuals; yet we are still a long way from a situation in which the recently developed innovations and advances in evaluation and assessment techniques for a full range of educational desiderata are automatically applied and in operation in educational systems and institutions. Even when education has been conceived of in the compartmentalized manner of sector provision, as has been done in the past, it is still yet scarcely possible to make valid and reliable judgments about its quality, efficiency and effectiveness, much less about the total range of student learning styles and educational outcomes, simply by employing the restricted and narrow range of assessment techniques that have been applied in educational testing and evaluation generally.

Thus a great deal of work still remains to be done in this connection, involving the development of appropriate technologies for the application of the new and sophisticated instruments and styles of evaluation; but even more needs to be done to achieve the kind of institutional development and transformation that will easily admit of, respond to and employ the tools offered them by such advances and developments.

There also need to be considerable changes in public expectations and perceptions of what constitutes valid, reliable and *objective* evaluation of learning gains for the various purposes that policy-makers and educators, societies and individuals have in mind.

When it is realized that some of the most ill-informed criticisms, objections to and blockages of the application and employment of recent developments in notions of valued knowledge, styles of learning and advances in educational evaluation have been articulated in some of the most redoubtable of a community's educating institutions, it has to be realized that the total challenge for change to be faced here is one of enormous magnitude and will require immense efforts of energy and time, if such objections are to be overcome.

A major challenge facing policy-makers, academics, system administrators and school-based educators is how to translate the vision of lifelong learning for all into a programme and a form that can be realized, transmitted and assessed, without in any way discounting, diminishing or destroying the complex, heterogeneous and multifaceted nature of the goals and outcomes at which it is aiming.

Chapter 6

Managing a Coherent Approach to Lifelong Learning

Over the years many proposals for schemes and programmes of lifelong education have been advanced, yet they have not gone forward to successful implementation. This has come about, in part as a result of a lack of clarity about the nature, aims and purposes of such an enterprise; in part due to lack of resources for clearly articulated policies; and in part because the structures and processes of governance and management in education and training were not adjusted nor altered sufficiently in order to adapt to and accommodate the necessary changes in policy, provision and institutional practice.

Current approaches to lifelong learning differ from those put forward in many previous proposals, in that they now stress the vital importance of the role played by various kinds of partnership in learning, rather than concentrating chiefly on the role of government as a monopoly provider of formal education and training. The new approaches embody the virtues and educational value of collaboration in the provision and structuring of learning activities, as well as making allowance for fundamental differences in the structure and processes of learning. These new approaches and the concerns they exemplify carry considerable implications for the changed role of governments and the expanded type and number of roles that can be played by other stakeholders in the educational enterprise.

A commitment to lifelong learning will necessitate the introduction of new approaches and styles of teaching and modes of student progress; new emphases in the forms and conditions of knowledge, skills and dispositions to be acquired and renewed; greater attention to the varied range of pathways, transitions and coherences in facilitating students' learning; and a greater sharing of responsibilities for the content, organization and resourcing of education and training systems.

All the various elements that have come together and are embodied in the new configuration of lifelong learning patterns and programmes will require the setting up of policy frameworks and strategies for implementation. It will be imperative that these frameworks and strategies facilitate and enable the development, provision and exercise of opportunities for individual and group initiatives, responsibility and choice, while at the same time ensuring the needs of both the economy and society are met. The striking of such a balance between these varied and distinct exigencies demands that attention be given to the question of the most appropriate approaches to governance and management in education and training. Above all, this will require a reconsideration of the role of governments in the light of these alterations and changed arrangements in learning and in the provision of opportunities for individual advancement and community benefit.

Questions guiding our deliberations on these matters include:

- What are the problems and challenges which governments face in devising effective policies and managerial strategies that steer development into the desired direction of lifelong learning for all?

- In recent times these policies and strategies have included moves towards decentralization and the creation of quasi-markets for learning, with an emphasis on partnerships, privatization and diversification and even de-institutionalization. What are the implications of these trends?

- What balance between central regulation and local decision-making by autonomous establishments and among actors and across functions best promotes the development of effective and efficient provision which fosters lifelong learning for all? Does this balance differ among sectors and education and training establishments and programmes? According to what criteria?

- How are the goals of inclusiveness, coherence, quality, efficiency and effectiveness to be promoted in a system with diffused and widely shared responsibilities?

- To what extent does present practice in governance, accountability and management promote such goals?

GOVERNANCE AND MANAGEMENT

Current approaches to the governance and management of education and training systems and institutions are now being increasingly challenged, as provision expands and agenda are broadened to adjust to the idea of a lifelong perspective on learning for all. Shifts in the balance between central direction and regional and local autonomy can be discerned in new approaches to governance and management, as well as moves towards the creation of quasi-markets for learning.

Accompanying such trends are moves towards partnerships, diversification and privatization in education provision and servicing. In the wake of these trends considerable challenges are emerging as regards the possibilities and limits of government involvement in standard setting, governance, steering and management in education. The question that faces governments now is whether they should maintain their involvement in the day-to-day steering of education and training systems. For they will recognize that, in the changed emphasis leading now to moves towards the adoption of a lifelong approach to education, there will be an emphasis not only on schooling and formal education and training delivery but also on non-formal, informal and alternative modes of delivery, and on provision well beyond hitherto 'normal' chronological guidelines. All these are areas in which government interest, activity and control have traditionally been relatively limited.

In the changed patterns of governance and administration across countries, it has been possible to observe a range of responses to the challenge of offering and managing the various forms of educational provision, especially in a time of budgetary constraint. Amongst these responses it is possible to discern a movement away from highly centralized and bureaucratic approaches to system-wide administration, and towards decentralization, devolution and, in some settings, the adoption of a more market-orientated approach.

The question that arises here, however, concerns the knotty problem of whether governments can influence the provision of education in a decentralized system or in some kind of educational 'market-place', if they relinquish their traditional control over the rules and regulations that govern the inputs, contents and processes of education, and, if they do so, what is the best way such influence might be exerted and exercised.

In this context a further question arises concerning the nature, type and extent of the roles played by central, regional and local governments in the control of inputs, processes and outcomes of education seen now from a 'lifelong' perspective. We might, for instance, ask whether the most appropriate response to the problem of provision of lifelong learning lies in the opening of more 'markets' for learning. Given that governments have in the past been mainly responsible only for formal education and within restricted confines of time, we might also ask how far the responsibility of governments for education should be extended to other areas of lifelong learning, not least to the areas of continuing vocational education and learning on the job. The question of the type and range of government involvement in educational provision also has an impact upon the question of the assessment and certification of skills and qualifications: we might reasonably question whether current government monopolies or 'single-system' approaches are worth keeping; whether there are viable alternatives; and who should be accountable to whom and for what.

WHY THE IDEAL OF LIFELONG LEARNING HAS NOT BEEN REALIZED

In his summary of the themes, challenges and issues raised at the First Global Conference on 'Lifelong Learning' held in Rome, December 1994, Sir Christopher Ball highlighted the main finding of the conference:

> Our traditional and inherited systems of education and training have
> failed to create 'learning societies' in which everyone is motivated and
> enabled to practise lifelong learning ... Existing systems of education
> and training tend to favour an élite of fast learners, to focus on teaching
> rather than learning, and to overemphasise initial education at the
> expense of lifelong learning. What is required is not more of the same. If
> we are to reach the unreached and include the excluded, more must
> mean different. The key principle governing provision in the future
> must be the primacy of personal responsibility for learning, encouraged
> and enabled by the support of the whole community ... For
> organisations the fundamental requirement is the development of the
> idea of learning organisations. For governments the threefold task is of

setting targets for learning, gradually transferring the resources for learning from those who provide teaching to those who undertake learning, and developing in cooperation a global system of qualifications, guaranteed by reliable arrangements for quality assurance.

Although the idea of 'lifelong learning' is not new – there has long been interest on the continent of Europe in the notion of *'éducation permanente'*, for example – there is still considerable discrepancy between different conceptions and practices, policies and their implementation, with respect to the various articulations of conceptions, interpretations and approaches to the provision of lifelong learning. Candy and Crebert (1991, pp. 3–17) maintain that this gap can be partly explained by the difficulty of devising practical policies and strategies to implement a notion of education that is based on and embodies a number of ideals.

The problem, they say, consists in the fact that lifelong learning has come to mean 'all things to all people'. There is an 'inter-related set of values' in lifelong learning (Candy and Crebert, 1991, p. 4), but nowadays, we might add, included among these values are some that are increasingly expansionist, facilitative and emancipatory for all members of the community. As we have argued in Chapter 2, the time is right to re-examine the principal philosophical underpinnings and educational values of lifelong learning, and to reconsider the place of this idea in the overall educational pantheon. For it is clear that the aims and programmes of lifelong education offer opportunities to, and are open to be taken advantage of by, a number of points of view and a diverse range of constituencies and interests, individual, social and economic. This gives lifelong learning, as it is now coming to be conceived, planned and delivered, an immensely heterogeneous and *protean* character – one that defies precise conceptual analysis and tightly co-ordinated and defined patterns and protocols of implementation and management.

Because of its fluid, dynamic, and cover-all character, 'lifelong learning' does not lend itself readily, particularly as regards orientation and programming, to the imposition of precisely specified government norms, controls and regulations, nor to the specification of a set of organizational, administrative, methodological and procedural criteria by which its progress and success may be measured. As Candy and Crebert remark:

> Lifelong learning is characterised by its unstructured nature, and is based on the philosophy that education should be openly and easily accessible to all at any time in life; it establishes that self improvement and enrichment are goals that are equally as important as the need to update professional and vocational skills; it relies on the understanding that such educational experience should be available either on a full time or part time basis when required; and it implies that some government funding is necessary to facilitate these opportunities. As well it signifies greater interaction between the universities and the community, and the establishment of stronger links between universities, secondary and primary schools, the profession, the graduate population and the community at large; and it implies the use

of alternative educational sources, such as television, radio, the press, computer learning packages and distance education. Integration for the individual occurs then on two distinct axes as he or she engages in learning throughout life – vertically (in sequential levels in chronological stages) and horizontally across the various aspects of a person's life as he or she interacts with different groups of people in different situations.

(Candy and Crebert, 1991, p. 7)

Before such a version of the ideal of lifelong learning can be realized, a number of changes will have to be made by governments and providers of learning, particularly in respect of the following concerns:

- funding arrangements;
- access;
- teaching and learning methods;
- provision of communications technology and access to new global information infrastructures;
- relationships between education providers and business, commerce and industry;
- adult and vocational education;
- schools and teacher training;
- universities and other tertiary sector institutions;
- informal education systems, the community and non-government organizations.

One of the challenges for governments in bringing about improvements and expansion of lifelong learning opportunities for all will be to implement the necessary changes in the above areas without compromising the best qualities in existing education systems. Another challenge will be to ensure that the benefits of lifelong learning and of access to new global information infrastructures, pathways and networks do not remain restricted only to those who have the means to enter the information super-highway. Instead every effort must be made to encourage the development of intermediate infrastructures through which such benefits can be extended to and taken advantage of by those most in need.

Despite the stated commitment of governments to the ideal of lifelong learning, some powerful factors have been identified that seem to function so as to impede progress towards realizing the goal of lifelong learning for all. Among the difficulties to be faced in order to realize the full possibilities of a commitment to lifelong learning, the following factors have been marked out (cf. OECD, 'Lifelong learning: from ideal to reality', a paper presented at the International Conference on 'Learning Beyond Schooling', 1994, pp. 7, 8):

1 *What some have regarded as a bias towards the provision of opportunities for initial learning in schools, in the primary, secondary*

and post-secondary phases of education and training. The perceived bias towards initial learning embodies the presumption of continuing public support for universal full-time schooling. Many argue that governments need to consider alternatives to present models of funding education in their aim to extend the emphasis upon initial learning towards a lifelong perspective. Some have asked, for example, whether there is a case for a shift in the balance of resources away from the idea of universal entitlement to initial education towards capitalizing upon new approaches to the concept of lifelong learning by introducing new forms of learning entitlements to be taken during one's life-span. Others argue that initial education is absolutely fundamental and indispensable to lifelong learning and all further progress in it, and, in the interests of a just and equitable society, substantial government provision needs to be made in order to give all members of society the requisite foundations upon which they can later build for themselves. In this regard governments need to consider the values as well as the economic dimensions of funding policies and arrangements for the whole process of education as a public service, and the implications these might have for the changes that may need to be made to the provision and funding of initial education and training, upon which an approach towards the provision of lifelong learning opportunities might be realistically based.

2 *The sporadic nature of adult learning.* Beyond schooling and initial post-compulsory education and training the most common times for adults to undertake further learning have been at points of crisis or substantial change in their lives or careers. There is a need to have learning accepted as part of the ongoing processes of people's lives, as a function of continuing self-development and the expansion of one's horizons, seen as part of the overall pattern of their growth. This highlights the importance of governments considering how they can help to create a stronger framework to motivate, facilitate and reward continued learning and in so doing create stronger demands for education and training among adults throughout people's lives.

3 *Evidence suggesting a strong bias in favour of those who already have education.* The higher the educational standards achieved in a person's youth, the more likely they are to take part in education in adulthood. The difficulty to be tackled here is the question of the ways in which governments can ensure the provision of learning opportunities on a lifelong basis is consistent with a socially inclusive and just society. The two major subsidiary parts of this question concern the question of whether governments, in their provision of lifelong learning opportunities and facilities, should draw a distinction between learning for work and learning for leisure, and whether they should give preferential subsidies to one or the other purpose, and to one group of learners over another.

A conference held jointly by OECD/CERI and the Japanese Ministry of Education, Science and Culture in Tokyo in October 1993 (OECD/CERI, *Learning Beyond Schooling*, 1993) highlighted the importance of governments grappling with a number of governance and management issues if they are to realize the goal of lifelong learning for all:

- There is wide agreement that governments need to assume a significant role in co-ordinating the provision of lifelong learning: for example, it is clear that governments have a role in providing the best possible information and guidance on the options available as well as validating them through a solid and well-articulated qualifications structure. The question to be faced is whether governments can create a sound framework for lifelong learning without necessarily becoming the monopoly provider. Where should government priorities in the provision and financing of lifelong learning lie?

- Although the possibility of achieving an equal balance in government support for the provision of initial and further learning is generally seen as an unrealistic expectation, there is increasing support for the view that there must be some scope for ensuring new spending on expanding provision takes due account of the learning needs of people at all ages. The question is whether, and if so in what ways, governments can create more just and equitable policies and methods for distributing resources between initial and other phases of learning throughout a person's lifetime, so that all members of society may derive optimum advantage from all the possibilities provided and available. As Rawls's principle of justice as fairness would demand, any distribution of scarce goods – particularly an unequal one – can only be regarded as just and fair insofar as those least benefited by it are nevertheless better off than they would have been, had no distribution at all taken place (cf. Rawls, 1972).

- Different countries assign different values and make different priorities in programmes of learning for investment, as opposed to the idea of learning as consumption; most, however, show a preference for funding certain kinds of courses rather than others. The degree to which the settlement of this question should be left to student demand is an important issue for further consideration by government. It is right that governments should begin to consider to what extent they should prejudge and prioritize those kinds of learning that they believe to be worthy of their support.

- Co-investment has been identified as a particularly valuable means of provision of facilities and opportunities for lifelong learning, partly because individuals who take a personal stake in their own learning are often better motivated to become effective learners. The nature of the process of co-investment, however, is still contentious. It is reasonable to ask how governments may encourage the devotion of a joint investment of money, time and resources to learning, in various forms of partnership with employers, groups and individuals, and then how they may together set up structures and processes to achieve the goal of lifelong learning for all.

The First Global Conference on 'Lifelong Learning' in Rome in 1994 concluded that the ideal of lifelong learning would not be achieved by means of tight centralized government control. As Sir Christopher Ball commented:

> ... [Lifelong learning] will involve the cooperation of both public and private sectors; and it must ensure that everyone gets the right start to their learning through the experience of good pre-school and primary education, provided in partnership with competent parents. The paradox of lifelong learning is that it requires that people start right.
>
> (Ball, 1994, p. 11)

HELPING PEOPLE 'START RIGHT': IMPLICATIONS OF NEW APPROACHES TO MANAGEMENT AND GOVERNANCE

New options for management and governance are being considered as part of a growing debate about the proper role of government in the provision of education and training opportunities throughout the life-span of individuals and communities. Whereas education is a central domain of government policy and a legitimate state involvement, the role of government is currently being developed in a new context, one that puts an emphasis on the allocation and use of resources on which there are many other competing claims. There is also an emphasis on the importance of the clear articulation and monitoring of outcomes; and on overcoming forms of inequity and exclusion that work so as to prevent some groups in the community from participating in the renewal and upgrading of knowledge and skills.

In order to address these concerns, governments are seeking to establish a more strategic role in the governance and management of education and training systems. A key question raised is the extent and form of the government's role: what balance is to be struck between central direction and local discretion or individual choice? And what should be the balance between direct government regulation and indirect steering by means of guidelines and incentives?

It is recognized that new approaches to governance and management have emerged as a result of a manifold set of factors. Whilst commitment to quasi-markets in education and to styles of corporate managerialism has driven changes in some settings, at the same time a commitment to democratic principles and an interest in encouraging widely shared decision-making have provided a rationale on the basis of which other governments have introduced new approaches to management and governance in education and training.

The multiplicity of rationales and the number of diverse interests now involved in education and training define both the context and conditions in which the roles of government are asserted. These require balancing to ensure such roles build on complementarities and address potential trade-offs. A key question here concerns the necessary conditions for the effective implementation and impact of governments' roles in new approaches to governance and management.

The extent to which governments intervene in the setting of goals and outcome statements, in regulating the scope for providers to exercise discretion at the local level, and in providing opportunities for the exercise of individual learner choice, varies in accordance with level of education and training.

THE GOVERNANCE AND MANAGEMENT OF SCHOOLS AND SCHOOL SYSTEMS

Differences in economic, social and political perspectives among parties debating the best way of ensuring quality in education have to do with the ethical and metaphysical commitments governments have to a set of beliefs regarding the nature of human beings and the ways they wish individuals to be, the most desirable form of society which will best facilitate their development, and the ways in which they can best arrange and institutionalize their relationships for the various purposes (economic, social and individual) they have in mind. Such differences of vision and perspective are fundamental to conceptions of the idea of 'public service', the public provision and resourcing of goods and services, and to governments' responses to questions associated with the governance, steering and management of education systems and schools (cf. Chapman and Aspin, 1995b).

The key questions in the provision of education, therefore, are ones that concern the form and content of our systems of values, codes of ethics and standards of conduct, that shall be translated into policy and become normative for both individual and society. In policy debates about the future of education, these questions are of central concern; arriving at agreements as to the substance of the values and agenda that shall underpin a country's educational norms and conventions must logically precede questions concerning the chronology or practical ways and means of their institutional realization and implementation. It is only when governments have settled their policies on decisions of principle, and secured some agreement about substance, that they can then tackle the further problems of operationalization, implementation and management. As policy-makers face the issue of the provision of lifelong learning for all, it is essential that they reconsider the questions of substance associated with the provision of initial education and its relationship to the goals of an economically sound society, yet one that is also democratic, socially inclusive and ethically just.

Some countries have traditionally supported the principle that opportunities should be provided for all individuals to have access to intellectual challenge and a high quality and empowering curriculum during the years of initial education. This principle is seen as being among the most important features of a more just and democratic society – one in which social justice and equality of opportunity become achievable goals. The provision of a structurally uniform and homogenously organized school system has been seen as one of the principal means of providing equal access to such opportunities for all (Aspin and Chapman, 1994).

Throughout the last decade, however, there has been increasing interest in and moves towards an approach to the provision of education and the resourcing of schools that incorporates and rests upon the philosophy of the market. This approach embodies a quite different set of philosophical preconceptions and moral norms from those that have hitherto featured in accounts of schooling arising from or associated with perceptions of education as a 'public good', access to which is deemed to be a prerequisite for informed and effective participation by all citizens in a just and democratic society – providing, as Sir Christopher Ball (1994) puts it, the conditions for helping people to 'start right'.

The philosophy which underpins a market-orientated approach places less emphasis upon such matters as equity and social justice. Inequalities in society are held to reside in and be caused much more by factors of individual make-up and personal motivation than those arising from structural features of society. From such a perspective the government response to the promotion and provision of education is of a much more minimalist kind, leaving a far greater degree of responsibility for achievement to individual motivation and talent and much more responsibility for provision to the market and for management to the local school site.

Recent moves towards a more market-orientated approach in education not only reflect specific ethical preconceptions and political and social convictions, but also particular preferences in economic theory. These have an impact on the provision of education in significant ways. Proposals for reform in the provision of education in many settings reflect broader changes in economic policy, variously described as 'liberalization', 'deregulation', or 'more market', and tend to mirror changes in public sector management more broadly.

The concept of 'the market' in education has wide currency in discussions on the financing of lifelong learning. One question that needs consideration, however, is whether the concept of 'the market' has validity and applicability in the matter of the provision of 'educational' services; and if so, whether it has greater applicability to one particular phase or sector of education over others – as, for instance, greater applicability to the domain of adult education, as compared to the domain of initial education and training. This issue is one of fundamental importance to decision-making pertaining to the provision of lifelong learning opportunities for all.

Supporters of the market approach tend to adopt the view that education is a 'commodity'. On this argument, the likelihood of an educating institution's success will be directly proportional to the range, quality and delivery of the academic products, goods and services that are offered by it. Enduring success will be achieved by the constant delivery of high quality products. Schools (and other educational institutions) that are freed from bureaucratic constraints and costs, it is argued, can accomplish their goals most effectively, with the minimum of interference and danger of resource misuse, by responding to market forces and concentrating on the most efficient and cost-effective management of personnel, plant and resources at the institutional level.

In a competitive environment, it is claimed, market pressures will work so as to force the school (or any other educational 'unit') to use its resources in the most economically efficient way and to develop the educational product in accordance with consumer preference. The absence of such competitive pressure in traditional government systems of education, it is asserted, has been to the detriment of achieving quality in schooling. This ideology of the market has led to certain conclusions: chief of these is the notion that the responsibility for the resourcing of education services should move away from the state and towards market providers and individuals functioning as buyers in the education market-place (cf. Chubb and Moe, 1990).

Reservations have been expressed, however, concerning the implications of the 'market' approach for the full range of values and interests vested in a public system of schooling. One of the results of the market approach, it is counter-claimed, may be the undermining of the public provision of funding for schools, so necessary not only to provide the 'right start' for young people and to promote the democratic ideal of an informed society of knowledgeable citizens, but also as a precondition of economic growth.

Critics of the market approach (Bridges and McLaughlin, 1994; Grace, 1994) argue that, as the market's role increases, the remaining public sector institutions and agencies become residualized. On the market model, the public sector becomes the bottom of a resource-availability hierarchy – the place for those without capital to exchange for services and goods. Within the public sector, such critics maintain that, if the ideology of the market prevails, tendentious differentiation and adverse discrimination will start to be made between schools, on the basis of academic and other criteria, and that some of these discriminations will become socially divisive.

Such different standpoints regarding the very nature of education lie at the heart of government responses in this conceptual and value debate. The patterns and procedures of the governance, steering and management of education cannot be determined and set in train without some clarification and decision about the key concepts and values that shall structure and define the administrative responses that governments adopt to the provision of initial education for all members of society.

For our part, we have a view on this issue, that arises from our adherence to the idea of 'education as a public good'. When we talk about 'aims of education', it seems to us that schools, colleges, educational institutions have at least four major concerns. These cluster around the purposes of education identified by the UNESCO commissioners in their publication *Learning: The Treasure Within* (UNESCO, 1996). They concentrate on the importance of the work of educating institutions as making people aware of the need to know, the ability to do, the power to live with other people, and the development of ourselves as persons – what the UNESCO commissioners call the power to be. *To know, to do, to live with, to be*: each of these concerns, and the undertakings that flow from them in our educating institutions, is shot through with values of particular kinds.

We accept and identify with these value concerns. And, with the values issues associated with these aims of education in mind, we can now say that we repudiate the notion that education is a commodity – something that one can obtain or not, depending upon whether or not one makes the choice to acquire it *and* has the means to secure access to it. For us education is a public good (cf. Aspin and Chapman, 1994; Grace, 1994); education is like social welfare, health, justice, law and order – all goods and conditions without which our future citizens could not even 'start right' on the process of coming to be able to *know* and *to do* and *to live with others* and *to be*.

These are all the qualities and characteristics that we desire to see as among the things that are added to people by their experiences and activities in our educating institutions. But unless young people are provided with access to the social and educational goods that enable them to develop those skills and understandings, attitudes and dispositions, then they are not going even to be able to get a purchase on the first rung of the ladder that will enable them to have some prospect of 'getting it right' for the rest of their lives.

The Redistribution of Governance and Management Responsibilities in the Schooling Sector

In the drive towards improving the quality of schooling and expanding the provision of lifelong learning programmes and opportunities, it is necessary for governments to undertake reforms which will have direct implications for the redistribution of power and administrative responsibility among the various levels and sectors within the education system (Aspin and Chapman, 1994).

During the course of the past decade, two trends in the administration of schools and school systems could be observed to be occurring simultaneously. On the one hand there has been a growing recognition that the key to the success of educational reform lies in the implementation and application of policy at the local and institutional level; as a result there have been consider-able moves towards providing for increased autonomy at the level of the local school site. At the same time a second trend could be discerned in the increasing emphasis being laid on the right and justified authority of government to formulate objectives, provide steering guidelines and monitor quality control.

Although many of these reforms in the governance and management of schools and school systems have been undertaken under the overt agenda of decentralization, or devolution, the situation is far more complex than this. A closer examination of data and practices suggests that any attempt to elucidate the redistribution of power is likely to encounter and to have to deal with a far more complex set of factors and variables than any account based upon a one-dimensional or linear account of changed relationships along the centralization–decentralization continuum would suggest.

What we need now is a reconceptualization of ideas and policies relating to educational decision-making and the administrative arrangements flowing from them. We need a policy framework and strategies for implementation, reflecting new sets and patterns of relationship and interactions, based on new concepts and categories. The old ideas are no longer useful in describing and explaining the complexities that are now involved in and operate at the different layers, levels and loci of decision-making among schools, parents, employers, community agencies of all kinds, and school systems.

The former bureaucratic notions, based on hierarchical positional power within a single school 'system', are now outmoded; other alternatives, developed in recent years, are proving similarly unhelpful. For example, the idea of a 'de-schooled' society functioning simply to provide a set of 'community resources', with their simple presence and availability for access by voucher-users, so celebrated by Illich and his like (cf. Illich, 1973), fails to do justice to the necessity of continuity in the early years of formal education, or to take account of the point that education requires the heteronomous activity of significant others, who induct and initiate our young into the heterogeneously constructed and transmitted sets of beliefs, norms and patterns of behaviour valued by society as a whole and that are absolute preconditions of their being able to make the 'right start' on their life and work in it.

Likewise the market vision of education, based on the analogy of educational institutions functioning like networks of business franchises, is regarded by many as providing an inappropriate model of the educational enterprise at the level of initial and compulsory schooling, particularly if education at this level is accepted as a public good.

New notions of administrative relationships in the provision of schooling in the framework of lifelong learning are, however, still at the stage of early exploration and articulation; they are highly tentative, lack specificity, and of course are yet to be tested. One challenge for policy-makers will be to explore ways in which new conceptions and models of altered administrative arrangements and relationships can be fully elaborated, delivered, implemented and appropriately evaluated in the real settings where the need for them to be implemented is so pressing. Fundamental to this reappraisal of altered patterns of governance and management will be debate on the matter of whether education is to be seen as a 'commodity' or as a 'public good'.

Those who, like us, see education as a public 'good' (Aspin and Chapman, 1994; Grace, 1994; McLaughlin, 1994) argue that access to and participation in a high quality and empowering educational programme of activities is a vital and indispensable preparation for life for all a community's citizens: the concept of participative democracy and social inclusion entails that all a society's future citizens have a common interest in securing access to and participation in educational programmes. For without admittance to such a 'good' our young people will be much less likely to progress rapidly towards those minimal degrees of personal autonomy and civic responsibility by means of which citizens in a modern democracy can ensure that there are in place and available to all those preconditions and mechanisms that are necessary for economically productive activity, the sustaining of independent existence, community participation, social justice or indeed any sort of advanced and sophisticated personal development.

Proponents of this view argue that in a public or government system of education there can be no such thing as a completely autonomous or independent self-governing school (Aspin and Chapman, 1994). To be sure, a certain amount of school autonomy may be readily countenanced and extended in certain areas of decision-making. It is a paradox, however, that autonomy can be rendered intelligible and made to work only within the confines of a relationship with the system and the community based on a mutuality of benefit and regard.

Schools conceived thus enjoy a mutual relationship with the government authorities or the system and the community of which they are a part. The government authorities ensure the basic protection of rights for all students; at the same time schools enjoy a mutual relationship with the community in which parents and other significant groups are able to have their voices heard in regard to matters of fundamental value and goals. There is also a mutual relationship within the school among school-based personnel, as decision-making is shared, owned and supported. In return the school enjoys a greater degree of autonomy in selection of community-related goals and the fitting of resources to meet those goals; it also enjoys a greater sense of its own standing and importance in providing community leadership, in promoting the value of education among all its stakeholders, and in this way promoting the idea of the learning community and the values of lifelong education.

On the basis of the values attached to autonomy and mutuality, it may be argued that, for the purposes of education, the governance and management of schools must be consistent with the values that form the basis for conceptions of individual worth and social and community harmony. This must necessarily include reference to the various forms of relationship emerging, evolving, or being deliberately created between educating institutions, schools and other agencies.

This will require that governments undertake an examination of a number of issues in schooling and educational provision more generally, in which the concepts of autonomy, mutuality and community get their major point of application. This will require the analysis of such matters as:

- The evolution and/or deliberate creation, between government, educating institutions and other agencies, of new relationships and the forging of new partnerships held to be conducive to the enhancement of education seen from a lifelong perspective.

- The ways in which new patterns of relationship between educational institutions and other community agencies and constituencies might facilitate and improve the more effective dissemination and acquisition of knowledge, skills and attitudes on the part of students.

- The ways in which new patterns of relationship might be created and expanded with new community constituencies and interest groups, in ways that will ensure schools can respond appropriately to and derive increased benefit from the increasing cultural, linguistic, social and economic diversity of schools and modern multicultural societies.

In addressing such matters and attempting to translate them into reality, policy-makers and educators will need to consider a number of issues, particularly with regard to the question of effective schooling:

- In seeking to draw upon and address the needs of all those affected by and having an interest in the educational process, policy-makers and educators will need to take account of the character and appropriateness of the balance to be struck between society's interests and the interests of particular constituencies, groups or individuals.

- Policy-makers and educators will need to consider the ways in which, in a more flexible, responsive system, with responsibilities for the framing of educational policies and funding decisions being more widely shared among a large and wider group of stakeholders, any alterations in structural and accountability arrangements will affect, positively or adversely, the formulation of policies and goals for schooling and lifelong education.

- How are the interests of stakeholders outside the formal education system to be taken into account by government authorities; what weighting shall be given to such considerations; and for what sorts of reasons?

- Policy-makers, educators and members of the community will need to examine the numbers of new roles and powers available to teachers and professional educators in the schools, and other stakeholders in the broader community outside them. They will need to identify ways and means by which a balance in responsibilities, competency and interest can be worked out.

- Consideration will need to be given as to how the distribution, acquisition and exercise of new responsibilities, particularly on the part of outside groups and constituencies, might or might not be causally related to such outcomes of schooling as examination results and other, less tangible, outcomes.

- Policy-makers, educators and members of the community will need to identify the new frameworks, regulations, mechanisms and procedures that must be developed at a system's centre in response to the new pattern of relationships.

- Investigations will need to be undertaken as to whether, and if so, in what ways, changes in organizational and administrative structures and work methods (including new relationships with a wide range of stakeholders) at the centre might be appropriate to the new roles and responsibilities at the other levels and in other arenas of the education system. Governments will need to reflect on what must now be done to encourage the development of new and more appropriate structures and methods at the centre and at the intermediary and local levels.

Changed patterns of governance and management in schools and school systems will also require an examination of the various models of school and family connections, including an examination of the basic obligations of parenting; the obligation of schools to communicate with the home; the involvement of parents in schools as volunteers and supporters; parental involvement in the child's learning, both in the school and in the home and other community settings; and – of especial significance in the light of the increased roles and responsibilities now being assigned to and taken up by parents and parent groups in the management of schools – parental involvement in school decision-making and governance.

In this context the various perils and pitfalls in the changing relationship between parents and professional educators will need to be identified and specific strategies for mediating and managing difficulties, and identifying bases for mutual respect, understanding and action will need to be put forward. There will also need to be a working out of ways in which parents and families can enhance the effectiveness of the contributions they make to quality schooling and education, by extending and broadening access to sources of support, advice and assistance available in and proffered by other sectors, groups and constituencies in the wider community.

Policy-makers, educators and members of the community will also wish to focus upon relationships between the school and school–business and other commercial, industrial and professional relationships. They will need to be particularly concerned to draw lessons from past dysfunctions in such relationships and to put forward plans to eliminate or overcome such dysfunctions in future partnerships. These could be drawn from an examination of more recent and current successful practices and partnerships, and of the features of those relationships that make them work well, in order to develop a set of proposals for educationally productive partnerships between such institutions, groups and bodies in the future.

They will also need to explore the impact of such relationships, as regards the enhancement of education, upon such important goals as better and more effective preparation of students for the workforce, creating shared goals among educators and employers and other industrial and commercial interest groups (such as trades unions and professional associations) and influencing the behaviour, plans and goals of business, industry and commerce. These joint endeavours must be put in the context of the interest both schools and such groups have in the formation of partnerships, whose positive collaboration and effective working can function as rich sources of community development.

They will also need, in their exploration of partnerships conducive to community betterment, to pay attention to the ways in which the school's activities, concerns and goals can be backed by the information, resource sustenance and moral support necessary for their enmeshment in the interests of all the various cultural, artistic, religious and minority ethnic communities, whose existence and orientations form an important and indeed indispensable part of the mosaic constituting the identity and enhancing the value of the community generally.

They will also need to consider the ways in which schools and other educating institutions can form part of and contribute to the cultural and artistic activities and institutions of the community; the ways they can provide an insight into and some understanding of the ethnic diversity of our modern multicultural society; and the need they will face to look into the various religious beliefs and practices associated with and embodied in different ethnic groupings, in the endeavour to increase racial and religious tolerance and to improve social harmony. Here too the school will want to draw upon the advice and assistance of a range of cultural institutions and resources, in order to make a contribution to the beautification and quality of the community and its environment.

In this endeavour policy-makers, educators and members of the community will need to address a number of important but difficult topics, issues and problems arising from changes in the patterns of relationships now subsisting between the school and the community. Among questions to be raised will figure such concerns as:

- As parents and other stakeholders at the local level take on greater responsibility for providing financial and in-kind resources, whether observable differences in the scale and quality of educational provision will be widened or narrowed.

- In systems relying more on energies and interests at the local level, what policies can be developed and what resources made available, and if so of what kind and over what range, to ensure the effective and appropriate involvement of all groups of stakeholders, such as parents from 'disadvantaged' backgrounds, in the endeavour to ensure equity is respected and quality for all participants in the educational process is being and can be delivered.

- How principals and teachers might deal with and overcome any fears they as professionals experience of being overwhelmed or 'overrun' by the increased number, powers and demands of the various new partners with whom they are required to work in the educational enterprise.

- How a sense of community and consensus might be formed, fostered and utilized at the level of the local school site, in a context of heterogeneity, diverse and sometimes competing pressures and multiple expectations bearing upon schools and all their personnel.

- How all members and sectors, public and private, of society might be encouraged to accept and fully exploit their changed and expanded roles, powers and responsibilities in the provision and enhancement of education. This will involve some exploration of the necessity of the education and development of the community and the forms the endeavour to bring this about might take. The aim here will be to conceive, characterize and manage the process of the transformation of the whole, in all parts and patterns of its independence and complementarities, for educational purposes into an aware, self-conscious and purposefully working, learning and teaching community.

To achieve all this policy-makers, educators and members of the community will need to be prepared to offer suggestions for the conception, development, implementation and monitoring of policies and programmes they believe to be appropriate for capitalizing upon and enhancing the potential contributions that can be offered towards a community's educational undertakings by the new patterns of relationship between schools and all other community groups with a legitimate interest in improving educational perform-ance and outcomes. Underpinning all this will be an acceptance of the notion and value of 'the learning community' as a fundamental precondition for lifelong learning.

The Management of Schools – Schools as Learning Organizations

In the OECD publication *The Effectiveness of Schooling and of Educational Resource Management* (OECD, 1994), countries investigated the effects of change and restructuring on educational institutions and the link that these might have with the production or emergence of effectiveness in schooling, particularly where such restructuring might be expressed largely in terms of the devolution of decision-making to the local school site. For devolution, school-site management and local management of schools seem to have been the main versions of administrative rearrangement found in proposals for systemic restructuring in many countries in recent years.

There has been, perhaps understandably, a certain scepticism among school-based personnel towards the motives behind policies urging or adopting moves towards school-site management or local management of schools. This has been encouraged by the fear that the consequences of restructuring have been mainly to displace problems and blame, particularly in respect of resource management, from the centre to the school. Notwithstanding such reserva-tions, data suggest that school-based personnel are nevertheless continually attempting to ensure that effectiveness is a part of schools' daily focus of attention and goals of activity: they work at it informally, formally, in struc-tured and unstructured ways, through decision-making, school improvement, school reviews, staff development, and in attempts to involve parents and the wider community in the life of the school.

One of the major difficulties for management at the local level, however, is that any change must be consistent with certain agreed principles and an overall philosophy, understood and owned by all parties in the process. If school-based personnel are poorly equipped to develop the philosophical under-standing necessary to give a sense of meaning and direction for effective school operation, the potential positive benefits of educational restructuring and school change are in danger of being lost. One of the most important next steps in restructuring, it would appear, is for authorities to empower school-based personnel, not only with the technical skills called for in the effective manage-ment and implementation of policies, but also with the knowledge and skills required for the identification and elucidation of problems and the policies appropriate for their resolution, the clarification of values, and the ability to provide cogent and persuasive arguments to justify the value-judgments involved in effective school management. For it is the professional educators who have to present rational arguments for policy innovation, change and confirmation to all a school community's stakeholders, not least of which are the parents of their students.

In respect of the promotion of parental involvement, what emerges as a key finding of research (Aspin and Chapman, 1994) is the widely held belief that one of the most effective ways to develop parent and community involvement is through a problem-solving approach, deployed in activities such as the formation and implementation of a school plan. The framing and shaping of school development plans, and their concomitant requirement for assessment and review, are believed by many to be one of the most critical factors in the whole process of school change and improvement.

Indeed some people go as far as to suggest that the relationship between schools and parents and the community is the most important relationship for the promotion of quality and the assurance of quality control. Building up the capacity of families to understand the educational needs and progress of their children and to make serious and informed contributions to the educational process; building up the capacity of teachers to understand children, their backgrounds and networks of relationships, and to relate to their families: all this is the essence of quality control.

The part of the principal or school leader in this relationship and its processes is absolutely vital. For it is the principal who will be an academic and professional leader for the whole school community in the formulation, clarification and adoption of a set of basic values and desired outcomes arising from being involved in programmes of activity in certain sorts of cognitive engagement. The total vision so composed will then constitute what might be called the school's philosophy, and this will then provide the epistemological, ethical and pedagogical underpinning, set the programme of cognitive activities, and determine the objectives of the whole educational endeavour in the school.

Furthermore it is the task of the principal or school leader to manage and deploy resources to create in the school an atmosphere in which people can relate to each other and perform well in their pursuit of the institution's learning goals. In this latter respect it seems clear that the creation of an environment or culture in which people are able to identify, formulate and commit themselves to some sort of mission, philosophy and set of objectives, and are aiming for similar goals, is perhaps the most significant role of the principal. As a secondary consideration in this undertaking, the principal may be able to perform this service and create that environment better as a result of having more responsibility for resource management and allocation.

In sum, then, there is a clear need for governments and system authorities to support principals, teachers and parents in their need and desire to make quality decisions in all these and other areas of new responsibility. For this reason governments and system authorities must make deliberate attempts to provide professional educators and school personnel, not only with the knowledge and skills referred to above, but also with access to the full extent of information, correlative implications and possible outcomes to enable them to see options, canvas opinions, and calculate and evaluate a range of possible outcomes consequent upon the adoption of some particular policy for school improvement.

This means being determined to provide school staff with the appropriate kinds of intelligence and training required by the skills of decision-making, policy implementation and evaluation. The sort of decisions that can and should be made depend very heavily on the knowledge-base with which school personnel work, on the question of who takes the decisions on important issues, and on the basis of what criteria. In this regard, for schools that are located in systems, the systems themselves have a direct responsibility to offer school-based personnel the appropriate information and support.

Given the above, governments and system authorities must come back to the difficult task of trying to measure the wide range of student outcomes, both quantitative and qualitative, achieved at the end of the formal education process. In the light of the complexity and difficulty of that task, and of the diversity and heterogeneous character of the goals and ends aimed at, and in a context in which accountability is a matter of such public importance, it would not be unreasonable to conclude that the assessment and evaluation of student impacts and outcomes poses one of the greatest challenges for policy-makers and school and system administrators in the years ahead.

Four messages emerge from work on the assessment of the performance of schools (cf. OECD/CERI, *What Works in Innovation: The Assessment of School Performance*, 1994, p. 6):

1 In national efforts to raise the standards of individual schools, both objective external assessments and advice from professionals or peers who know the school are equally important. For it is clear that evaluation systems need credibility within the school and in the outside world, while at the same time enabling schools to improve their performance.

2 Performance indicators can provide important evidence of a school's achievements but there should be a clear attempt to identify information which is genuinely related to the quality of education a school offers its students. Gathering large amounts of data and analysing them is expensive of time, energy and financial resources, and should not be engaged in for its own sake – or simply because the technical ability is there. In addition, it is important that only those data that can be clearly related to the establishing of quality and effectiveness in a school's operations should be gathered and subjected to analysis.

3 Simply making schools accountable, whether to parents, the community or others, is unlikely on its own to lead to improvements in performance. But to require accountability of a school's stewardship of its resources, mission and educational responsibilities is highly desirable in the interests of transparency and democracy in education.

4 Care should be taken to build on the expertise and professionalism of teachers, and to provide programmes of staff development which enable the staff of an institution to develop and extend their professional activities into new forms of autonomy. The key idea here, and the ultimate aim, is to build an unthreatening but effective climate of self-review in schools so that they become 'learning

organizations' capable of continuous improvement – and this means that all forms of development (institutional, curriculum, professional) must play a critical part in that process.

The notion of the 'learning organization' is particularly pertinent in our consideration of lifelong learning. As educating institutions, schools should model the characteristics of 'learning organizations' now being given such credence and prominence across the organizational and institutional arena. In his introductory address at the First Global Conference on 'Lifelong Learning' (in Rome, December, 1994), David Stewart identified what he regarded as some of the distinguishing characteristics of learning organizations. Such 'Learning Organizations' (Stewart, 1994):

- invest in their own future through the education and training of all their people;

- create opportunities for and encourage all their people in all their functions:
  - as employees, members, professionals, or students of the organization;
  - as ambassadors of the organization to its customers, clients, audiences and suppliers;
  - as citizens of the wider society in which the organization exists; and
  - as human beings with the need to realize their own capabilities.

- share their vision and sense of mission with their people and stimulate them to challenge it, to change it, and to contribute to it;

- integrate work and learning and inspire all their people to seek quality, excellence and continuous improvement in both;

- mobilize all their human talent by putting the emphasis on learning and planning their education and training activities accordingly;

- empower all their people to broaden their horizons in harmony with their preferred learning styles;

- apply up-to-date open and distance delivery technologies appropriately to create broader and more varied learning opportunities;

- respond proactively to the wider needs of the environment and the society in which they operate and encourage their people to do likewise;

- learn and relearn constantly in order to remain innovative, inventive, invigorating and in business.

In the knowledge society of the future, *learning* will constitute, furnish and make possible the principal sources of well-being, welfare, justice and economic self-sufficiency. This means that schools, and indeed all other educating institutions, will need to be *learning organizations* if countries are to achieve the objectives and capitalize on the possibilities and opportunities of lifelong learning for all.

Redefining the Place to Learn: Schools of Tomorrow

There is a further important question to be addressed at this point, however. We have just spoken about 'schools' as educating institutions needing to be become 'learning organizations'. Yet, given the rapid and large-scale changes taking place in the form and content of knowledge, in styles of student progress and learning achievement, and in the technologies by which such learning may be gained, assessed and utilized, the question arises as to whether the conventional concept of schools as physical locations, operating within fairly strict parameters of teaching time and student grouping, has much life left. There are those who believe it is much more likely that learning organizations in the future will be much looser, and much more likely to be operating nationally and internationally through the use of modern information technologies, such as CD-ROM, interactive video-disk and the Internet, with students sitting in front of their VDUs conducting, checking and applying their own self-directed and self-achieved learning.

As Susan Stuebing has pointed out (Stuebing, 1995), educators, architects and administrators have throughout the past decade been exploring the ways and means by which changing goals of education, new developments in approaches to learning, and incremental advances in information technology might change the places within which learning occurs. Information technology as a tool for learning is developing rapidly. These days computers are becoming all the time more versatile and more powerful; hardware and software are becoming cheaper; and applications are more wide-ranging and easier to use. In addition, changing educational methods are putting new demands on the use of buildings.

The fundamental question for governments arising from such developments must now be addressed: will schools and school facilities as we know them be required at all in the future, given the flexibility, independence and networking power of modern information technology, developments in student styles and modes of learning, and alterations and expansions in the character and content of knowledge?

Stuebing identifies (1995, p. 7) a number of vital questions that need to be taken into consideration in the design and use of modern learning environments:

- *Redefining the place to learn*. The classroom has remained a constant for nearly a century. With advances in information technology and new teaching and learning methods, will the classroom continue to be of uniform design? Or will new models for the place of learning develop? How will the design and use of the spaces and places in which learning takes place differ from the classrooms we have known? What are the implications of this for timetabling and school organization?

- *Building connections*. With the increased use of networking and the information highway, will the role of the school building diminish or are there new requirements which will be placed on the actual fabric of the built facility? Will distance learning significantly affect the requirements of educational buildings and facilities? What impact will networking have on urban and rural schools?

- *New building use requirements*. Are there new use requirements that will alter the ways schools are designed? Who will use the facilities? Will the use of information technology expand and open up the educational building for the use and learning enjoyment of a larger population than the traditional school-age student?

- *Transforming support facilities for learning such as libraries and production centres*. The increased use of information technology in teaching and learning requires increased teacher support and professional development. At the same time, however, a whole range of further and new materials is required, such as software, videos and other multimedia and database materials, as well as a comprehensive servicing and debugging facility. Expertise and maintenance requirements suggest the need for educational support centres to facilitate new approaches to learning, but what will be the requirements of such facilities and what will be their relationship to schools?

Those planning for these new facilities for learning must take into consideration the rapid rate of change in technology, the time it takes to design and construct new facilities, and cost.

In all this, one thing becomes clear. Schools as we have known them in the past are about to undergo a radical transformation, as indeed are also their personnel and teaching staff. The challenge for policy-makers and administrators is to ensure that this process of change is undertaken in such a way that the advantages offered by these new approaches to self-directed and successful learning are made available to all students, irrespective of gender, social origin, ethnic background or current location of abode. Governments must ensure that access to the opportunities offered by those new modes of learning gain and cognitive advance are provided on an equal, free and just basis. Such access must be open to students, not only in privileged schools located in privileged areas in the urban environment, but also to those from less wealthy backgrounds and from homes that may not have the sophisticated equipment required for such learning available.

This is the major problem with which governments must struggle: enlarging the pool of educated ability and talent open to them by ensuring that opportunities for engagement in such learning organizations are offered to all their future citizens, not to just some of them – to capitalize, in other words, on *all* their futures.

THE GOVERNANCE AND MANAGEMENT OF LEARNING BEYOND SCHOOLING

The Demand and Supply of Lifelong Learning

It is clear that governments are now taking learning beyond schooling to be as serious a matter as schooling itself. A radical rethinking of education beyond the compulsory years of schooling is taking place. Policy-makers, educators and members of the community are now analysing more precisely the nature of the demand for lifelong learning and asking how well existing structures cater for that demand. Strategies to remove such conventional barriers to lifelong learning as age, time, and place are being identified and a critical reappraisal of the missions, goals, policies, structures, finance and personnel of individual institutions and educational providers is under way.

The framing of policy strategies to promote learning beyond schooling appears, however, to be less straightforward a matter than that associated with the introduction of publicly supported school systems a century ago. Unlike compulsory schooling, the pattern of learning beyond schooling is seen as being beyond the direct control of governments and system authorities, not just because governments lack the resources to finance education and training on a lifelong basis, but because learning patterns are determined by a complex array of influences ranging from company attitudes towards in-service training to local cultural attitudes towards formal and informal study. As the authors of the OECD publication *Learning Beyond Schooling – New Forms of Supply and Demand: Background Report* (1994, p. 5) pointed out: 'Rather than being determined by nationally planned institutional provision, education and training activity beyond the years of formal schooling is influenced by a most complex and multifaceted interplay between supply and demand.'

On the demand side, although greater importance is being attached to learning beyond schooling by society as a whole (OECD, *Learning Beyond Schooling: Background Report*, 1994, p. 7), the nature and extent of this demand is often difficult to assess. The learning needs expressed by society or the skill requirements of industry are not automatically translated into manifest demands from individuals. A variety of factors influences participation in learning beyond the years of compulsory schooling: these include the existence of financial incentives, the context in which learning is provided, the constraints of time and place. In addition the diversity of the potential learning groups, with their varied needs, learning objectives and propensities to different learning modes and styles, makes direct quantification of the level of this sometimes latent demand difficult.

The diversity of the demand clearly needs to be matched by diversity of supply. This is unlikely to be provided by any *one* type of institution or even necessarily by a single nationally supervised system of education and training. It is for this reason that, in the eyes of some commentators, the supply of education services is starting to look less like the activity of one single form of provision and more like a whole range of activities offered by a heterogenous set of providers and agencies, both public and private – potentially with international as well as domestic points of connection.

There are a number of reasons to explain why the nature of supply is changing. These lead to a call for a radical reappraisal of the provision of learning beyond schooling (OECD, *Learning Beyond Schooling: Background Report*, 1994, p. 8):

- *The institutional framework is changing.* Greater variety is developing both within and between post-secondary institutions, in terms of delivery modes and target client groups. Many institutions are becoming open to part-time students, offering a greater range of courses of varied duration, and making efforts to combine on-campus with off-campus study, either through distance learning mode or through partnerships with work and community-based organizations. At the same time general-purpose, post-secondary institutions are facing competition from learning modes and agencies with no links to campus-based organizations. Any organization, public or private, may, for example, compare the advantages of sending an employee on a college-based course with courses possible in an in-house training scheme or the use of a specialized training consultant specifically hired for the purpose.

- *The technological possibilities are changing.* Information super-highways ultimately offer the potential for low-cost, real-time interactive communication between any group of people anywhere in the world in video, audio and written mode. As software applications become more sophisticated the interaction between learners and technology could put students more decisively in control of their own learning; the traditional conception and role of teachers as imparters of knowledge will become less important and teachers will have to adapt to a new relationship with knowledge, learners and technology. The supply of technology-aided learning packages will become more flexible with greater potential for export on a world-wide basis.

- *A new financial framework is evolving.* A key issue relates to the question of who pays for learning beyond schooling. The present and future development of post-secondary education and training is being considered in the context of shared funding responsibilities. Employers and individuals who benefit from an investment in learning are increasingly expected, and in some cases required, to contribute. Joint investment can enhance the effectiveness of learning by giving several partners a stake in the outcomes. But there is the danger that financial arrangements will inhibit participation by some groups in society and hence be socially divisive. The optimal division and distribution of funding responsibilities remains to be decided.

In this context some governments are starting to stimulate in limited ways the commercial dynamic of demand and supply by basing funding decisions on student choice rather than providing funds to institutions on a planned level of input. This has the advantage of ensuring that supply is sensitive to demand;

but the drawback is that institutions find difficulty in maintaining high quality provision when income flows are destabilized.

The OECD Conference on 'Learning Beyond Schooling' in 1994 pointed to a future likelihood of post-secondary institutions operating in a competitive and diverse market in the provision and supply of educational services. According to this view, post-secondary institutions will have increasingly to adapt to fluctuations of student choice and demand, rather than expecting stable funding based on their longer-term contribution as institutions operating in the framework of a single unified national system (cf. OECD, *Learning Beyond Schooling: Background Report*, 1994).

Towards a New Infrastructure for Learning Beyond Schooling

New demands for post-compulsory education and training are being generated by new government priorities and by the expansion of and proliferation in the range of knowledge and competencies which each individual is expected to come to possess throughout their life-span. Developments in the understanding of the learning process, and in the conditions needed for successful learning, and advances in technologies of learning are creating the potential for new kinds of learning, transcending traditional constraints of age, time and place.

However, although educational opportunities are expanding and becoming more diverse, there is evidence that they are not adequately matching new demands. At the same time, institutional, financial and other barriers appear to have restricted access to the various new forms and technologies of learning to a small proportion of the people who might benefit from them.

Technologies that improve the possibilities for open and distance learning are developing rapidly; theories about learning in new contexts are developing; and knowledge itself is expanding and increasing in sophistication and complexity at an alarmingly rapid rate.

Yet although new epistemologies, theories and technologies of learning are emerging, it would appear that mainstream education and training has still not adapted sufficiently to make full use of them. There is a great deal of latent demand among people who would benefit from learning, but this demand is not always manifested nor can it be responded to, unless learning is offered in forms that are accessible to the full range of potential learners.

The following issues and concerns have been identified as being important for governments' consideration in providing for learning beyond schooling (OECD, *The Context of the Conference – Learning Beyond Schooling*, 1994, p. 4).

- There is evidence to suggest that adults are most attracted to learning opportunities which depart from the conventional model of didactic and directive teaching. If this is so, we may ask why is not more being done to support self-directed as opposed to didactic learning?

- It is widely acknowledged that learning for work is most effectively achieved in the context of the work itself, and that workers are more likely to apply their new competencies when they have been acquired alongside colleagues. This invites us to consider whether the demand for 'on site' learning is being adequately catered for in learning provision.

- Traditional opening hours of educational institutions do not always suit the convenience and/or the varying needs of learners. While many institutions have attempted to become more flexible to meet these needs, study times may still be a constraint that deters potential students from participating in learning. In this connection we might reasonably ask whether providers are sufficiently flexible in their provision of opportunities and facilities so as to enable study opportunities to be available at times and at places suitable for learning and convenient for learners.

- With new information technology there is scope for a shift in the relationship between teacher and learner towards a more 'open' relationship, with the teacher serving as a guide, facilitator or mentor in conjunction with multimedia learning packages. There is also scope for new relationships among learners in taking advantage of electronic networks. Given this, we may reasonably ask whether information technology is being fully utilized and exploited so as to redefine learning provision and learning relationships, rather than simply as a teaching aid in subordination to existing models of teaching and learning delivery.

- Future technologies enhance the opportunities for distance education. There are many models of distance education whose development will be influenced by both technical and pedagogical developments. Alternative models of organization, management and delivery need to be considered in traditional distance education providers and in new dual-mode organizations.

- Information highways are developing in some countries, aiming at connecting work-places, schools, institutions of further and higher education, libraries and homes. The vision of such networks is one in which learning occurs in a variety of environments throughout the course of one's life. Such possibilities are bound to have a profound impact on the future provision, organization and management of education, and indeed on patterns of development and change in society more widely.

The creation of a new environment for learning depends on the management of complex and difficult changes in institutional cultures, in securing and training of personnel, in funding regimes, and in the intelligent application of communications technologies for educational purposes. In creating an infrastructure which removes barriers to the universalizing of learning beyond schooling and throughout the human life-cycle, governments will need to consider what kind of infrastructure is needed and the specific changes needed to bring it about. This will require consideration of (OECD, *The Context of the Conference – Learning Beyond Schooling*, 1994, p. 13):

- The creation of a set and range of more open institutions which permit learning to take place at the convenience of the learner.

- The creation of learning strategies that make learning more effective, rendering it possible to serve purposes and client groups that have not hitherto been catered for.

- The facilitation of learning in different places according to the needs of the learner, and the effective integration of activities inside and outside educational institutions, through the use of dedicated networks and eventually through a universal, more general link-up on the information super-highway, which transcend conventional patterns of social grouping and even international boundaries.

Challenging the Ideal of Campus-bound Learning: The Management of Learning from Anywhere

A number of governments are giving serious consideration to the types of institutional arrangement for learning beyond schooling thought to be appropriate to meet these changing circumstances. Among the alternatives being weighed are the availability and operation of institutions that have the vision and facility to alter their existing campus-based activities and programmes in the direction of the addition of a dual-mode operation. By the turn of the century, advances in information technology could well have the potential to transform the nature of learning institutions and of student–teacher interactions and relationships, whether students are studying on or off campus. The possibilities offered by multimedia, hypermedia and telematic learning are bringing together a number of strands of developments that have hitherto been separate – software for computer presentations, media corners, computer-assisted instruction, distance learning, computer conferencing systems and computer-assisted co-operative learning.

Dual-mode institutions incorporating the face-to-face mode usually associated with teaching and learning in more traditional universities, and distance mode, such as those in open universities and 'open learning agencies', would be able to shift emphasis from one mode to another depending on changes in the pattern of demand for particular courses. Dual-mode institutions also have the advantage of opening up continuing professional education at a time when innovations in telecommunications are making interactive learning at a distance a realistic possibility. Dual-mode provision also enables a flexible institutional response to projected increases in enrolments in prevailing climates of uncertainty about future funding regimes, and an entrepreneurial response to market possibilities for off-campus education associated with telecommunications technology (cf. OECD, 'The future of post-secondary education and the role of information and communication technology: a clarifying report', paper presented at the International Conference on 'Learning Beyond Schooling', 1994).

There are a number of reasons why dual-mode institutions present a viable response to the changing circumstances and demands of learning beyond the school, and these in turn help explain the rapid transformation of the relationship between distance education and face-to-face education:

- *Economic*. It is the hope of many governments that through economies of scale, unit costs of self-learning over the long run will be lower than for comparable face-to-face courses.

- *Institutional*. Distance education has often been seen as peripheral to the traditional post-secondary education system. The non-traditional learner and the non-traditional teacher often had lower status. As recognition of qualifications from open learning becomes more readily accepted, mobility of students from face-to-face mode to distance mode and vice versa will become more accepted.

- *Pedagogical*. Distance learning institutions have been innovative in the use of self-instruction, new forms of project-based collaborative and co-operative learning, interdisciplinary and problem-based approaches and new divisions of labour in teaching and learning.

- *Technological*. Information and communication technologies are breaking down the barriers of distance through networks of communication. Such technologies are also transforming conventional face-to-face learning by providing learners with new possibilities of self-learning. They are blurring the border between the two modes of education.

The introduction of alternatives in the institutions and modes of learning is, however, a complex and difficult process. A major challenge for management, for instance, will be for institutions to transform their internal structure and culture. The structure of educational institutions has often functioned so as to restrict access to learning rather than to promote it for all. Two common forms of restriction have been selective criteria for admission and participation, and rigid timetabling for both study and assessment. Higher education in particular has been traditionally selective.

A more inclusive policy for admission to institutions need not compromise academic quality as long as it is combined with diversification. A genuinely open institution would attempt to start by identifying student needs and design courses accordingly. One possible implication for higher education is that most or all courses might include at least some vocational components; one way of delivering these is in modular form aided by new technologies.

Technology has also multiplied the potential for restructuring the time devoted to learning. An open learning infrastructure should allow students to structure learning in more flexible ways over a day, a week, a year, a life-cycle. Where institutions are open to all and allow time to be structured more to the convenience of the student, it becomes easier for citizens to envisage regular returns to learning throughout their lives. But equal access to learning for people of different ages is not simply a matter of admission policy, time flexibility and internal culture; it is also one of finance. Governments may not be prepared to give equal subsidy to students of all ages. We deduce from this that the consideration of alternative funding arrangements is a key issue for the future.

As governments consider alternative approaches to the provision of learning beyond schooling, they may wish to note that there are now few technical barriers to prevent education from moving beyond national boundaries. There is now sufficient experience available to them to enable them to make generalizations about the practicalities of international exchange and co-operation in approaches to lifelong learning. At the practical level international co-operation demands the development of policies and codes of practice on copyright, on credit rating, on information techniques, and on costing. At a broader level, technological change is likely to influence the form of the synthesis that will emerge in lifelong learning from the dialectic of internationalization and autonomy (cf. OECD, *Distance Education and the Internationalisation of Higher Education*, 1994).

However, governments need to take into account the number of major stakeholders who are, as they are themselves, active or potentially active in the internationalization of the provision of lifelong learning. These include the private sector, supra-national bodies, non-governmental organizations, students, and representatives of higher education. Private sector interest in the economic purposes of the internationalization of education is often shared by national governments and supra-national bodies of various kinds, but not always by education institutions and non-government organizations. There are still many issues that governments need to resolve in the debate about the internationalization of education and lifelong learning. These include: lack of outcome studies, the absence of well-integrated and co-ordinated policy, the lack of agreement on equivalence, and the skewed distributional nature of student mobility (cf. OECD, 'The views and activities of stakeholders in the internationalisation of higher education', paper presented at the International Conference on 'Learning Beyond Schooling', 1994).

Markets for Learning

The need for the provision of learning beyond schooling presents a triple challenge for governments: how to provide a high quality education suitable for the economic and social exigencies of the twenty-first century; how to provide it, in a fair and equitable way, for all who need or want it; and how to provide it in the most cost-effective manner. Very many countries are planning increases in their provision of learning beyond schooling in all post-secondary education sectors but it is unlikely that they can meet these challenges simply by extending and broadening current patterns and models of provision.

Whereas, a generation ago, post-secondary education in most countries was regarded as a public good to be provided largely at public expense, the question of the provision and funding of post-secondary education is now starting to be viewed differently. As Renwick (1994) points out, the model of the provision of post-secondary education that is increasingly being proposed is one based on the notion of learning beyond schooling being conceived as a set of private goods that might be supplied by many sources, some of them subsidized by public money, some not, to students who will also be expected to bear an increasing portion of the costs of learning themselves. This approach implies a partnership between public and private agencies prepared to provide courses and finance for them, and individuals prepared to assume at least part of the responsibility for meeting the costs of such provision, in a mixed economy of educational provision.

Another model that is put forward to address this need involves recourse to a sophisticated and pluralistic model of the supply and obtaining of educational goods and services as dictated by the norms, conventions, standards for success and operating procedures of an educational 'market-place'. Support for the 'market model' as the answer to the challenge of providing learning beyond schooling is found in the report 'Markets for learning and educational services: A micro-explanation of the role of education and development of competence in macro-economic growth', a paper prepared as part of the OECD/CERI activity on *Investment in Education and Economic Growth*, 1994, p. 12.

The authors of this report argue that only by the mechanism of a sophisticated and pluralistic market for educational services can the challenge to provide for the educational needs of a wide variety of learners be met. A number of possible policy implications is derived from the conceptual and policy analysis presented in the report. They include the contentions that:

- Educational policies will not work unless they are supported by economic incentives that make it worthwhile for individuals to invest in their own development of competency. This means that the performance of the labour market and the social insurance system have to be altered to support educational reform. The authors of the report point out that this is difficult since it requires co-ordinating different political authorities and overcoming vested interests with radically different views.

- Educational policy has to rely much more on student effort and interest and less on public money.

- The financing of education has to be shifted away from the educational institution (the suppliers) and towards the individuals (the users) and the market. Financing incentives and control should remain with the individual throughout his or her working life. It is not seen as advisable to vest almost all responsibility for an individual's education in the hands of public authorities schools or employers.

- The length of time required to develop basic competencies means that strong incentives are needed to stimulate primary and secondary students to build the basis for profitable continued education, since the financial rewards of their investment are far off. Education is cumulative throughout working life and the leverage on later competency development of early education is large. To achieve a good early start in education, therefore, the authors of the report recommend a strong tilting of compensation schedules in favour of initial education.

- To prepare students for the conditions they will encounter in the labour market, it is argued that primary and secondary education should be more focused and more demanding on students; it should ensure the achievement of a minimum level of competence in communication skills; and perhaps cover a larger part of the scholastic year.

- If basic competencies have not been maintained and upgraded, it is maintained that the 35-year-old worker will face an almost impossible retraining problem. Therefore compensation schemes in the labour market should be set up to facilitate frequent job changes and to stimulate individual development. The labour market, it is contended, should be so organized as to compensate effectively those who actively pursue continuing education. This is essentially a call for deregulation of the labour market by eliminating restrictions on mobility and wage rigidities imposed by central bargaining agreements.

- It is asserted that there is mounting evidence of some over-investment in education. In this respect a case is developed to demonstrate that to increase subsidized higher education may actually be functioning so as to be performing a negative service to the economy through filtering talented young people out of manufacturing production jobs. Public subsidizing of higher education, it is averred, should be carefully analysed to minimize negative effects and to oblige people to take more personal responsibility for their job market and educational investment decisions.

In this analysis it is claimed that many significant decisions and a proportion of public resources should be removed from central authorities so that individuals take responsibility for their own development of competency, their labour market contracts and their social insurance arrangements. This requires deregulation and decentralization in all three domains. In this report it is held that if reforms aimed at conducting policy through efficient markets are not enacted, mature industrialized economies will not be capable of reorganizing themselves for the new demands of technology and competition in the future.

The authors of the report argue that it is crucial for the success of the public policy model outlined above that the social insurance system of countries function effectively in covering growing labour market risks and in being credible to individuals now increasingly at risk. This requires radical product innovation in the social insurance market, something that they argue is difficult to achieve in countries where a dominant part of the social insurance system is operated as a public monopoly.

The overall policy implication drawn from this analysis is that policy has to be formulated so that the problem of education, the labour market and social insurance is addressed and solved in one coherent context and in such a manner that the importance of individual effort and incentive is recognized. However, lack of sufficient information on the three policy areas makes it difficult today to formulate precise policies to ensure fewer labour market risks for the individual. Therefore, the authors of the report suggest that the following issues would have to be further analysed and clarified:

- the identification of the basic competencies or minimum communication skills that will prepare students for the job market;

- the clarification of the interdependence of educational and labour market performance; and

- the setting up of a distinction between the relative importance of education as a sorting or filtering device *and* as an investment in human capital.

We wish to point out, however, that proffering the model of the 'market' as a solution to the problems of funding and provision of approaches to lifelong learning beyond the years of schooling, based on the notion of education as a commodity, remains highly contestable. There are other answers to the problem, arising from the requirement to link together the various functions of educating the future citizens of a nation. This undertaking will involve helping them prepare to face a number of challenges: one, of moving towards the future with a high degree of economic self-sufficiency; another, of developing the capacity for entering into satisfying interpersonal relationships and contributing to making social relations in the community tolerant, harmonious and peaceful; and yet another, of allowing individuals to access all the various resources (financial, cultural, intellectual) they need in order, on the best-informed basis, to construct satisfying and enriching patterns of life-choices for themselves.

These latter two concerns are seen by many critics of the 'market model' to be equally important, if indeed not more important, than simply functioning as a productive unit to assist the community to reach a degree of economic viability and possible surplus. Moreover, these concerns are an inherent part of the 'triadic' account of the purposes of lifelong learning proffered in this book. For critics of the 'market' approach there are some things that are essential – such as learning how one ought to conduct fruitful, benevolent and principled relations with other people, and how to find springs of personal satisfaction by acquisition, use and enjoyment of a well-informed and creative imagination, such as will enhance one's own living. These are not catered for, nor amenable to passing on by any reputable pedagogy, in the calculus of the market-related aims of increasing private investment in the provision of goods and services and lowering the public sector borrowing requirement. On the contrary, the problems of urban decay, domestic violence, civil unrest and work-place discord, it is argued, cannot be solved simply by throwing money at them nor by contracting their solution out to the lowest competitive tender in some kind of 'market-place' in which individuals and groups are 'bidding' to offer solutions to such human problems and predicaments.

Colin Wringe (1994) argues that Adam Smith and his followers since have all missed this vital point. Wringe maintains that the operation of the market is not likely to prove beneficial in those cases when:

- activities are inherently detrimental to the public interest or subversive of essential social institutions;

- market transactions are unsuitable for the distribution of necessities which individuals are unable to meet through no fault of their own or which are beyond the means of ordinary individuals; and

- individuals are unqualified to judge their own needs or the quality of the services being offered.

On this basis Wringe concludes that the treatment of education as a commodity for exchange in a market-place is conceptually and morally inappropriate. In taking this view Wringe is supported by Terence McLaughlin, who, in the final chapter of *Education and the Market Place* (Bridges and McLaughlin, 1994), bases his own conclusion on the imperatives arising from our attachment to the concept of democracy. In a democracy, McLaughlin avers, there are certain higher-order values relevant to and only gained via the process of education – those, for example, relating to civic virtue and personal autonomy – and these constitute (broadly speaking) moral limits on markets and the idea of markets in education. These prime values, that are indispensable features of any citizen's life in a participative democracy, ought to make these principles both exempt from subjection to approaches redolent of the market and regarded as non-negotiable features of all educating institutions' activities.

The debate about the nature of the best model of provision, governance, management and funding for the courses and programmes that will meet the needs of learners beyond the compulsory stages of education is still unresolved. The question of the best model of provision, governance, management and funding constitutes the most critical issue in the debate about the optimum policies and strategies for any country's approaches to learning beyond schooling; it must be addressed as one of central importance to considerations of lifelong learning.

The key question, we believe, is: what are the alternative models for the provision, governance, management and funding of learning beyond schooling, that will both facilitate the whole range of learning needs and yet at the same time be economically efficient, socially inclusive and ethically just? If the market model is one that features distinctively among the proposals put forward for a resolution of this question, then we believe it needs to be asked what might be the limits that should be placed upon the market, given the moral imperatives embodied in the concept of education and the social and ethical goals associated with lifelong learning?

THE ROLE OF GOVERNMENTS IN LEARNING BEYOND THE SCHOOL YEARS

Many countries are reviewing or have recently reviewed their policy stances in respect of the governance, delivery and management of programmes and courses devoted to learning beyond the school years. Different emphases exist but there are some common themes:

- More responsibility is being devolved to institutions themselves to determine their own objectives and to take their own initiatives to achieve objectives within broad policy guidelines; increasingly institutions are being given greater autonomy to judge for themselves what is needed to be done in this area, in order to make the best use of their funds.

- Funding arrangements are changing and being made more stringent, at the same time as being focused much more on the target of each institution's output of qualified graduates rather than to such matters as input of staff, equipment, accommodation.

- Institutions are being urged to become entrepreneurial.

- Students, particularly for graduate and continuing professional programmes, are being required to pay a greater proportion of the costs of their courses.

- Some governments are removing barriers to private sector initiatives in a number of aspects of post-secondary education and training; some as a matter of policy are encouraging private providers to compete for contracts with public institutions. Long-standing distinctions between public and private providers of educational services and programmes are being removed. Previous approaches to provision and funding, which traditionally restricted access to and the provision of such services and courses solely to public institutions, are being broadened so as to offer a range of opportunities and arenas in which public sector institutions will be competing with private sector interests and with each other to attract students to their courses.

It has been argued that there has probably never been a time of so much ferment in post-secondary education as there is now (cf. OECD, *Learning Beyond Schooling: Clarifying Report*, 1994, p. 73).

In looking at the question of the range and kinds of post-secondary and lifelong education provision, the role of governments in making, planning and funding such provision is of key concern. Many believe there is a strong case for governments to play a *strategic role* in relation to sectors where they cannot be the main provider of services, but where there is value in influencing or providing a coherent framework including a range of incentives for a different type of provider. This strategic role might involve partnerships with providers and/or regulation, finance, monitoring results and fostering strategically important developments.

Some suggest that the distinctive role and contribution of governments in all these matters might reside most appropriately in helping institutions and agencies to formulate, shape and promulgate their own version of what they believe their society's overall interests and goals to be. Without such involvement, it is claimed, many activities relevant to the aims of lifelong learning might be provided on a haphazard and unco-ordinated basis. Some authors (OECD, *Learning Beyond Schooling – New Forms of Supply and Demand: Background Report*, 1994, p. 16) go further than this, however. Governments, they maintain, need to consider policies in respect of:

- *The harnessing of new technologies*. Communications infrastructure can be influenced by government regulation, financing and tax regimes. Governments will need to negotiate and collaborate' with the private sector in developing the technology of learning.

- *The position and nature of public funding*. Despite the practical impossibility of governments providing all post-compulsory education and training, it is likely that they will still play an important role in financing. In particular governments continue to fund the bulk of higher education in most European and many other countries and governments are the biggest single funders of post-secondary education in all OECD countries. In this connection a number of key questions arise and press for an answer: How should public funding for lifelong learning be structured? How should financing responsibilities be divided among governments, employers and individuals? How does offering a major role in provision to private institutions ensure better and wider market penetration: does it help to ensure that supply meets a wide range of demands? How might funding be reorientated in the light of internationalization?

Governments can also seek to create new conditions under which institutions are encouraged to adapt to changing conceptions of learning and societal demands for education. To ensure the flexibility of public institutions in meeting such demands funding may need to be less specifically allocated to predetermined inputs and more related to outputs measured by the criteria of certified learning progress. But governments may also have to help institutions to change by supporting in-service training and by adapting regulations to the needs and challenges of a new educational environment, in which a large proportion of learning takes place away from educational institutions.

A diversification of learning methods and content also needs to be accompanied by an adaptation of qualifications to ensure that learning outcomes are well recognized by employers and others. One challenge is to find ways of certifying the acquisition of competencies as well as substantive knowledge. Another is to devise a qualifications structure that measures learning outcomes regardless of the institution attended. Since the widest possible acceptance and interchangeability of qualifications is essential in a changing environment, especially as regards employment mobility, it is important for governments and educational institutions to work closely together with employers and others in providing and extending this key element in the learning infrastructure.

The authors of 'Investment knowledge and knowledge investment' (a paper presented as part of the OECD Education Committee's activity on *Further Education and Training as Investment* (OECD, 1993, p. 57) put it this way:

> Looking back over the post-world war period the existing human capital information and decision making processes may have been suited to conditions where the largest proportion of human capital investment was both mandatory (in the form of initial education and training for youth) and geared to inculcating a well established and economically functional set of cognitive and behavioural skills (punctuality, basic literacy and numeracy). Thus compulsory schooling combined with on the job learning experiences like apprenticeships not only met the demand for the labour market but also provided a set of signals adequate for the information needs of mass production and labour intensive service industries.
>
> Today however, faced not only with technological and organisational change but also the need to find entirely new knowledge based areas of economic activity, both the systems that generate information about human capital and those that guide the use of information are being challenged in most OECD countries. Pressures to innovate are provoking pervasive changes at all levels of society. This transformation encompasses both the means and ends of the knowledge acquisition and utilisation choices made by individuals, firms and governments.

The authors of this report suggest that one of the primary ways for government to encourage more effective information and decision-making systems is to establish the collective parameters and guard the general interest when it comes to defining competencies, assessment methods, and recording conventions. Effectively pursuing these tasks, they argue, requires processes that are simultaneously inclusive, decentralized, and based on a common general framework.

Measuring and recording competence acquisition requires the development of low-cost, universally accepted and labour-market-relevant systems for defining and assessing knowledge for use in the work-place. These systems, configured to specific attributes of domestic labour market institutions and labour market and negotiating practices, need to balance the competing interests of employers, employees, educators, professional associations, citizens, entry and adult learners and different regions.

One of the benefits of a national and universal system for assessing and recording competencies is its potential to reduce current fragmentation of certification and diversify the provision of knowledge by rendering knowledge acquisition method-neutral. That is, learning can be acquired by methods and/or in fora and by forms of study that are formal, informal, institutional, experiential and so on. In this way all sources, ways and forms of knowledge have equal chances of being validated.

In order to reap the benefits of these policies, governments must work closely with individuals and firms to ensure that new measurement and accounting practices, tax measures, labour market initiatives, and financial regulations – intended to reveal and recognize the stocks and flows of human capital – actually implement the incentives, disincentives and flexibility that are consistent with both competitive decentralization of power and general social welfare.

By undertaking the role of *transaction facilitator* and setting up the 'playing field' in this way, it is maintained, the state can help to generate a wide range of benefits, including:

- incremental investment;
- capitalization allowing firms to collatoralize and amortize;
- clear ownership allowing direct financing of knowledge acquisition;
- transparency of labour contract;
- validation of alternative learning acquisition;
- identification of investment patterns;
- discouraging prejudicial forms of discrimination.

The authors of the report 'Investment knowledge and knowledge investment' (OECD, 1993) have attempted to explain how and why rethinking the systems that determine human capital investment knowledge will improve knowledge investment, in the hope that – given the ascendancy of the learning economy – collective efforts to ensure more efficient and effective acquisition and utilization of human capital will lead to improved overall economic performance.

It must be pointed out, however, that this analysis is also predicated upon a highly economic and instrumental view of education. As previously argued, the broader-scale philosophical and values debate must be undertaken before the more technical issues to do with the achievement of the values, goals and purposes of lifelong education more broadly conceived come into consideration.

Among the broader issues for consideration, governments will also need to take an approach to the planning and development of educational communications, which includes all sectors of education and capitalizes upon all their various forms of potential contribution and benefit. The more widely that networks are shared, the greater the economies of scale. Governments, acting in consultation with carriers and educational institutions, need to develop policies for educational applications of telecommunications technologies, which provide equity of access, common standards and a unified network strategy including all telecommunications services, such as voice, data, fax, video, together with interconnections between institutions and with the external world via such information highways as the Internet (cf. OECD, 'The future of post-secondary education and the role of information and communication technology: a clarifying report', 1994, p. 118).

A unified network strategy will need to be accompanied by detailed analysis of the teaching and administrative applications required by institutions, in order to determine traffic volumes before appropriate technological decisions can be made. Continued emphasis on and investment in the information and communication technology infrastructure is required. In a number of countries consideration is being given to expanding networks, originally set up to serve the academic community, into national networks serving not just the universities but also schools, technical and further education institutions and adult and continuing education institutions of all kinds.

In this connection it is worth adding into the consideration of framing comprehensive policies for the conception, implementation and effective delivery of a range of initiatives for lifelong learning, the point that industry, commerce and businesses are also investing billions of dollars in new technology delivery systems and in the necessary programming for them. There is a clear opportunity for government and business to participate and co-operate in a shared enterprise that will provide the resources for and offer leadership in the provision of lifelong learning opportunities for all in the learning communities of the future.

CONSIDERATIONS AND OPTIONS FOR STEERING DEVELOPMENT TOWARDS A LIFELONG APPROACH TO LEARNING

Earlier reference was made to the policies and practices developed by some countries in response to current pressures on education exerted by the combined influence of the value-orientations, educational commitments and societal conditions identified as operating in those countries.

As revealed then, a key feature of new approaches to management and governance has been a redefinition of the role of governments as part of a general trend in which responsibilities for education and training have been redistributed. Often referred to as 'decentralization', the trend is perhaps better described as a movement towards a realignment of educational and administrative responsibilities. In this realignment the outcomes to be achieved by individual institutions and learners tend to be more tightly specified and assessed by central governments; in some countries governments have gone about this in greater consultation with learners, third-party clients, such as employers and parents, and other stakeholders in the 'learning society' at large. Decisions about the means used to achieve such outcomes are increasingly being left to individual education and training establishments, communities and learners themselves.

At a time when restructuring efforts have often involved major down-sizing and 'outsourcing' of educational bureaucracies, it was noted that governments are entertaining some reservations about the need to preserve some of the cross-institutional bulwarks of value, which were traditionally built into public systems of education. To ensure that in the move towards greater autonomy governments do not abandon or give up some of the most treasured values, on the basis of a commitment to which education has been provided as a public service, a number of key issues have been identified.

As governments move away from bureaucratic regulation, it is important, for example, that they should consider the important question of the ways in which they may safeguard the public values which previous governance and administrative structures and arrangements were designed and established to protect – values such as impartiality, the wider public interest, equity and fairness. It is right that governments should ask how they can ensure that increased autonomy does not widen the gap between the 'haves' and the 'have-nots'. Underpinning such concerns is the key question of how governments might fulfil their legislative responsibilities and obligations for the provision of education, at the same time as enabling maximum flexibility and autonomy for the individual and the individual institution, without significant compromise or damage to the rights and responsibilities of all parties.

It was pointed out that the distribution of responsibilities for publicly provided or publicly regulated education and training is a highly complex matter. Responsibilities are now more widely distributed and shared, not only from central government authorities to the region, to the education or training establishment, and to the teachers, but also to stakeholders and other 'interested' parties outside the traditional boundaries of education or educating institutions. Responsibilities are also more likely to be shared under the assumption of a mutuality of interests and an acceptance of the indispensability of partnership in shaping and determining educational goals, processes and outcomes.

We observed that, when governments are looking at the implications for governance and management in all types of education institution, account needs to be taken of research findings and experiences in different national settings as to governments' role in bringing about change in education and training systems. Such evidence as exists – quantitative school effectiveness studies and education and training evaluation studies, as well as more qual-itative case-study investigations of the change process at the level of the individual education and training site – points to the key roles of the teacher or facilitator, the parent and members of the local community, as well as the role of the individual manager or team, in the overall direction of teaching and learning at the local site.

All this has implications for governments' understanding of human resource development. A broader vision of the role of and part played by human resources in conceptions of and plans for lifelong learning gives greater weight to the choices of learners (and, at younger ages, the choices of their parents). When learners are provided with greater responsibility for their own learning, they may, through the decisions they take, serve as agents for change, both directly, with regard to their own learning, and indirectly, through the cate-gories and forms of education and training services selected. These concepts are important and need to be examined, in the light of some governments' experi-ences with a range of different roles played by human resources in the change process, by level and type of learning.

In their various approaches and in relation to unique contexts, many countries are attempting to fine-tune the balance operative between regulation, on the one hand, and autonomy, initiative and diversity of provision, on the other. Education policies continue to evolve in respect of the different levels and sectors of formal education and training and in the domains of informal and non-formal learning. Although few countries have yet to develop policies for management and governance with the necessary coherence across all levels and forms of learning across the life-span, nevertheless in some countries innovative strategies targeting this need are being progressively introduced. The hope is that, in due course, a proper balance between the claims of choice and accountability, individual autonomy and centrally determined quality control, public provision and private initiative will be achieved.

On this issue three questions need to be addressed by policy-makers and educators:

1 To what extent are reforms and new approaches to management and governance sufficiently connected to teaching and learning, and what roles can each of the relevant parties play in bringing about a blending of responsibilities for administration and management with those for teaching and learning?

2 To what extent do guidelines, regulations and accountability frameworks inhibit initiative by providers and learner choices? Can the government's role be formulated in such a way as to encourage learners, teachers and education and training establishments to be active and take initiative while at the same time ensuring the overall needs of the economy and society are addressed?

3 What are the costs, as well as benefits, of a wider sharing of responsibilities and a different government role, as governments and other agencies and institutions within the community assume greater responsibility for lifelong learning?

At the same time larger and deeper questions need to be raised, concerning the extent to which new approaches to governance and management can bring about improvements in teaching and learning, the achievement of identified outcomes (to include consequences for equity), and overall efficiency.

As governments shape their policies for the future they may come to feel that the accent needs to be placed on reforming their own roles in the provision of, and the formulation of, policy frameworks that will support change and development towards a lifelong approach to learning. The following questions point to the issues which governments need to consider as they move towards new arrangements for governance and management in the provision of lifelong learning:

- What policies might be put into place to overcome adverse consequences of autonomy and choice, specifically with regard to equity?

- What are the necessary elements of a development structure, as opposed to a maintenance structure, for central education authorities in the provision of lifelong learning?

- What regulation and financing mechanisms can be adopted to encourage all partners in the educational endeavour to contribute resources to learning, while at the same time ensuring the interests and needs of the economy and society are met?

- What forms and types of partnerships best promote a lifelong approach to learning? How can partnerships better enhance coherence through improved links with business and industry and with other cultural and community groups? What limits should be placed on partnerships in the interests of avoiding the dangers of inequity, inefficiency and uneven quality?

- What information must be provided to ensure dispersed and shared decision-making takes into account the costs, effects (individual and collective) and coherence of learning in the lifelong perspective?

In answering these questions, a tentative beginning may be made by endeavouring to identify options for policy frameworks, structures and processes of governance and management that governments will need to consider and conclude upon. Considerable assistance in this endeavour is offered by the analysis provided by Stewart Ranson in *Towards the Learning Society* (1994). Ranson recommends that:

1 Governments need to decide upon the organizing principles they deem necessary for the governance of democratic and inclusive educational provision. A precondition of such decision-making will be

- a resolution to the debate as to whether education is to be seen as a public good or a commodity;

- a delineation of the ways in which community fora, councils and advisory panels can enable public discourse to take place and make participation a condition of the workings of representative democracy;

- an acceptance of the need for progressive decentralization, with the direction of the realignment of power and responsibility being focused upon partnership and mutual answerability: 'responsibilities and powers should be distributed to each inter-dependent tier of education – the centre, the local authority, institutions and the community – so that each can make its appropriate contribution to the shared overall purposes of the learning society by enabling autonomy and citizenship through a system of comprehensive and equal opportunities' (Ranson, 1994, p. 114);

- a greater commitment to multiple accountability, an acknowledgment of plural centres of power – centre, locality, institution and community – which must collaborate if the needs of all are to be met, but which must also be willing to give an account of purposes and to be held to account on the exercise of responsibilities.

2 Governments will also need to determine the functions and powers of the tiers of government within a new structure of partnership.

(a) The centre should, according to Ranson (1994, p. 115), have as its primary functions:

- enabling and promoting national policy for the learning society;

- developing the infrastructure;

- developing strategic planning and resourcing;

- commissioning research;

- evaluating the quality of learning.

(b) Local authorities should have as their prime function the development of a systemic, public-minded and coherent approach to learning: providing strategic leadership, that will encourage local education partners to develop a shared understanding of and commitment to quality in learning and learning provision, and to the democratic concerns of a system of education provided as a public service for the whole community. This will involve:

- promoting a vision of learning that will generate understanding of the conditions and processes of learning necessary to release 'the powers and capacitates of adults as well as young people, and encourage them to make their responsible contribution to the development of their society' (Ranson, 1994, p. 122);

- strategic planning and resourcing;

- the provision of support and support services;

- evaluation of quality;

- partnership and networking;

- setting up structures and processes enabling participation, voice and accountability.

(c) Learning institutions, schools and colleges: the principal challenge at the level of the institution will be to enable reform of the learning process, in line with changing conditions affecting education – changing goals, changing epistemologies, changing theories of learning, and changing technologies. Ranson identifies the following organizing principles to enable such reform at the institutional level:

- valuing the capacity of all individuals to learn;

- an emphasis on the entitlement of all to a comprehensive and continuing education;

- a commitment to active learning;

- the promotion of partnerships with parents and the community.

(d) The community, parents and other stakeholders committed to the need for lifelong patterns of learning: Ranson maintains that a number of organizational mechanisms need to be developed, to support the identification of local needs, to facilitate participation, and to support the co-ordination of schools, colleges and other learning centres. Mechanisms might include:

- community fora;

- the appointment of community education officers.

Ranson's analysis, of course, presents only one among a range of possible scenarios for the realignment of governance and management powers and responsibilities in furthering the mission of governments to extend opportunities for lifelong learning to all. It nevertheless provides a starting-point for reflection on the conditions necessary for the conception, articulation and enactment of policies and programmes offering opportunities for lifelong education for all.

CONCLUSION: STEERING AT A DISTANCE

In this chapter we have started from the premise that there are three elements in lifelong learning: education for economic progress and development; education for democratic understanding and activity; and education for personal development and fulfilment. These elements are fundamental to the enterprise of seeking to bring about: a more democratic polity and set of social institutions, in which the principles and ideals of social inclusiveness, justice and equity, are present, practised and promoted; an economy which is strong, adaptable and competitive; and a richer range of provision of those activities, on which individual members of society are able to spend their time and energy for the personal rewards and satisfactions they confer.

To achieve these ends we argue that policy-makers and educators must undertake a substantial reappraisal of the goals of their education policies; the governance, management and resourcing of their education provision; and a major reorientation of its direction towards the concept and value of the idea of the learning society *and* lifelong learning for all.

We may infer from evidence gathered by contemporary analysts, such as those working on the OECD *Jobs Study* (1994), that the current dominant approach to education and training, based on governments' monopolies and a systematic provision of 'front-end' formal education and training, preceding entry to the labour market, is inadequate. On economic grounds alone, technological and other structural changes have led to situations in which certain jobs, skills and occupations become obsolete, to such an extent that the idea of a 'front-end' and 'once-and-for-all' conception of education as a preparation for one career is now seriously out of date. The slow rate of labour-force renewal through the entry of young, newly qualified workers cannot satisfy demand. As qualifications become outdated more quickly than workers retire, there is an increased risk of older workers becoming unemployed. Current education and training provision is not sufficiently broad-based to address those problems.

The implications for government of such trends in economy and society as the changing structure and pattern of relationships of the family, the changing pattern of employment and unemployment, population and demographic change particularly associated with an ageing population, labour-force participation rates, change in the nature of available jobs, the increase in the number of young people designated as being 'at risk', the increasing rate of technological change, increase in the amount of discretionary time available to individuals, and increasing globalization, are manifold.

Programmes of compulsory and post-compulsory education, and the availability of lifelong learning opportunities, must reflect and seek to address the requirements flowing from and generated by these trends, particularly as they have an impact on people's life-chances and their preparation for frequent job changes, periods of unemployment and increased longevity. For the educationally under-served and unskilled the implications of these trends will be especially acute, thereby highlighting the need for governments to adopt a multifaceted approach to policy development, governance and management in education, incorporating serious and detailed appraisal and considerations of the relationship between economic policy, education and social policy.

In respect to the administration of lifelong learning, governments are also recognizing the need for a multifaceted approach. It is clear that questions concerning the nature and number of the goals of education and training, the curriculum appropriate to deliver them, and the institutional and systemic arrangements necessary to secure them, transcend the immediate and limited character, constituency and remit of system authorities and of the local educating institution. Across very many countries now there is perceived to be a need for broad social and community partnerships to be forged between associated interests, groups and sectors in a range of community stakeholders. Clearly consideration needs to be given to the task of creating social consensus and partnerships that will assist in the realization of governments' policies for lifelong education.

Given many countries' concern for lifelong learning for all, an emphasis on the institution of schooling as constituting the main way of providing people with the groundwork for lifelong learning must be reconsidered. In recent years there has been considerable debate regarding changing conceptions of education, the public service, and the public administration of schools and school systems. The patterns and procedures of the governance, steering and management of education cannot be determined and set in train without some clarification of the key concepts and values that shall define and structure the administrative responses that governments adopt. As governments move towards a reappraisal and reconsideration of schooling and education now seen from a lifelong perspective, there is a need to provide an arena in which these conceptual and value issues can be addressed and the appropriate systems and forms of governance, steering and management decided upon.

At the present time new notions of administrative relationships in the provision of schooling, seen within the context of lifelong learning, are still at the stage of early exploration and articulation. They are tentative and lack specificity. Notions of bureaucratic relationships, of the de-schooled society, and of 'the market' have all been found to be outmoded or deficient, as new notions of administrative relationships in the provision of compulsory education are explored. For governments a major challenge will be to examine and decide upon ways in which new conceptions and models of altered administrative arrangements and relationships can be fully elaborated, implemented and appropriately evaluated in the real settings where the need for them is so pressing. Of particular interest will be an exploration of the ways in which the principles of autonomy and mutuality in governance and management can be elaborated upon and made meaningful in educational contexts. The hope is that in due course a proper balance between the claims of choice and accountability, individual autonomy and centrally determined quality control, public provision and private initiative will be achieved.

In the quest to realize the goal of lifelong learning, it is clear that governments are now taking learning beyond schooling to be as serious a matter as schooling itself. A radical rethinking of education beyond the compulsory years of schooling is taking place. A key issue in considerations relating to the provision, governance and management of lifelong learning is, of course, the question of who pays for learning beyond the compulsory years. The present and future development of post-secondary education and training is being considered in the context of a move towards shared funding responsibilities. Employers and individuals who benefit from investment in learning are increasingly expected and in some cases required to contribute a share of the cost. Joint investment can enhance the effectiveness of learning by giving several partners a stake in the outcomes. But there is the danger that financial arrangements will inhibit participation by some groups in society and hence be socially divisive. The optimal division and distribution of funding responsibilities for lifelong learning remains to be decided.

The debate about the best model of provision and funding for the courses and programmes that will meet the needs of learners beyond the compulsory stages of education is still inconclusive. The question of the best model of provision and funding constitutes the most crucial issue in the debate about the best policies and strategies for any country's approaches to learning beyond schooling. This question must be addressed as one of central importance to considerations of lifelong learning. The key issue is: what are the alternative models for the provision and funding of learning beyond schooling that will both facilitate the whole range of learning needs and yet at the same time be economically efficient, socially inclusive and ethically just? If the market model features distinctively among the proposals for a resolution to this question, then a further question needs to be asked: what are the limits that must be placed upon the 'market', given the moral imperatives embodied in the concept of education and the social and ethical goals associated with lifelong learning?

In considering the range and kinds of lifelong education provision, the role of governments in planning, steering, managing and funding such provision is a key concern. Many believe that there is a strong case for governments to play a strategic role in sectors where they cannot be the main provider of services but where there is value in their influencing or providing a coherent framework, including a range of incentives for a range of providers. Others see government as undertaking the role of transaction facilitator, setting up the 'playing field' for provision. As governments move away from the role of monopoly provider and towards one of partnership with other agencies and institutions in a 'mixed economy' of public and private provision, there is clearly a need to consider the range of roles available to agencies, institutions and governments, and to assist governments in selecting that role which they deem to be most appropriate to their initiatives, values and goals in the field of lifelong learning for all.

In exploring the range of roles available to those who have traditionally been both inside and outside the educational boundaries, the formation and extension of partnership relationships between educating institutions and business, industry, commerce and trade unions will be of increasing importance in the realization of lifelong learning for all. It will be particularly important to draw lessons from past dysfunctions in such relationships and from an examination of more recent successful practices and partnerships, so as to delineate and draw attention to the features of these relationships that make them work well. There is a need to explore the impact of such relationships as regards the enhancement of lifelong learning upon such important goals as better and more effective preparation for the workforce; creating shared goals among educators and employers, and other industrial and commercial interest groups (such as trades and craft unions and professional associations); and for influencing the provision of learning opportunities offered by business, industry and commerce. These joint endeavours should best be placed in a context of the interest all such groups may be said to have in the formation of partnerships whose positive collaboration and effective working can function as a rich source of economic, individual and community development.

In broadening the concept of educational partnerships and extending the boundaries of the learning society, there will also be a need to explore the ways in which educating institutions can derive the necessary information, resource sustenance and moral support from the various community, ethnic, cultural and religious groups that comprise our multicultural societies. Engagement with such groups and agencies will be a vital precondition for the enmeshment of education in the work of all the various cultural, artistic, religious and ethnic communities, whose existence and orientations form an important part of the mosaic of lifelong learning, and of the whole range of constituencies that comprise the learning society.

Governments will also need to enter into partnerships with those assuming major responsibility in the planning and development of educational technologies and communications. In forging these partnerships, governments acting in consultation with carriers and educational institutions will need to develop policies for the educational applications of telecommunications technologies which provide equity of access, common standards and a unified network strategy between institutions and the external world via information highways such as the Internet.

The realization of lifelong learning will also be heavily dependent on those who assume responsibility for management and for 'leading the learning community' at the institutional level. A significant effort should be made to identify, motivate and provide requisite training for the range of people within the community who can serve as leaders in the learning enterprise. The same concerns for autonomy and mutuality should animate approaches towards the conception, implementation and assessment of such training schemes and should feature throughout as part of the government's approach to the mutually supportive and interactive roles of those in educating institutions who are being trained to offer leadership and be agents of change in the implementation of policies directed at achieving lifelong learning for all.

Part III

Lifelong Learning through School and Community

Chapter 7

Connecting Schools, Families and Communities

In this section of the book we attempt to identify some of the ways and means in and by which the goals of lifelong learning may be achieved through the activities of schools working together with other agencies, constituencies and groups in the community. We begin with an account of the ways in which the interests of lifelong learners may be promoted and achieved by linking together the learning opportunities made available through the connections and forms of co-operation increasingly being developed between schools, families and other sections and groups in communities.

Many such activities take their starting-point from the concern of societies to educate their young for their future roles, rights and responsibilities as citizens in modern participative democracies and to promote and safeguard the principle of social inclusion which seeks emancipation for all citizens. Yet others begin from the premise that increasing the sense and the powers of individual autonomy is a key factor in helping individuals achieve some degree of success in learning about and creating a satisfying pattern of life-options for themselves, then choosing a range of activities with which that life might be fulfilled and its quality further enhanced.

Part of achieving success in these undertakings will involve bringing about some understanding of, skill in and progress at establishing and conducting relationships with other people, in the home, in the work-place, and in other centres of community life. Given the number of causes, factors and phenomena militating against balance, harmony and concord in community, social and personal relationships at the present time, this is perhaps one area where a stress on the need for lifelong engagement in educational undertakings of all kinds can be especially beneficial.

Schools have a vital part to play here. For, in offering entrée and access to opportunities for further learning among a range of individuals, groups, constituencies and associations of interest in the community, it will not only enable people to upgrade and extend their learning for vocational, political and personal growth purposes, but it will also lay stress on the ways in which group co-operation and joint activity can make learning easier, more rapid and more enjoyable. In this way schools offering themselves as centres of learning for sectors of the whole community can act as agencies of mutual understanding, healing, reconciliation and jointly supportive community development.

SOCIAL BETTERMENT, DEMOCRATIC PARTICIPATION AND PERSONAL FULFILMENT THROUGH LIFELONG LEARNING

Learning for Social Betterment

The notion of social betterment has a particular point of applicability when we come to consider ways in which the school and community can provide a forum for social learning through lifelong education. In this regard it is important that we move from thinking merely about effecting modification in society by means of education, to thinking and acting to promote social development, as distinct from social change, through educational endeavour of all kinds.

Commitment to the enterprise of social betterment through lifelong learning will be enhanced and made more effective if schools can look outside and beyond their current restricted mode and remit of operation. Schools can seek opportunities for outreach into their communities as a means of contributing to their community's growth and welfare. They can do this best by engaging in discussion with the various organizations and interest groups constituting their community and by setting up procedures and structures whereby each can jointly work out strategies that will better involve as many sectors of the community in the education process as care and claim to have an interest in it.

One of the principal agenda of such discussions will centre upon the shaping and framing of policy initiatives meant to cater for the differing needs of all parts of the community – mainstream, minority, and outlying – whose interests a school will serve. There will also be a need to concentrate on the agenda of community development at many different levels – the family, locally, organizationally, state, nationally, internationally.

Questions that will arise for schools in these deliberations are:

- What constitutes the concept of community with which we are working?

- Do we presuppose the model of some consolidated, all-embracing conception of community as some kind of unitary organic entity? Even supposing such a thing to be possible, is the development of a unitary, all-embracing version of community desirable?

- Or is our model of 'community' no more than that of the accidental geographical agglomeration of different cultures, ethnic groups, social classes, trade and vocational interests of various kinds, that form a set of impermanent alignments, relationships and associations, some of them consciously sought and deliberately entered into, others no more than fortuitous and unintentional clusters of individuals brought and held together in loose concatenation by economic forces, vocational necessity or religious affiliation?

In addressing these questions, one thing is clear: whether the association of individual constituencies into communities is accidental or deliberate, single or complex, different groups in society have often found and continue to find that their most important task is to work together for the benefit of society or their particular sector of the community, whether this is conceived in overall terms or with relation to particular parts of it.

Schools will form their own answers to these questions. It is clear, however, that they will see themselves as inducting their students into the life of their own community and offering an educational service more widely within that community.

One form this service has traditionally taken is for schools to act as a centre where young people are able to learn a range of skills and knowledge that will help them prepare for their future lives. Another form of educational service is for schools to work with other agencies in the community to make learning opportunities available to people who are not currently in paid employment, or are beyond the normal working age. Yet another is for schools to act as initiators or partners in joint ventures in the undertaking of targeted community aware-ness and assistance projects. In such fora and activities it is possible for the school to use community structures and frameworks more generally to promote awareness of and response to the ideas of lifelong learning in the interest of social betterment.

In these days of a fragmented society, many people are looking for friends and often find friendships in the opportunities for social intercourse provided by learning programmes offered in schools and other learning centres. For that reason it is important for schools and education centres to provide a welcoming and accepting environment and to be located in positions where they can be conveniently reached. This is important in changing people's perceptions of education and learning and for making that learning accessible. Accessibility is especially important if we are to enhance social inclusion through lifelong learning by encouraging and welcoming the participation of hitherto isolated or marginalized groups, the disadvantaged, the disabled and the elderly, in learning activities – and by helping them to enjoy a sense of success and achievement in doing so.

It is here that governments can work in co-operation with schools. Govern-ments can promote social inclusiveness and betterment through the period of formal education by taking such measures as: developing multiple pathways towards educational achievement, recognizing different ways of learning, valu-ing different kinds of knowledge, putting on programmes for the disadvantaged, for those in remote areas, for the long-term unemployed, and setting up youth initiative programmes; establishing a range of strategies for case management for those who need mentors and appointing people to take a professional interest in their advancement; offering labour market and counselling services for young people; and serving as youth access and student assistance centres. There are a myriad ways in which governments can promote the prospects of schools and other education institutions acting as centres for community learning.

Here we see the importance of values in our approach to providing for the educational needs of all members of our communities. For such endeavours as are described above require insight, understanding, reflection, imagination, sympathy, altruism and a commitment to democratic values.

Learning for Democratic Responsibility and Participation

In a democratic society, the need for and the stress on democratic values, civic understanding and the readiness and willingness to participate in community decision-making should be a thread that runs through all our education. Democratic understanding and being prepared to exercise our rights and responsibilities as citizens is an important part and function of lifelong learning, especially in a world where the task of understanding and judging on a whole range of policies aimed at social and individual welfare has become increasingly complex. Such civic skills are quite as important as social skills for the citizen in a modern liberal democracy. For the principle of that form of government requires of citizens not merely knowledge but also goodwill, tolerance, mutual respect and a willingness to bear civic burdens based on regard for the goal of maximizing individual benefit and social welfare. Thus civic education is not only about the political process; it is also about the free and willing acceptance of the burden of community participation and responsibility.

An education for this end will take a number of forms. These will include:

- educating young people in democratic understanding;

- promoting opportunities for parents and members of the community to participate in school decision-making;

- promoting involvement in community agencies in the life of the school.

In the USA, the Association for Supervision and Curriculum Development (ASCD) Panel on Moral Education asserted that at the heart of democracy is the morally mature citizen (1988, p. 7). Among the recommendations of the Panel were the following agenda:

- To urge all those involved in education to renew their commitment to promoting moral education in schools – as a powerful unifying and energizing force in the curriculum.

- Educators to form partnerships with parents, mass media, business and community groups to create a social and cultural context that supports the school's efforts to develop morally mature citizens.

- Schools to work for the development of a morality of justice, altruism, diligence and respect for human dignity.

- Education systems to make sure that their moral education efforts extend beyond the cognitive domain to include the affective and the behavioural.

- Socialization into appropriate patterns of conduct and education for critical thinking and decision-making to be included in the curriculum.

- Institutional practices of school life to be predicated on an adherence to these moral principles and to aim to contribute to the same moral growth.

- School teachers and administrators to understand clearly the expectations of their role and responsibilities as moral educators.

Bottery identifies these strategies for schools seriously interested in pursuing an education for citizenship in a democracy (Bottery, 1993):

- In primary schools begin the process of education for citizenship in an optimistic and proactive manner by enabling children to take a more active part in structuring their day's work, in completing their work, and then discussing how it went and how it could be improved.

- Use the fact that children are interested in politics and the running of institutions. Systems of management in schools should allow students to be knowledgeable in the running of the country, interested in participating in constructive and critical change within society, and feeling empowered to do so.

- Teachers, as role models, should be involved in the management of schools as a right and a duty. Teachers and parents must be seen as partners in the educational process. Principals must work democratically.

Bottery concludes (1993, p. 7) that ' ... the gradual citizenship education of pupils, staff, parents, and head, through the mechanisms of school management is perhaps the best hope of an informed and empowered citizenry of the future'.

Ranson reinforces this point. He argues that:

> Education will always 'fail' if the capacity of young people has to be sectioned off to match a pyramidal hierarchical society (the hidden curriculum of which is learned very early by young people), underpinned by a political system that encourages passive rather than active participation in the public domain. A different polity, enabling all people to make a purpose of their lives, will create the conditions for motivation in the classroom. Only a new moral and political order can provide the foundation for sustaining the personal development of all. It will encourage individuals to value their active role as citizens and thus their shared responsibility for the common wealth. Active learning in the classroom needs, therefore, to be informed by and to lead towards active citizenship within a participative democracy. Teachers and educational managers, with their deep understanding of the processes of learning, can, I believe, play a leading role in enabling such a vision to unfold not only among young people but also across the public domain.
>
> (Ranson, 1994, p. 129)

Learning for Personal Growth and Sound Interpersonal Relationships

Education can be seen as a social activity for all learners that speaks to their needs and also provides them with access to a large range of goods and sources of personal satisfaction. Awareness of the pleasure and satisfaction that access to such goods and sources can bring is important as a motive and a justification for providing lifelong learning for all people and attracting them to it.

To begin with, learning about personal health and interpersonal relationships is crucial if the conditions required for people to expand their lifestyles is to be secured. Life-threatening diseases such as those of the heart and various forms of cancer still need to be brought under control, quite apart from the dangers inherent in people's engaging in risk-taking behaviours of all kinds. People need to be aware of the ways in which they can minimize those risks and give themselves an assurance of a healthy life, in order that they may enjoy the activities that lifelong learning opportunities have opened up to them.

One of the most important preconditions for a life of personal satisfaction is the need for positive and harmonious relations with other members of the community. The incidence of such unhappy phenomena as work-place discord, interpersonal contention, child-abuse, domestic violence, teenage suicide and relationship breakdown leading to divorce is not decreasing in modern societies, and such things not merely cause individual distress, pain and unhappiness, but also take a great deal out of the community, not only in terms of the financial cost involved, but also as regards the damage done to the social fabric generally.

There is thus everything to be said for encouraging younger as well as more mature members of the community to be aware of the dysfunctionality of such factors, to learn ways of establishing and maintaining positive personal and social relationships, and to learn the skills necessary to manage interpersonal difficulties, discord and the peaceful resolution of conflict, in the home, in the work-place and in relationships generally. There *are* such skills and they can be taught, along with work in improving the disposition to follow such positive pathways to improving social harmony rather than responding with negative reactions to dysfunctional phenomena.

As much as anything else, people's time at school affects the development not only of the knowledge, skills and attitudes necessary for learning how to engage in positive and harmonious relationships with other people, but also of their awareness of their own identity as independent and autonomous human beings, with their own view of the world and their own worthwhileness as individuals. Thus, whatever other purposes it serves, education must be about enabling and helping people to develop a sense of their personal value, integrity and dignity, since this is a precondition for being able to develop satisfying and mutually beneficial relationships with others. Many of the activities and procedures of educating institutions will need to be planned and arranged to serve this end.

Students in schools will benefit from approaches to them that consider them and accord them the dignity of being treated as individuals worthy of recognition and respect in their own right. This is a principle that can be extended not only in the planning and delivery of curriculum activities and learning experiences but also in the procedures and arrangements of school organization, administration and governance. As a result of taking part in such procedures students can develop further increments of self-awareness and personal growth.

The awareness of oneself is enhanced by the growing realization that human beings live in a social world. As one of the best-known of Aristotle's aphorisms has it: 'Human beings are by nature animals that live in groups.' Individual autonomy evolves and increases *pari passu* with one's developing social awareness and acceptance of the obligations and responsibilities of the patterns of human relationship and interaction in which we are all enmeshed. Lack of attention to the need to sensitize our growing generation to the constraints imposed on us (as well as the privileges conferred) by the bonds of relationship and the claims of other people in the community has probably much to do with the increasing incidence of such dysfunctional social phenomena as marriage breakdown, domestic violence, child-abuse and teenage suicide. Whatever other purposes education is to serve, it has at least as much to do with developing an awareness of the need for agreeable and productive relationships between ourselves and others, if our autonomy is to be preserved and expanded and our chances of leading happy, rewarding and fulfilled lives are to be realized.

Some of these matters will certainly be covered in the formal curriculum, in such subjects as history, geography, literature, and in the understanding of other cultures and societies as is a necessary feature of learning a modern foreign language; but there is also a need in the curriculum to give more time and attention to the nature, structure and improvement of human relationships. Such attention could well concentrate on relationships in the home, in the work-place, and in the community. In all of these, people will make choices and follow paths of activity that they believe will not be inimical to their own welfare but will offer them opportunities of further growth and enrichment that will be of benefit to themselves and ultimately to others.

Some patterns of human relationships have changed and are still changing, of course: marriage may no longer be as tight or as permanent an institution as once it was, yet the majority of people still choose it as the focus and centre of what they see as a desirable and worthwhile form of life. So important is this institution as a part of people's lives that, if we are to enhance its possibilities and learn how to deal with its challenges and difficulties, we may quickly come to the conclusion that these are things that require overt attention and work in our educating institutions. There is a need for marriage education as part of lifelong learning in schools.

Given that children are offspring of close human relationships, there will also be a need to teach parenting skills, that can show people how to deal with the day-to-day exigencies of bringing up children but also increase people's consciousness of the larger moral obligations involved in the relationships brought about through being a parent. There is also a need for education in the ways and means of establishing and ordering tolerant and tolerable forms of family life and in the ways in which these can be secured through the understanding and acceptance of family rights and responsibilities.

Knowles and Scattergood (1989, p. 67), in reference to the 'Education for Parenting Program' in Philadelphia, show how this programme gives K-8 students the opportunity to gain knowledge about babies and toddlers through direct observation and a written curriculum covering pregnancy, newborns, infants between 6 and 12 months old, toddlers and partnering. They regard the value of this programme as consisting in the fact that it reaches students before they are sexually active and when they are still amenable to changing their attitudes. The programme teaches that parenting takes time, energy, knowledge and skill; and it makes students think about the consequences of becoming parents. In the view of the authors: 'If students have a more realistic understanding of parenting, we believe they will be more cautious about becoming parents.'

For very many people relationships, both in the family and much more widely, are their principal sources of strength and support. When relationships break down the resultant unhappiness not only affects the individual adversely but is also injurious to the health of the entire community. At the present time most schools fail to teach children how to reflect on and learn from their own life-experiences and those of others. Courses on human relationships need to be based on people's own experiences and to show how difficulties can be avoided, faced and dealt with, and how good things can be built upon and turned into blessings.

Because this is so important, education about healthy relationships has to start as early as possible, when children start school, or preferably before. A beginning in this can be made with stress being placed on the importance of such principles as fairness, respect for others, and consideration of their interests. Attention needs to be paid to how children treat each other and how they are treated; the Golden Rule of 'Do unto others as you would that they should do unto you' cannot be applied too early, even if it has to be articulated in some such form as 'How would you feel if someone did that to you?'

A particular example comes to mind in the case of bullying, which is widely agreed to be one of the most unpleasant features of school life. Recent Australian studies (reported in *The Age*, 1996) suggest that:

- Nearly 50 per cent of school students in one Australian state reported having been bullied at some time.

- About 10 per cent of schoolchildren are victimized 'often' or 'once a week'.

- Bullying is more prevalent in primary schools than in secondary schools and boys bully more than girls.

- The incidence of repeated bullying in high schools is greatest in the first two years.

- Children in single-sex schools experience more bullying than those in co-educational schools.

- The most common form of bullying is name-calling and teasing. Males tend to engage in physical bullying, while female bullying takes the form of verbal abuse or exclusion.

- About 7.6 per cent of female and 4.1 per cent of male students experienced bullying lasting months or more. Such bullying often continued because the victim did not retaliate and because such behaviour was tolerated by some students and adults.

These figures are dismaying and deeply shaming. They indicate that this particular form of anti-social behaviour is a major cause of personal unhappiness and distress. One researcher said that one former school student had written to say that 'he had left school in year nine to escape relentless abuse by other students'. It is clear that some students and even adults feel that this kind of behaviour towards other people is a tolerable and acceptable form of behaviour in other social milieux. We can postulate a link between that kind of violence and oppression in schools and the incidence of such forms of behaviour in society generally.

If society is to do something about bullying in the home, then schools and the education service generally clearly need to do something about bullying in schools. This emphasis gets a particular point of urgency with respect to the incidence of that form of aggression in the home that is often seen as being linked to bullying in schools – domestic violence. The experience of many groups working with the victims of domestic violence is that such people often had interpersonal difficulties, many involving bullying, at school. Many problems with domestic violence appear to begin as early as primary school.

There is obviously a need here for a large-scale attack on this problem, requiring address and overt action in educational institutions of all kinds. We need to educate children and adults to turn away from such antagonistic forms of conduct; we need to show them how damaging to individual lives and destructive of the social fabric such behaviour is; we need to bring students and adults to understand that such forms of action cannot be tolerated if our community is to be harmonious and supportive of the right of all its members to be secure from personal intimidation and oppression.

In sum, we need to teach children how to resolve conflict without resorting to violence and to acquire the skills of non-violent conflict resolution. For certainly children and young people will, in their later years, experience differences of opinion and values, problems in reconciling such differences, and substantial divergence of principle and behaviour in the home, the work-place and the wider community. This is where lifelong learning should begin, giving people confidence in their knowledge and ability to tackle problems, to realize that life is a learning process, to handle problems and to learn from them.

The conclusion of this is the realization that it is important to teach young people to take control of their own lives and not to be dependent on the judgment, approval or even the assistance of others. Children need to learn that they can change, develop, take control throughout their lives. We need to give all children experiences of learning that will enhance their sense of personal independence, interpersonal competence and equal social standing. These experiences will enable our young people to overcome the lack of self-confidence from which so many of them suffer, will help diminish and take away any sense of failure they might feel, and will encourage them to believe that they have the prerogative to take control over their lives.

The school can do much to promote these ends by planning and putting on courses devoted to those competencies and values. In offering such courses the school can work with other community groups, such as Women's Health Groups, which can give children a broader view of social issues and problems. In addressing such vital matters as teaching the skills of conflict resolution, schools should be working with other agencies and experts, such as Women's Domestic Violence Outreach or with MOVE (Men Overcoming Violent Emotions).

In promoting and providing access to such socially and personally important knowledge and skills, the school is not, of course, on its own. It can engage the goodwill and co-operation of other agencies, groups and constituencies in these vital endeavours – parents, members of extended families, churches, trades unions and professional organizations of all kinds. Schools will be helped by the realization that in seeking to address such matters they do not have the responsibility to do everything, but they do have an integral role to play in what is, after all, an endeavour that is essential to the health and welfare of the community – and therefore an undertaking in which all interested constituencies in the community are entitled and needed to play a major part.

BUILDING COMMUNITY THROUGH THE ACTIVITIES OF THE SCHOOL

The success of lifelong learning has partly to do with the individual and partly to do with the community. People's experience of learning to work together in all sorts of environments and milieux will encourage them to tackle further learning on both a group and an individual basis. Individuals will come to have a more informed understanding of the contribution they can make to the welfare and development of their community, while members of the wider community will acquire an increased understanding of the ways in which the community can support individuals in the interest of social inclusion and personal growth. Crucially, it is from their involvement as part of a group that individual learners will develop the motivation and courage to embark on extensions of their existing knowledge and skills for their own purposes, at the same time as acquiring knowledge, skills and values that will contribute to their community's broader social goals.

Schools have a responsibility to take the lead in building a sense of community. They have to learn how to develop strategic alliances with constituent groups in the community, frame their aspirations into intentions, and put their intentions into effect as activities for the school and the community at large. Schools can do a great deal to act as promoters and agents of change in developing positive community attitudes to the need for lifelong learning and encouraging engagement in lifelong learning activities. They can assist in providing a better integrated community of learning by facilitating people's participation in the educational and cultural life of the community; they can extend opportunities for learning for all members of the community beyond traditional barriers of space, time, age and location; and they can ensure further learning and recreational resources are available for and offered to people of all ages. Bringing members of the community into the school and offering them an entrée into some of their learning activities can open up, facilitate and stimulate people's participation in a range of learning ventures for people who might otherwise not have access to them.

Of course this proposition may be reversed: there can be quite as much material and experience in the external environment that can prove fruitful as sources and stimulators of motivation and growth in bringing about learning for students during the compulsory years of schooling. There are many opportunities offered by being placed in environments outside the school in which students will have experiences and encounter challenges through which they can gain knowledge, skills and insights that will be relevant to the demands they are likely to face in their lives. Such encounters with real-life situations have immense potential for promoting students' learning. These experiences can include taking part in some kind of study or work-place experience, spending some time on extra-curricular activities, or engaging in schemes of community welfare activities or community projects of various kinds outside the school environment.

People learn in, from and by their experiences and activities in all kinds of places in the community, many of which have little to do with schooling and education provision as it has been traditionally conceived. These sources of additional formal and informal learning to be gained through experience outside the school include television, radio, the work-place, the sports club, the ethnic cultural centre, the library, museums and art galleries, the church, and certainly the home, where access to computers and international information and communication systems is increasingly available and can open up a world of learning opportunities.

The important point is that schools must become aware of the potential and the opportunities offered by these additional sources and sites of learning and capitalize on them to the fullest extent of which they are capable and insofar as they meet the schools', the students' and the community's needs. For our younger generation, such learning experiences need to be integrated into the overall pattern of a student's learning and, at the present at any rate, this will occur largely in and through the school.

What is still vital is that schools should make it possible for all individuals and groups to avail themselves of like opportunities in a place which has been built and funded, first and foremost, for educational purposes and to provide educational services. It will be especially important that government schools have available to them the necessary resources to enable them to provide facilities and equipment for all children and young people to take advantage of the learning opportunities they provide. Without government provision of such resources the danger is that many children and young people will have restricted access or no access at all to those lifelong learning instruments to which private access is enjoyed by some of the more fortunate members of the community.

Facilitating the integration of all the learning resources existing within the community, providing facilities and encouraging the active involvement of members of community groups outside the traditional audience will ensure that schools begin to be seen as a major source of educational advice, service and support for the entire community. This will cement the community's view of the school as being actively involved in the development of community life. But this will occur only if there is a real sense of partnership in which there is a keen awareness, a strong understanding, and an acceptance that the community is going to be the beneficiary of the presence and activity of a vibrant and outward-looking educational institution in its midst. One teacher with whom we spoke during our research on lifelong learning gives an exciting account of how beneficial such a presence can be: 'I worked in a school that encouraged community participation. We had parents coming in to use the woodwork and craft rooms, when they weren't used by our day classes. We had a committee that looked at the needs of the community. We had a Drop-in Centre, where anyone could come in for a cup of coffee.' With models like this before us, it is hard not to agree that there must be greater involvement of schools in the local community. Community participation and partnership with schools can be a positive force for bringing the community together and giving people in it an understanding and sense of involvement in the learning process.

All this speaks volumes for the vital part that committed principals, teachers and parents can play in securing community involvement in lifelong learning. But it is clear that, in order to play a primary and invigorating role in leading the learning community, the school will need to be properly resourced. We have found that many teachers and principals in schools are receptive to the ideas behind lifelong learning in and with the community but there is a widespread agreement that, at the end, if there are few resources of personnel, funds, time and space, the chances of such an initiative's succeeding will be greatly reduced. With such resources, however, schools can achieve a great deal in community outreach and help to bring about an awareness of the importance of lifelong learning activities.

Resources can of course come to a school via a number of pathways – the employing authority, sponsorship from business, industry and commerce, special grants from non-profit-making organizations, interested community groups, churches, artistic and cultural agencies, parents and friends. In respect of the latter, however, we have to be cautious: evidence suggests that there is a dis-proportion about the ways in which schools can seek sources of financial support for their activities that can lead to some schools being starved of the funding necessary to run programmes. In some areas a large proportion of the parents are on some form of social or unemployment benefit; in others the proportion of such parents is very low. It is for such reasons that the impetus towards increasing community participation, particularly in funding the work of schools, can cause problems for some members of the community, parents and the schools them-selves.

Many schools have traditionally received substantial support and contribu-tions from their community, and that is a valuable starting-point for a community lifelong learning endeavour. This kind of approach is largely to do with financial assistance and the willingness to take part in school governance, both of which can be activities that are, relatively speaking, at some distance from the educational 'front-line': but this is only one kind of approach to enhancing educational opportunity. The challenge of lifelong learning with which we are grappling is much larger, extensive and more protean. Lifelong education is not so much a supervenient service to the educational goods provided by initial learning in the school: it involves all people in education and the wider community tackling the problem of transforming traditional conceptions of education and replacing them with an awareness of the importance of education across the life-span as an institution and agency of economic, social and cultural advance.

The appreciation of the need for such a reorientation of thinking could well take some time to permeate community attitudes and flow through to the activities of the school. For what is involved here is nothing less than the imperative to get people to accept and then become comfortable with the idea that they will need continually to improve and update their knowledge and skills. What has to be demonstrated clearly and persuasively is that an acceptance of the need for lifelong learning and an engagement in lifelong learning activities will bring benefits to all. All agencies concerned with education, particularly the school, need to engage in a process of the sowing and broadcasting of a set of seminal ideas and the enculturation of those ideas to the point at which acceptance of the benefit of a lifelong approach to education will grow throughout the community.

Many educators now appreciate that they should try to foster a growing awareness in the community of the need for lifelong education and a willingness to recognize the need for learning at different stages through life. One means of achieving this might be by way of an awareness-raising campaign; this can certainly be arranged through a variety of media outlets and broadcasting agencies. Another way of doing it is through the teachers and school communities themselves establishing exemplary models of constant learning and renewal: a start could be made by having a few pilot schools that are willing to undertake the exercise being given freedom to develop their own links with the community and document their experiences. The results can be disseminated so that other places have a basis of experience to follow.

In all such endeavours schools need to explain the benefits of lifelong learning so that acceptance of the need for it and the adoption of the requisite behaviours for it come about through the choices and actions of community members, not only through the work of professional educators. The important point is that greater attention needs to be given to integrating the educational activities – formal and informal – offered by the school, the work-place, the family home and the community centre, to make it clear that all can work together to improve and extend people's knowledge and skills and develop a quality of life which is intellectually and socially fulfilling.

One of a school's obligations in attempting to build new partnership relations with the various constituencies in its community is to be aware of and sensitive to the demands of the different social, cultural and religious commitments that structure and define productive, tolerable and agreeable forms of life for such constituencies. One of a school's most important tasks is to ensure that such groups co-operate with it for the benefit of the society they inhabit.

For some schools this will involve the discussion of cultural and religious issues. This will necessitate all sides attempting to appreciate differences in matters of religion, culture and value in order that understanding may be enhanced and capitalized upon and misunderstanding diminished. Such understandings will enable different groups to come together with more confidence on matters of mutual interest and concern affecting the future of their children and the community. Many schools already have considerable experience of working with different ethnic communities and religious groups, many of whom, while having their own views on events taking place around them, are nevertheless aware of the importance of inter-group understanding and social cohesiveness as preconditions for individual growth in a democratic and just society.

If schools are prepared to allow for, to tolerate and to welcome with understanding different religious and cultural groups as part of the school and the school community, there is likely to be a greater potential for the development of intercultural and interfaith understanding, tolerance and sympathy. This will ensure that, when contentious matters of curriculum content, student-centred styles of learning, innovatory modes of assessing student progress and unfamiliar approaches to discipline are discussed, parents and others from various groups will feel that they have a part to play in determining such issues and will be confident that their point of view is sincerely sought and welcomed.

Learning to be open in this way to the views of others is itself a beneficial effect of a school that is 'open' to its community. But such an attitude is not something that develops easily or quickly; in some people that kind of openness and tolerance takes many years to mature. This is another reason for seeking to develop an understanding of the importance of lifelong learning and a commitment to its value.

Such a commitment is not something that schools can impose on the community; it must be worked on and developed over a long period of time. Its growth will be facilitated by the way in which schools and other educating agencies can arrange for people to bring into schools their professional talents and their vocational skills and deploy them into the pattern of their functioning and engagements in their normal everyday lives.

Schools and all educating agencies have to spread the message of the benefits of lifelong learning so that more and more people will want to take advantage of them. If people become more aware of the advantages offered to them by engaging in lifelong learning they will be able to furnish education providers with information on the kinds of opportunities and activities they want to see laid on by schools and other learning agencies, as a prerequisite for accessing those good things that are conducive to social as well as individual betterment.

LIFELONG LEARNING AND THE LEARNING FAMILY

From the moment of birth, children are launched into a world of learning. Some of these learnings are formal and active, in the sense that children come to acquire them by activities involving directed attention, and work, with conscious and deliberate purpose, organized or facilitated for them. Other activities are more informal: these have to do with the ways in which children come to acquire patterns of belief and behaviour, with no overt intervention or directing action on the part of others. Yet other learning children acquire even more informally, by undergoing particular processes. Some of these types of learning – such as the processes of hand–eye co-ordination or body loco-motor control – are gradually mastered more as a function of the individual's physical maturation than through the direct intervention of others. Other processes, involving children's conforming to and gradually adopting particular conventions, customs or habits are acquired, not so much as a result of maturation but rather more by a process akin to that of osmosis. That is, by being immersed in an environment of interpersonal contact and interconnection, children learn how to communicate and how to behave in ways that do not offend other people.

Some of these skills can be taught formally in a school or other educational environment; others are so fundamental a part of our being human that they begin to be learnt in early childhood and in the company of other members of our family and extended family. It is here that we realize the cradle of lifelong learning is that in which the first stirrings of learning are experienced – the family.

The family informally begins the process which the school and other institutions later continue. The work of bringing young children into the social world and the world of learning begins inevitably and necessarily in the home. The basis of and the induction into the need to learn is set in train upon the arrival of the newly born child into the family's world. It is here that the stage is prepared for all the learning that the individual child will need to acquire on the way to developing independence and autonomy. The child's introduction to that need begins at the beginning of life in the family.

It is for that reason that children's parents are rightly seen as crucial agents of their familiarization with the notion of learning as a process and an activity that, one way or another, will continue throughout life. Indeed if parents are not convinced or concerned about the profound significance of this notion – the idea that learning, whether it occurs informally or is worked at consciously, is something that will and must continue throughout the whole of an individual's life-span – then it will be difficult for children to come to appreciate and value the concept of lifelong learning.

Parents' commitment to helping their children's growth in knowledge, awareness and skill will be exhibited and deployed via their encouragement of their children in their learning, their provision of resources and artefacts of various kinds in an environment that is conducive to learning, their seeking out and providing experiences and activities in which children can extend the boundaries of their knowledge and abilities, their attitudes to study and school, the way they speak to their children, their approaches to the media and the apparatus of modern information technology, their parenting skills, and their own interest in and engagement in attempts to promote their own continuing growth and development. All these things will contribute to a positive response to the question of whether their children have some conception of their own learning and some informed views on their own preferred styles and directions of learning for the future. These are important ways in which families can function as a source and a stimulus towards increasing the understanding of the meaning and value of lifelong learning.

Campbell (1992, pp. 2–3) has identified a number of characteristics of the family which encourages learning. Such a family has:

- a feeling of control over their lives;

- a frequent communication of high expectations to children;

- a family dream of success for the future;

- a recognition of hard work as a key to success;

- an active, not a sedentary, lifestyle;

- a perception of the family as a mutual support system and problem-solving unit;

- an adherence to clearly understood household rules, consistently enforced;

- frequent contact with teachers.

Schmidt (1986) has reported on a successful programme of 'Parents and schools as partners in preschool education' in Massoutah, Illinois, in which parents spend 90 minutes each week observing their pre-schoolers who have been designated as being 'at risk' engaged in learning activities. During the remainder of the week, the parents take the teacher's role at home. Schmidt concludes:

> With training and guidance provided by the teacher, parents are encouraged to assume an active role in the education of their children and to enter into a real partnership with the school. This partnership brings about changes in the home environment that benefit not only the child in the programme, but younger and older siblings as well. The children experience a more cognitively stimulating home environment.
>
> (Schmidt, 1986, p. 41)

The notion of the learning family and its link to lifelong learning has a number of dimensions and possibilities for the school. There are important areas of value and content in the school curriculum which all agree are vital to getting young people 'started right'. Families will understandably want to have a large say in and about the ways in which young people learn about human relationships; the rights and responsibilities of being a family member; and the beliefs, principles and practices arising from their commitments, some of which may be to particular religious denominations, for example. Certainly there is much that young people can learn about such important matters in environments external to the family and the school; but success in ensuring effective learning in all such areas will be promoted by incorporating the educative impulses afforded by the obligations and responsibilities of belonging to a family and a community into the life of the school.

One very powerful way in which this can be promoted and advanced is through parental involvement in their children's school learning activities. This may, in turn, necessitate providing access to lifelong learning courses for parents through the agency of their children's schools, using school facilities and other resources that can be formally and institutionally provided. Through various ways and means of involving parents in the whole range and time-span of their activities, schools and other educating institutions can do a great deal to build up a sense of community in the area in which they function as 'centres' of the different constituencies that constitute their particular 'learning community'.

Such an approach establishes between schools and parents – and indeed between them both and other groups in that community – a sense of partnership in learning. The start of this is making parents equal in the choice and direction of the educational experiences and activities being offered to and determined for the child. Parents' goodwill and active co-operation is enhanced by their being engaged in knowing how to participate in advancing their children's learning.

This carries the corollary that parents need to know and understand more, not only about the innovations in content which are being laid before their children, but also about current changes in approach to teaching and learning, so that they, for their part, can support and assist with their children's endeavours to gain understanding and attain the requisite degree of competence in the subjects of formal learning. There is an increasing need for parents to take courses that will familiarize them with recent developments in concepts of knowledge and theories of learning. This is an area in which schools can provide a real service to lifelong learning in the local community. For if schools and learning agencies generally can achieve success in getting more parents and other members of interested groups involved in the learning of the young, then it is likely that schools will succeed in getting broader acceptance of the changes in schooling that are being brought about as a result of the increasing emphasis on lifelong learning in schools, other educating institutions and society generally.

If we accept that schools and parents must share an understanding and work in partnership with each other for the potential of lifelong learning to be realized, then each side of the partnership has to listen to the other and feel that they will have their own concerns attended to; those concerns will also be modified by the effect that the legitimate interests of the other has on them. An example may be found in the concern of many parents that their young people should start learning to specialize at a relatively early age in those particular subjects that they feel will be of best use to them. One of the difficulties of early specialization is that it is often encouraged by parents because they still believe that early concentration on a particular set of skills and knowledge content will secure their children employment; for many parents getting a job for their children is the critical issue and the chief mark of success of education and schooling. Parents who continue to hold this view are, however, somewhat short-sighted. They need to be made aware that skills and content that seem to be important at the present time will be either obsolescent or redundant in ten years. They have not caught up with the message of lifelong learning, that the present generation of young people is being educated for jobs in the twenty-first century that have not yet been thought of, do not have a name, or for which no need has yet appeared. Schools need to look at ways in which they can help parents in the development and enlargement of their own understandings of social and economic changes, help them expand their own intellectual and cognitive horizons, and expose them to the importance of preparing young people to be adaptable and flexible in meeting the challenges of the future.

At the same time as there are contributions that the school can make to the potential growth of learning in and through the family, there are, from the other side of the partnership, an immense range and number of benefits accruing to schools' educational activity from the gifts, skills and contacts that parents can bring. One of the potential benefits of greater parental involvement, for instance, is that parents can provide the links necessary for connection to and engagement with other community agencies, groups and constituencies. Links with such groups and interests can be initiated by parents who have community, commercial or industry connections. Such connections can often start with the interests and activity of the parents. Sometimes the linkages are forged from the work of a teacher or a community group or a person from business, commerce or trade who has educational aims and purposes very close to the heart of their interests, be they industrial, social or political.

Strategies for Promoting Increased Involvement by Parents in the Education of Their Children, in the School and in Their Own Lifelong Learning

In the concept of the learning family, then, we see how one of the chief educating institutions of our society has its starting-point and offers further pathways for learning. This is why one of the main connections of schools to their host community must consist in and be measured by the linkages it forges with parents. It is important, however, that parental involvement in learning partnerships with schools and engagement in their activities should involve all elements of a school's community, not merely the few who can be relied upon to turn up at 'Parents' evenings', or those who have the time, money or knowledge to make a contribution to school management operations and activities.

The relationships we envisage here are far more complex and are closely linked to the lives and values of all members of the surrounding community. The complexity of the interactions and interrelationships between home, school and family lead rapidly to the insight that community involvement in schools is not merely about managing schools or helping in the raising of funds. The emphasis needs to be on extending and enhancing the ways in which students can more effectively and securely enjoy and succeed in their learning. This means that parents need to be involved in helping to plan and deliver those learning experiences and activities which will be conducive to good teaching and learning.

In this undertaking educating institutions will have to plan and put in place a range of strategies for engaging parents' attention and interest in learning, and for winning their collaboration and support. Such strategies will need to draw upon the capabilities for action and contribution that are specific and relevant to that community. There are some general principles, of course: parents need to be personally invited and engaged in some specific role and set of activities; they must be welcomed into the school: there should be a space, a parents' room, or a 'Drop-In' centre in the school, where parents feel at home, a place in which they feel they really belong in the school.

There are other ways in which a sense of partnership, co-operation and community may be developed in schools. These will include such styles and fora of engagement and interaction as are found in: establishing representative committees at local level; using a broad range of people on sub-committees; or developing special interest parent groups.

There is much more to such a partnership than strategies such as these, however. Schools can also offer a service to families and help the parents and extended family of their younger students by providing them with opportunities to engage in their own lifelong learning. Indeed, we might point out that parents themselves constitute one of the biggest markets for lifelong learning. Teachers often find that their children's parents are unaware of the magnitude and complexity of the changes in subject content or styles and technologies of learning that have appeared since the time they were themselves in school. As a result some parents are often confused, bewildered and occasionally even angry about what is happening in their children's education. Because some parents are unfamiliar with or do not understand the reasons for many recent developments, they feel that they have lost control over their children's learning and are far from being equal partners in what should essentially be a collaborative relationship.

It is for such reasons that some schools are now trying to inform parents about more recent changes in curriculum, teaching and learning methods, school organization, and so on. For all schools to do this and to involve their parents and community more fully in their work is one of the major forms of lifelong learning for personal empowerment and development. In order to educate children and young people well schools must also educate their parents. For their part parents need to be aware of their own role in, but also their own opportunities for, capitalizing upon and fulfilling their own lifelong learning, as well as that of their children.

This point is illustrated by Nuckolls (1991, p. 45) who comments that: 'When literacy becomes a family affair, the challenges for all concerned may be formidable – but the rewards are immeasurable.' Referring to the way in which the problem of family literacy has been approached by the 'Parents and Literacy' (PAL) programme in Tucson, Arizona, he notes that:

> [This programme] began with parent classes in school and has evolved into a home visitation model. Our collaborative curriculum emerges from students' needs and parents' skills. By pushing the limits of the parents' proficiency, we can also push the limits of the student's potential for school achievement.
>
> (Nuckolls, 1991, p. 45)

Nuckolls gives an example of one mother whose learning to read with her son not only changed the behaviour of the son but also changed the whole character and tone of the relationships between all members of his class: 'The mood and the dynamics of that classroom were changed by one mother with the courage to grow with her children.'

In addition to the support and personal and professional service such programmes provide, schools can offer additional learning opportunities for the whole family. A school can play a great part, for example, in offering and conducting programmes for introducing people to the skills of parenting and the ways in which parenting problems can be approached. Schools are well placed to offer parent effectiveness programmes and some schools and school systems have been particularly effective in integrating parenting programmes into the whole moral dimension and commitment of the school. The moral dimension is particularly important in modern times of changing family structures and relationships. The fragility of some family relationships can place enormous stress on some children and schools have an opportunity here to be a source of strength, support and practical assistance for such children, their families and others in the wider community.

In addition, in times of rapid economic change and increasing unemployment, when the need for the skills of literacy and numeracy is particularly pressing, schools can help parents and families address these needs: they can offer courses in literacy and be providers and presenters of Adult Literacy Courses. Similarly with respect to the skills of numeracy and mathematical thinking generally, schools can provide courses in numeracy and modern mathematics for whole families, in which parents and other members of the family who may be challenged in this way may profit.

This is particularly important with our communities' increasing use of and reliance on the communicative devices of modern computer technology, advances and developments in which bid fair to exacerbate and increase the generation gap between adults and young people. In this respect schools can be an immense force for good, because they can give parents a chance to keep up with their children. Schools can capitalize on the interest of parents in these matters and assist them to undertake lifelong learning courses in a structured way. They can offer various forms and styles of attendance on courses on computers, either in small or in large groups. All that is necessary is the realization that schools constitute a capital resource that is available twenty-four hours a day.

Wheeler (1992, pp. 34–5) identifies a number of things that schools can do to promote parental engagement:

- Keep records of school–parent contact, possibly with one teacher acting on behalf of all the teachers of a particular student. Contacts should be monthly.

- Initially use activities where children can experience success and report success, i.e. adopt a positive approach.

- Translate materials for students whose parents do not speak English.

- Listen to suggestions parents make about their children.

- Encourage parents to visit the school. Issue invitations to specific events.

- Get support from local businesses and community agencies – be specific.

- Offer parents fun, family and food at school functions.

- Provide support for parents on parenting.

- Build trust.

- When there is a serious problem, act at once.

Brandt (1989) also identifies a number of useful strategies for promoting parental engagement in the work of schools:

- Educators need to know their goals for parental involvement.

- Methods of involving parents must take heed of parents' situations, e.g. work commitments, location, etc.

- Parents want to work with their child at home and need direction in this regard.

- Effort must be made to secure parental involvement beyond grades 2 or 3.

- Communication from school to home needs to be in simple, readable, jargon-free English or in the language spoken by the family.

- Look for volunteer work out of school hours and involve people other than current student parents and community members.

- Develop new forms of recruiting and training of parental leaders.

- Appoint a lead teacher for school and family connections.

- If schools take parental involvement seriously and work to involve all parents, then social class and parents' level of education decrease or disappear as important factors.

Loucks (1992, p. 23) identifies the importance of strategies such as: parent/student switch day; parent/student fund-raising; teachers in the round; good news awards; newsletters; parent/teacher organizations; selecting parent/family volunteers/alumni events; parent classes/invitational events. Loucks concludes: 'Be creative and innovative, find out what your parents and students want, and then entice them and/or challenge them to become involved. The benefits are well worth the time and effort'.

Rich (1984), in a report entitled 'Helping parents help their children to learn', reveals the way in which the Home and School Institute has developed four rules for successful parental involvement programmes which have a link to the learning family:

1 Link parents' involvement directly to the learning of their own children.

2 Provide ways for families to teach academic skills at home – home-teaching projects which don't duplicate school work, but which parents and children can do together. The success of this experience indicates that all parents, even those with limited formal education, can help teach children.

3 Link the school's work to the community – set up family learning centres in schools and storefronts. Use senior citizens or teenagers to staff these rooms and share the teaching materials.

4 Provide for parental involvement at all levels of schooling.

Rich concludes that to ensure the acceptance of a home involvement programme, parental involvement must be seen as a legitimate activity of the school, and reaching the family must be considered as important as reaching the child.

Thus there are a number of strategies, ways and means by which schools can act as sources of ideas and action aimed at addressing the needs of one of the most important groups from among their constituents – parents and families. The three important points to be made in this discussion are that:

1 The family has an equal importance with the school as a place and context within which lifelong education can be instituted and protracted.

2 The school and the family have to work in a relation of partnership in order that the lifelong educational endeavours of each shall be maximized and any barriers and constraints lessened.

3 The school can act as a centre of lifelong educational opportunity and can be a provider of educational courses and resources to the whole family of the students who attend it on a compulsory basis during the years of formal schooling. In doing so it is acting out the full implications of its mission to provide educational service to and act as a leader in the whole learning community.

Some Challenges and Barriers to be Overcome

Notwithstanding the opportunities, there are also many challenges to be faced if partnerships between schools and parents in providing and capitalizing on lifelong learning opportunities are to be established and strengthened and the role of leadership to be realized. The incubus of past practices, the inertia of existing institutional arrangements and organizational structures, the inhibiting effect of the expectations and preconceptions which many people both inside and outside the school – teachers, parents, employers – hold about schools' proper role and responsibility as regards its educational purposes have all functioned so as to constrain the school's advance.

Harris and Associates (1987, p. 48) reported on the findings of the *Metropolitan Life Survey of the American Teacher* which:

> ... reveal that teachers and parents have somewhat different things in mind when they ... favour parental involvement inside the school itself. From the teachers' point of view, that involvement would include volunteer work, various supportive activities, and promotional efforts, but would stop short of any large parental role in decision-making over curriculum or school policies. Many teachers are very willing to consult with parents, but hesitate to place them in control. This is quite consistent with the tendency of teachers throughout this series of surveys to feel strongly about and indeed, to want to increase – their professional role in those areas which they consider to be mainly pedagogical in nature. From the parents' point of view, however, many are interested in the entire gamut of possible involvements, including many who would favor placing parents on curriculum committees and management teams with decision-making power. This is a surprisingly strong expressed preference from parents to be involved in all facets of education.

There are thus already in place many barriers: preconceptions about respective roles and responsibilities of teachers and parents, physical structure, organizational arrangement, vision, against the notion that there could be a place for parents to take greater advantage of the educational opportunities offered by schools or for themselves to assist in educational provision and delivery. It is plain that schools would be much richer and more thriving places for education if there were more ways in which parents could be encouraged to come into them, to be warmly welcomed, comfortably accommodated and challengingly involved in their work.

At the moment, unfortunately, the ways in which most schools are structured and run militate against the presence of any group other than children and young people, for whose educational needs and interest they are seen as being primarily established. For example, the idea that schools can be a community educational resource that does not shut down at the end of the formal school day is still strongly contested. Furthermore, many adults are not comfortable in a school environment which is usually child-centred rather than orientated towards an adult culture. Such preconceptions, structures and processes are still found all too often in many schools and tend to lead the exclusion of most other groups, particularly adults.

Of course the supervisory and 'custodial' role of the school is important, particularly in primary schools. A school's responsibility for the safety and welfare of its students at times when they are under its 'guardianship' means that schools and teachers have a legal duty of care towards those with whose progress in the formal and compulsory stages of education they are charged. Such a duty necessarily imposes conditions on the school's openness and accessibility to other groups of people. Notwithstanding this very proper concern, however, it is still important to make parents and other interested parties feel that they do have some sort of access to the opportunities for education offered by a school to all members of its community, even if such access has to be limited in some ways.

To turn this situation around, to redress what many see as exclusion, and to capitalize upon the opportunities for providing educational services to a wide range of members of the community is a major undertaking, requiring substantial changes of many dimensions. It will demand a considerable change in attitudes, a reconceptualization of schools' educational purposes, and of course the necessary funding and resources to provide for the extension of educational benefits and opportunities to the community more generally.

This will involve altering and reconstructing present conceptions and cultures in schools to make them more accepting of and acceptable to adults. Schools need to be demystified in the minds of considerable numbers of their constituents. Unless and until schools succeed in remodelling themselves, or being assisted or required to do so, and in bringing about and presenting a transformation of themselves and the ways in which they act and are perceived, there will continue to be groups of parents, especially those who themselves did not succeed in schools, who will feel and who will be isolated from them. At present, many parents are inclined to view schools only as places to go for advice and assistance when their children are in some sort of difficulty or trouble.

In order to transform such attitudes schools will have to work hard and often against the grain of existing preconceptions. They will need to dismantle the barriers that frustrate effective and co-operative school–parent partnerships. Such barriers include: apprehension of each other by both groups; lack of knowledge on the part of some teachers as to how to set up effective working relationships with parents and how to use them as agents of real educational transformation; and, in the case of some parents, particularly migrants or those of non-English-speaking backgrounds, some embarrassment about their deficiencies in language and communication skills. The need to care for other children at home or to go out to work are often barriers against the participation of some women in the school's work. One mother we spoke to in the course of our research on lifelong learning puts this experience, and the sense of exclusion and frustration it generates, very clearly: 'As a working mother I play almost no role in my children's school. I put down my name to help but I am available only evenings or weekends. I never hear a word. Schools will miss out if they don't learn to harness the energy of parents who aren't available during school hours. Schools have a role to assist parents in addressing some of the Lifelong Learning issues.'

Last, but by no means least in importance, are the traditional expectations that parents contribute to schools mainly by acting as providers of money, resources, time and effort in particular times or cases of need, rather than being seen as true partners with a mutual interest in the quality and excellence of the work of their school in their own community.

All such factors tend to inhibit the effectiveness of the co-operation between a school and this most important of its groups of stakeholders. Of course, schools will be realistic about this; they will accept, and some parents will make it clear, that not everyone wants to be involved in the life of the school. Most parents want the best for their children but they cannot be available for every form of service or make a constant contribution to the school's undertakings all the time.

There is a further caveat to be made regarding parent–school partnerships. Schools must respond to the reality that there will be members of their school population who are unemployed, living below the poverty line, or disadvantaged in other ways. Some parents may not be able or may not have the confidence or time to become involved in the work of the school, especially when they are in the poverty trap. The problems that schools must try to avoid are those caused by a situation in which it is only the more affluent parents who have the time, energy and confidence to engage in interactions with the school and who can benefit from school–parent partnerships and lifelong learning initiatives. It is here that issues of social justice arise. Governments have a responsibility to ensure that partnerships and lifelong learning opportunities are adequately resourced and inclusive, for access and equity to be assured.

Getting parents involved and active in the life of the school is fundamental to helping to bring about a lifelong approach to learning. But there is an important note of caution to be struck here: both school educators and parents will have to come to terms with and learn how to manage the reductions in stability and in a sense of security which can come about when students move out into the community as schools adopt a lifelong learning approach. Both schools and parents will best help each other when they realize that the dynamic social and economic changes that are doing much to set the stage for lifelong education are likely to take away some of the old certainties and securities and bring in instead a climate of uncertainty, instability and risk.

Given this understanding, schools will need quickly to locate and define the 'comfort zone' within which professional educators and parents can work effectively in partnership with each other. This area needs to be identified, established and then worked on with the aim of broadening and deepening the limits within which school–parent partnerships can operate most constructively and productively for the good of all members of the school's community. In that way schools will quickly learn how best to harness the energies of parents, how to expand parents' understanding of how schools operate and for what purposes, and how to make the fullest and wisest use of the full range of resources available in the community.

From the foregoing, one implication follows immediately. It is that learning about partnerships with parents – and indeed with all constituencies interested in the work of schools in the community – should be part of pre-service teacher education and training and should continue to feature in schemes of professional development. This is important if old stereotypes are to be demolished and negative preconceptions removed. Many teachers believe that, in respect of the education of children and young people, they have a particular professional responsibility and a clearly defined role, and that parents have another, but by no means the same, role. Teachers and parents need to communicate better so that they can work together, in a common direction, for the benefit of all those involved in and capable of benefiting from the education process over the life-span.

LIFELONG LEARNING AND THE MULTICULTURAL COMMUNITY

One of the most common descriptions that people apply when talking about the present composition of many societies is that they are 'multicultural'. What this term means, however, is less widely agreed. For many people it simply refers to the fact that a particular society is now the home of many different ethnic, racial and national groups who have, for various reasons, come from a point of origin in another country or society and settled there along with the original inhabitants of the place. For example, in Australia, since its first European settlement in 1788 most of the country's inhabitants have come to it from distant shores. At the level of historic description, 'multiculturalism' simply means that a country's population is now constituted of representatives and bearers of many different cultures. In this sense 'culture' connotes those structures and patterns of belief, value and practice that specifically character-ize a group observably different in particular physical features and/or certain distinguishing symbols, tongues and behaviours, from other groups. Nothing more than an accidental accumulation of such differences may be meant by 'multiculturalism'.

For many people, however, the arrival of representatives and bearers of different cultures evokes a different response. For people in some countries at earlier times of foreign settlement, the notion uppermost in the beliefs, values and attitudes of government and other civil authorities was that of 'assimila-tion'. According to this notion settlers from abroad had to adjust and accommodate themselves to the dominant culture of the 'home' group and become bearers of that dominant culture themselves.

Another view was that of the 'melting pot' mentality, according to which all new settlers to a new country had to make every effort, along with the existing and still incoming inhabitants of that country, to forge a new culture in which the individual contributions of all cultures would fuse to form a greater, and it was hoped, overall harmonious whole.

A development of this idea was the notion that modern society should be a kind of 'mosaic', in which individual traditions and cultures would maintain their own identity, independence and distinctiveness but would also be inte-grated into some kind of overall configuration, that would in its overall pattern and shape fuse a kind of differentiated harmony in a new political and social environment.

Finally there has been a notion of the desirability of separate development, in which groups from different geographic locations, races, tribes, creeds and colours would live within their own separate locations, maintaining a separate identity and form of life, which would in some way establish 'boundaries' against intrusions from external and incompatible cultural norms, conventions and demands.

These are only a few of the characterizations of the ways in which different ethnic and cultural groups come to constitute a nation's social fabric. There are others set out at greater length in works devoted to the topic (cf. Aspin, 1988). Of these characterizations it seems that, though there may still be, in certain quarters, continuing regard for the 'assimilationist' ideal, there would be few environments now that would base their immigration, ethnic affairs and indigenous peoples policies entirely on that notion. Similarly, recent events in South Africa and elsewhere suggest that, if there was ever anything to be said for the idea of cultural enclaves, that view has been refuted by a growing awareness and acceptance of the need for intercultural understanding and respect for ethnic and cultural diversity as a key feature of a tolerable form of life in modern participative democracies.

Many modern states are now endeavouring to work out various forms of 'mosaic' theory, some with greater, some with lesser, degrees of success. Behind and underlying all such attempts lies a set of principles: widespread acceptance of the need for mutual tolerance; respect for difference; consideration of other people's interests; concern that all should be accorded equality before the law and in all social institutions and political arrangements; and the determination that people should be able to exercise and enjoy full civil rights and entitlements freely and without being subject to duress. Thus any form of multiculturalism today takes as a basis the ethical principles of respecting all human beings and trying to work out ways and means of the various groups that constitute our society living harmoniously together while maintaining important cultural differences.

This task requires the work of educational and social agencies of all kinds. One way of building tolerance is to have people fully informed about the possibility of unity and differences in diversity. Beginning with children and young people in school, there is a need for people to understand others in their society, accepting and respecting each other's differences.

There can be problems on all sides here, though. Many migrant and minority ethnic communities are still relatively hindered in their attempts to achieve social recognition and emancipation because of their as yet restricted communication skills. Among ethnic and indigenous groups in many societies there are many who are information-poor and speech articulation-poor in the dominant language. There is also the view that some of the social practices of such groups are not congruent with the norms, conventions and values of the dominant society. From the perspective of some members of minority ethnic communities, their sense of dislocation from their own geographical origins and the desire not to 'lose touch' with the deepest parts of their identities lead them to adhere even more firmly to the cultural mores and values that they brought with them from their places of origin. This can lead to isolation from the bulk of the community.

Any society concerned about the integration of all its citizens into the body politic and concerned to have them fully taking up their rights and privileges, as well as answering to their social obligations and civic responsibilities, will want to address such attitudes, since they could lead to division and social tension. Modern societies with a commitment to social inclusion will want to try to break down barriers between their constituent cultures and bring people together.

This requires the work of educational and other social institutions. Schools and other educational agencies have a part to play in informing people and trying to give them the disposition to be open to the larger world beyond their parochial subcultures and local groups.

Included among the strategies that a school might employ are: initiatives of community development, the arranging of cultural and ethnic celebrations, and the arranging of social occasions where people come together and share. Schools can also work with different community ethnic, cultural and religious groups in the interest of community development more generally, particularly where community resources, such as schools, libraries, arts and cultural centres, sporting venues and recreational facilities and the like, are available and worthy of support and promotion.

In the effort to give such support and assistance to agencies and institutions that provide for and further the welfare of all sectors of the community, there will clearly be times when people from widely different backgrounds, and of widely different tastes and inclinations, can join together; where differences are valued and accepted. This means that learning communities more widely should respect the ethnic, cultural, spiritual and religious dimensions of the lives of their members. They can promote and achieve this by setting forth what the different ethnic and cultural groups can offer each other.

In this undertaking we already have some fine examples of some people and cultural groups acting as leaders in the learning community. In a suburb of Melbourne, Australia, for example, the imam of the local mosque tries to enlarge the strong relationship between his community and all the people around it by speaking to schools and other groups about his faith, life and work. Jewish organizations too are very active in promoting links with their community and in integrating their cultural activities into the broader community life.

There is a need to involve the whole range of ethnic community leaders and structures and organizations, television, press and radio in an attempt to increase social inclusion, emancipation and eventually a wider integration of such groups into society. The multi-ethnic and multicultural nature of many modern communities should be presented to students in ways that encourage acceptance of every individual as a human being to be respected. Schools can promote a spirit of working together to serve the needs and interests of all citizens – common, joint, communitarian and diverse.

A part of this will consist in providing opportunities for lifelong learning for members of ethnic groups. One way in which this can be tackled is through the provision of language and literacy courses. There are many older members of ethnic communities – and especially women – who still feel themselves inhibited from identifying and seeking out opportunities that would allow them to have access to a culture whose major language and cultural values are alien to them. There are major areas of need for lifelong learning for members of such groups: they lie in providing adults with general skills of literacy and numeracy and thus introducing them easily to English as a second language with its own world of listening and speaking skills.

Schools can also offer a service by running community programmes in their constituent groups' own languages. It is often the older and more recent arrivals who are disadvantaged in lifelong learning when schools and other institutions persist in restricting themselves to using only English as the language of instruction. Adult literacy courses can readily be conducted in a neighbourhood school, starting in the community language(s) and moving on to English as people grow in comfort and confidence. Helping ethnic minorities make progress in English in this way has other advantages too. It can be used as a focus to initiate people into the idea of lifelong learning. Literacy programmes can also be used as a focal point for integrating other programmes for the acquisition of life-enhancing skills. We know that adults learn better if the skills they are working to acquire are embedded in a process that is intelligible and has direct relevance to their daily lives. In addition, through language classes and other fora, greater awareness of the need for intercultural and inter-group understanding can be promoted.

There is a powerful and indeed overriding need for education institutions to work at increasing the community's understanding of indigenous people and their culture and to promote respect for these throughout the school curriculum. In the aboriginal community in Australia, for example, great value is attached to an holistic learning environment, in which all elements and persons are involved. Here it is important to have parents and members of extended families coming to and learning in schools, for this has the added advantage not only of helping adults to learn but also of enabling the adults' learning successes to serve as model and motivation for the efforts of younger indigenous people.

Schools, in planning multi-ethnic curricula and a multicultural programme of educational services, will need to stress the value of diversity. Part of this will be to promote awareness by various ethnic and cultural groups of their own educational potential and the advantages of looking outwards and going beyond the boundaries of their own religious and ethnic communities.

This last point needs to be stressed. For the multi-ethnic and multicultural composition of our society makes us aware that the learning community has not only cultural but also religious dimensions. Our policies for education and other agencies must be sensitive to this and be prepared to accommodate to such differences. Schools need to develop an inclusive language in respect of faith issues and to introduce students to different traditions of faith and practice in an inclusive rather than an excluding way.

A specially helpful way of doing this is in the ecumenical service model in operation in the involvement of religious leaders in the work of schools. Representatives of different faiths have their own part to play in increasing information and expanding the boundaries of tolerance and showing the ethical basis for the principle of tolerance. Such approaches will foster a process of growing together in the community. For, we might say, among the purposes of the school, two of the most critical are to pass on the cultural heritage we have and to challenge it critically, where it fails and where it can grow, so that the community that bears it can grow into a better civilization, more democratic, and one that lives the values of the moral commitments that embody its basic religious beliefs. Schools are being well served in this by contributions from a number of churches and religious organizations which are providing for school students services which themselves are manifestations of an all-over approach to lifelong cultural, religious and moral commitments. These also have potential for developing and securing lifelong learning.

LIFELONG LEARNING AND SOCIAL INCLUSIVENESS

Another part of promoting a policy of access and inclusiveness in offering lifelong learning opportunities to the community is to ensure that no one as a result of handicap or disadvantage is barred from taking advantage of such opportunities offered. In planning lifelong learning opportunities it is important that, in pursuit of the principles of equality and social justice and in the interests of a better integrated community, schools make facilities available to the disadvantaged and those with disabilities.

There are many forms of disadvantage, however, not merely those in which people are intellectually or physically challenged in some way. Disadvantaged groups include some seniors in our society, dwellers in rural environments or far distant locations, people who are housebound, and people who suffer from difficulties of all kinds that inhibit their taking advantage of opportunities. It is very important to build up networks in the community to act as points of reference and sources of support for the housebound, older people, and those who suffer from 'the tyranny of distance', and thus to make learning accessible to them.

Among those who are hindered from achieving easy access to sources and units of learning are those who suffer from anxieties of various kinds. Among such anxieties, one that can be especially disabling is anxiety about new modes of computer literacy and communication by means of modern technology. The new literacy of today includes technical literacy and if one is not adept in using it, there is a decided sense in which one is disadvantaged. This is particularly so for some seniors in our society: there is a real need for our senior citizens to become computer-literate, in order that they may be able to function more effectively in our community, as well, of course, as to add to their own sources of satisfaction and enjoyment. Banking and shopping, for example, can be made much easier for those with the requisite technical skills.

In this endeavour an important step forward will be to target specific groups who need access. In order to identify such groups it is important to make liaisons with key agencies in the local community and make use of the information that can be provided to schools and other education centres by doctors, clinics, local council employees, and so on. Where schools have outreach programmes responding to the needs of the whole community, they should aim to have the maximum use made of their facilities, making them accessible to people with disabilities and people of all ages in the community.

There are many forms that such access could take. There is, for example, a strong interest in life writing courses. These can be taken on a correspondence basis by people who are housebound. There can also be telematic links built into these activities. Sometimes people simply want to have someone with whom they may have contact and share their learning about writing: lifelong learning can have enormous value in simply providing a form of social contact for the isolated in our community. One other avenue to explore will be to develop and target programmes to expand people's leisure options and in this way to give them an entrée into community groups and the larger society.

Lifelong education programmes can also help people who are in some ways challenged or disadvantaged to become better aware of their civic, political and social rights and privileges. This can start at the level of helping people in Ministry of Housing projects to establish where to go and how to handle particular sorts of difficulties they may encounter with the fabric of their homes or the range and level of services available to them. Such an approach can broaden into a form of thoroughgoing political education that could end with some learners seeking to represent their constituency's interests by standing for election to public office. These are examples of some of the beginning points for those lifelong learning activities and structures that can promote and enhance social inclusion.

THE SCHOOL AS A LEARNING COMMUNITY

In opening up opportunities for lifelong learning and in modelling the learning community, schools should look beyond their current mode of operation, which often tends to be inward-looking and focused only on providing education to those students who come to them on a full-time basis during and shortly after the compulsory years of schooling. Schools need to transform that approach, to look beyond their boundaries and to consider their communities as areas for expansion of their educational effort. Schools can try to identify what they, in consultation with other groups, believe to be community needs for educational provision and then work jointly to develop and articulate strategies that will involve the community more fully and better in the education process. It is, after all, part of the role of an organization to examine itself and make an assessment as to whether or not it is fulfilling in its role in the most effective way. Offering educational services to individuals and groups in its surrounding community who have learning needs that the school can satisfy is part of the school's *raison d'être*. Schools that understand this and have envisioned for themselves a broader role in serving the community are more likely to open up their facilities and to develop them more extensively for the use and benefit of all the community.

It is unfortunate that traditionally many school doors have been firmly closed against the entry of the community. It is difficult for schools, that in the past have seen themselves as closed organizations, to change their attitudes towards becoming open institutions that can provide many sources of information and possible avenues of expansion to cater for the needs of people who have very different learning requirements from those of children and young people. Yet schools are a community resource; they are funded and supported by the community, and part of their responsibility is to be open, available and accountable to the community.

This means that schools need to consider being open for many more hours, making their facilities and skills a general community resource, serving the community of which they are a part. They must keep in mind that adults operate on different agendas of time and other conditions that will facilitate easy learning. In future we need to envisage schools expanding their roles, being far more community-based, with different groups coming in, mixing, interacting with and affecting each other. We need to see the school as a resource centre which is open and available, where facilities are made available to those who have learning needs of any kind. For accessing these resources is going to enrich the community and help people to improve the quality of their lives.

Schools can provide training and recreational venues for the community, in the daytime as well as in out-of-school hours. This might mean setting up forms of organization, administration and teaching and learning that differ considerably from more traditional methods and procedures. Groups of adult learners can, for example, run courses in the school for the community, in which they provide the resources, staffing, and the curriculum while the school provides merely a room and a whiteboard. Schools can also be seen or constituted as cultural venues, just like community centres, libraries, public buildings, and other facilities for public edification and enjoyment. Indeed in small or rural communities they can be the main cultural venue for the local community.

The above are among the many reasons why schools must use their available time, space and resources to offer educational services to parents as well as children, to older members of their community as well as to the younger ones. They must want to have a broader role in the community. But, as we have noted, one of the key preconditions for succeeding in fulfilling this role is accessibility, and providing and guaranteeing that accessibility is one of the key issues for lifelong learning. This accessibility can be best secured and more widely encouraged by schools participating with other groups and agencies in their environment for the extension of educational offerings in and to the wider community.

Schools need to be contributors to the management of their own learning environment by seeking help, advice and resources from those cultural, ethnic and religious organizations in the community that themselves have a strong part to play in promoting learning. In this endeavour schools can connect with neighbourhood houses, community libraries, health centres, the police, child care providers, hospitals, universities, colleges, industry, trades unions, local councils and libraries, Probus groups, and radio and television stations. All of these agencies, service-providers and institutions need to interact, collaborate and form links and interactive networks by which their promise and provision of more numerous and more frequent occasions of educational benefit can be assured and more diverse and sophisticated collections of learning resources may be generated and afforded them.

One might argue that there needs to be some sort of local community arrangement or structure to make possible the setting up of some kind of process for bringing the various community groups together. Local councils could have a role to play in putting such structures and processes in place, to enable projects of community value and benefit to be undertaken by groups working together. People can experience considerable individual benefit from working on a project that has some meaning both for them and for other groups in the community.

Schools could publicize and provide information about all kinds of lifelong learning activity in the community. They could provide a one-stop shop where people could go and identify things they might want to learn about or courses they might want to take. As things stand at the moment, few people can use schools to access the requisite or appropriate information, let alone identify the actual courses they might take. The task of setting forth and of offering lifelong learning opportunities is increasingly devolving upon community centres and non-traditional forms of education. To add schools to this list of centres of provision could easily be arranged through the work of such bodies as local councils, Councils of Adult Education and other agencies, which could work with schools and help with the provision of support.

One source of such support comes from people in the community itself. There is an enormous resource of people in late middle age and those who are older who are looking for a continuing role in society and need to feel that they have some part to play as useful members of society. There must be ways of making links with those who have expertise involving them. There is a whole range of possible structures and procedures, formal or informal models of arrangement or institutions, such as, perhaps, something like a mentor scheme that could be considered and examined creatively, so that people of all ages and conditions might be provided with space and time for lifelong learning. This is one way in which community providers can identify and reclaim those for whom schools have not provided an adequate foundation for lifelong learning and provide them with sources of inspiration and alternative avenues of advancement.

Enrichment of community life by the networks of schools, local councils, community organizations and agencies of all kinds has the potential of fostering a sense of responsibility, community involvement, social trust and reciprocity. For, insofar as people engage in giving to the community and contribute to the setting up and running of community activities, by so much does the community benefit.

Chapter 8

Establishing Relationships with Business, Industry and Commerce

The importance of there being a range of relationships between schools, business and industrial and commercial concerns is not a matter of the rhetoric of school–community relations or of schools seeking philanthropic benefits from their links with such agencies. Such partnerships are seen these days much more as a matter of survival.

In this chapter we shall focus upon the relationships and partnerships that schools can forge with particular groups in business and other commercial, industrial and professional groups. We shall be particularly concerned to draw lessons from past dysfunctions in such relationships and to delineate those features that make them work well. We shall explore the impact of such relationships upon such important goals as better and more effective preparation of students for the workforce, creating shared goals among educators and employers and other industrial and commercial interest groups, and influencing the behaviour of business, industry and commerce. These joint endeavours will be put in the context of the interest both schools and such groups have in the formation of partnerships, whose positive collaboration and effective working can function as rich sources of community development and lifelong learning.

DECENT CORPORATE CITIZENSHIP

The need for a new approach to the building of partnerships between educational institutions and the industrial and commercial sectors arises from the increasing recognition on the part of both business and education that education and training is now the critical resource for any kind of growth and development in the economy, society and community. How such growth is to be assured and such development strengthened is not fully clear but the realization of the vital importance of the linkage between education, industry and commerce and economic growth and development exists, and business appreciates that it must play a part in promoting that relationship and that it must get involved in schooling.

It is clear, then, that there must be a range of relationships between schools and the education and training sector generally, and business and industry in the private sector, in order to promote ends to which they both subscribe. There will be a multiplicity of such relationships and the forms these take will be complex, varied and multifaceted.

Merenda (1989) draws attention to the number of different *levels* at which partnerships between private sector business and commercial interests and schools operate. He describes the various levels at which such partnerships and business involvement in schools operate in the USA:

1 Partnerships at the level of policy in which co-operative efforts are made by businesses, schools and public officials to shape the public and political debate about schools, leading to changes in legislation or governance.

2 Partnerships in systemic educational improvements, focusing on the identification of needed reforms and then working to bring them about.

3 Partnerships in management at the school level.

4 Partnerships in teacher training, in which businesses become involved in teacher and career counsellor training and professional development, providing opportunities for professional educators to update, upgrade or maintain skills or to learn about the labour market in the community.

5 Partnerships in the classroom, in which volunteers from the business and industrial sectors bring business or occupational expertise into the classroom or take the class to the business.

At the moment, unfortunately, such a sophisticated and multifaceted approach to the establishment and deployment of school–business partnerships has not developed in all settings to the extent that it might. The forms that such relationships might take and the ways in which they can be played out for the benefit of those concerned is often poorly conceived. At the moment industry gives much to education but, in many settings, this has been on a voluntary, sporadic and very much ad hoc basis. Clearly a new conception of possible relationships between schools and industry and the opportunities they offer for mutual advantage needs to be worked out. There is a need for consultation and communication between all parties involved in creating the new partnerships that are vital for planning the range of opportunities for education and training on a lifelong basis.

For this reason it is important that the basis of the relationship for school–business partnerships be reconsidered. Business, industry and commerce are beginning to realize that the need for their active involvement in education and training has to be put on a rational, coherent and purposive basis. Their commitment to education and training will need to be conceived and played out in ways that will encourage their involvement to be specific, formula-based, targeted and integrated into the overall pattern of the educational investment of the community. For their part schools have to begin approaching this important sector of their local community in different ways – by promoting their image as vital, integral and co-operative partners in the community's educational enterprises.

This becomes especially important with respect to the whole community's interest in lifelong learning. Insofar as all sectors of the community have an interest in lifelong learning and a part to play in making opportunities for engaging in it available and accessible, there will clearly be a role and a responsibility for the corporate and business sectors in promoting lifelong learning and indeed in providing some opportunities for it. For, inasmuch as all institutions, agencies and individual members of society have civic and social responsibilities and rights, duties and privileges, then the business and industrial and commercial sectors are also to be recognized as being, in a quite decided sense, among the leaders of the learning community. It is for that reason that communities need to develop the notion of decent corporate as well as individual citizenship.

THE DEMANDS OF A CHANGING ECONOMY

One of the commonplaces of the movement for lifelong learning is that the knowledge and skills of a nation's workforce will be foremost among the factors that make a country economically competitive.

It is this realization and the impact of competition that have forced companies to become more sophisticated in their market strategies and in their approaches to the preparation, appointment and deployment of their workforce. Their future employees will be confronted with an ongoing need to change and adapt, and many of them will find this disturbing and possibly even destabilizing. The workforce is faced with the reality that changing forms of paid employment and changes in the skills and competencies required to perform in it will necessitate a commitment to continual periods of updating existing knowledge, redirecting old skills and learning new skills. And they may have to do this five or six times in a working lifetime: for many people who are being retrenched from existing industrial or commercial concerns, the options of getting work of exactly the same kind in exactly the same area of industrial or commercial activity are probably relatively limited.

Our community's young will be taking jobs in society that have not yet been named or created, and using equipment that is still found only in science fiction novels. Nowadays therefore schools have to guard against a situation in which their graduating students will be leaving school with skills that are already obsolescent or which can become easily and quickly outmoded.

In industry it is necessary to keep reskilling in the use of the latest tools and equipment and, where a firm's work-people cannot use the latest tools, firms must offer opportunities for retraining, reskilling and possible career redirection. In future, many of a firm's work-people will be exposed to training on the job as a requirement. This means that firms must institute their own education and training programmes and arrange for them to be delivered on site – where, as and when necessary – so that people might learn while continuing to earn. They will also need to arrange for work-release for the upward-skilling and multiskilling of their work-people, and for other industrial concerns or businesses to come together to provide training courses or centres if these are not available through their current provision. The object of schooling then must be to prepare and help people to be constantly reskilled and able to move through a range of occupations during their working lifetime. As part of this, students should be exposed to the demands and differing styles of a range of working and learning environments.

The dynamic character of the expansions in knowledge and the changes in skill called for in employment require a realistic approach to the kinds of knowledge and skill we teach in schools and to the kinds of outcomes which we are looking for in those leaving school. But to prescribe the right kind of curriculum and to educate in the right kind of values and attitudes necessary to face these changes in the wider world of employment is a problem not just for the school to tackle: it is a community problem and the entire community must contribute its resources to its resolution.

There is a further important point to be made here: everyone agrees that there is a legitimate need for the continual upgrading of our vocational skills and an emphasis upon the development of skills of 'learning how to learn', that will be a vital part of work-place change and upward-training. In some quarters, however, this has given rise to a perception that business is not interested in other aspects of lifelong learning. It is a matter of vital importance that when government, business and education leaders meet to discuss education, training and lifelong learning they do not underplay the importance of other aims of lifelong learning – democratic empowerment, social inclusion and personal formation and expansion. Government and businesses would do well to realize that one cannot expect high degrees of productivity from people who are suffering, whose family relationships might be breaking down, or who feel excluded from having a say in the governance and future direction of their society. By contrast, it is widely agreed that when one has a wide range of external interests and is well adjusted and happy in oneself, one's activity and productivity in the work-place improves and one becomes a much better and more effective worker. There is a very real significance in the point that the nature of the goals of lifelong education is triadic: for economic effectiveness; for personal development; and for democratic inclusiveness and empowerment.

In taking account of the interconnectedness of the employment, the personal and the social aspects of people's lives, business and industry can appreciate how much of a benefit they would receive from the interrelationship of all three elements in lifelong learning. They might then reasonably expect to be presented with the justified proposition that they should contribute to all the different aspects of that process as well. Perhaps a beginning could be made on promoting the other vitally important goals of lifelong learning by stressing and making available forms and institutions of work-place democracy and opportunities for individual growth and development in the range of facilities and activities provided available by a firm to its employees. There already exist many examples of such provision in the practices of industrial enterprises of various kinds in Europe and Japan and this should surely be made more widely available elsewhere.

At the same time individual employees must, as autonomous human beings, take greater responsibility for developing their own lives and careers, not merely in business and industry but also in political and social institutions and in the fabric of society generally. In getting citizens to take greater control over and have a sense of direction concerning their own career development, we are moving away from the notion of a paternalistic role for business. It would be even less justified to consider governments adopting such a role: no government group or institution could carry out that particular responsibility. On the contrary, it is the function of industry and government to assist people in developing the strengths and capacities that are vital and indispensable parts of their taking control over the direction of their lives and careers for themselves. That is also a part of the contribution that business and industry can make to lifelong learning. Business and industry cannot be expected to succeed in such an endeavour if the first foundations for it have not been laid down in schools.

A Note of Caution

It is therefore important to observe that the involvement of business in lifelong learning must not result in its being conceived in a narrow vocational way. To start from the premise that lifelong learning is only about technical, vocational and economic goals is to risk simply creating or implementing policies for education and training that are narrow, instrumental and predicated upon the present and the particular. The outcome of such policies might well be the emergence of a population whose concerns for further learning are concentrated purely upon the immediate expediencies of employment objectives and thus make for a society that is narrow and short-sighted in its vision and inward-looking in its concerns.

There is also a danger that an emphasis on vocational education might well perpetuate the myth of a separation between those who work with their heads and those who work with their hands. This might well enforce a cleavage between those who have a vocationally-based education – studying the 'useful' subjects – and those who have been educated in the 'liberal' and non-applied arts and sciences.

Another danger in schools succumbing to pressure to concentrate on educating children and young people on the basis of a utilitarian, vocationally based view of education and training is that schools will really not think hard about offering other educational opportunities for those who may never find employment, showing them what society can offer, helping them develop real life skills separate from employment skills, and preparing them for extended periods of discretionary time in which they will have many opportunities to make choices as to the most fruitful ways in which they can spend their time. In the current social and economic context schools must change their attitude to those who have or are going to have difficulty finding employment or in some other way have difficulty in adjusting to the imperatives and exigencies involved in responding to the challenges and demands of living in modern-day society.

Schools nowadays need not only to help young people acquire the knowledge, skills and competencies requisite for employment, but also to educate people in a sense of civic awareness, duty and social obligation, to be responsible for and to each other, in order to promote their concern for the survival of democracy and their respect for individual autonomy and dignity. For this reason schools need to address the broader range of issues involved in lifelong learning, beyond skills formation, and overcome the narrowness of focused courses by showing that the distinctions some make between 'education for jobs' and 'education for quality of life' are spurious and rest on a misunderstanding of the necessary interrelatedness of vocational and liberal, individual and moral education activities and concerns.

The current emphasis upon skills and competencies in the service of employment and economic development should be employed to show that economics is one of a range of tools and instruments with which we seek to make life better. Nevertheless it is a higher and broader range of values than merely the economic that drives schools as educating institutions, and these values – the moral – are paramount. For they encompass our most basic beliefs and commitments about the kind of society we want and the kind of life that we as individuals and social groups desire to live in it. It is part of the task of schools and the wider community to help children and young people to clarify what their own vision of the best form of society and their ideas of their own best place in it might be. For these values will help them define and direct their preferred pathways of growth and development in the overall learning community.

Thus there will need to be a whole range of general academic and vocational education opportunities made available to all, with parity of importance and esteem given to each and an emphasis upon the diminution and disappearance of separation and division between one group of educands and another. We need to offer educational opportunities of all kinds to the whole populace, for its members are 'all our future'.

A Learning Workforce

A learning workforce and a trained workforce are different things. The former idea incorporates the acceptance of the need to have people's knowledge and skill constantly updated and expanded by on-the-job further education and training, and sees the present state of educational achievement as a *terminus a quo*. The latter idea simply accepts the employees' current state of training as a fixed *terminus ad quem*, without reference to any need for further extensions of excellence. In the current economic climate the need for training and retraining is being placed very high on the agenda of both business and education institutions.

It is on the basis of the connection between the ideas of vocational training and a wider and more liberal notion of education that both employees and businesses will understand that they benefit from the availability of wider educational opportunities for their employees and from their employees' engagement in them. It should be widely agreed, accepted and legislated that workers should have an entitlement to education and to make their own choice of courses from among those on offer. There has to be a widespread acceptance of the idea that a learning workforce is not only productive and profitable but a critical resource in the future development and expansion of that productivity and profitability.

For their part people in employment and preparing for employment will come to accept the need for continued learning while they are active in business, industry or commerce. The knowledge and skills they will constantly require are not such as they will necessarily have acquired while in school; indeed there will be much further learning that employees will have to acquire while they are 'on the job' and in the work-place. What is important is that schools can provide the necessary basis for this kind of lifelong learning by helping their students to master the wide-ranging and generic cognitive competencies that will furnish them with the resources that will facilitate will further and fresh learning later on. These will include such skills as learning how to learn; learning how to do research; learning how to solve problems; learning how to scan, apply, monitor, evaluate, correct and redirect the fresh knowledge and additional skills they need for effective performance in the work-place; learning how to communicate their needs to others who can then work collaboratively with them to correct mistakes, overcome problems or expand their skills; learning how to construct and to work in teams that will act co-operatively to acquire new knowledge quickly for the benefit of all; and learning how to think creatively and imaginatively to solve problems they encounter in the work-place and elsewhere.

As a representative of the business sector to whom we spoke commented: 'There is a general level of skills that schools must produce, and then responsibility for specific job skills rests with tertiary education or the employing bodies themselves. Industry pours millions into getting the right people and upgrading their skills, but it doesn't expect education to deliver the fine detail of the particular skills and competencies they need their people to have at specific times and places in their industrial activity'. Readiness for this generic kind of learning is a part of the new student-centred approach to learning. Schools are now starting to operate on the basis that their students' best learning is generated from within, so that they get a better understanding of themselves as people and a full appreciation of the limits of their current cognitive repertoires, together with an awareness of the gaps where their new knowledge will fit and the connecting points from which their new knowledge can grow. An emphasis in schools on the co-operative dimension of people working together can expand and assist in lifelong learning and can provide a model for much of the later learning that will be necessary in the work-place.

STRATEGIES FOR SCHOOL–BUSINESS PARTNERSHIPS

Effective, co-operative and productive relationships between schools and business and industry will be fostered when everybody in each community is able to see the need for such relationships and the ways in which the interests of each can complement the other. Just as industry and commerce need to sensitize schools to the realities of their world and the need for economic productivity, growth and development, so too can educators help businesses to understand what schooling and education more roundly and widely conceived are about. In these days education and training involve not merely the acquisition of one set of skills, not just training for one job. Students need to acquire a much broader picture of the world and an understanding of the speed, complexity and dynamism of changes in the knowledge and skills required for the world of work.

There is thus a need for a much stronger set of linkages, connections and partnerships between business and commerce, and schools. In fostering such relationships, leaders of industry and their education liaison officers might work out ways in which they can become more involved with the work of schools by going into schools and seeing what they are doing. Business and industry need to improve their understanding of the part they can and do play in education and training, instead of adopting the approach (adopted by some politicians too) of 'Why aren't you doing and producing what we need?' The time is long past (if it ever existed) when negative attitudes of that kind were of any real help or practical utility in contributing to the debate about the role schools and other educating institutions can and should play in forming the future of a society.

As part of this process, perhaps there might well be further significant inputs of funding, time and personnel on the part of business, industry and trades unions towards assisting the processes of lifelong learning in schools. In this way they will help all citizens in the community appreciate that there must be constant attention to the demands generated by the need to offer products and services that will be admired and acquired by people seeking access to the range of goods involved. For both industry and education appreciate that, from the point of view of the national interest and in the international arena of globally competing economies, what our nation seeks and needs to do is to compete successfully in those areas where our greatest strengths lie.

For many developed countries, there has been an obvious decline in the level and range of primary manufacturing and secondary production industries. Many of the needs for manufacturing and production are now being satisfied by the building or relocating of factories into countries of the developing world. For many western countries, economies are becoming orientated much more towards a service-based society, with the emphasis in the hospitality, tourism, culture, communications and financial services sectors. This means that many business and commercial concerns are having to adjust to a new way of doing business, to a new clientele, and to new forms of employment; many business enterprises are now realizing the need for change in the kinds of knowledge and skill required from their employees in these sectors.

In seeking excellence and international recognition in these fields, such enterprises will achieve success by placing greatest weight not merely on the quality of our products and services but also on the quality of the education, knowledge and competencies of the workforce that has produced or offers them. This can be the starting-point for their engagement in activities of a lifelong learning kind, that will encourage them to move on and develop initiatives to further democratic emancipation and personal growth.

We might now think it worthwhile to suggest some specific strategies and ways forward in which business and education can co-operate, that will properly prepare our young people for effective performance in these fields:

- There is a need for both sides to develop a common vision and purpose in the ways in which they conceive and give expression to all the positive and productive forms of their partnership. Partnerships between education and business should not merely be concerned with raising money, sponsorship and additional funding.

- There need to be mechanisms by which students can be made aware of the range of options and choices in business and industry that are open to them after the end of their period of formal educational attendance.

- There is a need for students to be exposed, allowed access to and have active experience in a variety of work-places and extra-curricular activities which widen young people's experience of the worlds of work and the demands of modern industry, business and commerce.

- As a part of this process, schools should be taking children into business and industry from the time of primary education.

- We should accept that there has been a certain naïveté in some previous and existing work experience programmes. If there is to be any integration of experience between school and the world of work, it has to come about as a result of programmes of planned activity, begun early in a young person's life. To facilitate this process there needs to be more resource material made available by industry and greater opportunities too for teachers to become more aware and better informed about the demands of the world of work and the relevance of work-related issues to teaching and learning in schools.

- Examples of school–business links include such schemes as work-placement programmes; the employment of career counsellors who have recent experience and knowledge of industry; and the arranging and instituting of teacher–industry placements and interchange. In one setting, some business enterprise centres arranged interactions between schools and major industries by way of work-experience and open days. This sort of approach to 'opening up business and industry' could be more broadly applied in order to give students experience in different working environments.

- Business–school partnerships might well be promoted by the formation of 'Work-Experience Teams': groups of young people who go into industry where they are presented with a problem which they then have the responsibility to solve. These must be real problems, and the students' work on them can make a solid contribution to their work and progress in school.

- School–business programmes can be promoted by businesses instituting something like an 'adopt a school' programme. In one school, for instance, students became involved in building an aeroplane and received enormous help and advice from the aeronautical industry in the provision of parts, instructors, equipment, advice, and so on. These types of learning activities and experiences have the potential to confer multiple gains and benefits on all the parties involved in them and have great lessons for the wider community of learning too.

- Students will benefit by learning skills for work: this may be facilitated by experience of studying at the work-place on a particular project, linking the acquisition of knowledge to a particular need, seeing how this is relevant to and interconnected with many elements.

- There is a need for business–school links to arrange for some form of client service. This might take the form of making available the services of a craftsperson who will help schools and students, take their wishes and views into account, and in general act as a mentor for young people. In many such linkages this kind of service is already being provided as a form of 'case management'.

- There is a need for authorities and business–education agencies to make sure that interactive satellite learning networks are in place, to deliver programmes to schools on emerging business issues. It would be quite easy for schools to employ the same mechanisms and access the same networks which small business concerns use to keep themselves abreast of and informed about current issues having a bearing on or directly affecting their work.

- Agencies of all kinds can offer opportunities for learning, the effects of which will be lifelong. In such a case, for instance, the Australia/China Chamber of Commerce has applied Australian standards regarding protection of the environment and effective labour relations in their work practices with Asia. In turn the members of that Chamber have been able to share the expertise gained with young Australians and in this way offer them important lessons for the future. Organizations such as the Australia/China Chamber of Commerce are increasingly prepared to be attached to a school or cluster of schools and work with students on these and other issues of importance to them for the future.

- Rotary International has also played a role in working with young people, not only through Rotaract and the provision of Rotary International scholarships, but also by teaching them about effective telephone communication, assisting them in mock interviews for employment, and with such matters as Jobsearch and the preparation of job applications and resumés.

Such schemes and strategies can be used as models for new school–business partnerships. Both school and business sectors can in such ways work collaboratively for their mutual benefit and also for that of the community generally.

Hirsch (1992) notes that partnerships involve a gradual building of trust between the two sides. Early on, activities tend to be kept simple and often symbolic but in the longer term partnerships need to find ways of changing aspects of education systems (rather than just running 'one-off' activities), thus leading to new joint goals based on a common understanding of what needs to change. This is more effective than 'one-off' activities. Hirsch identifies the following partnership types:

- Simple forms of co-operation between a company and a school, e.g. work-experience placements, visits to companies, shadowing and teacher secondment.

- Activities within schools of curriculum development such as the establishment of mini-enterprises.

- Direct help from companies to schools and students including one-to-one mentorships, 'adopt-a-school' initiatives and donations of equipment.

- Partnerships that go beyond specific activities based on a company's relationship with a school, such as a compact whereby employers in an area agree to give jobs to pupils who meet certain standards, and improved career guidance for students in upper secondary schools in a locality connected with particular employment possibilities in the transition from school to work.

Hirsch concludes that the process of co-operation between schools and the business/industry sector is itself important in building trust and in formulating common goals. As partnerships mature they change in character and content and improve their ability to bring about significant change. Hirsch comments that: 'The challenge for business is to maintain enthusiasm and the fresh eye of the outsider to education, at the same time as becoming a regular part of the process of mainstream educational change' (Hirsch, 1992, pp. 17–22).

Some Particularly Effective Strategies and Practices

Work-experience

The emphasis on the acquisition of such key competencies as literacy and numeracy, oral and written communication, problem solving, team building, interpersonal relations, and such generalizable learning strategies as learning how to learn and learning how to do research, should help students emerge from their formal educational experience as highly motivated, creative and multi-skilled future employees. The need for access to a workforce having such abilities has been recognized by a number of companies, which have collaborated with education institutions in the creation of programmes that will facilitate and enhance the acquisition of such knowledge and skills. One example of this is the dual recognition programme where students are placed within local industries to do parts of their work in the last two years of their schooling and in specific Year 11 and 12 subjects. When such students complete their final Schooling Certificate, they also have a first-year trade qualification granted by an institution for technical and further education (TAFE).

A representative of the business world to whom we spoke in the course of this study has described ways in which useful partnerships could be formed, with respect to the overall educational undertaking:

Members of the Australian/China Chamber of Commerce are extremely generous of their time and are interested in young people and the kinds of training they are getting. They would be interested in contributing more in some organized way. The Chamber might adopt a project and encourage members to support it for a defined period. Kids in school can benefit from and enjoy contact with people in real life work and planning. Some redesign of present work experience should be possible. Children need to work through real problems and see how people in the work-place do it, with their weaknesses and strengths. It is important that children get an understanding of what Australia is doing in Asia. It's not just knowledge but an attitude.

If meshed in with a wide-ranging programme of work-experience, such an approach could go far towards ensuring that in future educationists will work with other sectors of the business community to bring together their world and the world of business and industry. They might perhaps ensure that schools would be exposing their Year 9 and 10 students to as wide a range of work-options as possible, while, towards completion of such students' full-time education, there would be the possibility for more intensive, specific and extended work-placement.

Indeed there is nothing to prevent work-experience from being expanded to periods of up to a year or so, starting, say, at Year 9. Such an arrangement would provide students with valuable opportunities for learning at first hand about the kinds of experience and activity, successes and satisfactions offered to them by the world of work, and in a non-threatening, non-pressuring environment. Such an arrangement could also offer them one of the best vocational preparation programmes to which they might ever be introduced. Such a programme has to be well co-ordinated, of course, and well planned, so that the students themselves are getting educational learning value out of it – and are able to see that this is so.

The integration and co-ordination of work-experience between schools and the world of work has to be an ongoing planned activity, and moves towards introducing students to it should thus begin fairly early in their school lives. For the more effective and targeted planning of the process, there needs to be a great deal more material made available by industry in conjunction with education authorities. Furthermore, there need to be greater opportunities for teachers themselves to become more aware and informed about work-related issues. The practice of teacher release to industry should continue, but the numbers of teachers engaging in such exchanges should be sufficient to make more widespread the levels of knowledge, skill and understanding required for such schemes to work successfully.

This process could be materially assisted by the involvement of local firms and other agencies in the community in planning and arranging for such schemes to have maximum benefit. There needs to be a great emphasis on the importance of forging links between schools and business and industry in local communities, together with a move towards the establishment of more comprehensive work-placement programmes in the final two years of school. The employment of career counsellors and the deliberate setting up or conscious development of networks of teacher exchange with industry would provide major positive impetus and points of purchase for such initiatives.

Following such a beginning, schools could move to arrange work-experience on a basis of an annual activity after Year 9, for a few weeks at a time. Firms in business and industry would need to work out with schools the precise and most educationally beneficial structures, forms and processes such experience should take, if the students involved in that experience are not to be treated as cheap labour engaged *pro tempore* on trivial tasks. In arranging such schemes there has to be an educationally targeted approach. This means that work-experience should not be pursued for its own sake. From an educational point of view, it is better to ask what educational goals such experience should achieve.

Clearly, the availability of work-experience needs to be enlarged and expanded so that children and young people can have greater success in acquiring more extensive and informed knowledge and understanding about society and work. The good things about work-experience should be embellished in appropriate forms of relationship and interaction with firms in industry and commerce, that will provide students with access to knowledge and experience of the ways in which organizations work. Exposure of students to work-places and post-school work activities is enormously important, and this exposure should also make them aware of industrial notions of work-experience and the industrial relations elements that figure so largely in people's working life.

This is important inasmuch as students in schools often get very little exposure to and engagement in forms of work-experience. It is nevertheless noteworthy that young people are often engaged in business and commercial activity, particularly as part-timers and in retailing, because they work in a local supermarket, or in the service industries, where they will often help out in restaurants or tourist-related enterprises in which there is always demand for casual workers. One wonders how much of that experience gets to be discussed as part of their formal school curriculum work and how much business needs to encourage the interest of young people not just as mere casual employees but rather as potential citizens who could and should receive additional increments of training or development in their work-place engagements.

'Adopt a school'

In the USA some firms in industry adopt a school in their local area and try to educate people about that industry. There is benefit for each partner in such organized forms of association. The firms open up their plants to school families and thereby influence people's view of them and attract the interest of potential employees. For their part schools can consider the advantages of adopting some of the approaches and practices they observe at work in the business or commercial world. In such ways and through such schemes business and industry can assist in providing resources for schools. Schools in turn have to be realistic: they will understand that the assistance they get from firms is often not totally altruistic and that the firms that help them will often want some benefit that might accrue to them. At the same time schools will appreciate that they in their turn have to be more entrepreneurial to attract such sponsorship and to forge the necessary linkages of support from firms in the business or commercial sector.

In the USA, compacts, such as one scheme known as the Boston Compact, are developed between business and schools. These take into account the whole profile of the students, the school and its place in the community and then make available to the school advice, support and practical help. It is especially important that industrial enterprises should offer the support and assistance available through this kind of relationship to schools that might otherwise have to struggle to set their students on the pathways of lifelong learning.

Links between schools and small businesses

Specific businesses are beginning to link with schools in innovative ways. In Australia one particular scheme has met with some success in achieving this kind of linkage. Small Business Victoria (SBV) has produced and is currently seeking to introduce materials on small business into the school curriculum. A product called 'The School Report' provides a series of exercises for secondary schools to demonstrate the potential of small business for employment, designed to run with the involvement of the local community and small business people. SBV produces 'Kits for Graduates' to enable technically highly skilled work-people such as carpenters, electricians and plumbers to acquire the necessary business and commercial knowledge to enable them to establish small businesses for themselves. The instilling of an entrepreneurial spirit and the idea of taking up a small business as a career needs to be established among students early in their thinking and planning for the future. For this reason SBV is also currently working with teacher bodies to produce a curriculum kit for use in primary schools.

Similarly, the Australian Centre for Retail Studies' training and development programme is aimed at extending people's awareness and capabilities and fostering their personal growth, while at the same time helping management in such businesses to understand that they have an educational role to play in developing people's careers. The programme, which was developed with funding from a large public learning agency, the Victorian Education Foundation, offers formal education programmes, by means of distance education.

The importance of the small business sector being engaged in such activities is evident from the fact that this is the sector which, in Australia at any rate, has experienced the greatest growth in the last few years: nearly 85 per cent of firms that have begun commercial activity over that time have had twenty employees or fewer. Unfortunately, at the present time in the case of smaller retailers, very few firms offer or engage in any education or training and development activities.

It is important that educators recognize that in the past small business has been a very difficult area in which to promote the idea of lifelong learning. Yet the need of those who work in this sector seems clear. Representatives of the 'small business' world realize that electronic developments are going to have an impact on small businesses. Schools could run awareness seminars for small business people, using their networks of support in the business world to attract the attention of 'small business' people and get them into the schools that could help them in these ways. Getting people used to going to schools for information and learning could then be expanded to make possible and to facilitate the opening up of a whole range of interactive lifelong learning opportunities.

Clearly we should look at the developments, expansions and ability to respond to change offered by such lifelong learning activities for the benefit of small business organizations and industry, and seek to form alliances between them and education providers. Equally schools and other education providers need to co-operate in running courses for them at the work-place; several such agencies and institutions could combine to provide occasions and fora for a range of training and upgrading activities.

There is almost no limit to the ways and means in which all partners in the learning community can work together to provide lifelong learning in schools, learning centres, the work-place, the community centre, and the home. The schemes and courses that can be provided are limited only by the imagination and vision of those providing access to all the various forms in which people can take advantage of such learning.

POTENTIAL PROBLEMS AND TENSIONS IN SCHOOL-BUSINESS PARTNERSHIPS

At the moment much hesitation is felt in both schools and the commercial sector about relationships between schools and business; in some places this betokens lack of interest, in others it amounts to scepticism, in yet others there is distrust on both sides. Some people in business feel intimidated about the idea of forming relationships with educating institutions or are not clear on the best ways to do this; sometimes too there is a lack of confidence on the part of business people in schools and in the teaching profession generally. Similarly, there is often a lack of trust on the part of educators concerning the motives and intentions of business people who involve themselves in education.

A cultural shift has to occur in the attitudes and beliefs of both groups about each other: both need to realize that they are working towards the same objective. It is vital that attitudinal change should take place on both sides, lest the move towards co-operation be slowed down by reservation, hesitation and mistrust about each other's motives.

Some of this hesitation comes from the fact that, while education is something that is relatively long-term – 'Education can't be put on like coats of paint' as Edward Lear remarked – most businesses have very specific short-term needs that have to be met in order for them to survive. In setting priorities among these needs the notion of having a responsibility to the community sometimes does not come high on the list. Generally, however, more well-established businesses have learnt to be decent corporate citizens as well as effective commercial enterprises, and to accept an obligation to contribute something to the wider welfare of the community.

The extent to which schools will be able to work with business and industry depends on the extent to which they can capitalize on the notion of decent corporate citizenship and on the contributions that organizations and institutions from those sectors want to make to the work of the educational community. Such contributions will have to be appropriate to their skills, activities and resources. Schools' interaction with such agencies will likewise be appropriate to their nature and function: the first obligation of schools is to educate, not to raise money. This means that any relationships schools develop and any particular partnerships they set up should not be such that they compromise, inhibit or interfere with the core values of the educating institution.

There is much that is already being done in the business and commercial world to promote and profit from lifelong learning. In the private sector already business organizations are increasingly thinking of themselves as learning organizations and are trying to empower and encourage their employees to think for themselves, to learn better from experience, to discuss and challenge and so to improve their practice.

A part of this is the increasing recognition that a learning workforce and a trained workforce are very different things. Extending work skills into learning of a more general kind and studying broader and more humane concerns is an important part of promoting ideas of best practice for all a firm's employees and sets a benchmark for an educated workforce in the work environment generally. A shop steward is entitled to have a knowledge of the management of database operations, for example, so he or she has a broader view of the organization's operations. A fitter and turner who wants to take a course in philosophy should have access to information and networks that will enable him or her to pursue such an interest.

The key consideration underlying such interests and concerns has to do with the larger question of how a trained workforce is to be turned into one that is constantly committed to learning – of both specific and more general subjects. For a learning workforce is not merely a useful and productive layer over and above a trained workforce; it is one that will focus upon more general and humane concerns: the innovation or improvement of good practice in the workplace, the personal growth of all its members, and the ways in which they can be further emancipated as citizens contributing to the common wealth and welfare of the community.

IMPLICATIONS FOR THE TEACHING PROFESSION

Suggestions and proposals for school–business partnerships have clear implications for the preparation and continuing development of the teaching profession. What is clearly required is that teachers should have an informed understanding of and positive attitudes towards the world of business, industry and commerce, and some working knowledge of its operations. This will enable them not merely to advise and counsel their students in making their career choices but to act as their guides and leaders in introducing them to the learning opportunities offered by that world, empowering them to start right on the learning pathways open to them in it, and helping them afterwards critically to reflect on their experiences and so to extract maximum learning value from them.

Of course no one expects that teachers will be experts on industry but it is a reasonable expectation that members of the education profession will know enough about it to make their students' preparation for it personally challenging and educationally valuable. Similarly, no one demands that industrialists will be experts in education. Nevertheless local education agencies and private providers of learning courses, technical and further education (TAFE) colleges, government bodies, institutions of industry and commerce, employers' associations, professional organizations and trades unions can all work together with schools to develop programmes in virtually every aspect of schooling, education and training.

The cross-fertilization of thinking and planning that will undoubtedly occur in the exchanges between these different bodies will provide schools and school-based personnel with the sort of information on vocational matters and personal career development that they want. These plans can then be adapted to and adopted in schools' and students' ongoing curriculum activity, either during normal school times or outside those times, in the evenings and possibly at weekends.

Teachers will have to prepare for such engagements as part of their teacher training and as part of their continuing development once in the profession. There are many ways in which this can be done and many benefits, too. One example is provided by schemes of teacher release to industry in which teachers work in industry for twelve months. This is a sound idea for it enables industry to show people the kinds of qualities and skills it needs in its workforce, while at the same time enabling teachers to develop an interest in and a play a part in developing those training opportunities in business and industry to which their own skills and knowledge relate.

There is of course a slight danger in this. Many good things are happening now in schemes in which much of the specific training in the industry or business is being planned and given in industry by teachers. It is the entrepreneurial educator who finds out what is needed and offers training in certain areas. In one setting, so impressed have some sectors of business and industry been with the knowledge and skills of the educators joining up with them that they have offered employment to them and those educators' expertise has been lost to their schools. But this risk can be offset by the number of people crossing over to the educational sector from the business and industry sectors, some of whom have already found that their *métier* lies in teaching and working in the education service. Many workers in the commercial world have been able to offer immense insights of wisdom and provide examples of the kinds of excellence of which they had been practitioners in their former environments. Nothing but good for both students and staff can come of this.

There might well be much more of this sort of interaction: the connections between the two worlds need considerable freeing-up if there is to be the greater benefit to both that a lifelong learning approach for all requires and makes possible.

Chapter 9

Cultivating Connections with Constituencies in Culture and the Arts

A TIME OF CHANGE

The previous chapters have made it clear that we are living in an age where there have been profound and considerable changes in economy and society. These changes are not without their effect on the worlds of culture and the arts.

In this chapter we shall explore the ways in which the school's activities and goals can derive the necessary information, sustenance and support for their enmeshment in the work of and service to the interests of various cultural and artistic communities. The existence and orientations of such communities form an important and indeed indispensable part of the mosaic constituting the identity of and enhancing the value of the community generally.

We are now entering an era in which our societies have the potential to cater for people's material needs without the necessity of all people being in full-time employment. This raises all kinds of questions about the importance of employment in people's lives and about the psychological and emotional needs that people's vocations and work occupations satisfy. Certainly there are sufficient changes in the nature and availability of regular paid work to make us realize that the days of full-time employment until the ages of 60 or 65 for all members of the community are coming to an end.

Changes are also taking place in the nature of work. Employment in the manufacturing and productive sectors has been decreasing; workers are now being trained in a range of skills so that they can play a part as multiskilled members of work teams that can function in a variety of capacities and places. The number of jobs in the actual manufacturing and production of goods has been decreasing in proportion to the greater numbers involved in design, presentation and marketing. Meanwhile the number of jobs in the service industries have been increasing – jobs that are often episodic, casual, part-time – and the need for which is constantly changing.

Existing alongside high rates of mass production is an emphasis upon quality service to the customer – on preparing products and offering services that are precisely tailored to individual needs. This stress on standards of excellence in the provision of high quality goods and specialized services calls upon specific knowledge and creative skills possessed by individuals determined on the continuous improvement of the goods and services they currently offer and on the inspiration, creation and provision of new ranges of attractive products and specialized services.

Rapid change in the production and service industries has led to a broad-based knowledge requirement in the work-place. In this context, we have had to get used to the notion of leaving the industrial age, with old forms of communication, production and working disappearing, and of entering the information age, with new forms of literacy and communication emerging, that often leaves print behind.

These changes require a reshaping of our modes of thinking, working and creating. We are looking at a new reality that we can shape now, much of which is graphic and non-verbal. Increasingly oracy and literacy are expanding, as the requirement to be able to operate in graphic forms of communication begins to impinge upon our theories of learning, thinking, imagination and creativity, that are helping redefine, expand and recreate the world we share in the new information and technology age.

The dominant technology of the future will increasingly be a union of computers and communication, which emphasizes the increasing importance of multimedia technology in the presentation of information in words, structures, images, melodies and rhythms. These are going to be the new modes of envisioning and communicating messages and developing new forms and modes of interpersonal significance between people and between worlds, not merely black and white print on a page or chalk on a blackboard. We are therefore going to need people to be able to frame and deliver such messages, possessed of a range of qualities and competencies: they will be articulate people, divergent thinkers, effective communicators. Such qualities are related to the demands of the new forms of service industry and to creative and imaginative ways of expanding employment opportunities.

At the same time as creativity and specialized service provision is increasing in importance, in some spheres of human endeavour direct human involvement in the provision and monitoring of other products and services will be taken over by technology. People will in future be able to send messages, read books and newspapers, do their shopping, attend to all their personal financial affairs and have their appliances serviced by computers, robots and all the other devices of modern information communication and multimedia technology. In the future, from the point of view of industrial engagement, some highly able and information-rich, computer-intelligent people will be needed to create, apply and service all these increasingly sophisticated devices, while fewer and fewer people will be needed to do the jobs that such devices have steadily taken over from the human sector.

We have to accept all this as part of the change in employment prospects for the future. We need to realize, from the point of view of economic capacity, that, for the foreseeable future, there are sufficient resources and means of generating finance for many members of our society without all members of society needing to be in full-time paid employment.

This means that our society is going to need to find ways other than full-time paid employment to occupy the time, energy and understandable aspirations of significant numbers of its population. It becomes clear that one of the places and forms of activity in which such time, energy and creative enthusiasm can be expended lies in the world of culture and the arts.

New Concepts of Learning and Engagement in the Creative Arts

It is possible to look at the importance of the creative arts in the context of lifelong learning by pointing to the revolution that has taken place in concepts of knowledge and theories of learning. These have altered our thinking about and approach to education, in a major way.

Knowledge has ceased to be absolute, factual and coercive upon us. What we have now is the notion of knowledge as temporary, provisional, conditional and constantly changing. Knowledge now is much less like the fixed, stable and permanent structure of an architect-designed Greek temple and much more like a constantly shifting web in which all parts are integrated on to another. Knowledge is experimental, tentative and problem-orientated; above all it is criticizable, corrigible and subject to change.

Learning is now such that students are no longer viewed as receptive jugs waiting to be filled, as it were, in a classroom that is essentially didactic in its pedagogy, in which students receive and teachers deliver. Learning is now highly differentiated, student-centred, with a multiplicity of different styles and modes and individual paces. Our metacognitive research has highlighted the importance of learning being student-centred, motivationally driven, self-monitored, contextually relevant and individually created and developing.

Knowledge and learning are now viewed as best engaged in and achieved on a cooperative rather than a competitive basis; knowledge and learning are enabling and empowering. They provide us with concepts and categories that make sense to us because it is we who work to integrate them into our patterns of existing knowledge and understanding. This enables us to work out and set in place our own models and paradigms with which to work in our appraisals of things which we can then bring under our cognitive control. This kind of self-directed learning is rigorous and very critical. We are forever correcting ourselves, forever going back and 'getting it right', particularly if we are working on computers. We now realize that by collaborating with each other and correcting each other's work we can all as a group make progress faster than if we are shielding our work from each other.

It is particularly as a result of changes in communication that these changes and advances in learning have been brought about: they have been facilitated by the revolution that is taking place in information technology. The ability to communicate globally and internationally expands our awareness of increasingly wide boundaries and previously unknown territories of knowledge in this newly interconnected, interactive network of computer communication. This new world offers immense resources for enhanced learning and creativity: information technology and modern communication is infinitely resource-rich. This is a world of information and resources that are always available. It is personally controllable. It is immensely patient. It never gets angry. It never gets tired. It is universally accessible; it can provide us with an entrée to far wider archives of information and banks of data than are ever available for us on the shelves of our school and local libraries, however well funded they are.

In this way communication and information technology is helping to

219

redefine the place in which people learn and the ways in which they learn. In higher education, for example, it is now a readily accepted part of the pathways to personal advancement that are available through registration in institutions of higher education that students can complete degree studies virtually without leaving their bedrooms and without accessing hard print media or even, because of virtual reality capabilities, these needing to go into laboratories. Such possibilities of and access to the availability of learning from a distance and at any time of day or night are now also available to children and young people enrolled in our schools. These new modes of retrieving, handling and communicating information enable learners to construct new thought worlds for themselves, of innovation, imagination and immense creativity.

Implications for the Arts of Changes in Economy, Society and Learning

Changes in society, economy, theories of learning and the powers of modern communication technology have an impact upon but are also promoted by work in the creative and performing arts. In all these things the arts provide us with paradigms. They set the example of the revolution in theory of knowledge, in style of learning, and in communication. They are demanding. They require strict criteria of accuracy and attention to detail, common clarity and rigour. Crucially they are iconoclastic: they alter the moulds of all that we do and create, and help us to look at reality in new ways and make judgments about it according to new canons of appraisal. This can be done through the arts because it is one of the chief features of the arts that they call existing categories and concepts into question and create and apply concepts, categories and criteria of significance that are uniquely their own.

In this they are analogous to and equivalent with the sciences. Workers, performers and creators in the arts are leaders in framing and forming new modes of thinking, new categories of working and imagining. The arts are paradigms of corrigibility and criticism. The concept of 'getting it right' in the arts is something which exemplifies itself with every stroke of a brush, every movement of a violinist's bow, every move of a dancer's limb.

At the same time works in the arts bring all our learning, knowing and understanding together in one complete fusion, one complex web of thought and action, creation and imagination, because they 'de-differentiate' all the constituent parts of the one organic entity that we see as the work of art (Ehrenzweig, 1976). They bring together into one particular consummate whole entire layers of meaning that cannot be split off from the whole work in which they are embodied, without radically distorting or destroying its meaning, intelligibility and value.

We might, as an example, consider the poem by William Blake, *The Sick Rose* (cf. Greger, 1972). This consummate poem, so small as to consist of only eight lines, has as many meanings in it as there are audiences to listen to them and to discuss the poem. Yet these cannot be differentiated out as though we could strip off the various layers of meaning and somehow come to a central point. They are one perfect fusion. It is in this way that the arts are paradigms of the integration of knowledge and the relatedness and interconnectedness of all things (cf. Arnaud Reid, 1969).

The arts are student-centred too, in the stress they lay on the individual as learner, creator and performer. In the arts teachers can only help, teachers can only facilitate, teachers can only accompany and assist the student. It is the learner who stands in the middle. Furthermore, the arts are models of individual effort yet co-operative endeavour. Arts are productive in that they actually seek to expand people's horizons and co-operate in offering enrichment to them rather than being competitive.

The idea of lifelong learning can find particular expression and challenge in the world of the arts. People's painting, writing, poetry, dance and music give them interests, skills and commitments that are life-lasting and which revivify their imagination. The arts show us alternative visions of what it is possible to be. They can help us work out ways of creating satisfying and life-enhancing possibilities for ourselves to create a pattern of preferred life-options.

Finally, the arts are examples of the democratic spirit at work: the arts are paradigms of the open society. Karl Popper's view that it is only through trying to solve problems, seeking and attending to criticism from whatever quarter it comes, not merely delegating responsibility but also engaging the notice and attention of all those who have an interest in the work, that we can create an 'open' society, is particularly exemplified in the arts. For this is the way in which the creative and performing arts work – facing problems, setting up hypotheses as solutions to those problems, trying to criticize the tentative solutions our productions offer, and being prepared for criticism and attempted correction or improvement of the work we put forward – this is the daily experience of any visual artist, actor, dancer or musician. In that way the arts are models of the democratic life at work.

The artistic life is one of constant challenge. It is the task of the educator, particularly those working in the arts, to help the learners in our community – of whatever age, of whatever interest, with whatever gifts – to make the search for artistic expression and aesthetic experience in their own lives and that of the community the focus for their search for quality more generally and to make the achievement of quality not quite not so difficult and perhaps a little less rare than it might otherwise be.

THE ARTS AS A FOCUS FOR COMMUNITY INTERACTION AND INVOLVEMENT IN LIFELONG LEARNING

There are thus many good reasons for seeing the arts and cultural activities as focuses of community involvement and lifelong learning. Many people are drawn to the arts and cultural activities because of the opportunities for social interaction and the practical enjoyment of creative activity that they offer. But it is important that enjoyment of the arts should be made accessible to all social and ethnic groups and be available in all geographic areas – urban, suburban and rural.

To preserve equity and access it will be important to monitor the availability of such developments and activities and to watch for the emergence of high-priced structured courses and costly pursuits, for these will clearly dis-advantage some groups. Schools can provide a key cultural venue for engagement in cultural activities and artistic pursuits. Schools are in a position to promote the widest possible participation in cultural life, and this will be of major assistance in the aspiration and commitment to create a better-integrated community. It is to make possible and promote such a community integration that schools must develop more accessible cultural and artistic programmes.

One strong reason for seeking to make such programmes more accessible is that the arts have the potential to provide meaningful learning experiences for individuals and groups who might otherwise feel marginalized. There is a need for educators, in partnership with other groups, to lobby for the right of all members of the community to have access to cultural activities and artistic pursuits and to courses of training and education in the arts – especially for those with disabilities or those who may be disadvantaged or marginalized in other ways.

One example of a successful programme to achieve this can be found in the work of Arts Access in Australia. This organization has put together a special programme for young people having special needs and this has proved success-ful in offering an introduction to and guided activity in the arts, in ways that give people a real sense of inclusion in the educational milieu, where such activities and experiences were being made available to everyone. This is just one example that provides evidence of the hunger for cultural enlightenment that can find rich expression and fulfilment in community involvement in the arts and culture. This kind of work needs to be integrated into the work of schools and educational institutions of all kinds. It is important that there are comprehensive cultural programmes available and accessible to all.

In such programmes the school and the community can join together in and engage in a joint exercise of offering people opportunities to engage in life-enhancing activities. One can see the possibility of dual community–school centres, where there can be provided courses and programmes in the arts, crafts, leisure activities, theatre – a whole range of learning activities in the arts for young people and for the community more broadly. Schools have the infrastructure, a hall (often with a proscenium, theatre lighting and amplifica-tion), a piano or even a music suite, art rooms, a gymnasium with a sprung floor – maybe even a dance studio – wheels for pottery and kilns, woodwork and metalwork shops, and other such facilities and resources. In many schools, however, such resources and facilities are often locked away for a large part of the week. These could all be opened up to the community in the interests of lifelong learning for all.

Such schemes can be especially exciting and educative if the schools and community centres used as places for learning and enjoyment in the arts can be staffed by those having qualifications and who are actively working in the arts. This could involve expanding upon such schemes as 'artists in schools' and/or 'artists in the community' but also capitalizing upon the contribution that people trained in particular crafts or trades can offer to such programmes.

Professional craftspeople who are at the forefront of their profession are able to offer a great deal to schools and lifelong learning.

One note of caution needs to be sounded, however: the practices of artists and craftspeople are often focused rather more on individual creativity than orientated towards the interests of an organization or institution. This individuality will need to be respected as well as carefully managed. Yet the talents and creative efforts of such people could be put to immensely beneficial use: they could be encouraged to become more involved in arts and educational activities, showing the benefit of and highlighting the importance of cultural endeavours to the general population, as well as instilling greater enthusiasm for and securing larger audiences for their work. Larger audiences, larger involvement in arts and crafts activities, and greater community engagement can only lead to greater understanding and personal illumination. Increased participation can only benefit the arts, the schools, the community and society.

This last point might serve as the principal objective in promoting the arts and lifelong learning in schools and centres of community learning: to benefit both the individual and society. There are, however, also important economic benefits made possible by and accruing from engagement in arts programmes. It is worth noting that integrating the arts into the school might be a means of assisting the school in income generation. Of course this would require a different way of thinking about resources in such areas; but some modern approaches to local school management, including finance and budgeting, suggest that the raising of additional funds is a critical part of any school's success.

Awareness of this kind of emphasis in the direction and management of schools offers a new challenge for the arts community. But such an approach is important in planning and delivering all kinds of educating programmes; it has very serious implications for management and for the role and functioning of schools councils. Arts educators would do well to remember that, among the reasons for setting up programmes and schemes for the arts in schools, one important reason is the potential they have for assisting institutions to bring in further resources of finance, equipment and facilities, and a further range of personnel with skills and interests that complement those the school already possesses.

There will of course always be some barriers to integrating the arts in schools. These will include 'political' considerations as to their inclusion in the curriculum on grounds of their perceived status; there may be some difficulties arising from their need for resources; and management may find that the iconoclasm that is endemic to successful arts work militates against management approaches privileging direction and control. In the past many enthusiastic arts educators have ended up disillusioned because artistic and cultural activities have been squeezed for space on the timetable, poorly resourced and managed, and often belittled and demeaned by people some of whom should really know better.

Many of the worst effects of these factors can be mitigated if teachers and educators appreciate that there is a need for co-ordinated co-operation. Often this can be achieved with more people in the provision of arts and culture programmes and in arts management at the community level. A positive approach to such provision and effective management could operate in ways that complement what is already being done, and could be brought to bear in the attempt to set in motion and draw upon the synergy of a range of diverse groups working together in a planned and strategic way, bound together by a common interest, concern and set of aspirations.

SPECIFIC STRATEGIES FOR MAKING CONNECTIONS

There are many ways in which the arts can offer opportunities for integrating the community into the life and activities of the school and for providing openings for lifelong learning. Examples of schemes integrating the arts into schools include: artists in schools or artists in residence programmes; holding exhibitions; and providing studio space for dancers, painters and musicians with the expectation of performances as an outcome of such arrangements. Some schools have set up enrichment programmes that facilitate lifelong learning; others make arts groups welcome to use the school hall; others involve their students in mixed arts groups with local drama productions; yet others arrange for suitably qualified and artistically or culturally significant people in the local community to act as mentors in arts and craft activities. One other strategy to enhance learning in the creative arts might be for schools or other centres of learning to arrange for the conduct of master classes in schools with leading musicians, dancers, singers or writers. The ways in which the school can serve as a centre of provision of and access to forms of life-enhancing learning for the community are limited only by the range of ideas people have for bringing work in the arts and cultural pursuits to the notice of people in the wider community and then encouraging these people to take advantage of the schemes they offer.

One other forum for engaging the community in the activities of the school or learning centre might also be through programmes of Media Studies and media teaching. With multimedia communication growing as it is now and likely to expand even further in the future, people are going to use media quite differently from the way in which they use them now. All the various forms of communication media are changing rapidly and people need to be skilled to keep abreast of these advances. Students will find there is practically no end to the uses to which they can put their work in media and communication studies.

Students can use media access to contribute to local newspapers, to assist in the development of conference newsletters, to participate in taking photos of the elderly for local histories, and in helping compile archives of such history for study and expansion. Learners of all ages can read books, newspapers and reference materials on the world-wide net, access and distribute information out of their homes, do much of their personal business and even develop their personal relationships via the increasingly sophisticated devices of modern information technology. And what is perhaps of vital educational importance is the way in which use of these new media can be especially helpful when one is working with the visually impaired or those with learning difficulties. For them and for many others the new media provide educators with great aids to literacy and indeed give equal access and a sense of personal empowerment to all their users, whatever their personal capacities or talents.

There are of course some problems. Among these will figure the epistemological problem of the veracity of the images and information represented in and through the media. One picture, one report may tell both a thousand truths and a thousand lies: it is possible to manipulate pictures, to skew information, to process data in such a way as to distort, misrepresent and even falsify. Similarly it is quite plain that the Internet now gives users access to some things that our society might regard as undesirable – access to pornography, instruction in civil unrest, and the making of explosive devices. In some instances, computers can focus attention on the presentation of life in an oppositional mode; this comes about when information is processed only through binary logic – on/off, yes/no, bad/good – and can thus incline people to view reality through lenses that offer only antithetical, adversarial and generally conflicting perspectives. To learn how to deal with these phenomena, to adjust for possible distortion, to criticize and counter-bias, to learn to evaluate the images and information that are presented – all this must be part of any education in the use and exploitation of the media and the information made available to us through them. The 'open societies' of the arts have particular strengths here.

There is a further point to be made. A curriculum of arts activities and cultural practices, be they crafts, visual arts, dance, drama, media work or music, should not be presented simply or solely as recreational pursuits. A programme in the arts should also focus on getting people to see them as vocational areas in which opportunities for possible future employment or application to employment can be clearly seen. Some work in the arts can help young people develop the knowledge and skills requisite for their entering a profession, vocation or industry involving the visual or performing arts or musical experience, or can help them develop skills that are transferable to other areas. The arts can be related to the possibility of securing future employment in a range of activities. As Arnold Packer (1994) put it, 'Properly taught, knowledge of the arts can help youngsters with the know-how needed in the twenty-first century workplace'.

Experience in the arts requires students to acquire knowledge and develop a range of skills that can be transferred to the work-place. Many forms of artistic activity and creation, in the performing arts for example, call upon and develop highly complex skills of the management of time, space, resources and personnel. These are matters of daily artistic necessity experienced by the choreographer, the composer, the drama producer and the visual artist. Moreover the activities of people in the arts make many demands on their technological competence: they have skills in lighting and set design, modern musical electronics, and forms of effective multimedia presentation. Furthermore the necessary skills of working in a team, negotiating, communicating, acting as a leader or being willing to be led, are exhibited in each artistic performance. Each of these must be integrated into school programmes in the arts.

There is the further point that effective work in the arts occurs only when people have learnt the skills of articulate, clear and sophisticated forms of communication. Those who have sought to develop their understanding of and ability to communicate in dance, drama, literature or the presentation of images through film, will have gained invaluable lessons for work in places that call upon such skills, whether in the professions, business or the local council chamber. They will have been immeasurably assisted by their hard work at acquiring the powers given to them by the concentration of the arts on conveying complex and heterogenous ideas and kinds of meaning in clearly intelligible, vivid and compelling forms.

This emphasis upon communication of ideas in the arts often involves the production and transmission of material that is iconoclastic and innovative. As it is expressed by John Berger (1971), art demands that people do not ever 'see the same way again'. As Edwards Tufte put it (1991, p. 3), communicating 'ideas through the body', expressing musical ideas, interpreting dramatic materials, and creating visual works in order 'to effectively communicate ideas' are all parts of the methods, procedures and forms of signification that are central to work in the arts. All these qualities and operations show students of all ages and levels of competency how important it is to be effective communicators in this information age.

Central to our awareness of work in the arts is the notion that their approach involves problem solving and this is something that can be taken by practitioners of the arts straight into any other work-place. These days those firms that are determined to excel in service and performance are engaged in a constant endeavour to improve the quality of their products and procedures, and are constantly exploring ways of bringing creative solutions to bear on the problems and challenges with which they are continually beset. Arts learning makes such a problem-solving approach a central part of their endeavours. Arts lessons demand all the time that students do the best work that they can, that they integrate all competing considerations into a balanced composition, and that they weigh all the intangibles and incorporate them into an integrated whole.

This kind of approach can give students a far more realistic experience of making judgments in a complex world than other subjects that concentrate more on showing them how to 'arrive at the right answer'. The logic of the arts is not binary: it is multidimensional – as are most of the problems with which students will be faced in their employment and in their personal lives.

The kind of thinking and operating in which students of the arts will learn to proceed requires them to be aware of the ways in which parts fit together to produce a comprehensive whole. Their work entails a planning, conceiving and delivery process that involves constant checking, monitoring, evaluating and trying to ensure excellence and the highest standards in the final product or performance. This kind of achievement is made up of activities that call upon many of the skills and key competencies called for in modern work-place know-how: as *Mr Holland's Opus* graphically demonstrates, the planning and putting on of a play or a musical performance, the production of a film, the design of an exhibition of students' work, all demonstrate ways in which the skills called for in the arts and the world of work can be conjoined.

THE INVOLVEMENT OF MANY PARTNERS IN PROMOTING CULTURE AND THE ARTS

Employers may like to consider the ways in which they can persuade school councils to promote work in the arts on the programme of a school's activities as one of the best ways in which their future employees' readiness to engage in divergent and creative thinking can be demonstrated, encouraged and developed. The concept of work in the arts which we have explicated here shows that it is very much in employers' interests to confirm and strengthen the place of the arts in the curriculum and to promote and ensure that access to courses in the arts will be laid open to all students.

Educators, parents and employers will want to ensure that arts subjects are given similar status in the activities of a community's educating institutions to that given to mathematics, science and technology. For they will all realize that the lives and work of future employees, responsible citizens, and fulfilled adults in the community are likely to be enriched just as much from the experiences they enjoy, the lessons they learn and the explorations they make in dance, drama, music, and the visual and media arts, as they are in calling upon their knowledge of science, technology or mathematics.

Opportunities for the promotion of the arts and other cultural activities in the life of the school are also likely to have a definite 'roll on' effect. These activities offer openings for the development of micro-economic activities and small business works, such as cinemas, bookselling, print-making and picture-framing, domestic interior design, cultural tourism and the like. There is the further point that integrating the arts into schools could also generate income for local artists. Arts education also affords opportunities for training people for positions in community arts management. In these ways schools can forge strong links with the wider community, particularly in respect of activities that have come to be regarded as constituting a prime part of our culture and community identity, and that make contributions to the welfare of that community of an economic and cultural kind. No one who has seen the contributions made to European or North American economies and culture by activities, productions and exhibitions in graphic arts, theatre, music, dance and film can be in any doubt as to the importance of such work.

For their part arts educators need to realize that they too are part of the changes occurring in school and community. Teachers who in the past worked largely alone are today having to learn to work in teams; teachers who once relied entirely on chalk, pens and the printed page are coming to the realize that modern methods of learning require them to be expert in the educational use of e-mail, fax, modem, and video communication. Schools must adapt quickly to these modes of communication: those brought up and trained in one culture are now having to learning how to operate in others. Arts educators need to become adept in showing how their students' experience in setting the highest standards of endeavour and excellence for themselves in the arts can be applied to quality work elsewhere.

Arts educators need to show how the learning they offer their students is a demonstration of a deeper underlying purpose. Those in places of learning have to be able to argue that there is a direct connection between what their students learn and their ability to lead a responsible, productive and fulfilled life. Teachers of the arts have a powerful responsibility to communicate the part their subjects can play in forging the connection between work in the arts and leading a responsible and satisfying life in the community.

Any educational experience involving activity and achievement in the arts will quickly show us that work in the arts enhances the quality of life for everyone. For the development of rich sources of personal fulfilment, for training in the skills called for in participating in an open, democratic society, the arts can also do far more than giving people expertise in some complex and highly important skills that can be transferred and redeployed in the workplace. They are also a major factor in the conception, construction and launching of individual learners into a responsible and fulfilled life.

This was well put in the Report of the SCANS Commission, US Department of Labor, 1994, quoted in the pre-conference paper prepared for the 'Arts Education for the 21st Century American Economy' Conference held in September 1994 in Louisville, Kentucky by Arnold H. Packer, a nationally regarded economist, labour expert and former US Assistant Secretary of Labor, now a Senior Fellow at the Johns Hopkins University Institute for Policy Studies:

> We understand that schools do more than simply prepare people to make a living. They prepare people to live full lives – to participate in their communities, to raise families, and to enjoy the leisure that is the fruit of their labor. A solid education is its own reward ... We are not calling for a narrow, work-focused education. Our future demands more.

It is this kind of thinking that will stimulate and inspire those educators who see in the creative and performing arts a powerful force for motivating members of the community to respond to the opportunities offered to them by access to teachers, facilities and resources for extending their own learning beyond the period of formal engagement in full-time compulsory education. This will be most clear through such encouragement as can be given to them to engage in creating and communicating with other people by becoming literate and active in the arts. For in these particular subjects they might begin to explore the possibilities offered in them for developing their own interests and capabilities, for learning to live a productive life, and for contributing to the enhancement of society.

THE ARTIST AS A MODEL OF THE LIFELONG LEARNER

Early experience in home and school is essential to the development and promotion of interests and engagement in cultural and artistic activities. Children must be exposed to and engaged in these areas while they are young. To promote and support learning at school, schemes such as 'artists in residence' make it possible for individual schools or groups of schools to have their own artist-in-residence programme at little or no cost. Then there are ways of bringing people in from crafts and other arts professions, offering students and learners in the local community the experience of supervision and crafts-mentor schemes; and there are self-development programmes, that are helpful and important in promoting community engagement, as are contributions from community arts groups, that can stimulate the arts in schools.

In turn, schools and other educating institutions can open up their facilities and infrastructure to the arts community, offering their hall for dance, a stage for local theatre, access to a piano and other musical instruments, a pottery facility, a studio for hi-fi and multimedia exploration, or simply by offering the use of underutilized space to artists for exhibitions. In such ways as these schools can become more closely connected and involved with the activities, interests and values of important groups establishing, building and contributing to the maintenance of culture and value in the community. In return for the use of school resources and facilities artists and craftspeople can provide activities, exhibitions and performances for students and members of the school community. After-school programmes can be offered for work in dance, drama, the visual arts. Perhaps a one-day-a-week multifaceted arts programme after school hours could complement the after-school programmes offered in sports. The school, the students, the community and the artists can all benefit from such initiatives.

Already there has been considerable progress in taking the arts into schools. Cultural artists working in schools have been very successful in involving ethnic parents. In one setting, for example, at one local school a choreographer devised a dance evening with the school's students, and 42 different nationalities attended the performance, the first time that all of them had come together in one place. The programme recognized the needs of working parents by picking up and looking after the students involved during rehearsals that were held at weekends. Another programme drew refugees together, enabling them, through work in the arts, to reflect on where they came from, and helping them begin positively to look to the future.

In short, the involvement of artists, craftspeople and designers with schools can be an excellent vehicle for creating a sense of community involvement and cohesion. The projects they tackle can be simple, such as developing a sensory garden for disabled students, or more complex such as creating a playground for children living in an urban housing area. In such projects the skills of artists and craftspeople can be used to draw resources together, to provide a focus, and to stimulate people to be creative and productive in a non-threatening and supportive environment. In this way creative efforts operate as agents of change for the whole community.

For their part school students exposed to and engaging in such creative activities benefit from interaction with the artists. The artists also benefit from access to facilities that they often have difficulty in providing for themselves, and are enabled to develop personally and professionally. For all such individuals and groups, work in the arts or an arts-based education offers a richness that is valuable in itself, no matter what people do later.

Schools committed to lifelong learning through the arts can run visual arts workshops, painting and drawing classes, garden design courses, work on theatre or musical performances, and have a mixture of young and older people working together in them. Schools can see their communities as places where people create and exhibit what they do, participate in creating endeavours and pass on their experience and achievements to other learners. As one example of this, one school had some wonderful essays and explorations of dinosaurs in their art work at the time when interest in the study of dinosaurs was strong among school students; the school exhibited some of the art work in the local post office. At the same time, the post office was running a stamp collection on dinosaurs. The two together made for a splendid combination of artistic endeavour. Schools could do more of this kind of thing and could be even more open to community interaction.

These are the kinds of connections that enable schools to build and maintain links with their community and at the same time create environments that encourage people to think aesthetically. Schools and other learning centres can do much to provide a culturally rich environment and to be a catalyst for people's growing interest and development of knowledge, understanding and capabilities in the arts. They can do this by maintaining links with people in the community, including different arts, cultural and ethnic groups.

There are of course centres for developing interests and capabilities in the arts and culture other than in schools. One thinks here of art galleries, arts centres, museums and film and TV studios where there are untold opportunities for lifelong learning, in which such institutions' education or education liaison officers are most anxious to play a part. They can do this at every level and in every way. Within many arts centres, for instance, there are programmes for kindergartens, families and schoolchildren.

It is only when we encounter the work of artists and craftspeople that we start to attend to the meanings and possibilities available in partnerships between schools and those constituencies involved in culture and the arts. It is very much part of the function of artists working in the community to assist in the development of people's self-awareness and aesthetic understanding. Understanding of aesthetics and comprehension of form and composition can be related to anything within the visual arts – landscapes, architecture, cityscapes – and can take place in a range of social, cultural, educational and religious milieux.

The artist can serve as a model of the lifelong learner, continually striving for new means of communicating, or extending the use of a particular medium, continually extending the use of a particular technique, continually extending the boundaries in which they operate, looking for new experiences to extend themselves, and looking for new networks of possible meanings in which they can explore the expanding boundaries of the worlds they create. The quintessential artist is the best example of a person involved in lifelong learning. Pablo Picasso was quoted as saying that every child is an artist. The problem is how are children and young people to remain artists once they grow up? This is the task for schools and lifelong learning.

Chapter 10

Forging Partnerships among Schools and Other Providers of Learning

The idea of lifelong learning clearly implies that, while education may start during a period of experience and activity in a formal and compulsory school setting, it will clearly extend far beyond that, continued, extended and developed by experience and activity in a variety of settings, in a range of other institutions, and following a multiplicity of pathways. This implies that there will be a number of agencies involved in offering opportunities for lifelong learning, some of them formal, some informal, some fairly traditional, some innovatory. Lifelong learning is a concept of co-investment.

There is thus a need, not merely for connections and exchanges between schools and a whole range of educational providers, but also for a set of alliances among schools and the other organizations, agencies and institutions offering educational opportunities. There is now a wide range of institutions, organizations and agencies that provide educational services and opportunities in some form or other. In addition to schools there are universities, technical and further education (TAFE) colleges, tertiary education institutions, hospitals, Neighbourhood Houses, broadcasting corporations, firms and industrial enterprises, trades unions, local councils, Councils of Adult Education, the University of the Third Age – the list goes on. The presence and activity of a multiplicity of providers shows that it is a mistake to assume that any one institution is the one best focus for educational provision. We are now entering a stage where the separate, complementary and mutually supportive contributions of a wide range of providers of lifelong learning opportunities need to be taken into account and various forms of relationship between them made a matter of pressing educational concern.

One of the vital parts of such relationships will be the acknowledgement of the need for clearly defined and flexibly articulated pathways of interaction and connection between them. These will make possible the definition and demarcation of a whole network of linkages, not merely operating in the same sector of provision and on the same level, but also between different levels and sectors.

A good model here is that of the complex articulations of the climbing-frame, in which people do not simply get to the top by one particular route in one single linear and uninterrupted progression (Smethurst, 1995). Instead they may choose to move across, backwards and down before again proceeding along and upwards towards the top in a different area. This is why people desirous of making use of education services – those coming to climb the frame – will need much advice and assistance in being shown and led to move on to different stages. The educating institution that is the school may be seen as constituting only one part of the whole framework of educational opportunity, interrelated and interacting with a multiplicity of other elements and constituent parts of the networks.

Given this model we can now see that, for policies of lifelong learning by a multiplicity of pathways to be really effective, relationships between the various institutions that constitute the totality of educational provision need to accommodate to the range and complex interplay of possible pathways for learners. Connections and alliances between educating institutions need to be based on a notion of individuality and difference, yet providing comprehensive and interrelated coverage overall. This implies some complementarity among and between separate providers.

Indeed if lifelong learning policies are to be constructive and productive, there ought at best to be some integration of effort and balance among the enterprises and undertakings of the different agencies. Part of this involves an awareness of the value of better co-ordination and synergy in the provision of educational services. Such provision, and a wide awareness of both its existence and the ease with which people may pass through it, will enable people to make connections with other groups and individuals with related, even if not necessarily similar, learning needs. That way there will gradually emerge a real community of learners rather than, as at present, pockets of separate interest.

This will only be possible if there is wider knowledge about and greater consideration given to the possibilities of growth and development afforded by the various types of relationship and modes of interconnectedness between different areas and sectors of educational provision. All the community's learning resources need to be made available, their assets and different services combined, and the pathways between them connected in such a way that the diverse needs of all learners in the community can be met.

STRATEGIC ALLIANCES AND ARTICULATED PATHWAYS

Overcoming Barriers and Obstructions

A start can be made on this undertaking by addressing those factors that inhibit attempts to dismantle the existing obstructions to the establishment of closer relationships between schools and other educating institutions. If there is to be co-ordination between the efforts and resources of a community's educating agencies, many of the barriers between different sectors, levels and institutions need to be dismantled, so that present and future generations of students can move easily from one institution to another and so accelerate their progress in learning.

As an example of the restrictions on opening pathways to progress, one may cite the difficulties created for education in some countries by the fact that currently there are a number of different state, province or territory educational systems and these do not easily permit articulation or transfer. To promote easy movement and individual styles of progression, there needs to be established and developed a complex and sophisticated set of arrangements offering cross-sector linkages, easy credit transfer, and recognition of qualifications across sectors and geographical locations and boundaries.

To establish such linkages and to make movement along them possible, a great deal of planning is necessary. This will be especially important if schools are to create strategic alliances with other agencies and organizations in the community. There will be a need for some nurturing in the early stages of collaboration if all the many possibilities of cross-fertilization among schools and other learning providers are to be realized and capitalized upon.

In the past such co-operation has been often very difficult to foster and maintain; hence there have been exciting educational innovations proposed that have not come to fruition and there have been learners who have not been able to profit from all the various opportunities that were in fact open to them. In fostering the ideal of lifelong learning for all, schools, the community, government organizations and private agencies will find their mission of service enhanced by espousing a philosophy of co-operation in provision of opportunities for learners, as well as simply setting up channels and mechanisms of co-operation.

An illustration of the dysfunctions to which the lack of such a philosophy can lead is provided by the fact that, until recently, there has not been much progress in the development and extension of relationships between schools and technical and further education providers. One of the causes of this is the fact that the systems are administered separately. Indeed we may say that in general the structure, funding and administration of different educational providers has not hitherto functioned in such a way as to facilitate co-operation. Consideration of the ways in which such dysfunctions can be diminished or removed must be a matter for future policy attention and action. If lifelong learning were to be the informing precept for such policy considerations perhaps some of the structural, funding and administrative barriers to effective and mutually supportive interaction might be overcome.

A further challenge to effective co-operation in the provision of lifelong learning opportunities has been the lack of linkage between private and publicly funded institutions. In future the co-ordination and integration of private providers into the overall provision of education will make a substantial addition to its assets and resources. Areas of present or possible future contiguity, connection and overlap have to be recognized, gaps of provision identified, forms of relationship and strategic alliance worked out and the development of a range of partnerships working in concert on the common cause of lifelong learning made a matter of educational priority.

Governments can play a leading part in efforts to facilitate reforms of this kind. They have the status, power and means to assemble groups of key players together; they can offer incentives and targeted programmes, and try out various proposals for reform and innovation at the level of local institutions, rather than having always to work through layers of intervening and potentially inhibiting regional or local authorities and mechanisms.

However, one might perhaps want to approach such endeavours with a degree of caution: the possibility of co-operation among agencies offering educational services can often be challenged or compromised by government promotion of competition under the overt agendum of their concern to promote quality. The tendering basis for the provision of educational services or the supply of educational goods often diminishes possibilities of co-operation. If governments wish to continue with the policy of seeking tenders for the provision or supply of educational goods or services, they will need to point to the need for co-operation among agencies involved in tendering for the bid, perhaps with specially designated funding of clusters, targeted on those organizations and agencies that can combine in ad hoc or more permanent co-operative provision centres in the development of joint bids as part of the tendering process.

This kind of joint activity in the development and submission of bids promotes co-operation among agencies, formal and informal, public and private. Indeed if funding arrangements are such that clusters or partnership arrangements are required or promoted, then one of the more productive ways forward in developing provision and programmes of lifelong learning may be via the combination into co-operative provision centres of a whole range of learning organizations and agencies some of which will be community-owned, independent, autonomous, self-governing organizations with their own committees of management.

The development of such clusters of co-operation is facilitated by the approach to course design and construction now adopted by many institutions. The emergence of modular-based programmes offers the opportunity for a variety of providers to contribute to one course. The place of delivery, the circumstances of programme design, the number of elements combining to produce one overall programme, course or unit, all these are opening up a range of possibilities and pathways for co-operative endeavour among a range of providers. One of the roles of government is to promote this kind of interaction and it is a role that should be expanded.

Such forms of co-operation have many other benefits above and beyond the merely financial, in that they can overcome some of the more negative effects of maintaining separate status and operating on a competitive basis. For example, if an institution feels that it must compete with other institutions in seeking financial support for the development of lifelong learning programmes, it may be less inclined to make it easy for students to enjoy the advantages of portability and as a result tensions may arise between institutions and their clients. If an institution is competition- rather than outcome-driven, there are more likely to be unhealthy tensions of this kind, and this will not be conducive to the well-being of the students, who need the kind of portability, credit transfer and interactive access to the programmes of other institutions that a policy of co-operation would encourage. In this endeavour, different providers and agencies will need to meet to clarify objectives to determine possible pathways and to agree upon accreditation procedures and credit transfer. At the present time there are a range of different levels, styles and standards of qualification and accreditation, and there is little possibility of mutual recognition or cross-transfer between many of them.

Further barriers to the establishment and extension of co-operative undertakings between schools and institutions and agencies in the post-compulsory education sector have been the different approaches to teaching found in them. Contrary to many approaches to delivering education in schools, much of post-compulsory education is not subject- or discipline-based. The highly compartmentalized approach to teaching found in some schools may lead to some teachers in schools feeling that they have little to offer adults, and/or to adults feeling disinclined or being unable to have access to and participate in teaching and learning programmes offered in schools.

Another source of difficulty may arise from the perceived emphasis that schools and some other educational institutions put on examination success and qualifications of various kinds. For many people concerned to develop their own interests and to address their own learning needs, interest can wane as soon as there is mention of credentials to be obtained and examinations to be taken. Some people find it irksome and counter-productive to feel that they must be locked into some kind of rigid examination programme.

Another barrier to access and participation in lifelong learning opportunities arises from the part played by issues of gender. Present evidence suggests that in some settings women tend to take courses which are not accredited whereas men take courses that offer credits. There needs to be some reassessment of the whole issue of equity in access, attendance and forms of credit. It should be possible to provide opportunities for people to accumulate various forms of recognition, credit or qualification available to them by means of their success in passing through various stages of proficiency that match their particular circumstances and needs at particular times or places. Schools have a particular role to play here, in making learning accessible to women and providing a starting-point from which women may pursue further learning.

The age of students is also a factor that might attract similar consideration. A flexible approach to discerning and following different pathways of educational opportunity will quickly make young people familiar with the precept that in extending their learning after compulsory school attendance there is not one fixed way of doing things and making progress. Learning will not follow a preordained pattern of linear progression along a series of fixed points; virtually any order of progression and style of learning will be possible. The days when knowledge was locked up in libraries or the minds of professors, open to access only by those who had ascended a prescribed set of ladders, is now long gone. The individually designed climbing-frame is the model that is now seen as most appropriate for lifelong learning. Part of the material for construction of such a frame will be found in learning centres located in the community and open to people of all ages. The existing presence and work of schools can provide a foundation on which learning centres of this kind can be built.

Links Between Schools, Providers of Technical and Further Education and Other Agencies of Learning

There can be no doubt that, even prior to the now growing emphasis upon lifelong learning, relationships and pathways between the various education levels and providers – schools, technical and further education (TAFE) colleges, universities, Adult Education Councils, the training institutes of particular professions or trades, other private agencies, the University of the Third Age – have increased and proliferated. Much of this development has come about through the demands made by learners for the availability of wider ranges and types of recognition for achievement in a variety of courses and for portable credit and transferable results. Many of these developments have also come about through the concerns of national governments for an increase in the provision of vocational education and training, for the establishment of links between short and long courses, and between award-bearing and non-award-bearing courses, and the achievement of credits for articulation among and between such courses and programmes. More remains to be done, however: the range, strength and multiplicity of such linkages could be enhanced.

In the pursuit of increased interaction between educational providers it is obvious that there is a growing need for articulated pathways between schools, TAFE and university. Schools and TAFE colleges are making moves toward further co-operation and are developing initiatives aimed at increased inter-connectedness. Some universities are also increasing the strength and range of their connections with secondary schools. There are of course problems with bringing about such forms of interaction: the particular requirements for access, structural arrangements, forms of recognition and student and capital funding might militate against the development of some forms of inter-articulation.

In some settings schools, TAFE, university and community providers work very well together, yet there are still considerable gaps in conversation, communication and co-operation. Such gaps ought to be closed, to the benefit of all kinds of institutions. TAFE institutions have much to offer in these relationships. A TAFE college environment provides a good model of sound student-centred and self-selected learning. Many TAFE lecturers have adjusted to recent developments in learning theory and new learning technologies, and on the basis of students' interests many have developed branching pathways of learning that are of use not only to the student involved but also in setting up guides and markers for others to follow and develop further. Such models of good learning provide exemplars that could be better utilized.

Unfortunately one of the principal sources of resistance to the establishment of positive and productive articulation between schools, TAFE and other providers of learning resides in the university sector. If a range of opportunities for learning through life is to be realized, some change is needed in the climate, culture and mindsets of some people within the universities as to the status of knowledge and learning offered by other providers in the community. When people in some universities talk about partnerships in developing learning opportunities, they still seem to operate with the tacit assumption that they alone will determine and control content. Such people have to show the much greater flexibility and recognition of the value of learning that people in other institutions have already adopted and are exhibiting. Perhaps such shifts in thought and practice might be promoted and accelerated by changes in funding and support policies put in place by governments committed to the ideal of lifelong learning for all their citizens.

There still needs to be more work done on the processes likely to be called for and involved in strengthening relations between schools and TAFE. There is a need to develop more flexibility in learning in schools and a way of doing this involves establishing links between schools and TAFE with students attending half-days at TAFE colleges or TAFE students attending courses in senior years in schools. There are places where such arrangements are now in place and are operating successfully.

This kind of interchange is enhanced when such liaison and interchange arrangements can be made for credit to be exchanged between work done in later years at school and early years in TAFE or even in university courses. There are already increasing possibilities for schemes of dual certification to be arranged, in which students at school can gain credits towards TAFE or university studies.

Independent schools often seem to lead the way in such schemes. Part of this comes from their freedom to utilize their own resources to delegate some person to go out to other institutions, do the necessary research, establish the relationships on a solid basis of mutual understanding and commitment to co-operate and help set in train the appropriate forms of implementation. Such arrangements benefit all parties to them: school–TAFE partnerships enable young people to get credit towards their School Certificates and towards a TAFE certificate for work they do in TAFE colleges (an example of this would be the work they produce as part of their design and art portfolios). The TAFE college for its part benefits from training (by the school) of its staff in the different learning and assessment styles of the various forms of School Certificate. One of the advantages of partnerships between TAFE and schools lies in the opportunities they provide for professional development for teachers in different learning and assessment styles.

Such relationships might, however, be seen as causing problems for some schools. It is quite possible that some students in the later years of schooling, having experienced the benefits and freedoms found in their work in the alternative setting of TAFE colleges, might decide they would prefer to move to a TAFE institution. If the number of students desiring entry to TAFE and consequently leaving schools increased, some schools might feel that the range and style of courses they could offer to students in their later years would be restricted. In this way the range and quality of their more advanced courses could be under threat.

This challenge has been met by some schools which have chosen to register as private providers and have obtained the necessary statutory permission to offer TAFE courses. Some schools are offering the entire first year of a TAFE course; some are offering more than that – an advanced certificate or even an associate diploma. In other places 'Advanced Standing' courses are being negotiated between schools and TAFE colleges, but this is a process that is not considered to be doing very well at the moment.

Stronger and more articulated connections between TAFE colleges and schools could serve the interests of a much wider range of students, whose needs may not be met by current arrangements. For instance, a greater range of pathways to TAFE colleges needs to be provided to help those school students who are not concerned with academic learning. In addition, many TAFE colleges have resources and facilities that can improve and extend the learning of students from other sectors and institutions, who would benefit from participation in one or two courses that are relevant to or supportive of their main learning elsewhere. Arrangements can be made to facilitate students' auditing such courses and taking the credit for their success in them back to their own institution.

There are many kinds of interaction and co-operation already in existence and increasingly possible. TAFE colleges often have the most splendid facilities, that are already being made available to the community. Also the organization and course provision of TAFE institutions often have much more flexibility than schools and universities in the things that they can offer to and do with the community.

Partnerships between TAFE and a range of other agencies should be varied and diverse: it would be superfluous for them to co-operate to the point of providing 'sameness'; such different institutions work in different contexts and maybe with different audiences, even though they may be concerned with similar, even common, objectives. The current stress on students' acquiring various 'key competencies' might provide a suitable framework for movement in pursuit of a set of overarching goals.

In all this, the TAFE sector can provide leadership to schools: TAFE was founded and funded to provide the courses and programmes that help people construct the building blocks for making progress in lifelong learning: literacy, numeracy, language, self-esteem, and the fundamental elements of specific vocational preparation, democratic participation and personal growth. Many TAFE institutions in the past have been very heavily concerned with vocational preparation activities. Such activities carried out by TAFE institutions are becoming more innovative and responsive. TAFE colleges have long experience and have developed considerable expertise in working with local industry, business and commerce; they have learnt to be responsive and efficient in identifying training needs for industry. Working with employers they have provided courses on the clear premise that people should be taught relevant and up-to-date knowledge and skills that will advance their work-place adaptability.

The concern of TAFE institutions that their courses should be skill-acquisitive can provide a strong foundation for their leadership in opening up to their students more doors and opportunities. The staff of TAFE colleges are very much aware of the need to point the way forward from what they do for their students: they put in a great deal of work to ensure that the ethos of their courses and the culture of the college is consistent with lifelong learning, providing recognition of prior learning, new vocational opportunities, and increased knowledge of further pathways of personal development.

Sometimes these opportunities are constrained by the times at which students can get access to them: usually people work during the day and have to attend courses at night or at the weekend. To offset this many TAFE colleges try to take education to the community by offering access in many ways and at different times and places to suit the convenience and the needs of their students. TAFE colleges now bring their courses to people in all kinds of settings: at college, in the work-place, at the community centre and in the home, through television, work off-campus and on-site, during the evenings and at weekends.

Many TAFE institutions are doing all they can to provide for the interests of particular groups whose learning needs merit special consideration. Special entry provisions are made for single parents, for students from non-English-speaking backgrounds, for women, aboriginal students, the physically disabled and the socially disadvantaged. Pastoral care is provided and guidance and counselling offered by specially appointed people. Such people also offer assistance in solving problems of transport for students both younger and older, looking to their security and safety and helping to oversee their activities while their relatives or friends are occupied elsewhere in work or in their own learning.

On occasion there can be some competition between local adult education and the TAFE providers in respect of courses offered to members of the community. The negative effects of such competition are exacerbated when some TAFE institutions compete with universities or other 'prestige' institutions in an attempt to increase their own standing and status in others' eyes, rather than looking at the job they should be doing and at the range and type of learning opportunities they should be co-operating in offering.

Clearly this is dysfunctional and wasteful. There needs to be a greater degree of co-operation between the TAFE short-course system, the adult education system, community centres of learning and schools. There is a need for a system in which each kind and level of learning organization can interact with, complement and support the activities of the others. Higher education institutions are not immune from this requirement: they need to offer easier access, greater flexibility and increased possibilities of cross-accreditation. In too many institutions there are still many programmes and courses where students can get locked in for many years, yet not sufficient account is taken of, nor credit given for, their previous learning experiences and achievements. A commitment to lifelong learning will ensure that such difficulties are addressed and attenuated or removed altogether.

TAFE institutions have a vital role to play and a critical job to do in helping to provide leadership to members of the learning community, taking lifelong learning as a concept, a value and a set of opportunities to people from schools and other institutions and sectors, orientating people into the awareness of the ways in which they can augment and increase their skills, while at the same time helping them to gain high levels of self-esteem.

Connections Between Schools and Other Community Organizations

Many other organizations and agencies offer educational opportunities. The possibility of linkages between schools and other providers is very wide: they include Neighbourhood Houses, community libraries, community health centres, child care providers, University of the Third Age and other organizations, whose educating agenda can be said to be overt. But there are also other agencies active in the community, such as sports clubs for example, which are recognizing that they too are learning organizations and that they have something to contribute to the education of children, young people and citizens generally. Some attempt needs to be made to enlarge and elevate the vision of people in such organizations to the opportunities for co-ordinating their educating functions. Churches too could move beyond their primary faith mission to a broader educative function in the community and there are settings where this already takes place.

Many forms of linkage and co-operation can be mutually beneficial. For example, the grounds and other facilities of schools can be used by various outdoor clubs in the evenings and at weekends. Equally there can be joint efforts by government, local council, local community and school to build sporting facilities, such as swimming pools, basketball courts or children's play areas. Schools can also become involved in community learning projects, such as those provided for people suffering particular forms of handicap. There might be some difficulty in co-ordinating such activities with the formal school curriculum but equally schools might find such an involvement of real help in illuminating their efforts at integration of learners with disabilities into the mainstream of the school's activities.

One very fruitful ground for developing further learning initiatives lies in the presence and openness of 'Neighbourhood Houses'. Such places are very much concerned with increasing social inclusion by providing support and services to people with language difficulties, people with disabilities, or people with low incomes. Sometimes Neighbourhood Houses work with schools and get their support to run programmes, making use of school facilities, and advertising in the school newsletter.

Some schools seem not to be aware either that Neighbourhood Houses exist or that they can offer adult members of their local school community, particularly women, an entrée into further learning for their own needs and interests. Many community organizations of this sort are deeply concerned about the importance of second-chance opportunities: they are aware that women often begin their second-chance learning in Neighbourhood Houses. Yet, when some schools have opened up their facilities to community organizations such as these, many have charged full costs plus depreciation. Many members of the community, particularly the unwaged, feel that they cannot afford to pay the sums involved and also feel unwelcome in the face of such requirements.

It is sad that the culture of very many schools still seems to be centred around the idea of working with children only. They seem to take the view that the only learning that should take place is what they provide to the students. It is difficult for a Neighbourhood House to work as a centre of learning for adults in the vicinity of a school imbued with that culture. The presence or absence of such an attitude is very much dependent on the principal's attitudes and school policies; fortunately there are many who do not have such a restricted vision of their responsibilities for continuing education beyond the school level. Indeed there are very many people who teach at the Neighbourhood House in the evening and who also teach at school during the day.

A complication in the work of many community educating agencies is the complex financial system and cycle in which they have to operate. This can often lead to tension in relations with government for many community providers. In order to get government funding many community providers feel that they need to act in a way that complies with and even appeases the government's requirements. The concern for community agencies is how to seek financial support without compromising or losing their integrity as an organization.

There is an important point to make here about the autonomy and independence of community educating agencies. They would be less effective if they were merely agents of or implementation arms for the government and government policies. At the moment there is an amount of sensitivity and even abrasion in the interface between the government and such agencies, as they learn to move into new relationships. Government is conscious of accountability pressures, while for their part community groups sometimes feel that their freedom is being constrained. But this is part of the process of transition in the relationship between government and agencies which are no longer operated on the principle of complete financial dependence.

The autonomy of such educating agencies is vital if their function of offering leadership or providing a service to the community is to be preserved. The Australian Conservation Foundation is a good example of such an organization. Its independence has enabled it often to run counter to government decisions: it works with schools; it provides an information service; it has had seconded teachers working in it; it has shown ways in which students can take part in the preservation of their environment. Yet some of the recent resource restrictions on schools have definitely affected its outreach capacity. Notwithstanding its success in such activities, the Foundation has never spent core resources on long-term education, though this is something it deplores. But its educational thinking has been constrained by financial concerns: it has been expected to be politically effective in the short term and has not had the resources to do more. Had that not been the case the Foundation is clear that it would have done more to advance environmental awareness through educational initiatives of various kinds.

Another community educational resource is to be found in the activities of service associations such as Rotary and Lions Clubs, which often provide educational material and resources about life skills. If such clubs had the resources and time, they are clear that they would work with schools to set up and run programmes centring upon and answering local community learning needs. At the present time, however, the level of funding provided does not succeed in enabling them to meet all such demands. Notwithstanding this concern, such clubs believe that they have much to offer other community organizations: what they are doing, they say, is basic to the health of the community.

There are other small private sector groups and organizations which are responding to specific needs in the community. For instance, there is an increasing interest in business courses, and in courses that show people ways in which they could turn their interest in chocolate making, for example, into small home businesses. Other small private sector groups are aware of a demand for recreational, outdoor and leisure courses generally, as well as computer courses. They also appreciate that the availability of self-help health programmes is an area of deficiency in current community education provision.

The provision of learning opportunities of a wide range requires local networks of information and publication. Publicity needs to be given to good examples of lifelong learning. Much of this can be done through local newspaper and television networks: the media can publicize news of good education practices, while education departments and ministries can use their own newspapers or access to media outlets to increase awareness of a range of opportunities for lifelong learning.

There are other places and means by which people can not only be informed about opportunities for developing their interests and capabilities in further learning for all the various purposes they have in mind, but can also be provided with a place to learn in and can enjoy access to courses of direct relevance to those purposes or of wider interest. Certainly such community cultural and knowledge institutions as public libraries, art galleries, museums, community centres and film and TV studios can serve as sources of information about and indeed offer opportunities for many kinds of lifelong learning activities. To provide such sources and to offer fora for such activities is part of the function of such institutions' education officers; some places, such as museums for example, even have education departments, members of which see their role as offering learning opportunities to a range of people and groups who might not normally be among their public. They offer regular programmes of activity for members of the community and their young, from kindergartens, to school groups, to families, to seniors of all ages and ranges of interest.

One of the institutions that has done a great deal to develop and deliver a range of learning activities for seniors in the community has been the University of the Third Age, branches of which are now in existence and flourishing widely across the world; and Councils of Adult Education and other agencies are active in offering similar opportunities in seniors' centres and retirement villages. No one who has seen the enthusiasm exhibited by seniors and their readiness for hard work, often at the most demanding and sophisticated levels of operation, in subjects such as advanced mathematics, philosophy and literature, can be in any doubt as to the major difference that engagement in such work makes to the quality of people's lives and to their sense of personal autonomy, dignity and worth. Such is the aim of all learning and educational endeavour – it is for the welfare of individuals and the communities in which they live.

Relationships Between Schools and Providers of Technology and Communication

One of the major areas in which the imperative of providing opportunities for learners throughout their lives is carried out is that of technology and communication. The ways in which schools communicate their information and publicize their activities and resources needs to be re-examined, as do the ways in which the new modes of communication are employed. The information technology revolution and the powers made available by interactive multimedia have had an enormous impact on the ways in which schools and educational institutions of all kinds work. Similarly various forms of interactive communication have made enormous differences to the world of work and will clearly go on influencing the ways in which work is organized in a very large part of industry, business and commerce in the future. Education programming is central to this type of activity.

This means that schools have to reappraise and reorganize the ways in which worthwhile knowledge is conceived and presented, how curricula are categorized and delivered, and how learning is arranged and promoted. Schools have to find ways in which they can help people to develop the now vital skills of learning how to learn: pushing their cognitive progress forward themselves, directing and controlling their own intellectual growth, learning how to be curious and how to do research, being imaginative and creative, self-monitoring, self-critical, self-correcting, and pacing their own learning. In addition they need to find ways to provide multiple pathways and openings for people in which they can work at their own pace. Information technology can help in all this, in a major way.

At the present time, unfortunately, many schools are not teaching all members of the community how to live with and exploit the opportunities offered by information technology. Clearly this should change: there is now so much information available and so many means of handling it that the skills involved need to be taught. Schools and other education institutions have a role to play in helping people to manage information and to prepare themselves for the immense opportunities it offers, in increasing vocational preparedness, personal growth, social inclusion and democratic participation.

Before showing members of the community how to use technology, schools need to emphasize the many advantages offered by information technology: they need to help students be clear about the purpose and benefits offered by this form of communication. One of the main advantages of modern information technology is that students will be much more empowered to select and travel along learning pathways that they can construct for themselves and use for their own personal growth. Computers are immensely resource-rich; they are operable at any time; they help us correct our mistakes in an unthreatening manner; they enable us to communicate with the high and the low – with all those who have an interest in communicating in these new ways too. Such technology can also play a part in increasing our sense of equality and shared interests: it can be socially levelling in that the forms of language or kinds of regional accents that in the past helped define social class do not come into play on the Internet.

These are among the many reasons why in the future students will be logging into learning centres around the world from their schools, their homes and their work-places. The range of information channels and learning pathways available will be immeasurably enhanced. In the future, modern information technology, including audio-visual channels, will facilitate communication between communities, individuals and groups who share common interests.

For this reason educators will need to re-examine their reliance on linear models of community and communication, since one of the essential components of the new technologies is that random access is possible, that navigation through different informational elements is possible, and that the linear structure institutions are applying to their current course structure design is not necessarily the appropriate one. Video on demand allows students to feed their own non-formal, non-traditional and non-linear requests for information and other questions into the system and get responses that suit them. This means that education audiences are no longer passive and this raises massive questions for those providing access to education services through modern technology media. Program designers in schools and other educating institutions will have to establish how they develop programs and design messages that cater for the needs of the active individual learner.

New technologies will help people explore subject areas from their own particular interest or vantage point, such as developing their understanding of personality, social history, or family background. The challenge for educators and service providers is to design an educational product and process that makes this possible. Educators will need to use audio-visual communication to communicate with their constituencies and will for that reason need to become completely audio-visual-literate and develop that literacy further – in a process in which their students are probably already far ahead of them in terms of competency, imagination and innovation.

Already the Internet is broadening the communication of learners beyond all previously accepted boundaries. One school has students communicating with others in Israel, Russia, Argentina and France; another has them working on a project called 'Holocaust', that looks at the issue of racism today and the matter of values and respect for others through interaction with people in other cultures and societies; yet a third has students looking at issues of environmental pollution, population and food supply, accessing international sources of information. Very quickly students realize that when they are communicating on the Internet they are part of the global community and that what they do in their communication within it is helping them to gain experience in communicating with those of a different race and nationality.

There are immense advantages in students learning to be part of the international network of communication but there are some problems too. Technological barriers to communication may be breaking down but some cultural barriers remain. People now have the capability of developing their communication skills to the point where they could in principle communicate with anyone in the world. Nevertheless people's cultural assumptions are different and in consequence they see the world differently, and schools need to assist students to be aware of and to respect these differences.

Increasing competency at communication in the international community can, if handled properly, expand people's intercultural awareness and interpersonal sensitivity, though these are qualities that are not themselves provided by or embodied in any computer program or file-server. Indeed, although modern information technology provides people with many greater opportunities for communication, it does not necessarily lead to the development of good relationships. Educators need to work at ensuring human relationships do not suffer with the expansion of technology.

Television can be a source of risk in this regard: it can simplify or trivialize cultural identity and cultural difference. As yet, television has not proved a positive source of help to people seeking to understand each other better. The television industry is, however, a major catalyst in change: television has the power to become one of the major agents, sources and organizers of information distribution. The power of television to supply information means that those in the education sector must become successful and highly literate audio-visual communicators and program designers or they will be left behind.

In the classrooms of the future, with students using computers and media of all types, with satellite interaction, and with communication on the Internet, special attention will have to be given to preserving the humane virtues. Helping students acquire the skills of sensitivity, interpersonal understanding, empathy, altruism and beneficence is not a matter that is amenable to the on/off, yes/no constraints of binary logic. Appreciating other people's needs, respecting their rights as persons, tolerating their points of view, and considering their interests as if they were our own, call for the most sophisticated skills of appraising, weighing, judging and drawing of implications for response or action and are not the kinds of thing that we can learn from a computer screen or file-server.

Moreover, the individual emphasis in modern information technology has the potential to work against community; it may be desocializing, impersonal and isolating. Schools and other educating institutions have to work against these negative desocializing effects. Educators are helped in this by the facts of human nature and human development. Human beings have not shown any predisposition to opt for a totally electronic life: people still need human contact, human interaction and human warmth. People still desire and choose to reach out and touch each other.

These are among the qualities and virtues called for in assessing the information we can access on the Internet. For file-servers give us access to good things and bad, horizon-expanding and horizon-distorting matters: the question is how are we to educate young people to react to the realization that they can access pornography, racial hatred and recipes for making drugs or bombs by searching out or simply coming across such things on the worldwide web? In these matters young people need to be helped to develop the powers of making judgments about what things are life-enhancing and what are not, when they encounter such material or have it disclosed to them. Such skills of judgment lie beyond the capacity of the computer itself to teach them. Students need to be shown how to acquire and deploy the fine-drawn skills of articulate and sophisticated discourse and the ability to make moral judgments. These are the *proprium* of the educator acting as a guide, philosopher and friend to accompany young travellers along the road of self-discovery and personal growth.

There are a host of questions and a wide range of other such issues associated with developing knowledge and competency in using the new technology. Instances include such problems as the question of how one copes with plagiarism in the global community; how one ensures and preserves privacy; how one counters the possibility of outside interference and control; and how one makes it possible for all sorts and classes of learner to have access to and achieve competency in using these new forms of information storage and exchange, in ways that do not compromise our commitments to equity and social justice.

These are problems calling upon the virtues of consideration and sensitivity to other people's needs that are among the most important outcomes of the educative engagement between students and teachers, learners and the place of learning.

This is why schools will still need to exist and teachers will still occupy a central place in their classrooms: technology will not take away the vital educational role and function of the school and the teacher. Educators have major responsibilities for the growth and development of their students, in the moral and the emotional as well as the sheerly communicative elements of their being. Students still need teachers to show them how to weigh, to balance, to assess and to judge, for reflection, insight, motivation and right action. It is in this that the real function of the educator of the future consists.

The Role of Universities in Working with Schools to Promote Lifelong Learning

Universities have a particularly strong part to play in acting with schools and other educational providers to promote lifelong learning. In major part the initiatives that universities can take in this enterprise spring from the nature and purpose of universities and their traditional role as educating institutions. But just as schools are changing, in response to changing social and economic circumstances, changes in conceptions of knowledge and changes in styles and technologies of learning, so too universities are having to adapt to similar new challenges confronting them. In the case of the universities, the need for this kind of adaptability and flexibility are reinforced by two major factors – the globalization of knowledge and the move to mass higher education.

The objects of a university's attention and academic interest have traditionally fallen into three domains: the natural environment in which it works – the nature of things; the interactions between that environment and its inhabitants, and their influences and effects upon each other; and the nature, activities, pursuits and aspirations of those inhabitants, both in their relationships with each other and in and for themselves. Such categories as these generate the raw material upon which university scholars direct their inquiries.

They do so for a number of purposes: for the intrinsic value of the gains to knowledge; for the value of the increased understanding of past and present; and for the functional utility of being better able to predict, direct and plan for the future. Every piece of material that comes before those working in universities, from one or other of these various realms of study, may be taken as evidence, examined and explained from a wide number of theoretical perspectives and a variety of interpretative constructs, and concluded upon as increasing the sum of understanding of the way things are or the stock of wisdom concerning the way things ought to be. In this way our theories about these things are extended and refined. These give clearer, more comprehensive and diverse accounts of the problems we encounter in seeking to understand and improve our grasp and control of nature, people and their interaction.

It is to promote such inquiries that universities are founded, funded and run: for the increase of knowledge; for the teaching and dissemination of that knowledge; and for personal and community development and welfare, that the availability and exploitation of such knowledge permits. It is part of any university's mission to extend the boundaries of knowledge, increase people's discernment and offer tentative solutions to problems, for the increase of human understanding and the enlargement of human benefit. The problems are presented by nature, individual human beings, and the community: the tentative theories for their solution are developed inside the university for application back in the place where the problems arise and are still sited. In these endeavours it is clear that the university, the school and the community must combine in a mutuality of benefit for epistemic advance and community welfare.

In the current context, the concern for extending the provision of lifelong learning opportunities offers a great opportunity to reassess the academic and professional beliefs, values and attitudes that have traditionally been embodied in the operations of universities. Such a reappraisal is necessary if universities are to join with schools and other educating institutions in making a positive contribution to the process of educational change for the benefit of the community.

Universities can no longer be seen as some people have traditionally represented them – as repositories of traditional knowledge and procedures, as élite institutions of learning concerned to keep the unlearned beyond the gates of the citadel of privileged knowledge. On the contrary in the current context the role of universities has changed: now their prime motivation must be to promote openness, dynamism and organic change in the interest of offering high quality education and training for all. They will do this through:

- the advancement of knowledge through research;

- the transmission of knowledge through teaching; and

- the diffusion of knowledge through communication.

In these activities the mission and work of universities is made manifest and in them the value of the university stands. It is from these starting-points that universities can offer opportunities for learning for all who wish to take advantage of them and so improve the community and the institutions that serve it. The benefits of university education, including the development of intellectual and personal maturity through university education, are best achieved in the light of the principle of continuous learning. Universities must be flexible and creative in offering lifelong learning opportunities from which all members of the community can derive benefit.

Many universities are already aware of this responsibility and are taking steps to offer such opportunities widely across all sectors of the community and to students of all ages, coming to them from a range of informal, unusual and non-traditional education backgrounds. Many of them have appreciated the importance of the lifelong opportunities that they can offer, from different perspectives. Some people see their careers as involving the need for lifelong professional development, and for constant updating of their professional knowledge and skills. Others view community outreach and lifelong learning courses as being of a much more social and individual remit, concerned with the idea of personal development, social inclusion and political awareness, none of which is at all cashed out in career terms. For universities hitherto, however, most of the lifelong learning debate has been more focused on the changing needs of the work-place, career development, and vocational extension. Only when people have looked at other forms of university-type offering and have considered the role of the University of the Third Age, have they recognized that other impulses and motives concerned with the idea of expanding horizons and adding to one's repertoire of existing knowledge, are equally valid as parts of the mission of tertiary education institutions generally.

There is of course no reason why the two undertakings need be so disparate. In one system both are highly desirable and to the extent that one of them, that concerned with career development, is of such importance that it can command certain resources from industry and government, to that extent it could cater for the other interest at the same time. An example is provided by the work of Open Learning in Australia. That particular agency was established primarily as a kind of pathway to a first degree, because it was thought initially that there were too many people who had not had an opportunity to go to university and wanted such a 'second chance'. And yet always from the beginning it was recognized that such an agency would serve the other market as well. There were going to be people, professional people, other people who took a new degree or a new sequence or unit of study, purely out of interest or as a form of further personal growth. In this way one motive provided for the other.

Some of the newer universities already have considerable experience here. Some of them were founded in places in which they would be able to look at the idea of mature age entry for that group of people who had not had much opportunity to take tertiary education studies. One of the interesting features of opening up such opportunities to mature age students was that a large number of those students, particularly women, very soon, within a period of two years or a year, carried on their studies from motives of developing their potentialities and promoting the wholeness and quality of their life. In the Open Learning Agency those who interview students report that students often state that they want at first 'to do one subject out of interest'; they state that they are unwilling to take a greater chance on something that appears more threatening. But of course this often leads on to much wider and more complex avenues of inquiry.

As has been already remarked, Smethurst (1995, p. 43) comments that there is often a very great deal of development and interconnectedness here; his preferred metaphor for such development is that of a climbing-frame – a very useful idea particularly for articulating some of the pathways of connection between TAFE, school, universities, other tertiary institutions, and other private providers. The importance of this metaphor is underlined by the realization that the kinds of education background that many jobs are now requiring cannot be delivered adequately by any single pathway. In this connection one notable development has been the success of a system of the double awards that have put TAFE and university work together, in combination, interchange, or in sequence. Many students now accept that in order to get into work and to manage the transition successfully they have to have some kind of practical 'hands-on' experience and further specific training based on learning gains of a more general type than they have already made.

Many governments, employers and other sectors in the community see the many advantages of such an approach. Governments are now willing to fund universities on the basis of targeted numbers of students entering them as 'new to higher education' rather than 'school-leaver' and this clearly gives place to entrants to universities coming to them from non-standard pathways. One of the more common movements that can now be observed is the number of students who have completed or partially completed university degree courses going to TAFE institutions for the courses they offer. For one Australian TAFE college its largest source of students is the local university: students with degrees or partially completed degrees who want more 'hands-on' experience and base-level training to help them into the workforce. In the same way there has recently been an increasingly diverse range of provision and of pathways for students who enter TAFE institutions and then want to move across to university studies. The credit transfer arrangements facilitating this kind of movement seem to have been easily arrived at and properly accredited, all of this being to the benefit of those who wish to profit from the availability of such transfers.

Yet a third pathway is one that makes it possible for students simultaneously to undertake both training courses and higher education studies. This might be by some system of double awards, based on the notion of a double degree to complete which takes four years rather than three, at the end of which students emerge with a diploma from the TAFE sector and a degree from the university sector in complementary but not highly overlapping areas, such as Bachelor of Tourism, Diploma of Hospitality, Bachelor of Communication, Diploma of Professional Writing and Editing, and other similar areas. The idea of students having a greater range of opportunities for taking two programmes is enormously attractive. This is facilitated in those cases where two institutions are located on the same campus or on campuses close to each other; otherwise the problem of geographic separation can intrude on the prospects of the co-delivery of mutually supportive courses. Some of the ways in which such problems can be overcome is by flexible delivery, multimedia learning or resource-based learning arrangements whereby institutions can agree to deliver at least one or two years of the university part of the programme into the TAFE. The more that institutions can co-operate in making such arrangements for flexible delivery, the more they can offer these sorts of mutually interactive and complementary programmes of study.

This kind of interactive arrangement could also operate between some schools and other providers of courses. One way to start on this would be to encourage linkage between the TAFE sector and schools, and some institutions have already set such arrangements in place. In one state in Australia there are now many schools – particularly in the private sector but also some government schools – that permit and facilitate the completion of a TAFE Certificate programme alongside that of the School Leaving Certificate. If schools and other bodies are willing to allow credit for such arrangements, then a much greater portion of schools' Leaving Certificate courses can be taken from the training sector. Students ought to be able to take on such courses as part of their courses for Leaving Certificates, so that they are not disadvantaged later. Schools could co-operate with the TAFE sector in putting on such courses and operating flexible delivery arrangements. Similarly TAFE ought to be able to service the schools, rather than the schools becoming private providers of TAFE; both again lead to flexible delivery arrangements.

Another opening is for schools to co-operate with universities, as they seek to cater for students of above-average ability and learning achievement; some schools may look for ways of offering opportunities for such students to take university subjects as part of the School Leaving Certificate. This is already being done in some places, although one of the biggest drawbacks is to find practical arrangements for delivery of the programmes into the schools. The students involved get credit (a) as part of their Leaving Certificate and tertiary entrance scores; and (b) when they go to university for courses related to work they have done in this way. Such students get credit for the university study they have already completed.

There are various ways of achieving this end. There is one approach which says that schools can teach university subjects. All the universities have to do is train the teachers of those subjects, or make sure they are qualified to teach them, and then assess it. This approach is not quite analogous to the American 'advanced placement' but is very similar. Perhaps the American 'advanced placement' approach has more integrity in that the tertiary institutions involved do not leave teachers so much on their own once they have been 'recognized' as qualified as some schemes do. The problem here is that some universities have reservations about handing over to teachers the responsibility of providing a university learning experience. Experience here in subjects such as mathematics or accounting, where subjects are assessable by examination, suggests they are less unhappy; for others, subjects such as literature or history are regarded with much greater caution.

Another approach, the extreme opposite, is one in which universities accept the school students as bona fide students but insist that they join university classes. The university does not provide any special programmes for such students. The schools in a way are losing control of the direction of their students' study but simply join the universities in taking advantage of their programmes which are open to all.

Some universities have tried to find the halfway house between the two extremes. They have done this in two ways. One philosophy is that about half of the learning should come from school-based resources, and half from university-based resources. That has been delivered in two ways. One can find or set up a cluster of schools that can bring together a class after school; in this arrangement the class is jointly taught by teachers and university staff; in addition the students come in to further classes in the vacation and over some weekends. Half of the instruction comes from the university, half from the school and there are many benefits accruing from such an arrangement. The school staff become quite involved with the appropriate departments in the university and the advantages of the development of such collegial relationships for both institutions are fairly clear.

The limitation there is that one has to get viable groups together. So the second way in which such mutually complementary relationships can be set up is by distance education. Here students in more isolated situations can benefit from such arrangements and these are operated by multimedia and resource-based learning. Such institutions use telephone or e-mail to keep students in constant contact with the university staff and a mentor in the school. The notion of a mentor in the school is quite important for those students working in such courses, studying from resource-based learning material, coming to vacation schools, over weekends, but maintaining constant contact by telephone or e-mail. This seems to be one way in which courses for such students can work well. Such students' results are excellent.

The next generation of this approach involves substituting the attempt to get academics out to school cluster groups by delivering some of the learning material by video or over the Internet. This involves institutions working to upgrade the services and materials they provide to the isolated students so it is not quite so print-based but reproducible in resource-based form and materials. At present a number of departments in not a few universities are working on producing a resource-based package that can be provided to a school or indeed any learning centre. In this way there is a manageable amount of additional university input. But there is much more university involvement in the preparing and delivering of material than simply in those approaches that hand such a task, and the teaching of it, over to the learning centre.

One of the chief impulses behind such initiatives is in encouraging the development of ways and means by which universities can co-operate with schools to advance both their mutual interests. One example of such mutual benefit has been in one university's scheme of having a number of teaching fellows. These have often come from schools that were doing enhancement studies, where a teacher is brought in to work in the department for a year to assist with transition arrangements and be better acquainted with the first year course. When such teachers return to the schools they are effectively a fully qualified first year university teacher. The advantages of having such people with intimate knowledge of both schools and universities is clear and the arrangements seems to work well.

In one university this has extended so far as setting up formal schemes for helping school students make the transition to university study easier and more enjoyable. In partnership with schools a video has been prepared and distributed to all schools in the state, giving school students information about university, showing how life in one is different from that in school, and helpful guidance on how students can better prepare for it. The same university organizes visits to schools by its Student Theatre Department, in which the university students enact performances based on stories from students about their experiences in the first year at university. Following these performances discussions are conducted between students from both institutions, designed to help the school students prepare for their own first year in the university. Such discussions lead to ongoing dialogue between schools and the university about transition issues and findings, in a form of partnership designed to maximize the help each institution can give to the other.

In another example, some universities have arranged for some of their medical and engineering students to go out into schools, helping school students learn about important matters in their domain of intellectual and professional interest and so extending school students' understanding of and interest in issues that are at the leading edge of intellectual inquiry and professional development. In the case of at least one university this has become a formal course unit offered by the Faculty of Education to the Faculty of Medicine, in which the university students undertake a school-based project concerned to help future professionals to develop an understanding of children's learning about health issues and of the values which children bring to their view of themselves and the world, and to learn how to work with professionals from another field. The university students, some of whom elect to work with students in primary classes, are able to take these activities in schools as 'options' that obtain them credit in their courses and that can be sources of ongoing professional and academic interest to them.

In both these cases, and in others, the whole idea of partnership is underpinned by the notion that institutions that have interests in common do things better together than they can do separately. It is clear that opportunities already exist for strengthening and extending various forms of partnership between universities, schools and TAFE. What needs to be further developed is the realization that immense potential exists for this relationship to become triadic. However, this kind of partnership approach is currently only in operation between universities and schools with students of accelerated learning potential. The question is whether it could be further developed to involve other kinds of provider and extended forms of such interaction.

There is also the question of whether such partnerships could apply in the case of would-be students who are disadvantaged or challenged in some way, perhaps by rural isolation, people with learning difficulties, and so on. Some universities are aware of the needs of such groups and are beginning to respond positively to their demand for access and participation in tertiary study by identifying the groups and perhaps by having special admission arrangements to get them in. There are, however, some steps that universities might be well advised to take. They would be wise to make sure that the transition and resourcing of such students' first year (at least) of study is monitored and appropriately delivered. One area where institutions have done this well is with Aboriginal students. They have arranged for such students to have a special year of preparation and during at least their first year in the institution they are given some special help so that they can work at the level of those students coming from different backgrounds.

Universities agree that there are groups of students who potentially could benefit from admission to their courses of study, though that depends not just on the issue of selecting or putting them in but on providing ongoing support and counselling systems. There are such schemes in place in some institutions in some countries but this whole area still needs considerable development. It is an area in which there could be much greater co-operation between universities and schools than perhaps exists at present with respect to the levels of support and the pathways institutions provide to prepare such students realistically for further study, to secure them entry, and then to monitor and assist with their progress once they are in.

One way in which universities could be more proactive here is by extending their schemes of community outreach, of taking lifelong education programmes out to the community. Some universities institute and strongly support such initiatives. There are of course some questions to be addressed: how are such initiatives to be funded and resourced? Some countries have a curious attitude as to how education is to be funded. In some places people are loath to make a contribution to paying for tertiary education, higher education. Yet such an attitude might need to be reconsidered, if universities with already restricted budgets are going to achieve much more of such outreach initiatives. In the case of the enhancement approaches mentioned above, which are after all a kind of outreach programme, one generally finds that there is a willingness on the part of such students to make some payment. In the case of the professional programmes that are now being offered in the work-place, employers are paying or individuals are paying.

Thus many universities feel that, provided there can be some scheme in place whereby there is some willingness on the part of the community, the individual or the employer, to make a contribution to having such initiatives adequately resourced, then the provision of such outreach undertakings is part of their mission. It is here where use of the new technologies will play a major part in assisting an appropriate level of resources and materials to be made available to interested groups and target audiences. Lecturers, instead of having to go out to distant locations each week, can appear on a large screen, or talk to the students in a computer tutorial and in that way costs associated with general provision can be reduced. The new technology has made that kind of interaction much more possible.

CONCLUSION

What is vital in all this is that institutions co-operate with each other. This is not only crucial in respect to the problems of reducing costs, securing appropriate accreditation and cross-crediting arrangements, and in providing appropriately qualified staff. It is also a feature of the productivity of such partnerships operating at this level in education that there be a sense of equality and equal commitment to the educational purposes of such enterprises.

This is more likely to be achieved if there can be a sense of contribution, ownership, monitoring by the crediting institution, and jointly supportive and mutually complementary arrangements for delivery. It is vital that universities have confidence about the work being carried out in the schools. Similarly, the more that schools, TAFE staff and university staff work together, the greater the likelihood of the development of a willingness to agree that certain materials could count in the others' courses. The question here is how might teachers play a part in the kind of programmes where this cross-boundary and cross-institutional course linkage is occurring? Such partnerships will only prosper and flourish when there is more of an involvement and more of an interaction between the staff, and the students and staff, across their different institutional boundaries. If arrangements to ensure this can be put in place, then we may hope to see greater progress in providing a wider range of articulated pathways in which all institutions in partnership can achieve better outcomes for their students.

It is, however, going to be very hard to achieve the full potential such partnerships have, unless there is genuine movement in – possibly even some levelling of – the boundaries between institutions, together with an emphasis on securing a sense of involvement and a real sense of ownership by all the parties involved. That is what real partnership in promoting lifelong learning for all involves – and it is to building such real partnerships that all such institutions must now turn, if the aims of lifelong learning for all are to be realized.

Part IV

Conclusions and Recommendations

Chapter 11

Leading the Learning Community

This final section of the book will provide an opportunity to offer conclusions and recommendations which might assist in identifying the key roles and responsibilities for governments, system administrators, schools, community agencies and other providers of learning in developing a lifelong learning strategy and in distinguishing the key policy areas requiring attention. Particular emphasis will be placed on the development of policies which will meet the challenge of working out ways in which better relations can be fostered between the school, education and training systems, and other organizations, agencies and instrumentalities of society, to make sure that a coherent and integrated approach to policy development and practice is put in place to ensure the realization of lifelong learning for all.

ARTICULATING A PHILOSOPHY OF LIFELONG LEARNING

These are times of enormous economic, social and political change. At such a time governments and policy-makers accept that no country can have a significant number of its population who are outside its social institutions and work organizations. Such an exclusion cannot be afforded economically or socially: there is an overlapping concern for society to have an educated workforce and an educated community and insofar as the community does not maximize the potential of all its inhabitants to contribute to both, it suffers by the loss. Community leaders generally – employers, educators, agents of social and welfare institutions, members of political, cultural and religious groups – are coming to agree on the need to recognize the vital importance of people's undertaking further learning, for this is nothing less than an investment in the whole social and economic fabric of our community.

Opportunities for people to secure access to the advantages of engagement in employment and involvement in social institutions are promoted by lifelong learning. The extension of these opportunities to all potential learners in a society is founded upon arguments about equity, social justice and the chance to participate in all the various 'goods' made available by lifelong education opportunities and programmes. Lifelong learning is thus an ethical issue, as well as an educational and economic issue and there are ethical, economic, educational and social arguments to justify it.

Commitment to lifelong learning is a long-term matter: and articulating and establishing policies and programmes of lifelong learning for all involves not merely addressing the conceptual problems, but also the political problems.

Lifelong learning requires an educational and political strategy that will see a country over its next two or three generations. In order to cope with implementing such an approach, governments need to move out of their short-term time-frames.

Those who take an instrumental view in these matters argue that there is a need to convince the electorate that an investment in lifelong learning will pay dividends, both in increased wages and other economic measures, such as increased employment flexibility and adaptability that will give one a modicum of job security.

However, simply pursuing lifelong learning with these ends in mind might militate against other key values and goals, for modern participative democracies, of social inclusion. The fear is that lifelong learning, pursued with merely economic interest as its principal motivation, risks enlarging the gap between those who have access to education and those who do not – of marginalizing those people who, without access to such opportunities, become alienated from the operation of the social institutions that are there for their benefit. This danger is exacerbated when there are ideological tangles over what ought to be formal and publicly funded education and what not, with respect to the goals of social inclusiveness and/or international economic competitiveness.

There has also been some ideological debate about different conceptions of valued knowledge and different approaches to learning, and further, over the question of prescribed knowledge content as against mastery in particular sets of competencies and skills in subjects studied as part of the formal curriculum. But this is a reductionist and narrow debate: the debate about optimum learning, the access people shall have to it and the uses they shall make of it in the future, needs to become more educationally informed.

It is by now quite clear that lifelong learning has a benefit for society in general: the more engaged in productive and worthwhile activities people are, the more engagement they will be likely to pursue politically and socially. The two elements cannot be separated from each other. Governments must therefore address the issue of multiple priorities. And, in doing so, they might think it of importance to look at the whole range of benefits likely to accrue to the economy, democratic institutions, and social relations from the adoption of lifelong learning policies. In the past, and still in some quarters today, there has been perhaps too much emphasis in the formation of education policy on finding cost-effective solutions to problems rather than in seeking to achieve a more comprehensive form of understanding of the multiple issues involved.

Lack of clarity on this matter is perhaps a function of past history: until relatively recent times changes in policies and provision of lifelong education opportunities have tended to be introduced in a piecemeal fashion, with people being unaware of any underlying philosophy. In leading the learning community the philosophy behind lifelong learning needs to be made known to and understood by all members of the community, by, in and through all the various forms and fora of public communication, public and private, formal and traditional, non-formal and alternative. Governments need to be forward-looking, positive and committed to making it clear that, in promoting lifelong learning as a touchstone idea in education, they are promoting the general well-being of the community, in social, economic and individual terms. The whole idea behind lifelong learning is the increase of autonomy, for state, society and individual.

To repeat, then, lifelong learning is a touchstone in education; it is embodied in everything we do in schools, colleges, TAFE, tertiary institutions and other agencies of learning, underpinning and permeating all our endeavours in them. Because of this lifelong learning has to be addressed from a variety of entry points: the community needs to move away from the idea of linear progression to develop a more branching, articulated and expansive notion of education and lifelong learning. The concept of lifelong learning involves the importance of people having a sophisticated understanding of the context of their lives, and the skills they need to function in society. Part of this involves an awareness of the need for better integration of work, family and leisure in all our lives – such an integration can be assisted by lifelong learning opportunities and approaches. One part of this may involve asking some questions that seem to have been forgotten as being important in educational provision: how can we bring about an approach to education that allows people to value the learning of things they enjoy doing?

There needs to be a sea-change in our attitudes to offering lifelong learning for all: until now, many countries' approach to education has been exclusive rather than inclusive. Education has been geared too much to those who enjoy academic success. Clearly this must change if we are to help the community capitalize on the benefits in learning gains that can be achieved from all a community's people, not just a privileged part of it.

In this enterprise we might, with reason, ask where and in whom there exists a clear grasp of the 'big picture' issues of social inclusion, equity, economic advance and lifelong learning. And this immediately raises a problem because, in attempting to determine where the establishment of such 'big picture' views might lie, we have to discover who are the principal formative influences and what role they play in articulating a philosophy and developing policy.

In the development of 'big picture' perspectives leading to the implementation of lifelong learning policy initiatives, we might think it important to determine what are the respective roles of government, business, special interest groups, schools, other educating agencies and individuals. There is a problem for democratic representation and agreement if we establish that policy is being determined by the larger powers of government, big business, and other powerful players all at one end of the spectrum; equally worrying for the interests of the representation of all views in a democratic society, would be a scenario whereby our search established a powerful and determinative role being played by the private sector with its own special interests in policy formation.

What is needed is some kind of balance: there is a need to move away from the paternalistic role of government and the intrusive and exploitative approaches adopted by some private interests. Overall, we need, in articulating a philosophy and in setting up policy-making and administrative arrangements for lifelong learning, to see some balance maintained between overall government priorities and the interests of the local community, between central and local control, between large and small constituencies, between publicly and privately funded organizations and institutions. In this way the interests of all members of the community might have some chance of being considered, addressed and safeguarded.

PARTNERS IN LEADERSHIP
Leadership by National and State Governments

In responding to this challenge there is a role for governments at a number of levels. At a macro level there is a role for governments in insisting on the significance of lifelong learning, articulating arguments which will show its benefits to the electorate and legislating policies which will help realize its benefits. Governments will have a responsibility in promoting well-functioning systems of education and training in respect to: developing policy; establishing an appropriate institutional infrastructure; creating linkages between different forms of education and training and different sectors; and improving the relationship between traditional providers of learning and newer arrangements provided by community agencies and private providers functioning in the market. Governments can help develop the frameworks for better information on training opportunities, assessment, and the recognition of acquired learning and competencies (OECD, *Jobs Study*, 1994).

Outside the traditional education sector governments can also act to reduce the uncertainty of firms' investment in further training by considering and advocating the making of changes in financial accounting and reporting practices, thus improving the transparency of training costs and demonstrating the value of knowledge and competencies. Governments can reduce the risk and cost of 'poaching' through the imposition of training taxes and levies – although evidence suggests that caution should be exercised in this regard and that a more systematic solution lies in governments' encouraging diversity in the institutional settings in which education and training are provided and in the teaching and learning methods employed. Public authorities could also improve access to education and training programmes for small and medium-sized companies by encouraging the establishment of training co-operatives and in this way permitting economies of scale or encouraging public institutions to provide the requisite training capacity as well as advice (OECD, *Jobs Study*, 1994).

In all these efforts there will need to be a movement away from previous emphases upon partition, demarcation or compartmentalization. Cross-sectoral co-operation, institutional interrelationships and curriculum integration are key concepts in the provision of lifelong learning. It is this kind of interchange that is likely to make the organization and provision of lifelong learning opportunities in the 1990s and beyond much less difficult than previous attempts at the implementation of this notion. In such interchanges there will be a premium on goodwill, lateral thinking, and a whole range of supporting mechanisms to bring about change. It will be important to approach the implementation of the concept of lifelong learning with flexibility and adaptability, respecting the multifaceted and variable nature of lifelong learning provision.

At a macro level, the role of government in lifelong learning can thus be summarized as being:

- overseer of policy conception, development and implementation;
- facilitator of policies among different sectors;
- dismantler of barriers;
- creator of community connections.

In exercising these functions the agenda of a government committed to lifelong learning is to stimulate debate, to plan for the delivery of services, to provide funding, and to assist in the development of clear policies to facilitate implementation at the institutional level. There is a need to refocus policy, and to develop a strategy that is interactive between all the various agencies and constituencies having an interest in providing or benefiting from lifelong learning opportunities.

Government also has a nurturing role in respect to generating, encouraging and supporting 'bottom-up' change. This can take many forms: governments can be involved in providing seeding funding to communities and community groups on the basis of the learning needs identified by those communities; it can help community groups to generate income and become more independent, and to increase opportunities for all their members and constituencies. An increasingly important role for government will be to enhance the process of connecting what already exists in the community and encouraging it to grow and expand from the wealth of sources and resources either already present or having the potential to be generated from within the community. Governments can help communities focus their attention both inwards and outwards and address needs that are both local and yet also national; they can provide incentives that encourage local communities to take all constituencies' interests into account, to weigh them and then to balance micro and macro decision-making – to balance self-interest against the general interest.

Lifelong learning needs a co-ordinated government approach and commitment; it needs structures and resources if quality processes and outcomes are to be achieved, not merely within the various ministries in which the concept has developed but also in other ministries – Health, Social Welfare, Employment – in all the various sectors, levels and sites where responsibilities for educating citizens might also be thought properly to lie. At the policy execution level this will require considerable oversight and administrative co-ordination.

However, sectors go through periods of change and this is the case in respect to the provision of lifelong learning at the present time, especially in respect to the multiplicity of agencies that are involved in its provision and delivery. For the purposes of realizing the benefits of lifelong learning, there is a need to rework some relationships. Governments with a commitment to lifelong learning should go out and learn what it is that partners in educational provision want, who can contribute, and how the various agencies can complement each other in securing it.

One role for government could lie in the provision of a communal infrastructure which enables schools and other educating institutions to have much greater access to the community. This might be brought about through government and local funding of learning centres and through the supply of human resources to meet the needs of schools and other institutions.

Governments with a commitment to the imperatives of lifelong learning will appreciate that such an approach implies a new approach to the distribution of funding. Governments may need to provide seeding funding to support the development and extension of a range of lifelong learning initiatives. One of the roles of government lies in providing incentives for such new enterprises, and in giving them the necessary 'kick start'. Many community agencies that would play a key role in providing learning opportunities are not necessarily well endowed financially and would value highly any assistance they were given to make the provision they see as vital in promoting community interaction through lifelong learning programmes and courses. Consortium-type arrangements can be set up between such local agencies and ongoing relationships established. Incentives are required to put such consortium-type arrangements in place and to start them working. This would perhaps attenuate some of the problems agencies often encounter when seeking financial support.

One of the problems in new patterns of relationships has to do with the issue of competition or co-operation. Competition for resources between agencies – for instance, by responding to government invitations to bid competitively through tendering – could act against the interests of co-operation and partnership. A more co-operative and targeted approach could do much to eliminate the wastefulness and abrasiveness often caused by such competitive processes, as well, of course, as respecting government's responsibility for continuing an overview of the range and proliferation of lifelong learning opportunities being provided.

There are other reasons for governments having such oversight and for making the information thus obtained more generally available. There is need for better communication about what is available in respect to educational provision across the community. If people are to accept greater responsibility for their own learning they need not only a directory of courses but a process to help them think through where their own knowledge extension and skill development might lead them. People always need information and often need assistance to plan their personal and career development. Without such assistance there is a risk that people could miss out on opportunities and pathways that would be advantageous to themselves, the polity or the economy. People can fall through the networks of educational opportunity through bad luck, lack of information or changes in circumstances. Often it is only later that such people may be daily confronted with the repercussions of such deficiencies in their access to information about educational opportunities, and it is up to individuals, the community and the government to do all they can to provide the information, openings and encouragement to ensure that the possibilities of individuals missing out on opportunities can be minimized.

One of the ways in which individuals might suffer such a fate is if they are ignorant or have apprehensions about current methods of evaluation and assessment and find current approaches to assessment intimidating. There is good reason for arguing that current approaches to assessment and accreditation do not always promote lifelong learning; clearly new approaches to questions of evaluation, assessment and accreditation should be designed to promote the aims and purposes of lifelong learning. In this endeavour, one principle should be held equal to all the others: to promote the value of learning for its own sake rather than for examination success. Another principle should rest on the concern for the transferability and multiple utility of a range of forms of assessment and qualification. One might also consider the notion of building up credits in some type of learning bank. But as flexible and multi-faceted an approach to such matters should be in operation, as that relating to the conception and provision of lifelong learning courses.

Another important principle should rest upon the emphasis upon autonomy and choice in the selection of courses. There needs to be a demand-driven rather than a provider-driven approach to lifelong learning. Individuals in the community need to be placed in a better position to recognize their learning needs and be able to seek out and find the appropriate providers. This position will be enhanced if different organizations or agencies can work at providing courses that will enable them to capitalize upon their own strengths, resources and missions, while also working for the wider or the common interest.

Leadership by Local Governments

In this endeavour local government can serve to provide information about the range of services offered by local providers, in ways that enable them to combine and co-ordinate their activities. In this way local government might well reorientate its thinking towards the extension of forms of community support. Local government departments and offices have the means and opportunity to play an important part in developing lifelong learning linkages, as well as having an important role to play in community and cultural development. For this reason it is important that schools and other educating institutions and agencies establish multiple liaisons with a range of local agencies and institutions – especially with their local councils. Local governments need to ensure that all parties involved in delivering lifelong learning have an awareness of common areas of interest; these will include:

- co-ordination of activities serving common goals;

- sharing of resources;

- provision of maximum possible access to all avenues of inquiry regarding vocational training and personal development;

- provision of a wide range of information and other resources;

- co-operation among providers in ensuring that resources such as municipal libraries and the like complement what is being done in schools and other institutions.

In such undertakings it is vital that local councils become involved in planning the provision of lifelong learning. A first step may be to conduct local

needs surveys to identify the areas and kinds of requirement. Local governments have a leading part to play in such an activity, as they are often situated
in a central position in the local community: the importance of location in
networking with the local community cannot be overestimated. A main part of
such networking will be the way in which local councils and other authorities
and agencies can work together with schools and other educational institutions.
Crucially, there needs to be a systematic documentation of good practice.
Exemplars of such practice will be found in the work of those schools whose
involvement with the local community has succeeded in providing opportunities for all people through strategies such as after-hours learning. Local
councils might institute a programme of awards to schools that take a comprehensive approach to lifelong learning. The availability of such awards could act
as an incentive for other schools and learning providers.

Leadership by System Administration

At the level of system administration it is also clear that aspects of the present
configuration of institutional provisions and prevailing practices militate
against the realization of a lifelong approach to learning for all. The data
provided in contemporary analyses such as the OECD *Jobs Study* (1994) lead
one to the conclusion that the desired gains in economic efficiency and social
equity can be achieved only through more universal completion of upper
secondary education, or its equivalent; more predictable and certain entry of
young people into the labour market; and greater increases in skills and
competencies, that in turn can be matched to those skills and competencies
required in the work-place.

The causes of early school-leaving are multiple: some are related to characteristics of education systems, such as secondary education policies and
practices biased towards preparing young people for higher education and early
compulsory leaving ages; others are associated with the young people and
dysfunctional factors in their socio-economic environment: poverty, ethnic
minority status, and adverse family factors. The negative impact of these
factors when combined increases exponentially.

A major priority for the achievement of the goal of lifelong learning chances
for all must therefore be to reduce, through preventative and remedial measures, the number of young people who leave school before completing a
secondary education or its equivalent. Evidence shows that some countries do
better than others in reducing early school-leaving. The highest retention rates
occur in European countries with a long tradition of highly organized systems of
education and training with clearly defined, collectively organized and accepted
responsibilities. The systems of education and training in these countries are
characterized by inclusiveness. This is particularly evident in countries with
dual systems (OECD, *Jobs Study*, 1994).

In recent years a number of countries have introduced strategies to
increase education beyond the lower secondary and pre-apprenticeship level.
Strategies have included introducing greater diversity in upper secondary
education through the development of multifaceted programmes offering

alternative pathways for education and training; providing greater choice in post-secondary destinations; diversifying the content and learning methods at upper secondary level; and offering richer choices at upper secondary level including balanced opportunities in vocational and general studies. Achieving such diversity requires co-ordinated action with labour market actors. In systems that postpone vocational education until after secondary education, diversity is possible through the introduction of different teaching and learning techniques, such as laying greater emphasis on computer-based learning; and changes in the organization of courses, such as sandwich courses. Better quality education and quality control, achieved through changes in curricula, approaches to teaching, and improved assessment and reporting mechanisms and practices, may also help to address this problem. A structure of incentives to reward teachers who use more varied teaching modes and reach more students may also be a way forward. Other strategies to reduce early leaving have included establishing targeted programmes designed to meet the particular learning needs of those 'at risk': these can include programmes that target individuals (e.g. as in Germany and the USA) and those that target geographical areas (e.g. as in France and the Netherlands). The approaches that target individuals which appear to be the most successful are those that embody a systemic and systematic approach to the prevention of student drop-out and link targeted programmes with mainstream programmes and institutions (OECD, *Jobs Study*, 1994).

Yet another strategy to reduce early leaving has been to provide a foundation for success in upper secondary education and lifelong learning built on the provision of education at all levels: this involves adopting a longer-term preventative approach to reducing the chance of educational failure and early school-leaving, through educational and related interventions at the pre-school, elementary and lower secondary level. Although it is difficult to isolate the impact of early childhood programmes on educational performance there is increasing attention being given to early intervention strategies in the expectation that they have a positive impact on subsequent school performance and thereby reduce the risk of early school-leaving. Facilitating co-operation of family, social partners, government and the community at large has also been seen as an essential element of all strategies to address the problem of early school-leavers.

However, even when young people have acquired satisfactory initial qualifications their success in winning entry to employment and in their transition to employment is often difficult. There is considerable variation across countries with respect to the smoothness of the school-to-work transition for young people. There are two major orientations to the process of transition: (a) 'sequential', where largely full-time attendance at educational institutions is followed immediately by entry into the labour market; and (b) the dual apprenticeship system. Improvements in the processes of young people's transition to work require the development of new institutions and new attitudes on the part of system administrators, employers, workers and unions. Market mechanisms also need strengthening and interactions among institutions and market mechanisms need to be co-ordinated and mutually supportive.

Evidence suggests that there is no single best approach to improving transition. In the debate regarding the relative advantages of school-based or employer-based approaches there is some suggestion that a school-based approach is the better way to proceed. This is because: firms cannot be expected to provide remedial education on any long-term basis; firms are vulnerable to changing business conditions which may lead to fluctuations in the provision of training; there is a risk of inefficient or insufficient investment due to market failures or lack of mechanisms of co-ordination between employers to overcome 'free riders'; and finally, in enterprises which have organized their division of labour inefficiently or around outmoded technology, certification programmes and practices modelled too closely on firms' existing perceived requirements can simply perpetuate inefficiencies. Evidence shows that the most effective transitions for young people depend on partnerships that link formal systems, young people and employers (OECD, *Jobs Study*, 1994, p. 154).

Partnership is also the key in respect of control and funding schools and school systems. In this regard there needs to be some recognition of and agreement about what constitutes core activity for all schools. But this will best be achieved by a consensus of the voices of all those who have an interest in the work of educating institutions. System administrators do not need to be directive of what goes on in individual schools. Schools should be accountable to government and community, but should run as more autonomous institutions, with the principal as managing director, responsible to a board which in turn should be representative of the community. The chief function of the system administration should be in providing funding, research assistance, guidance, information, support, helping all interested parties in setting out terms of reference for effective school operation, ensuring equity and social justice in provision, and then assisting with the implementation of that process.

At the level of individual teaching staff, system authorities could offer incentives for teachers to participate in professional development work in preparation for lifelong learning if they are to transform the teaching service in the way needed. Options might include offering teachers one year off for such preparation, in lieu of 20 per cent of their income over a number of years, say, four to five; or an employing authority might arrange for especially gifted teachers to take a year, with appropriate higher duties allowances, as leaders in other institutions, places or fora where different patterns of lifelong learning programmes were in operation. The availability of such incentives is important for people with obligations to families, mortgages and other commitments, and must be made part of an education professional's normal pattern of career development, if countries and communities are really serious about promoting lifelong learning.

Leadership by the Community

Lifelong learning has to do with the development of a range of interactions between educational institutions and their host communities, working co-operatively to sort out, in a general sense, what all partners are about in seeking to promote the value of learning in the community. All are concerned to develop a learning community where learning is valued, where innovation is esteemed, where development – individual, social, communal – takes place, and where facilities and resources can be shared.

This means that lifelong learning has to be addressed from a wide range of perspectives, offered by a wide range of entry points, and to the whole age range of students, actual and potential. Everything that is happening in the community needs to be matched by changes at the levels of schools and all other types of educational institutions, to bring all such ranges of provision and resources together. Everyone working in such institutions has to understand the concept of lifelong learning and be committed to it. This is especially important in the case of schools, where students learn to take the first steps on the road to the learning they will need during the rest of their lives. To promote this, schools with an appropriate infrastructure of both human and building resources need greater integration with the community.

Many community organizations, by their nature, actively involve members of the community in their activities. These organizations already have a very positive attitude towards lifelong learning and play a positive part in bringing it about. Community organizations must be recognized as providers of learning and be brought into line with those other forms of lifelong learning provided formally in schools, systems and other institutions. One reason for this is that many of the people working in community organizations at the local level are vocal, intelligent and dedicated. They are often highly imaginative, innovative and creative, and are already involved in the process of lifelong learning for themselves and others. However, new approaches are needed for people who may be reticent about approaching an education centre but who nevertheless seek or would benefit from having access to further learning. This may involve the provision by local agencies of such activities as running a programme for elderly people in their own community hall or at their retirement village. Indeed, for lifelong education to succeed, there has to be a shift in thinking about the learning potential of older people: we need to move away from the notion that it is only younger people who are enthusiastic and capable of learning. One of the chief advantages of a lifelong approach to learning is that it highlights the need for structures in communities that use the abilities and wisdom of older people.

Community organizations have been successful in their attempts to provide lifelong learning opportunities because they have been able to address the needs of many people who need a personal approach to teaching and learning. Through involvement in community-based learning activities such people have come to gain confidence from each other, which enables them to go on to lead much fuller lives. Direct access to further learning opportunities in people's homes or in local community centres contributes to greater social cohesion in society generally and can only enhance the feeling of involvement, inclusion and sense of personal worth of many citizens, some of whom might otherwise be marginalized in the community.

With respect to younger people who may have already dropped out of the system of formal educational provision, much remains to be done. Welfare groups such as the Brotherhood of St Lawrence and the Salvation Army certainly give many young people much help, though this tends to be on a welfare rather than an education basis. Such young people and such caring agencies could benefit in a major way from links with education providers, though this might necessitate both working with new people and in new ways. In the future, effective interaction and positive working partnerships can be forged between welfare agencies and learning providers in the interests of lifelong learning.

Partnerships between education providers and business and industry will also be an important aspect of realizing lifelong education for all. At the moment the concerns of business and industry are very powerful in influencing much government consideration of policies for education.

Some employers expect schools and other educating institutions to train their future employees before they employ them. For such people education is something that must be run along business lines, seeking and targeting markets, addressing the needs of clients, providing marketable goods and services, and being subject to the judgments of market forces. There are many disadvantages and dangers in such an approach which ignores the other equally important considerations of education, to do with extending justice in society and enabling individuals to grow and develop as mature and autonomous adults, able to contribute to the political economy and the democratic running of a society.

Increasingly, leaders of business and industry are taking a larger societal view and, in part, this has come about from the partnerships between education, business and industry which have been developing over the last decade. It cannot be entirely fortuitous that the very metaphors which are now emerging in approaches towards business improvement are those which are centring around the ideas of 'education' and 'the learning organization'.

Business and industry have much to contribute to education: they have now appreciated the importance of developing the whole person. There is much work for business and industry to do in promoting and furthering the values and aims of lifelong education by the opportunities that they can provide in the work-place or help provide and strongly support in the community. Many firms and employers are already doing this – and finding that it enhances the quality and success of their organization, its modes of operation and levels of success.

Partnerships between schools and constituencies in culture and the arts will also be an important aspect of realizing the goals of lifelong learning for all. Schools can function as centres of arts and culture for their communities, offering opportunities for learners of all ages to practise, create and exhibit their work in various forms of artistic and cultural expression and to participate in creative endeavour with other learners. The learning emphasis in schools could make them be seen as among the best places in which people could get started on the development of artistic interests and cultural pursuits, in forms of interaction embracing other people and groups from the whole community. In this way schools can build and maintain links with their communities and create environments that encourage people to develop and extend their cultural activities and artistic interests, and refine their powers of aesthetic judgment. Such an environment can be a catalyst for people's growing interest and capabilities in culture and the arts. Schools can also promote such developments by forming partnerships with other institutions devoted to such purposes: art galleries, arts centres, museums, libraries, theatres, concert halls, radio and film and TV studios offer many opportunities for extending lifelong learning and all these can be capitalized upon and their facilities and resources used to good effect.

Leadership by Other Learning Providers

At the present time most countries have an educational framework in place which offers the opportunity for people to gain qualifications at all levels from school right through to post-graduate education. But, while we have a continuum of qualifying bodies such as schools, TAFE colleges and universities, there seems in many places to be a lack of close connection and co-operation between them. For the furtherance of all ways and meanings of lifelong learning there needs to be greater integration between providers and a greater inter-relationship one to the other. The important point is the availability of a network of pathways and possibilities of movement between sectors, levels and institutions, and along the various routes for learning.

Universities are vital parts of such a network of pathways and opportunities. Now universities make their own decisions about entry, and about their work in all the various fields of knowledge and understanding in which they are active; but there is a perception that they have a relatively restricted awareness about developments in other educational sectors. There is clearly a need for greater cross-sectoral co-operation and integration between the various sectors and levels of any education system but how this is to be achieved is another matter. This is something that needs urgent address.

Cross-sectoral co-ordination would also do much to clarify the differences between the visions and missions of universities and those of the TAFE and schooling sectors. The issue of 'mission' becomes very important to all sectors of the education service given the increasing importance attached to lifelong learning. Within the TAFE sector, for example, there is an ideological divide between those who, in emphasizing economic goals, advocate funding for vocational training, and those who, in placing stronger emphasis on social inclusiveness and the fulfilment of the individual, seek more funding to achieve these ends. Those who support the latter position urge greater interaction between TAFE, schools and community providers. In the recent past, for example, we have seen the emergence of adult literacy courses attached to schools, courses that are also taught in TAFE. There has also been considerable progress made in dual recognition of qualifications by the school and TAFE sectors and in joint enrolments in school and TAFE courses. Much would be gained by stronger partnerships in which the two sectors co-operated more in such areas of potential mutual interest, support and interactivity.

Many professionals in education will probably feel very much under threat if lifelong learning achieves the point of application in the range of sectors and levels described above. Some people in schools believe that their institutions have their own dedicated place in society, community groups have theirs, TAFE colleges have theirs too. The idea of working co-operatively on areas of mutual interest and educational concern may not come very easily to such people.

However, one of the factors that is now forcing the pace of change and adaptation is technology. Open Universities and distance education agencies are opening up opportunities for people who traditionally never had access to higher education. School-age children and young people are accessing education through personal computers in the home. More traditional providers of education can be helped to adapt to and profit from the opportunities offered by more flexible patterns and technologies of learning by thinking differently about the ways, times and places in which people learn most effectively. They can do this by entering into partnership with those in the communication and technology industries who can work them on putting these kinds of adaptations to good educational use. The culture of lifelong learning must be developed so that learning resources are not focused on the concept of students attending a 24- or 40-hour course delivered on some linear programme basis in one particular institution at one particular time.

RECOMMENDATIONS

In the light of the foregoing we offer the following implications, conclusions and recommendations for all those offering leadership to the learning community in the interests of realizing lifelong learning for all:

1   The three elements in the triadic nature of lifelong learning – for economic progress and development; for democratic understanding and activity; for personal development and fulfilment – are now seen as fundamental to bringing about: a more democratic polity and set of social institutions, in which the principles and ideals of social inclusiveness, justice and equity, are present, practised and promoted; an economy which is strong, adaptable and competitive; and a richer range of provision of those activities which individual members of society are able to spend their time and energy on for the personal rewards and satisfactions they confer. To achieve this governments need to undertake a substantial reappraisal of the provision, resourcing and goals of education, and a major reorientation of its direction towards the concept and value of the idea of the learning society *and* lifelong learning for all.

2   The current dominant approach to education and training, based on a systematic provision of 'front-end' formal education and training, preceding entry to the labour market, is increasingly being shown to be inadequate. Technological and other structural changes lead to situations in which certain jobs, skills and occupations become obsolete, to such an extent that the idea of a 'front-end' and 'once-and-for-all' career preparation is irrelevant. The slow rate of labour-force renewal through the entry of young, newly-qualified workers cannot satisfy demand. As qualifications become outdated more quickly than workers retire, there is an increased risk of older

workers becoming unemployed. Current education and training provision is not sufficiently broad-based to address those problems. The 'front-end' approach to education and training is clearly inadequate in a situation in which the pace of change demands new knowledge, skills and competencies, and when individuals need to prepare themselves for a number of careers and career changes over their lifetime.

3   The implications for education and training of trends in economy and society, including changes in employment and unemployment, demographic change, especially associated with an ageing population, changes in the structure of the family and family relationships, labour-force participation rates, technological change, and globalization are manifold. Programmes of compulsory and post-compulsory education and lifelong learning activities must reflect and seek to address the requirements flowing from and generated by these trends, particularly as they impact on people's life-chances and their preparation for frequent job changes, periods of unemployment and increased longevity. For the educationally under-served and unskilled the implications of these trends will be especially acute, thereby highlighting the need for a multifaceted approach to policy development, incorporating serious and detailed appraisal and considerations of the relationship between economic policy, education and social policy.

4   Aspects of economic policy will impinge upon, affect and facilitate the realization of the goal of lifelong learning for all. The setting of appropriate macro-economic policy; enhancing the creation and diffusion of technological know-how; increasing work-time flexibility; encouraging entrepreneurship; increasing wage and labour cost flexibility; reforming employment security provisions; expanding and enhancing active labour market policies; facilitating international co-operation; and improving labour-force skills and competencies – all these have been identified (OECD, *Jobs Study*, 1994) as ways in which governments may realize the ideal of lifelong learning for all. Policy recommendations for changes in these areas must be considered in framing a set of agenda for education in the twenty-first century.

5   Contemporary analyses of the economic context have provided a powerful rationale and justification for the realization of the idea of lifelong learning for all. That justification is linked directly to economic policies and performance of countries and to the concomitant need for the continuing availability of a high quality, skilled and knowledgeable workforce. But this is only one of the goals of countries' lifelong education policies. The others – democratic engagement and personal fulfilment – are quite as important as economic goals, if the goals of social inclusiveness and personal development are to be achieved. Given present

governments' concern for the multifaceted character of lifelong learning, and its relationship to a broader and more diverse set of goals, it may well be that, in setting agenda for education in the twenty-first century, a more comprehensive analysis of the various dimensions and features of the nature, aims and purposes of policies for lifelong learning for all will have to be tackled, and a more wide-ranging set of justifications addressing the differences in those aims and purposes provided. In this way policies pertaining to lifelong learning endeavours are more likely to be developed and articulated in a way that reinforces a government's appreciation of the need for a multiplicity of initiatives to increase the emancipation and participation of all citizens in its various political arrangements, economic initiatives, social institutions, and cultural activities.

6   In promoting well-functioning systems of education and training, a set of roles for government has been identified (OECD, *Jobs Study*, 1994). These include: developing an appropriate institutional infrastructure and improving the relationship between a range of learning providers. Governments can help develop the framework for better information on training opportunities, assessment, and the recognition of acquired learning and competencies. They can also act to reduce the uncertainty in investment in further training by considering and advocating the making of changes in financial accounting and reporting practices, thus improving the transparency of training costs and the value of knowledge and competencies. Governments can reduce the risk and cost of 'poaching' through the imposition of training taxes and levies. They can also encourage diversity in the institutional settings in which education and training is provided and in teaching and learning methods employed. Public authorities can also improve access to education and training programmes for small and medium-size companies, by encouraging the establishment of training co-operatives and in this way permitting economies of scale, or encouraging public institutions to provide the requisite training capacity, as well as advice. In setting agenda for education in the twenty-first century governments will need to address the challenge of providing for and planning the detailed realization of these roles and responsibilities.

7   The ideal of providing all members of society with access to lifelong learning can be realized only if all people are capable of and willing to engage in learning. People's capacity and willingness to learn throughout their lives will depend to a considerable extent on whether they enjoy constructive experiences and draw positive lessons from their period of initial education. A primary prerequisite for lifelong learning is that schools and other institutions for initial education and training offer experiences and activities that enable students to experience a sense of self-worth, a sense of excitement and challenge in learning, and a sense of success and lasting

achievement in making their learning gains. Governments have a responsibility to ensure that in sustained periods of compulsory education young people are given the best opportunities to learn and a strong foundation for lifelong learning. Attention needs to be devoted to the task of ensuring that the foundations of successful learning offered to young people in compulsory education are strengthened and, in turn, developed and extended in post-compulsory stages and institutions.

8   In planning and arranging for lifelong learning for all governments are recognizing that questions concerning the nature and number of the goals of education and training, and the curriculum appropriate to deliver them, transcend the immediate and limited character, constituency and remit of the local educating institution. There is perceived to be a need, in framing educational goals and curricula, for broad social and community partnerships to be forged between associated interests, groups and sectors in a range of community stakeholders. Consideration needs to be given to the task of creating social consensus and partnerships that will assist in the realization of governments' policies for lifelong education.

9   As part of facing the challenge of laying down an appropriate and solid groundwork for lifelong learning for all, there needs to be a re-examination, a reappraisal and a reconceptualization of the ways in which, and the bases from which, it is proposed to construct a curriculum suitable to address and deliver the educational and learning imperatives emanating from the adoption of the concept of lifelong learning. A reappraisal needs to be made of existing and developing conceptions of knowledge and the ways in which these translate into sets of content for delivery and engagement in the curriculum, particularly with respect to helping learners to acquire the range of cognitive structures and contents into which later learning can be integrated.

10 In providing a foundation for lifelong learning, governments and education systems will find it important also to take into consideration the emerging research, knowledge and understanding relevant to the ways in which people learn. It is on the basis of their mastery of the skills of research, knowledge expansion and learning to learn that students will be able to recognize situations in which such skills can be applied and utilized in the acquisition, internalization and appropriate deployment of new facts, information and knowledge. For policy-makers and curriculum planners the challenge is to ensure that learning to learn ceases to be a haphazard enterprise and instead becomes an integrated part of the content, style, structure and organization of all learning.

11 The interplay of epistemological and axiological elements and considerations, in association with reflections drawn from the

psychology of learning, the sociology and anthropology of learning institutions, and the values – individual, economic and social – attached to and embodied in institutions of learning by the society in which they are located, will occupy a central place in discussions about lifelong learning and the effective development of education and training for all in the 1990s and into the next century.

12 Given the international concern for lifelong learning for all, the nature, role and function of schools in providing the groundwork for lifelong learning, and the complementarity of services provided by schools, tertiary institutions, the work-place and other agencies in the community concerned with learning, must now be reconsidered. Lifelong learning reinforces the imperative of examining anew the content, structure and organization of appropriate and necessary pathways towards the acquisition of new learnings throughout an individual's life-span, and the various modes and cognitive styles by which individuals can best make progress in achieving such learning gains.

13 In providing a foundation for the world of work and for lifelong learning, there is a need for a much greater convergence of theoretical and practical elements and styles of learning throughout the educational experience of all young people. A convergence of the theoretical and the practical, and the general and the vocational, would give participants in the compulsory and post-compulsory years greater possibilities for transition to the full range of further education and training opportunities. There is a need for a review of policies and procedures for access and admission to all higher education and further education institutions, and a whole new range of relations and interactions between such institutions. In this way governments will be enabled to build up and assure the availability of a continuum of learning opportunities throughout the system for all categories of students for lifelong learning.

14 The provision of lifelong learning is heavily dependent on the skills, knowledge and professional competency of the teaching profession. To date the emphasis on teacher quality has tended to focus upon the preparation, development and retention of the teaching force to serve in institutions solely concerned with the compulsory years of schooling. Now, however, as a function of the broadening and deepening concern for education to be extended far beyond the compulsory years, a major challenge will be to extend this educational impulse into teaching and learning activities in the post-compulsory years, in both formal and non-formal institutions, and in settings beyond those of the traditional boundaries of the school, tertiary institution and the work-place.

15 Those training for work in the education and teaching service will in the future need to be helped to the realization that recent advances

in conceptions of knowledge and styles of learning, as well as changes in social and personal goals, betoken a gradual disappearance of the role, function and activity of teaching as traditionally conceived, and a move towards a new conception of the activity of those who carry responsibility for the facilitation of others' learning. Helping teacher educators and trainers, as well as teachers' associations, to bring about an understanding, acceptance and a positive embracing of these changes, will be among the major challenges for the future.

16 Teachers and teacher educators will also need to be helped to appreciate that previous notions of schools and other educational institutions are rapidly becoming outmoded. Given the stress on the importance of opportunities for learning throughout life, the days when schools were seen as institutions whose presence and work in a community was restricted solely to those falling within the age range of compulsory education are numbered. Teachers, educational administrators and curriculum policy-makers and planners need now to train for helping learners of a wide variety of ages, backgrounds, abilities and interests to take advantage of the learning opportunities available and consciously offered to them by and through all the human and technical resources of an educational institution. Schools are no longer places with walls: they need to be reconceptualized as centres of community learning for all.

17 The changing nature of economic and social demands plus the changing values and conceptions of knowledge and learning, which are having an impact on educational goals, has brought to the fore new requirements in standard setting and monitoring at the primary and secondary levels, which have yet to be subject to systematic analysis. Moreover, while some work has been undertaken on standard-setting in the vocational area, there is still a need for further inquiry into standard setting in the domain of vocational education and training generally, and most particularly in the provision of education on a lifelong basis, by the whole range of agencies outside the traditional boundaries of educational services and institutions. A major challenge will be to assist governments in the reformulation of standards and the methods of assessing student and system achievement relative to those standards and their relationship to the goals and ideal of lifelong learning.

18 Trenchant criticisms have been offered of existing practices in the assessment of standards. In the light of developments in epistemology and cognitive learning theories, there are now some valuable insights available about new directions for the assessment of learning and educational achievement, that are also likely to ensure that learning activities and achievements are more consistent with the changing goals emerging from changing economic and social circumstances. A major challenge is how to translate the vision of

lifelong learning for all into a programme and form that can be realized, transmitted and assessed, without in any way disvaluing, diminishing or destroying the complex, heterogeneous and multifaceted nature of the goals and outcomes at which lifelong learning is aiming.

19 In recent years there has been considerable debate regarding the changing conceptions of education, the public service and the public administration of education. The patterns and procedures of the governance, steering and management of education cannot be determined and set in train without some clarification of the key concepts and values that shall define and structure the administrative responses that governments adopt. As governments move towards a reappraisal and reconsideration of education now seen from a lifelong perspective, there is a need to provide an arena in which these conceptual and value issues can be addressed and the appropriate systems and forms of governance, steering and management derived from them.

20 New notions of administrative relationships in the provision of lifelong learning are still at the stage of early exploration and articulation. They are tentative and lack specificity. Notions of bureaucratic relationships, of the deschooled society, and of 'the market' have all been found to be outmoded or deficient, as new notions of administrative relationships in the provision of lifelong learning are explored. A major challenge will be to examine and decide upon ways in which new conceptions and models of altered administrative arrangements and relationships can be fully elaborated, implemented and appropriately evaluated in the real settings where the need for them to be implemented is so pressing.

21 In new conceptions of lifelong learning the relationships subsisting between schools, other educating institutions in the community, and universities should be among those subject to review, particularly with regard to their increasing potential to interact easily and fruitfully and so enhance and multiply opportunities for lifelong learning. From a lifelong learning perspective, the school, the community and the university must inevitably combine in a mutuality of benefit for individual cognitive advance, for economic development and for community welfare. This relationship cannot lie inert: it must be organic and dynamic. In assisting in the development of this relationship governments may wish to consider: the contributions made by schools, universities and other educating institutions in the community to the extension and proliferation of flexible and interactive programmes offering a range of activities for lifelong learning; the ways in which such institutions, and other community learning agencies, can contribute to and support a relevant and progressive research agenda devoted to the increase and improvement of openings for lifelong learning; and the

interaction between schools, other educating institutions and universities in conceiving, developing and evaluating positive schemes of community service and development.

22 Relationships between educating institutions and business, industry, commerce and trades unions will be of increasing importance in the realization of lifelong learning for all. It will be particularly important to draw lessons from past dysfunctions in such relationships and from an examination of more recent successful practices and partnerships, so as to delineate and draw attention to the features of those relationships that make them work well. Policy-makers can provide a service in exploring the impact of such relationships, as regards the enhancement of lifelong learning, upon such important goals as better and more effective preparation for the workforce; creating shared goals among educators and employers, and other industrial and commercial interest groups (such as trades and crafts unions and professional associations); and influencing the provision of learning opportunities offered by business, industry and commerce. These joint endeavours should be best placed in a context of the interest of all such groups in the formation of partnerships whose positive collaboration and effective working can function as a rich source of economic, individual and community development.

23 In broadening the concept of education to one encompassing lifelong learning and extending the boundaries of the learning society, there is a need to explore the ways in which the activities, concerns and goals of educating institutions can derive the necessary information, resource sustenance and moral support requisite to their enmeshment in their work and service to the interests of all the various cultural, artistic, religious and ethnic communities, whose existence and orientations form an important part of the mosaic of lifelong learning, and to the whole range of constituencies that comprise the learning society.

24 The realization of lifelong learning will be heavily dependent on those who assume responsibility for 'leading the learning community'. A significant effort should be made to identify, motivate and provide requisite training for the range of people within the community who can serve as leaders in the learning enterprise.

25 The vision of a networked society with equal access to knowledge and information made up of communities and individuals, themselves in charge of their own learning environments and progress, and governments, educators and the private sector working in partnership is fundamental to the evolution and achievement of a democratic, free, economically stable and just society in the twenty-first century. But realization of this vision will require a close examination of the content, style and structure and organization of modern methods and technologies of learning, particularly in respect

of the new possibilities offered by the emphasis on student-centred and self-directed modes of progression, together with an examination of the purpose and function of educational institutions and their use of electronic technologies to meet new educational needs. Governments may wish to direct their attention to an exploration of the ways in which the availability of modern information technology devices and new modes of student progress in learning will affect, make possible and shape frameworks for curriculum content, styles of assessment and structures of organization in educational institutions, in ways that will enable the realization of broader social goals.

26 In the knowledge society of the future, learning will constitute, furnish and make possible the principal sources of well-being, welfare, justice and economic self-sufficiency. This means that schools, and indeed all other educating institutions, will need to become learning organizations themselves, if countries are to achieve the objectives and capitalize on the possibilities and opportunities of lifelong learning for all.

27 A key issue in the provision of lifelong learning is who pays for learning beyond schooling. The present and future development of post-secondary education and training is being considered in the context of shared funding responsibilities. Employers, and individuals who benefit from an investment in learning, are increasingly expected and in some cases required to contribute a share of the cost. Joint investment can enhance the effectiveness of learning by giving several partners a stake in the outcomes. But there is the danger that financial arrangements will inhibit participation by some groups in society and hence be socially divisive. The optimal division and distribution of funding responsibilities for lifelong learning remains to be decided.

28 The debate regarding the best model of provision and funding for the courses and programmes that will meet the needs and desires of learners beyond the compulsory stages of education is still unresolved. The question of the best model of provision and funding constitutes the most crucial issue in the debate concerning the best policies and strategies for any country's approaches to learning beyond schooling. It must be addressed as one of central importance to considerations of lifelong learning. The key question is: What are the alternative models for the provision and funding of learning beyond schooling that will both facilitate the whole range of learning needs and yet, at the same time, be economically efficient, socially inclusive and ethically just? If the market model features distinctively among the proposals for a resolution to this question, then a further question needs to be asked: What are the limits that must be placed upon the 'market', given the moral imperatives

embodied in the concept of education and the social and ethical goals associated with lifelong learning?

29 In considering the range and kinds of lifelong education provision, the role of governments in making, planning and funding such provision is a key concern. Many believe that there is a strong case for governments to play a strategic role in sectors where they cannot be the main provider of services but where there is value in their influencing or providing a coherent framework including a range of incentives for a range of providers. Others see government as undertaking the role of transaction facilitator, setting up the 'playing field' for provision. As governments move away from the role of monopoly provider there is clearly a need to consider the range of roles available and to assist governments in selecting that role which they deem to be most appropriate to their initiatives, values and goals in the field of lifelong learning for all.

30 Governments will also need to take an approach to the planning and development of educational technologies and communications that includes all sectors of education and capitalizes upon all their various forms of potential contribution and benefit. Governments acting in consultation with carriers and educational institutions will need to develop policies for the educational applications of telecommunications technologies which provide equity of access, common standards and a unified network strategy between institutions and the external world via information highways such as the Internet.

31 As governments consider alternative approaches to the provision of lifelong learning, they may wish to note that there are now few technical barriers to prevent the offering and receiving of education from beyond national boundaries. Governments and communities may wish to consider the potential benefits, practicalities and problems of international exchange and co-operation in approaches to lifelong learning.

CONCLUSION

Community expectations that schools should provide citizens with all the education necessary for the remainder of their lives used to mean that, as society changed, more and more demands were placed on schools. These ever-expanding expectations became an impossible burden for teachers who had to maintain the quality of the work they had been doing while, at the same time, adding more and more to the curriculum. As a result, the community has begun to realize that schools alone are not able to provide all the education and training required by the contemporary world.

It is not only schools that are affected by the changing society. The work-place now demands more flexible and more skilled workers and managers; the state requires more informed citizens able to participate actively in government and community affairs; and individuals, with more leisure time and longer lives, require avenues for personal growth.

Learning for Employability and National Economic Growth

- In this changing work-place employers no longer expect their new employees to be fully trained when they move into the workforce. Even if it were possible to train students at school for specific jobs, current work-place realities would soon reveal a need for retraining – new technologies, new work-patterns, new skills and new jobs all make on-the-job training essential. Some employers meet the challenge by setting up training courses in the work-place, others prefer to use courses provided at TAFE colleges or other institutions, while other organizations prefer to use both these strategies. This means that the demands on schools have changed. They are still seen as having a role in ensuring the future employability of their students but this is no longer seen as job training in specific skills. Instead, business and industry are seeking young people with generic skills and aptitudes: skills in communication and information technology; societal skills; literacy and numeracy; an understanding of history and its implications for the future; lively and open minds; the ability to work in groups, take responsibility, engage in critical analysis and make judgments; and an openness to and understanding of totally different religions, cultures, art forms and languages. They want prospective employees who have the right attitudes and skills, who are able to be trained in the necessary specific skills, and who are flexible enough to be able to be retrained as new needs arise.

- Business and industry now need to forge strong links with schools to ensure that students and teachers gain a better understanding of the world of work. This can be aided by opening their organizations to provide work-placements for students and teachers and by representatives from the organization visiting schools and working with the people there. The main purpose of these links will be not merely be to develop work-related skills but to foster understanding of the role of business and industry, its importance to the well-being of the community, the challenges it faces and the possibilities for the future.

- For this to work, those already in employment will need to think again about restrictive work practices which exclude or limit students from gaining work-experience. Employers need to work with their employees to ensure protection of wages and conditions while at the same time providing opportunities for young people. Once this is achieved each organization needs to work closely with the schools to develop school programmes that are relevant to the needs of both the students and the work-place. Some organizations find the best way to do this is to adopt a particular school and thus establish an ongoing relationship.

- Of course, it is becoming increasingly evident that all who leave school will not find the employment they want. As this problem has increased and become more manifest governments have set up their own programmes or have helped fund training programmes run by voluntary and community groups. These groups have found that life-skills are an essential element in their programmes.

Learning for Participation in a Socially Inclusive and Just Democracy

- A thriving democracy requires informed citizens who are actively involved in community affairs and are prepared to work for good government. To achieve this the foundations of lifelong learning need to be laid from the earliest years. To the extent that students are encouraged to take responsibility for their own learning; work co-operatively together; and engage in problem-solving activities and gain an understanding of the world at large – business and industry; local, state and federal governance; and the different cultures and practices in other parts of the world – they will become active participants in building up democracy. The processes of lifelong learning will inevitably aid democratic involvement.

- Those who are imbued with a belief in lifelong learning will seek out further opportunities for learning and, when those they want are not available, will become actively involved in setting up such opportunities. Apart from the benefit of the courses the instigators will find themselves networking with others in the community, with educational institutions, and with governments and business organizations that may help provide funds. All these activities provide a practical course on democracy in action.

- Committees provide another training ground for involved citizenship. Groups such as Neighbourhood Watch and Citizens Initiative Referenda encourage and provide opportunities for involvement in issues affecting people's everyday lives. School Councils which are responsible for the management and resourcing of schools also help train their members in useful processes for achieving desired outcomes. To ensure these groups do not become the exclusive province of the advantaged who have the time and resources to be able to become active members, governments should seek ways of enabling access for all.

- Membership of committees such as those referred to above will also enable people from different backgrounds, cultures, religions and ethnic groups to find a common meeting ground and begin the process of achieving unity out of diversity. Only when all members of the community feel that they are valued will democracy flourish.

Learning for Personal Growth

- Concentration on academic or vocational education in schools has often meant that processes and courses to promote personal growth have been neglected or given so little time and recognition that students have discounted their value. In response, community groups, technical colleges, church groups and certain individuals have set up courses to meet those needs. These courses range from hobby classes, arts and crafts, music, literature, languages and public speaking to philosophy and theology. At the simplest level they consist of small groups of like-minded people keenly pursuing a common interest according to their own wishes. The organization is fluid and demand-driven, the processes are learner- not teacher-centred.

- As these courses have proliferated two interconnected problems have emerged. After the initial stage when processes are fluid and emerging, structures begin to be put in place and there is a tendency for bureaucratic practices to take over and begin to drive the process. The need for funding has exacerbated this problem. Those providing the funding often prefer courses that lead to clear, measurable outcomes. This can mean that some courses do not receive funds. The only way they can survive is to seek increased fees from their members and this, in turn, can lead to the exclusion of disadvantaged members of the community who have most to gain from such courses. When 'user pays' is the means of entry those most in need are excluded and society as a whole is the loser.

- Finally, it is essential that all those involved in the learning process – schools, further and tertiary institutions, employers' and trades unions' associations and learning and training programmes, community groups – should build networks, communicate regularly with each other, support each other, and work out ways of sharing resources to ensure maximum and effective utilization.

Every member of society has a responsibility for ensuring that co-operative learning becomes a core activity of the community. Technology can assist in the process but it is a means to an end, not the end itself. The individual person must be the one who drives the learning process, for that is the only way that the full benefits of that process will be achieved by the individual and society as a whole.

Chapter 12

Schools as Centres for the Learning Community

In this final chapter of the book we shall be particularly concerned to explore the changes in the roles, powers and responsibilities of school leaders that follow on from moves towards the adoption and implementation of policies and programmes of lifelong learning. We shall examine the impact of the range of new partnerships and structures of shared governance arrangements on school leadership, in particular with the aim of helping school leaders reconceptualize their roles from that of being the apex of a pyramid to one of being much more a centre of a network of human relationships and resources. The range, complexity, sophistication and demands of the new knowledge, skills and capacities now increasingly required of school leaders, especially in respect to such key public communication activities as strategic planning, quality management and control, marketing and promotion, public relations and community outreach, will be discussed, and strategies, plans and programmes for the corresponding leadership development will be adumbrated and justified.

LEADERSHIP AT THE LEVEL OF THE SCHOOL

The aims of education generally include giving people the necessary knowledge to enable them to face the challenges of daily living, to be aware of their responsibilities and obligations to others, and to plan and work a pattern of satisfying and personally enriching life-options for themselves. Young people need a well-rounded education for contemporary life and part of the task of education will then be to develop people who are able to communicate, who are broad-minded and understanding, and who have the high levels of competency needed to cope in today's technological society. Children and young people should leave school with a conscious awareness that they have acquired skills that they can then apply in a range of settings. Schools need to model an approach that establishes learning not simply as an academic exercise but as an awareness that the exigencies and possibilities of daily life make necessary a rounded commitment to learning across the life-span.

To date, an awareness of the ways in which students can make appropriate applications of fundamental knowledge and skills has not been fully developed as part of the curriculum. Young people do acquire basic knowledge but often they do not see the relevance of that knowledge to their situations in the world. Schools can promote awareness by organizing the curriculum in a way that formally and informally reinforces learning as valuable and as ongoing. Schools can stress that people learn by doing things, by talking to others, by mixing with others, by exercising judgment, by exerting their democratic rights. An understanding of and commitment to lifelong learning will embrace and value all these approaches to learning, for, unless the seeds are planted for this lifelong learning approach at school, they will not take root. Lifelong learning requires thinking differently about what a learning process and an educational task might be; it also requires a different approach to and different notions about the outcomes of schooling.

In these times there is also a different role for schools because of the knowledge revolution: the idea of schools as primary transmitters of knowledge and information is rapidly becoming outmoded. Students and learners of all ages now realize that knowledge is available to them from a wide range of sources, particularly from information technology, to which they can secure direct access and then direct and monitor their own acquisition and application of knowledge by themselves and for their own purposes.

These days too, because of the new ways in which the map of knowledge is being redrawn, a considerable reframing of knowledge in the curriculum is going on, and this is doing away with the more traditional barriers between discrete blocks of knowledge content and subject areas. Students and teachers have realized that it is possible to think about the curriculum in more integrated, lateral and expansive ways.

Some of these new approaches to knowledge will involve bringing into the whole curriculum learning activities in areas and along pathways that were previously thought to lie beyond its boundaries. Students may obtain knowledge and information from a diverse range of sources, many of them made available and explorable by the avenues opened up through new information technology. This ensures that students will stand increasingly at the centre of their own learning, shaping and extending it in ways that fit in with the demands of their own psychology and their own styles of cognitive growth and awareness.

Students will quickly become aware that merely acquiring more information is not equivalent to gaining understanding and wisdom. In future the values import of gaining knowledge will be something that requires overt and direct address: this will be the function of schools. Schools will, along with families, churches and other such organizations, be the social institutions that are overtly concerned with values, since the ethical and moral aspects of education must still be addressed. It is schools and other kinds of educational institutions that now have an enhanced role in those matters. Though literacy, numeracy and other skills are essential planks in the construction of an approach to lifelong learning, equally indispensable is awareness of the values that individuals and communities hold, as well as some skill in moral decision-making.

The kinds of skills involved in the deliberation and judgment required in such decision-making are best learnt through a guided process in a social setting. In order to give its young people an education in such powers and values the community will continue to need schools and other deliberate educating institutions. School leaders will help orientate the community education process towards the education of the whole person, helping individuals learn how to build self-esteem and develop positive attitudes to themselves and learning. Some schools have always been concerned with a more holistic lifelong approach to education and other schools too are already beginning to treat students more as whole persons, helping them make choices, respecting their decisions, supporting them through their setbacks, helping them learn from their failures. This kind of approach, involving as it does critical learning and questioning by both students and their helpers, is much more conducive to lifelong learning than traditional methods of accumulating information, acquiring knowledge and making progress by means that are largely didactic and instructional, rather than pedagogic and supportive of one's own endeavours.

In future the chief issues in planning educational curricula will be the ways in which educating institutions can best promote and help students acquire the habit of employing a spirit of critical inquiry in managing and directing their own learning. They will appreciate the need for some immersion in subject content, and for reflection on it, as well as the need for continuing flexibility and the spirit of curiosity.

We may go on from this to establish that a fundamental part of lifelong learning is the recognition that the learner is in a continuing process of growth and development. The trouble with some schools today is that they sometimes kill the love of learning. Some people leave school with a reluctance ever to undertake formal education again. An essential part of getting people started on the right path is to give them a sense of satisfaction in what they do, as well as a sense of accomplishment. Schools are failing children and adults, often those already disadvantaged, if they do not allow them to experience some sense of success at school. The notion that, early on in their experience of learning, children can be told they have failed should be opposed by all engaged in education.

Schools can make a good beginning on promoting a lifelong commitment to furthering one's own education by making learning a pleasure, encouraging the motivation for and interest in lifelong learning and increasing their students' awareness of the need for it. They can begin by stressing that learning can be fun. We have to promote a sense of joy in the whole process of learning and remove failure, with its dysfunctional effects, from the schooling experienced by many. Schools must reassess notions of success and failure if they are serious about encouraging a positive attitude towards lifelong learning.

Too often, unfortunately, it is the stress laid by schools and others on the passing of examinations, and the concomitant disvalue attached to not passing – to failing – that militates against students acquiring a love of lifelong learning. Schools will be constrained in promoting lifelong learning so long as they are preoccupied with helping students get high marks for passing examinations of various kinds. The emphasis in some schools on successfully arriving at prespecified terminal outcome points – on achievement for achievement's sake – runs counter to the whole ethos and spirit of lifelong learning.

There is a need for young people to be acknowledged and recognized for those things that they do in schools which do not get marks or scores or ticks. There is a need to recognize the value of broader learning experiences and to create a learning environment for children and young people that is happy and co-operative, and in which they all have equal rights and responsibilities in the pursuit of excellence of all kinds – where the achievement of excellence lies in introducing an inclusive curriculum that will encourage and assist all young people to become self-starting, self-directing and self-managing learners.

Schools need to understand better the sorts of approach to learning, teaching and inquiry that create a lasting interest in various areas of work and subjects of study. With an approach that concentrates on students building knowledge for themselves, on managing and directing their own learning, students can come to see and value themselves as part of the process of recreating knowledge.

Most important is that young people are not overtaught: much more important is the fostering of a sense of inquisitiveness and a determination to achieve and enhance their own competency in acquiring knowledge, the encouragement of curiosity, and giving courage to learn, to give them a sense of the world – particularly the world of knowledge – as something they can control and that they can play a part in shaping. In sum, we need to keep the spirit of inquiry and enthusiasm for learning that exists in primary school going for much, much longer – for the rest of people's lives, in fact. And this brings us on to the question of the ways in which we can bring this about, particularly through strengthening the relationships between the school and the community.

If we are to achieve the goal of promoting lifelong learning through school and community, one of the first tasks on the agenda will be to link them together more closely. In the past schools have in general been too compartmentalized, too shut away from the community, with many of them having an attitude of erecting barriers to keep outsiders excluded. This is illustrated by the notices that some schools used to put on their entrance gates: 'Parents stop here'.

Not only have the boundaries to community involvement in the work of schools been territorial and locational, however: they have also been conceptual. Many schools have inhibited the spread of the diverse ranges of approach and the multiplicity of pathways for lifelong learning, by the ways in which and the extent to which they have held fast to theories of a linear and compartmentalized progress through fixed stages of learning, embodied in and co-ordinated accordingly with a parallel linear journey through schooling.

Another barrier has been epistemological – the past tendency to compartmentalize knowledge and styles of learning, to separate learners in horizontally organized groups divided according to chronological age and to departmentalize in subjects undertaken in classrooms remote from real-life experience and application. As long ago as Dewey, and more recently, new theories and advances in epistemology and learning theory have called such lines of demarcation into question, if not decisively refuted them. There is no epistemic warrant for such theories, whose main status is revealed to be that of an educational dogma.

Refutation of stage theory in learning and partitioned set theory in concepts of knowledge and the curriculum suggest that other educational shibboleths should share the same fate. We might now, for instance, consider breaking down the traditional barriers between the classroom and the learning that can take place outside the school. Indeed the very structure and organization of classes and classrooms is likely to change. Instead classrooms in future are much more likely to become multiskilled, multi-aged and multi-language with an emphasis on inquiry and experience-based learning, and where the acquisition of knowledge and information will be available to students, not only from books and other resources located within the school but also from computers, the Internet, and other information sources around the world. These developments will entail that one major barrier to flexibility and independence of learning direction – the timetable as it is now structured – will have to go, though of course schools will have to give a lead to learners, at least initially, in organizing the programme of the 'learning' curriculum and organizing learning groups.

Moreover, if in future schools are to become centres for the benefit and use of learners from all sectors of the community, then there is a need to open them up to community access. Such an approach of course has implications for the traditional custodial role of schools and this needs to be respected, especially during the years of statutory attendance. At the same time, however, the physical barriers which schools erect – even if in observance of their statutory 'duty of care' – are themselves an obstruction to the concept of lifelong learning and to young people's sense of the interaction between their learning experience in school and learning 'on the outside'. Achieving a balance between the custodial role of the school and the need to open up the school to greater community interaction will be a major challenge for school leadership.

The point is that learning does not take place only in schools. Nowadays we are already redefining the place to learn: learning takes place in libraries, cultural and religious centres, through technology, in the home, and in work settings. School is just one form of concentrated learning and the sooner school personnel appreciate the need for adjustment to this, the easier it will be to develop a multiplicity of fora for and approaches to learning for all kinds of student. Given the multiplicity of student needs and choices, and the multiplicity of learning pathways open to them, in the future schools and other learning institutions will be able to offer real choices through flexible programmes, modules, and alternative courses of many kinds.

Indeed in the future there is likely to be considerable relaxation of the classroom environment with teachers working much more as directors of study with individual students, working teacher aids, and auxiliaries of various kinds, to assist students in their learning. In future years there is likely to be an increase in moves to a 'tutorial' approach to learning, rather than an emphasis on having larger taught classes: in future teaching will be seen rather as 'companionship in learning', with teachers taking the role of what in Germany is called a *Lernbegleiter*. Such an approach does not mean 'throwing the baby out with the bathwater', of course: educating institutions will have the sense to maintain those forms and styles of learning that are most efficient at doing particular jobs. Schools can be places where both formal and informal learning is integrated and this integration is also reflected in choice of learning and teaching delivery: in the senior years of schooling many schools have already adopted a mix of technology-based learning in the school and the home with some traditional approaches to learning in school settings.

In sum, schools are now coming to operate much more pragmatically. They will utilize whatever mode of approach will give students greatest access and benefit, and they will use their experience, expertise and best professional judgment in deciding which of the various approaches best suits the particular learner's case. This is gradually bringing about the emergence of a recognizable concept of a community of learners, in which we speak of 'thinking schools' and thinking people, linked together in interlocking circles of interest.

We know of course that in certain schools there are many things that are not working. For change to take place in such schools there needs to be a reconsideration of philosophy, structure, organization and resources if society's concern to start children and young people on the road to lifelong learning is to succeed.

These days there is wide acceptance in schools that learners should accept a greater degree of responsibility for their own learning. This principle can be imparted from the earliest stages of schooling. It can also be modelled by the ways educating institutions go about their business. Educating institutions will be increasingly pressed to ensure that people take responsibility for their own learning and for achieving the outcomes deemed important. These days we are entering a stage of educational development where this will be a much more widely shared responsibility – shared between schools, individuals, families and community.

In this task the creation of partnerships will be vitally important. A range of relationships of this kind is a good way of assisting educating institutions to meet the challenges they face as they attempt to cope with the enormous range of expectations that are currently being placed on schools. The traditional institutions that we have known as schools are not structured to respond to the demands of the changing economy and society or to respond to the need for a large-scale cultural change in their notion of the work with which the community charges them.

Schools working in these ways with their community will need educational leaders who have the vision to encompass the aim of introducing students to lifelong learning practices and to create an environment which fosters a close relationship between school and community, policy and practice. Educational leaders need to develop skills to plan for change, to participate in and to reflect on change. There is a need for consultation, discussion and debate among all those seeking to bring about a transformation of people's educational vision, creating a climate of change in which there will be constant infusions of fresh ideas from people in the community and from people already in schools. Lifelong learning needs leaders in the dialogue seeking such a transformation, not simply managers in this organic and dynamic context.

The move to an emphasis upon opening up pathways to lifelong learning will involve large-scale cultural change in schools. Such a move will probably necessitate looking at school tasks, responsibilities and experience with a fresh eye: to bring about the necessary change in school culture one will need people who have had wider, extra-school experience.

In this new context schools need to work hard at avoiding the minefields of organizational and cultural change that such moves often create. One of the problems in seeking new pathways round difficulties is that with some people ideas are fixed – they are unable to change. One of the problems here is the classic one in the administration of many schools and educational systems – people get locked into positions, attitudes, beliefs and values, and are apprehensive about the risk of upheaval. School leaders will be able to surmount such problems by encouraging people in management teams to realize that organizational change is made much easier and more flexible when people move sideways as well as upwards.

But the impulse for lifelong learning cannot be a responsibility that is 'added on' for teachers: existing school personnel cannot be expected to take on the establishment and extension of lifelong learning activities themselves as some sort of 'add on' to existing duties and demands. There is a need to create positions for community education officers in schools to co-ordinate activities and achieve co-operation between the community and schools.

Any school offering leadership in learning and in administering learning communities will find that they face many problems from their client community and will find it necessary to overcome distrust among many groups. Not only will school leaders have to work hard to overcome the inhibiting effects of the inertia of existing institutional structures, arrangements and procedures, but they will face mistrust, malice or often simply apathy. These are major obstacles for school leaders to overcome – and they will not be assisted in their endeavours to do so by the resistance they will undoubtedly meet from other sources above and beyond the level of the school. Often it is the people working in schools and community agencies who have the really creative ideas to promote lifelong learning but equally often they feel they have no way of influencing the politicians and those with power to make the difference. This is one way in which governments can be of help: the channels for exercising influence need to be opened up to allow for local school initiatives and community-led change.

Part of the policy, organization and structure of schooling, particularly with respect to the provision of courses for a whole community of learners, should be concerned to transform the thinking of all educators towards the need for more entrepreneurial activity. School leaders need to be encouraged to take an entrepreneurial role with the community. A problem here is that some schools have a more positive mindset towards such activities, have more experience at it, and are in a better position to take advantage of revenue-generating activities, especially in the use of facilities. These schools not only have the better facilities but they have the managerial infrastructure to service their use.

It will, however, remain a problem requiring constant attention in the opening up of schools to the community, that in such an approach there is at least the potential for the commercialization and politicization of the schools' activities: schools need to be reassured that opening up to the community will not interfere with the programmes they are implementing for their students. There is always going to be tension between the aim of providing a good education for the students who are in school during the day, the aims of the system, and the need to create extra funding to provide the kind of education the community wants. In all this it will be vital that schools do not lose their primary focus – which is its concern with values that are educational in character, rather than political or economic.

LEADERSHIP BY SCHOOL PRINCIPALS

Principals who have read this far could, by now, be prey to at least two conflicting emotions – excitement at the possibilities and challenges presented by lifelong learning, coupled with horror at the thought of the amount of time, energy and resources required in the attempt to implement this approach in the school and beyond. Of course, principals would be right to reject lifelong learning if its implementation merely required more activities being added to an already overloaded schedule and list of commitments for all members of the school community. However, strong and persuasive arguments have been presented for the value of lifelong learning for all, and if the benefits of lifelong learning are to be realized by current and future members of society, ways must be found for schools to integrate it into current practice.

The first thing to note is that lifelong learning cannot become reality by simply adding things on to current content and processes in schools. What is required is a sea-change in the attitudes and expectations of all sections of society and a willingness to translate this sea-change into actions that support the progress of lifelong learning at all levels. This is an enormous expectation: a commitment to lifelong learning will not be brought about overnight; yet unless the first steps are taken, it will not happen at all. School leaders can be encouraged by the knowledge that some progress has already been made in many schools in many parts of the world. These successes need greater publicity.

Principals should therefore be encouraged to start or continue the process in each individual school, seek allies among fellow principals, and develop networks with other like-minded individuals and organizations. While this could be seen as a somewhat daunting undertaking, it is not an impossible one provided one is prepared to follow the maxim *festina lente* – hasten slowly. The concept of lifelong learning has so much merit and its practice is so rewarding for those who engage in it that others will be encouraged to join in.

The first step in the process is a recognition that the role of the school in society has changed. While early home experiences and the education received at school are still an essential basis on which an individual achieves a rewarding and fulfilling later life, they are no longer sole contributors to this. Learning can not be seen as something engaged in during the early years of life, completed by the end of schooling, and never revisited. Increasingly the demands of changing work requirements and social environments underline the need for the learning process to continue throughout life.

Schooling must now meet this new reality. Already, as the amount of information on any given topic has grown exponentially, teachers have begun to place less emphasis on the acquisition of knowledge and more on the processes by which students can access information. This, however, is not enough. For lifelong learning to become a reality, those leaving school need to take with them the following:

- an enthusiasm for learning;
- a recognition of the value of learning;
- the ability to synthesize, analyse and question data;
- the ability to earn an income and contribute to the economic development of the country;
- the skills required for engagement in and contribution to democratic processes;
- an understanding of how to maintain a healthy lifestyle and the will to do it;
- an awareness that life consists of more than physical and material realities, it also has a spiritual dimension;
- an appreciation for artistic and creative endeavours and a willingness to take part in and support such endeavours.

To achieve these outcomes schools need to:

- generate an enthusiasm for learning;
- facilitate the learning process through appropriate structures, resources, curriculum, teaching styles and climate;
- ensure that students acquire the skills necessary for them to access and process information then put that information to use;
- value the different forms of learning and maintain a balance between academic, vocational, physical, creative and spiritual activities;
- insist on high quality work from all students;
- put in place assessment and reporting procedures that reflect the commitment of the school to learning as a top priority;
- develop links with other groups which are providing learning experiences outside the confines of the school; these experiences can then be made available to school students either in the school setting or in the wider community;
- provide the community with a working model of effective learning.

What then can individual principals do to ensure their schools achieve these outcomes?

1 Demonstrate and maintain a personal commitment to lifelong learning

- Establish an environment where learning is valued. This must become a core value in the school so that the efforts of all members of the school community are directed to this end. The first step in this process is for principals to model the kind of behaviour desired. If the principal is manifestly excited by learning, demonstrates an inquiring mind by challenging and questioning ideas, undertakes and openly enjoys learning activities, welcomes and encourages questions, and encourages the same behaviour in others, then learning will be seen as a pleasurable experience that is engaged in by adults and is not confined to school years only.

At the same time the principal must make every effort to motivate teachers to model the same kind of behaviour through innovative activities in and outside the classroom, by the encouragement of lateral thinking in their students, and by the establishment of a positive climate in which students are rewarded for what they have achieved.

- Establish an environment where people are valued. The principal should, at all times, demonstrate respect for all members of the school community and ensure that the tone of the school encourages respect for others. The less able and variously challenged members of the school community should also be given a sense of confidence in their own worth and a feeling that they have something to contribute. Under these conditions learning thrives.

- Members of the school community should also be assured that all their learning achievements, whatever they might be, have value. To bring this about the principal should discourage the labelling of actions and/or people as failing and instead encourage a positive attitude to mistakes and errors which should be seen as a natural part of the learning process and as stepping stones to further learning. Children learning to walk are not labelled failures when they fall down: they are encouraged to stand up and try again. This approach should become a model for all later learning activities.

- Because there will inevitably be some difficulties in establishing a climate of lifelong learning it is important for the principal to maintain balance and perspective. Universal education is a relatively recent concept in the history of humankind but, in just over a hundred years, it has been accepted all around the world. Lifelong learning will not become reality for everyone tomorrow but it will, in fact, it must be worked towards over time. This recognition of the long term nature of the task will enable the principal to maintain and convey a positive outlook despite inevitable, short-term setbacks.

- It is also important to remember that school provides only one of many learning arenas in a person's life. If one were to consider an individual's linear time line of learning it would be evident that the most intensive lifetime learning experiences occur before that person even sets foot in a school and that, after formal schooling is completed, formal and informal education continues in a variety of ways.

- This extended learning sequence is paralleled by the range of learning experiences being undergone at any one time. An in-depth snapshot of students engaged in full time attendance at school would show that they are simultaneously being educated through a number of different sources such as parents, clubs, television, church groups, part-time employment, computer networks, and formal 'after school' classes. School members need to be conscious of these other sources of learning, encourage students to incorporate them into their 'school work', and develop linkages to them.

2 Establish processes that assist members of the school community to realize, in action, the value of lifelong learning

- Staff and students need processes and structures in the school that encourage responsible decision-making and which provide working models of democracy in action. It is difficult for students to learn the benefits and responsibilities of living in a democracy in a school setting that is hierarchical in structure and where all decisions are handed down from above. Such practices encourage either passivity or rebellion and such attitudes can be carried through into later life to the disadvantage of both the individual and society at large.

  Decision-making on matters such as curriculum, school goals, codes of behaviour, reporting and assessment procedures, acquisition and use of resources can be undertaken by those at every level of schooling (Kindergarten to Year 12) provided that those involved in the decision-making have an interest in the outcome and some understanding of the issues involved. The decision-makers also have to be made responsible for the outcome. In this way commitment to the process and its successful outcome is engendered and mistakes become part of the learning process, while successful decisions bring a feeling of accomplishment and reinforce learning.

- Schools which see themselves as part of lifelong learning need to ensure that their goals, methods of assessment and school reports reflect this. The principal, in turn, needs to ensure that processes are established that enable the school and community to articulate its goals and then decide on how the progress to these goals is to be measured and reported on and improved or redirected if necessary.

- To encourage the growth of lifelong learning the goals towards which the curriculum is directed must make it possible for each pupil to engage in the three elements of lifelong learning and thus move towards the achievement of economic progress and development, democratic understanding and activity, and personal development and fulfilment.

- These elements require much more than just information giving and receiving. For their successful achievement teachers must give due attention to processes, not just content, and must help students develop skills of analysis and synthesis, not just information gathering. This approach then requires matching recording and reporting procedures to ensure that the outcomes of the learning experience are recorded positively and reflect the goals of the school. For example, portfolios of work or reports that set out the expected outcomes and the progress of the student towards these outcomes give a far better view of what the pupil has accomplished than do percentage marks. They also indicate the way ahead for future learning activities.

These forms of evaluation, however, are more time-consuming and not as easy as the ranking of schools and students by marks scored in examinations. Further, familiarity with the process of ranking is deeply ingrained in community consciousness. It is relatively simple to achieve but it favours students from advantaged backgrounds and it tends to assess performance that can be quantified in numerical terms, rather than advance in some of the qualitative aspects of schooling. For other forms of assessment to be seen as acceptable, there will need to be a considerable change in school and community attitudes towards assessment. Principals have a major responsibility in bringing about this attitude change. In some communities, however, this change is already well under way. The leaders of business and industry, recognizing the need for more articulate and socially skilled employees, are urging schools to develop these attributes in their students.

3 Recognize that during times of change those engaged in the process need help and support and that the introduction of new technology by itself will not necessarily lead them to change their practice

- Staff need to develop skills appropriate to their work. The principal can assist in this process by such things as encouraging attendance at in-service sessions, developing mentoring practices within the school, drawing attention to articles or events and facilitating visits to organizations that may prove helpful. As staff grow in skill and confidence they will be better equipped to try out new ideas and to involve students and parents in the learning and decision-making processes.

- The establishment of a supportive atmosphere and the new skills acquired will give staff the courage to be adventurous – to try out those new ideas, to take on new roles, to expand their area of educational activity beyond the confines of the school. As they model the processes and outcomes of lifelong learning they will be demonstrating to students what it means to be self-reliant yet socially involved.

- At the same time, while encouraging change, the principal must retain a sense of stability for all members of the school community.

This can be achieved by clear goals that have been agreed on, by open communication and discussion, by involvement in decision-making and by ensuring that the good features of the school are preserved. In this way lifelong learning will be built on strong foundations.

4 Locate and provide resources for the effective functioning of the school

- As the concept and practice of self-managing schools becomes more widespread, principals are expected to identify what resources are needed, to acquire them and then to see that they are used effectively to enable the school to achieve its goals. A lifelong learning climate will assist in this process by encouraging the school to widen its search. This will involve generating lateral thinking processes within the school, setting up information networks with people outside the school, and using the ideas and information gained to convince people and organizations to assist in the provision of the required resources.

- It is also important that the principal encourages effective use of resources – buildings, grounds, equipment, personnel – already within the school and encourages staff and students to do the same and looks outside the school for additional resources.

5 Build collaborative relationships with neighbouring principals to develop a climate of lifelong learning in the local area

- One outcome of the advent of the era of self-managing schools and economic rationalism is that competition rather than co-operation can become the accepted *modus operandi*. In this competitive climate, schools, fighting for survival, may retreat into a new isolationism. While this may advance the interests of a particular school, it ultimately has negative effects on the community as a whole. Lifelong learning thrives in a co-operative atmosphere and should not be limited to just a privileged few. All members of a community gain from the social cohesion generated when everyone is involved in the creation of a learning society. Principals need to be conscious of this and work with other principals to bring this learning society to fruition.

- It is therefore important for principals to meet and discuss their ideas on lifelong learning. In this way they can expand and clarify their understanding of the concept, share experiences, learn from each other's successes and failures, and provide support for each other. This does not mean that schools will lose their individuality. Even though goals may be similar, the practices involved in reaching those goals could be quite different, depending on the composition and needs of the school community.

- Such meetings could also lead to a mapping of the resources available in each school leading to the opening up of those resources to each other, e.g. personnel (staff and students), buildings, equipment and sports facilities. Students could be involved in cross-age tutoring or mentoring programmes, specialist staff could provide advice, there could be joint access to libraries, and so on. The benefits derived would come not only from access to the resource but also from the actual processes of sharing.

- Further, these meetings could also provide information on resources available in the community and open up new possibilities for school and community activities. The same processes as occurred between schools could apply.

- As schools gain a greater understanding of each other and begin to recognize that they share a set of common purposes it may also be possible to set up joint in-service activities for members of the school communities, thus increasing communication and understanding.

6 Build collaborative relationships with the local community

- Traditionally it was the principal who provided the community with the school's 'public face'. While this is still true it is equally true that many other school members could, and do, perform this role. Some people active in schools in roles such as that of careers counsellor must necessarily work outside as well as inside the school. However, all members of the school community should be encouraged to build these collaborative relationships. This means that the principal needs to highlight their importance, give recognition and encouragement to those who establish such links, and ensure that the local media give publicity to the school's efforts to reach out into the community. These efforts can take many forms – art displays in shopping malls, meals-on-wheels, visits to retirement homes, student-run computer classes for adults. The list can be endless and in each case the learning is a two-way process

- All community–school activities do not have to take place outside the school buildings and grounds. Principals, staff and students need to make the school a welcoming place for parents and community members. Ways need to be found for these people and groups to make use of school facilities without placing impossible financial, supervision and work load burdens on the school. Getting people to make use of school facilities will not happen unless the school is open to suggestions for the sharing of facilities; then, once a climate of co-operation and sharing is established, schools must be prepared to enter into detailed discussion and negotiation to ensure that both groups gain maximum benefits from the arrangements. In the early stages it is particularly important that the community use of the school facilities works well or the initiation of other promising schemes could be jeopardized.

- Other community members may simply wish to join school classes in certain subjects (while subjects remain part of school organization) or to gain certain qualifications. The principal, staff and current students should explore the pros and cons of such admissions with the prospective students and reach agreement on whether such admissions are possible and on what terms. Principals also need to ensure that their schools establish policy on the admission of mature age students.

7 Build collaborative relationships with other educational organizations

- The lock-step approach to schooling where cohorts of same age students progress through the various stages of the system has too often led to each stage in different institutions operating in isolation from each other and those involved being critical of each other's outcomes. At present, schooling also proceeds in a series of stops and starts which bear little relationship to the way effective learning occurs. The lack of continuity and communication between teachers often leads to overlap between different levels and also overlap between different subjects at the same level. Students, not surprisingly, find these disjunctions unsettling and the consequent repetition boring. These problems, while not easy to overcome even within the one organization, are compounded when they extend into other levels of schooling, and sectors of education. This lack of coherence and continuity works against the encouragement of lifelong learning.

  Principals therefore need to encourage the interchange of information and ideas between teachers within and across organizations. This would lead to greater understanding of the different learning requirements at the different stages of schooling and may help teachers provide approaches to learning that match the students' needs. It has long been accepted that students who pursue their music studies outside the school can progress through the various grades of these studies according to ability rather than age. Very young students can be working at the same level as much older students. A study of such practices may open up possibilities for new processes and structures within the school.

- Principals should encourage their school communities to undertake mapping exercises to identify both their short- and long-term needs, to ascertain how well these needs can be met by resources within the school and then to identify whether those needs could be met from outside the organization. Once this has occurred negotiations for the joint sharing of resources can be started.

8 Play an active role in regional, national and international principal organizations to ensure that they work effectively towards the achievement of lifelong learning for all

- Individual principals or small groups of principals may influence events in their own schools but, for lifelong learning to become a reality for society as a whole, principals need large and effective organizations that can provide support, research, a voice at the political level and a vehicle for gaining media attention and support. Also, as noted earlier, principals are busy people. Many of the suggestions above take time to put into effect, perhaps more time than some individuals feel they can afford, but principals' associations and centres, adequately staffed and resourced, can provide services for their members that reduce the individual workloads.

- Principals who are attempting to create a school climate that encourages the development of lifelong learning need access to publications that generate and maintain enthusiasm and that give practical assistance by publishing case-studies of successes and failures around the world. They need in-service programmes that give them confidence in the use of new technology, that explore new approaches to learning, and that provide training in such areas as decision-making, and the introduction and management of change. Some may also need help in moving from a hierarchical to a collaborative leadership style. Finally, a large principals' organization has credibility when approaching other large organizations and can gain entrée for its members who can then take part in educational visits, set up collaborative arrangements, and gain experience and a wider perspective from activities such as work-exchange programmes.

- It is also important that moves towards lifelong learning are informed by a solid research base. Many people, both in educational institutions and the community, will require evidence that what is being proposed is better than what exists at present and is worth the extra effort involved in implementing change. Such research is beyond the resources of most individual schools or even local groups of schools, but principals' centres, for example, could undertake such studies, especially if principals expected this of them.

- Those in education seem to have difficulty in gaining publicity for their ideas and actions and often find themselves reacting to adverse criticisms or calls for change rather than presenting educational issues in a positive light. Many people in the community have little knowledge of the changes that are taking place in education and, when they do hear of change, have little understanding of its purpose. Principals' organizations need to identify members or employ professionals with media skills so that issues in education can be presented in an interesting and positive way, discussed fully and openly and become a means of increasing the understanding of the community at large. For lifelong learning to become a reality there must be understanding, acceptance, involvement and support from the whole community. The media should be the principal's allies in this.

- Governments, rightly, accept responsibility for ensuring that all members of the community receive basic education, even though the interpretation of 'basic' differs from country to country and may range from some years of primary education through to some form of tertiary education. The wealth and well-being of a country depends on the education level of its citizens but governments, in their quest for financial savings, are seeking ways of moving much of the funding of education to other sources. This immediately creates concerns about justice and equity for those in the initial stages of the lifelong learning process but, because of demographic changes, e.g. ageing population, declining birthrate, more dual-income, childless or single-child families, the community is less vocal in its opposition to the suggested funding changes than it should be.

  At the same time, the schooling stage is not the end of education. There are cogent arguments to show that reliance on initial education alone is no longer sufficient if a country is to prosper, if its citizens are to play an active role in its affairs, and if people are to find their lives fulfilling.

  Principals who support lifelong learning are therefore faced with a difficult task. Governments are looking for ways of reducing their financial commitments in all areas, including education, so principals have to fight for the educational futures of the children in their care. At the same time, they have to strive to widen the understanding and vision of those in government and the community and encourage a commitment to lifelong learning with its consequent resource implications. They therefore have to find ways of ensuring that this is achieved without the government diverting resources from schools.

  It is only by developing a strong voice through their associations that principals will be able to help the community understand the implications and benefits of lifelong learning: they will want to demonstrate what schools can do, how they can go about it and the outcomes of their actions; to publicize their activities and needs; to seek resources from government and industry; and to establish links with other educational groups – TAFE, universities, the University of the Third Age, community groups – to present a united voice and to devise practical ways to implement ideas together.

The way ahead for principals is challenging, exciting and rewarding. Changes can be effected in individual schools that will have a positive impact on society as a whole. However, if principals extend their collaborative approach outside the confines of their own schools to neighbouring principals, community members, other groups and organizations involved in education, and principals' associations, they will have a much stronger voice and be able to present a united front. They will also be able to devise ways of making more efficient use of funding as they work together to rationalize their use of resources. Finally, and most important, they will help society move towards the achievement of lifelong learning for all.

TEACHERS AS LEADERS

A commitment to lifelong learning requires quality teachers. This in turn presupposes and requires high quality professional preparation and development programmes for teachers. Those who will serve education in schools and learning institutions of the future will succeed at introducing their charges to the challenge of lifelong learning only if they themselves have a strong commitment to and a passion for learning and inquiry. Students of the future need to be in contact with people for whom learning is exciting and enriching and teachers are a key to showing them living proof of this. There is a need for teachers to show the value of learning and to excite and motivate people to take up a lifelong approach to it.

One of the problems of the present is the low level of investment on the part of education systems and institutions in the ongoing professional development of their staff. Yet professional development is vital if the impulse for lifelong learning is to be carried forward and brought into effect. Among many teachers there is confusion about what is expected of them and this is in danger of being exacerbated by the phenomenon of an ageing teaching force. It is clear that, to introduce new thinking into the 'thinking' schools of the future, one needs a considerable infusion of new blood: a mix of youth coming in, supported by the experience of older and wiser teachers.

Teachers working in schools now and those entering the profession in the future will need to be properly educated if they are to adopt a lifelong approach to education. In schools of tomorrow teachers will have substantially changed roles and responsibilities: they will be organizers, co-ordinators, mentors and guides responsible for groups of students, who will also have access to many more people and sources of knowledge in the community. This means that teachers need to be facilitators of learning rather than repositories of knowledge. They have to become adept at knowing or being able to find out where the resources of learning reside and to bring them together at an appropriate time.

This will require a change in the attitude and culture of professional life in schools. For this change to be brought about, there is a need to build up the skills of teachers as networkers. Teachers need to become more highly skilled and more multiskilled; they must be able to engage in a more constructive dialogue with other professionals and members of the community about what constitutes learning attainment and what are the various modes of learning procedure.

A problem for the profession is that teachers have been perceived as being unable to articulate the considerations and criteria on which they base their decisions and judgments as regards learning needs and appropriate programme design. Teachers need to develop the ability to diagnose students' needs and capacities. It is all too often the case that many teachers are working with outmoded theories of education, learning and human development: they have to face the challenge of theoretic and practical catch-up. There is an enormous task of professional training and retraining to be done here to minimize the time and energy needed for teachers already in the profession to adjust to the changes in theories of knowledge and learning that are now characteristic features of modern approaches to lifelong education and training. Teachers themselves need to have knowledge and experience of learning in different ways and according to the dictates of a range of learning styles and modes of progress. Teachers will operate well as models of lifelong learning if they can engage in co-operative learning among themselves.

As part of their professional development, however, teachers will need to be brought to face another issue – that of changes in the power relationship between students and teachers. The access that young people have to knowledge and information reduces teachers' control over knowledge. One aspect of this relates to increases in the sophistication and technical literacy of students. As a result young people are likely to demand that teachers alter their approach to teaching and learning and make particular use of modern learning technology. The problem here is that many teachers have not kept abreast of more recent developments in technology; yet if they are to work well as guides and facilitators of learning for their students, they will need a knowledge and understanding of all the various sources of knowledge and pathways to learning that lie open to them. Thus teachers must push themselves, or be pushed, to keep up with technology: they have to become a part of a learning community, in which there are many modes for the organization and advancement of learning as well as of teaching.

Another aspect of this issue is the shift from passive learning to students taking responsibility for their own learning. This involves the creation of an active learning environment. It requires that teachers transfer some of their control over the curriculum, teaching and learning to students. Often teachers' 'expertise' in a subject or discipline prevents students from getting a point of purchase in their learning; teachers need to adapt to making students their active partners in enquiry and cognitive advancement – their own, as well as that of their students.

All this betokens a quantum change in the ways in which universities and employing authorities educate teachers and prepare them for life and work in the education service. Educators will need understanding of, competency in and commitment to new ways of working, new knowledge and new teaching and learning procedures. As part of the move towards a lifelong learning approach, the teaching profession, and those institutions preparing people for entry into it, must realize that they themselves will have to adjust to the new forms, modes and sites in which professional expertise can be gained and mastery of professional knowledge and skills achieved. The teaching profession and the training institutions need to become just as multi-form, heterogenous and flexible as the lifelong approach requires learners themselves to be. Motivating and introducing such a change is going to call for a radical reappraisal of existing methods, structures and forms of induction. Some teacher training institutions may find this quite agonizing even though they are already convinced of its importance.

At the moment, however, the move towards lifelong learning, increased interaction between the school and the community, and redefining the place to learn relies heavily on the goodwill and volunteer efforts of a select number of the teaching profession. Of course it has always been the case that able and dedicated teachers see their role and teaching responsibilities extending outside the school, and many are working hard at these responsibilities already. Yet, though their teaching remit does increasingly extend beyond the walls of the classroom and the school, actually taking learning outside is not done by all teachers. It will take a considerable change in professional attitudes and training for educators to appreciate that there is a need for far more outward-looking and broader approaches, employing the new learning strategies and technologies and beginning to move more deliberately into the changed and extended roles now required.

To draw upon the opportunities provided by work-place learning, by the arts and culture, sport and religion, and all the other activities in which the community has opportunities to learn new things, tomorrow's teachers will need to know what schemes, facilities and resources exist within the community and to integrate them into the curriculum at the appropriate time. This means not only an expanded range of relationships that encourages teachers to work with parents and many other individuals and groups in the community: it means an altered approach to the terms and conditions of teachers' service in education. For example, the division of labour and demarcation problems that are often involved when students undertake work-experience are issues for which teachers must be prepared and which they must be shown how to tackle, for the benefit of their students and the business or union involved. This is one example of an opportunity for government, unions, employers, parents and representatives of the wider community to come together with teachers to prepare and carry through effective and stimulating schemes of work-experience for the benefit of their students and the community generally.

In the light of the foregoing we offer the following conclusions and recommendations regarding the role that teachers can play in leading the learning community and offering lifelong education opportunities for all:

1 Attitudes to learning established at school affect the future of both the individual child and society as a whole. In the teacher the child discovers the first adult whose life is dedicated to teaching and learning

- This first contact can have a profound influence on the child's approach to lifelong learning. If the teacher plays the active role of imparter of knowledge and the child plays the passive role of receiver of knowledge then the basis of lifelong learning is gradually eroded. If, on the other hand, the teacher encourages a spirit of inquiry, critical thinking and reflection on the implications of actions and ideas, then the child is equipped with the means of pursuing learning.

From the earliest stages, therefore, teachers must encourage children to become active participants in their own learning; the child must be given the skills to do this successfully. Positive attitudes to learning need to become part of the child's being.

- It is in the early stages of development that children learn the essentials of literacy and numeracy – reading, writing and arithmetic. The massive growth in and access to various technologies has not reduced the need for these skills. On the contrary, their effect is to increase the need as people access the Internet and communicate with others around the world. The quality of our thoughts is governed by our facility with language and citizens with impoverished language skills will have less to contribute to the social well-being and economic growth of their countries. The child's acquisition of a foundation of knowledge and skills is a primary responsibility of the teacher.

- During their years of schooling children need to gain other essential skills: keyboarding skills to ensure they can exploit the opportunities made possible by the computer; media skills; arts and crafts skills; physical skills in games, gymnastics and swimming; the list goes on. Just as important as acquiring the skills is the development of an awareness of wider issues relating to each of the skills. For example, many secondary schools have driver education programmes. These programmes can be concerned only with the mechanics of driving and rules of traffic safety or they can become a vehicle for helping students to consider the role of the car in today's world, its effects on people's lives, its environmental effects, and its influence in shaping our homes, cities and transportation systems. As teachers encourage critical reflection on taken-for-granted aspects of everyday life and as they help the students discover creative and constructive ways of responding, they are ensuring that students achieve a sense of control over the future.

- Awareness of the importance of respecting and conserving the environment has led young students in some school settings to plant trees; to take part in programmes which monitor water pollution then help in the reclamation of the waterways; and to engage in creative efforts to recycle waste materials. Some of these programmes, such as Water Watch, are worldwide as students communicate with and encourage each other by sharing the results of their efforts on the Web. When learning, in this way of critical exploration and active response, students often begin to engage in a co-operative mode of learning. They learn to work together, to explore ideas and to implement solutions together.

- One of the dangers of the new technology is that it can create an even greater sense of isolation and anomie for some students. Correctly used technology can develop learning clusters of critically aware students able to work together to generate ideas and put them into practice. The intelligent use of modern learning technologies is one of the challenges facing teachers as they prepare young people for lifelong learning.

- It is vitally important that teachers model the kind of behaviour they wish to see in their students. Students need to see teachers who have a wide range of interests both inside and outside the school. Teachers need to reveal themselves as people who obviously enjoy exploring ideas with the students and are not threatened when students challenge an idea or statement; as people who phrase questions to encourage critical inquiry rather than rote responses; who welcome others into the classroom and take the class out to other learning environments; who are themselves still happily engaged in learning activities; who play an active role in establishing community contacts, welcoming parents, finding resources; and who take part in the decision-making processes in the school. Teachers also need to display an appreciation for the arts and demonstrate by their behaviour that they respond to the cultural and spiritual dimension in their lives.

2 Teachers play a number of other roles within the school that have an effect on the students even though these roles are performed outside the classroom. These too will have an influence on the attitudes to learning developed by the students

- As the world changes, and as more and more is being demanded of schools, it is important that teachers be actively involved in curriculum development. This should not merely be seen as deciding what new activities should be added on but rather it should engage teachers in a careful appraisal of how their current curriculum meets the needs of students, what should be jettisoned, what should be added and how the curriculum should be translated into practice. Students too could have useful input into this exercise and would benefit from working co-operatively with teachers and other students on this task.

- There are other decision-making fora in the school where teachers can play an active role by membership of committees, contributing ideas at staff meetings, initiating discussions, and so on. This not only benefits the school by the improved quality of the decisions but it also provides the students with a working example of democracy in action. Teachers who are confident of their own skills in decision-making are also more likely to involve students in decision-making processes, thus helping them learn in practice the rights and responsibilities of citizens.

- Teachers can also demonstrate their initiative and negotiation skills as they work out ways of sharing the resources within the school.

Students can also be encouraged to engage in lateral thinking and seek out new and original ways of resourcing projects.

3 Teachers can take co-operative learning outside the confines of the school into the community

- In ancient times, it is claimed, the Greeks believed that men had a certain number of teeth and women a different number. Nobody, so the story went, bothered to look in people's mouths and count the number of teeth. Too often, in the past, schooling separated the theory from reality. Lessons on local government, for example, remained in the abstract, taken from books. Instead, as some teachers have discovered, if children are taken on a visit to the local council chambers and see a council in action they can begin to understand how local government works in practice. Some councils also encourage the establishment of junior councils that discuss real local issues. In ways like this the students can move out into the community with confidence.

- When teachers arrange for students' work to be on display in the local shopping mall, help their students involve older people in a local history project, or offer their technology or media skills for use by community groups, then the community can see what the students have accomplished, gain some understanding of what is happening in schools and benefit from the interchange.

- This interaction between school and community has the potential to reach quite high levels of sophistication. Val Wilkinson, a teacher at Bendigo Senior Secondary College in Australia, has conceived an innovative plan for breaking down the compartmentalized examination system in the final two years of schooling; team building within the college; building links with business, the community and other schools; providing an ongoing source of revenue; and providing meaningful, ongoing learning while addressing a real need. She has called the scheme 'Bendigo – Tourism 2001' involving the development of a state-of-the-art, interactive hypermedia tourist database on the Bendigo district. The students do all the research, writing, photography, audio-taping, editing of material, packaging, consulting and marketing of material. In time it is expected that the students will produce CD-ROM laser discs, point of information terminals for international airports, and an information bulletin to go round the world on the Internet. Such a project involves a variety of skills from a range of subject areas, it has a real outcome, and it requires patience, dedication and organizing skills. Inevitably the barriers that separate the school from its community are overcome by activities such as this.

4 For lifelong learning to become a reality the concept and practice must be adopted by society. Teachers, therefore, need to play an active and visible role in the educational debate promoting lifelong learning for all

- Adults in the community are concerned about the education of their children and often make assumptions that schooling has not changed since they were at school or, alternatively, that the changes that have occurred are not in the best interests of the children. Leading community figures and organizations offer educational comment and solutions often without any real understanding of the implications of what they are suggesting. Teachers need to enter into these discussions – preferably in a constructive and not in a reactive or a defensive way. They need to develop their ability to communicate with the community so they make clear what they are attempting to achieve and how they are going about it. They also need to stress that helping young people develop their own learning skills is complex, may involve some risk and takes time but the end result for the individual and community will be worthwhile.

A Note of Caution

This may all sound very idealistic and it would be wrong not to consider the difficulties teachers are likely to face as they move towards an even greater involvement in lifelong learning. What is being proposed by the current focus on lifelong learning is a change in teachers' relationships with their students, their peers and their communities, as well as a change in their work patterns and practices. This can be very threatening for people who may feel that there has already been too much change in too short a time. It is therefore important that teachers be given every opportunity to understand the reasons for the change, control the rate of change, and are given, through professional development, strategies for managing change. Lifelong learning will have much more hope of success if this happens and if the teacher can be assisted in conceptualizing the following aspects of their role in different ways:

- *The teacher's relationship to the child*. Over time many have assumed the ideal classroom atmosphere to be one where a cohort of same-age children sat in separated ranks and quietly proceeded with work provided by the teacher. Of course, this assumption has been gradually eroded as schools experiment with multi-age and multi-level classes, seating at round tables, conversation corners, and so on. But considerable change must be brought about in the interests of lifelong learning. It is also true that the teacher–child relationship has been a custodial one. The child is in the teacher's care in the organization of the classroom and patterns of class interaction. In this situation the teacher is the person in control. Clearly it will be necessary for many teachers to learn new attitudes to enable changes in relationships to students engaged in the learning endeavour.

- *Teachers' expanding roles in the school and their relationships with their colleagues.* The teacher's role is complex, time-consuming and often exhausting so teachers will need to be convinced that time spent on committees, on decision-making activities and in-service programmes designed to further the implementation of lifelong learning will benefit the students and not have an adverse effect on their current work. It should be the teachers who decide priorities. Excessive time spent on trivial decisions will be counter-productive and discourage participation and professional growth in areas pertaining to the implementation of lifelong learning.

- *Relationships with the community.* Building up community relationships can also be time-consuming so it is important to target a few productive activities and networks early in the process. The enthusiasm thus generated will then help build bridges to ongoing exchanges. In the initial stages both sides could feel threatened as they engage in new and different activities. Resource centres could help generate ideas and publicize successful programmes. Some 'lighthouse' schools could also assume responsibility for the 'diffusion of ideas' as part of their mission.

- *Working conditions of teachers.* As the community members begin to see schools as learning centres for all the community, they will begin to seek greater access to school facilities and resources and this will inevitably lead to changes in teachers' working evironment. Flexible working hours, weekend and evening work, and flexible class sizes will substantially alter the working life of the teacher. Teachers will need extensive retraining to ensure that they are equipped to meet these challenges.

- *Changes in the teaching career structure.* The changing nature of the school will demand the creation of new roles and the abolition of others. Teaching aides may be used to train students in technical activities thus freeing teachers to play the more challenging role of helping students develop higher-order skills such as: understanding issues; thinking laterally, critically and reflectively; clarifying values; and creating new learning experiences. Teachers who have fought to improve their conditions and to ensure that only registered teachers can teach in schools may find these ideas difficult or impossible to accept.

Change is inevitable and it is always less threatening when those affected have the opportunity to manage it. Some teachers have already started down the road to lifelong learning and are reaping the rewards as they:

- encourage self-directed learning in their students;

- work closely with their peers to develop schools as co-operative learning centres;

- are open to a two-way exchange with parents and members of the local community; and

- demand and engage in professional development activities tailored to meet their particular needs.

As others take up the challenge, the realization of lifelong learning for all will move closer to reality and teachers will find their future exciting and rewarding as their roles expand to meet the new demands.

CONCLUSION

There is a major difficulty for those committed to the promotion of policies designed to increase lifelong learning opportunities for all. It comes from the realization that a period of some ten to fifteen years might need to elapse before there can be a change in social attitudes and a broad-scale acceptance of the idea of lifelong learning for all. And, in order to make sure that a range of lifelong learning strategies is in place and at work, a policy perspective extending to 30 or 40 years might be required.

Yet, if countries are to start on the path to the economic success, social inclusiveness, democratic participation and personal growth, there are certain steps that must be taken. To begin with, all members of the community will need to be made aware of the reasons why the achievement of such goals is a matter of vital importance, locally, regionally and globally. In this there is a need for advocacy as well as education: lifelong learning requires an attitudinal and cultural change on the part of governments, policy-makers, providers of education, learners and the entire community.

It will be crucial to the success of the enterprise to demonstrate the benefits of lifelong learning to all parties. In the face of this undertaking there may be some initial reluctance or difficulty; yet the more that people experience the growth and excitement of learning, the more chance there will be for the emergence of the political will and societal commitment to invest in lifelong learning, on the part of both the community and the individual learner.

Policy-makers, professional educators, members of the community and the media need to act in concert to articulate the benefits of lifelong learning: these agencies provide a powerful mechanism for spreading the message: they have the means to make the concept of lifelong learning a reality in people's lives.

In articulating policies on these matters and in putting them into effect, governments are in a position to allocate large amounts of money and thereby encourage the development of an awareness and an understanding in the community as to what it is important to foster. This can drive the engine of policy implementation and the extension of community action.

There is much more to the success of lifelong learning initiatives than government intervention, of course. Local communities need to be actively involved. This entails a number of moves. The first is that our society as a whole must value learning, support those who continue to learn and make the value of learning part of their country's culture. Then there is the question of providing an adequate level of resources – always a problem. This problem can be tackled in the community by affirming and promoting the notion that education serves the community in ways that extend far beyond the economic concerns of society: the full potential and promise of lifelong learning will only be realized if there are other moves in the community to give it value.

It is important too that consideration be given to making all kinds of opportunities open for personal advancement through education; it will be important for students and continuing learners that a multiplicity of pathways are created for them and that they are given the capacity to project their plans for further learning and development into the future. This will involve the creation and articulation not only of a variety of pathways but also laying emphasis upon a range of goals and objectives, not restricted to those relating to further education and training, though these are highly important. Until now, we have generally asked children 'What would you like to be?', with the expectation that the answer will normally fix on some occupation; in future it will be equally important to ask young people what they want *to be* as human beings, and as contributory members of society.

Lifelong learning entails a greater responsibility for growth and advancement lying with the individual. With respect to future development, individuals need to start seeing themselves differently, to see the need to manage their own career, and to accept responsibility for learning across the life-span. Unless one sees the value of learning for oneself, one fails to see its value for others. Development of the notion of valuing learning has to come as much from people themselves as a strong personal commitment, as from the wider community.

There are thus many difficulties to be worked through, many barriers to be removed. For many people formal education institutions are threatening and alien, closed communities with their own rules, regimented, impersonal, unwelcoming. Changing such an image of a learning institution will be another in the list of major priorities – and it will require huge investments of time, effort and resources.

It is up to schools and other educating institutions to break down these barriers to freedom of imagination and diversity of planning in people's learning development; to act as part of an overall educational service in which lifelong learning will be on offer to a large extent outside traditional educational institutions. Schools will have to draw parents into their campaign to include all the people in their community. In this way they will be able to help people realize that in these times educational opportunity lies open everywhere and anywhere.

In sum, people need to be educated more widely and to come to understand that all experience can generate lessons for learning; successful learning and growth does not merely come about as a result of directed work with pen and paper. There are all kinds of experiences open to us in nature and society that help us to grow: these things are changing all the time as well, and we grow in consequence. Cicero put it well: 'Tempora semper mutantur, et nos cum temporibus' ('The times are always changing, and we ourselves with the times').

Appendix 1

Organizations and Departments from Which People Were Interviewed

During the course of this study, tape-recorded interviews were conducted with a range of school-based personnel and people from the following organizations:

Adult Community and Further Education Board
Adult Education Association of Victoria
Anglican Marriage Guidance Council
Arts Access Society
Arts Victoria
Association of Heads of Independent Schools of Australia
Association of Neighbourhood Houses and Learning Centres
Australia-China Chamber of Commerce
Australian Capital Territory Department of Education and Training
Australian Centre for Retail Studies
Australian Chamber of Commerce and Industry
Australian Chamber of Manufacturers
Australian Conservation Council
Australian Education Union
Australian Greek Welfare Society
Australian Institute of Family Studies
Australian Institute of Management
Australian National Training Authority Research Advisory Council
Australian Parents Council Incorporated
Australian Teachers of Media
Business Education Round Table
Catholic Education Commission of New South Wales
Catholic Education Office of Victoria
Commonwealth Department of Employment, Education and Training
Council for Christian Education in Schools
Council of Adult Education
Crafts Council of Victoria
Directorate of School Education, Victoria
Employment and Skills Formation Council
Federation of Parents and Citizens Association of New South Wales
Federation of School Community Organisation of New South Wales
Footscray Community Arts Centre
Hawthorn Community Education Project
Higher Education Council

Islamic Society of Victoria
Jewish Cultural Centre
Local Government Industry and Training Board
Monash University
Museums Australia
National Board of Employment, Education and Training
National Industry Education Forum
New South Wales Primary Principals Association
Office of Training and Further Education, Victoria
Policy and Projects, Directorate of School Education, Victoria
Research and Planning, Directorate of School Education, Victoria
Retail Traders Association of Victoria
Rotary Youth Training Extension
Salvation Army
SBS TV and Radio
Small Business Victoria
The New South Wales Parents Council Incorporated
University of the Third Age, City of Melbourne
University of the Third Age Network
Victoria Council of School Organisations
Victorian Aboriginal Education Association
Victorian Adult Literacy and Basic Education Council
Victorian Association of Directors of TAFE Colleges
Vietnamese Community in Australia
Women's Domestic Violence Outreach

Appendix 2

Questions Asked in Interviews

1 How can the targets of high quality education and training for all be realized through a policy of 'lifelong learning' that is designed to promote both social and economic goals?

2 How might lifelong learning promote social inclusion and sustain and develop democracy, as well as economic growth?

3 What are the barriers to lifelong learning? What is the value of a lifelong learning approach in relation to the perceived weaknesses in current educational provision and practice?

4 What is the readiness of current education and training provision to meet the challenges posed by competitive and global knowledge economies and the need for social inclusion and democratic participation? What changes need to be made, if any, to achieve these goals?

5 How can schools create an environment conducive to a lifelong learning approach?

6 What are the elements of a high quality foundation of essential knowledge and skills, that all young people should acquire and all members of society should possess, as a basis for lifelong learning? How should students acquire such a foundation; what should be the content of the curriculum for it; and should the same foundation be common to all institutions? If not, what should be the different contents of different curricula, and for what reasons?

7 How can trade-offs between excellence and exclusion and consolidation and expansion be better balanced and which skills and knowledge acquired at one stage or in one setting provide the best basis for learning at other stages and in other settings?

8 Is there a need for a complete overhaul of current curricula and methods of teaching and learning in school to bring about a realization of lifelong learning for all? If so, in what directions should changes seek to take curricula and pedagogy in the future?

9 What are the implications of lifelong learning for the teaching profession? What incentives might be needed to change attitudes and upgrade knowledge and competencies?

10 What are the implications of new epistemologies, new approaches to learning and styles of student progress, and new technologies of learning for the content, style, structure and organization of learning in schools and for the nature of schools as learning organizations and educating institutions?

11 How can existing goals of education contribute to the development of educational provision in schools, which fosters lifelong learning for all?

12 How should education standards be set, monitored and evaluated, in a coherent approach to lifelong learning for all?

13 What are the problems and challenges which governments face in devising effective policies and managerial strategies that steer development into lifelong learning for all? What balance between central regulation and local decision-making by autonomous establishments and among actors and across functions best promotes the development of effective and efficient provision of schooling which fosters lifelong learning for all?

14 How are the interests of stakeholders outside the formal education system to be taken into account by government authorities in their consideration of lifelong learning? What weighting should be given to such considerations and for what reasons?

15 What new frameworks, regulations, mechanisms and procedures must governments develop in response to the new pattern of relationships associated with the provision of programmes aimed at promoting lifelong learning for all?

16 How do various constituencies outside the formal education system and institutions of government see themselves as contributing to the goal of lifelong learning for all?

17 As parents and other stakeholders assume greater responsibility in the provision of education, is there a possibility that the scale and quality of educational provision will be widened or narrowed? Does this represent a danger or an opportunity?

18 How might principals and teachers deal with and overcome any fear that they as professionals experience of being overwhelmed or overrun by the increased numbers, powers and demands of the various new partners with whom they are required to work in the educational enterprise?

19 How might a sense of community and consensus be formed, fostered and utilized, at the level of the local school site, in a context of greater heterogeneity, diverse and sometimes competing pressures on schools, and an increased emphasis on greater school autonomy, that also enhances the cohesion of the local community as a self-conscious learning organization?

20 How might all members and sectors (public and private) of society be encouraged to accept and fully exploit their changed and expanded roles and responsibilities in the provision and enhancement of programmes, opportunities and occasions for lifelong learning for all?

21 How might acceptance of the notion and value of the learning community as a fundamental precondition for lifelong learning for all be developed?

22 As schools themselves will need to become learning organizations, how will schools better integrate work and learning to inspire all their people to seek quality, excellence and continuous improvement in both?

23 Will the conventional concept of schools as physical locations, operating within fairly strict parameters of teaching time, space and student grouping, exist in the next century? If not, by what kinds of institutions, organizations, structures or educational processes will schools have been replaced?

24 What are the various perils and pitfalls in the changing relationship between parents and professional educators in the provision of lifelong learning? What specific strategies might be put forward for mediating and managing difficulties?

25 What are the ways in which parents and families can strengthen and enhance the effectiveness of the contributions they can make to quality schooling and lifelong learning?

26 How might school relations with business, industry, commerce and trades unions foster lifelong learning? What lessons can we draw from our experience of past dysfunctions in such relationships? What successful practices can be highlighted to delineate and draw attention to those features of such relationships that make them work well? Can recommendations for joint endeavours be put forward, where positive collaboration and effective working can function as rich sources for the development of the learning community?

27 What are the ways in which schools can form part of and contribute to the cultural and artistic life, institutions and activities of the community? What are the ways in which those institutions and activities can contribute to and join together with educating agencies to enhance the range and type of opportunities, possibilities and programmes necessary for the development of lifelong learning for all?

28 How can schools provide insight into and reflect the ethnic diversity of our modern multicultural society, in ways that will increase racial and religious tolerance, improve social harmony, and enhance opportunities for lifelong learning for all a community's members?

29 What might be the relationships between school and other agencies and providers of technologies of learning and communication in the question of providing programmes and opportunities for lifelong learning for all?

30 How might schools draw upon the advice and assistance of a range of cultural institutions and resources in order to make a contribution to the beautification and quality of the community and its environment?

Bibliography

Ackerman, B. (1980) *Social Principles and the Liberal State*. New Haven, Conn.: Yale University Press.

Adler, L. and Gardner, S. (eds) (1994) *The Politics of Linking Schools and Social Services*. London: Falmer Press.

Age, The (1996) 'The Options Project' of Monash University reported in *The Age*, 5 March 1996.

Allen, J.M. and Koehler Freitag, K. (1988) 'Parents and students as cooperative learners', *The Reading Teacher*, May, 922–5.

Allman, P. (1982) 'New Perspectives on the adult: an argument for lifelong education', *International Journal of Lifelong Education*, 1(1), 41–51.

Applied Behavioral and Cognitive Sciences Inc. (1993) *The WELL Strategy. Workforce Education and Lifelong Learning for Education and Economic Reform*. San Diego, Calif.: Applied Behavioral and Cognitive Sciences Inc.

Arnaud Reid, L. (1969) *Meaning in the Arts*. London: Allen & Unwin.

ASCD Panel on Moral Education (1988) *Educational Leadership*, May, 4–8.

Aspin, D.N. (1988) '"Critical openness" as a platform for diversity: towards an ethic of belonging' in B. O'Keefe (ed.), *Schools for Tomorrow: Building Walls or Building Bridges*, pp. 27–51. Lewes: Falmer Press.

Aspin, D.N. (1996a) 'Logical empiricism and post-empiricism'. Chapter 2 in P. Higgs (ed.), *Meta-Theories in Philosophy of Education*. London and Cape Town: Heinemann.

Aspin, D.N. (ed.) (1996b) *Logical Empiricism and Post-Empiricism in Philosophy of Education*. London, Cape Town and Sydney: Heinemann.

Aspin, D.N. and Chapman, J.D. with Wilkinson, V.R. (1994) *Quality Schooling: A Pragmatic Approach to Some Current Problems, Topics and Issues*. London: Cassell.

AVCC (1992) *Report of the Committee in Response to the 'Quality Reference'*. Canberra: AVCC.

Bagley, C. and Hunter, B. (1992) 'Restructuring, construction and technology: forging a new relationship', *Educational Technology*, July, 22–7.

Bagnall, R.J. (1990) 'Lifelong education: the institutionalisation of an illiberal and regressive ideology?', *Educational Philosophy and Theory*, 22(1), March, 1–7.

Bailey, C. (1984) *Beyond the Present and the Particular: A Theory of Liberal Education*. London: Routledge & Kegan Paul.

Bailey, C. (1988) 'Lifelong education and liberal education', *Journal of Philosophy of Education*, 22(1), 121–6.

Ball, C. (1993) *Life-long Learning and the School Curriculum*. Paris: OECD/CERI.

Ball, C. (1994) Summation of the Conference at the conclusion of the First Global Conference on 'Life-long Learning'. Rome.

Bauch, J.P. (1989) 'The transparent school model: new technology for parent involvement', *Educational Leadership*, October, 32–4.

Belanger, P. and Gelpi, E. (eds) (1995) *Lifelong Education*. Dordrecht: Kluwer.

Benson, G.M. (1994) *The Lifelong Learning Society: Investing in the New Learning Technology Market Sector*. Stephentown, NY: Learning Systems Engineering.

Berg, C.A., Klaczynski, P.A., Calderone, K.S. and Strough, J. (1994) 'Adult age differences in cognitive strategies: adaptive or deficient?' in J.D. Sinnot (ed.), *Interdisciplinary Handbook of Adult Lifespan Learning*. Westport, Conn.: Greenwood Press.

Berger, J. (1971) *Ways of Seeing*. London: BBC Publishing.

Berman, L.M. (1984) 'Educating children for lifelong learning and a learning society', *Childhood Education*, **61**(2), 99–106.

Bernstein, R.J. (1983) *Beyond Objectivism and Relativism: Science, Hermeneutics and Praxis*. Oxford: Basil Blackwell.

Binkley, M., Guthrie, J. and Wyatt, T. (1991) 'A survey of national assessment and examination practices in OECD countries'. Paper presented at the General Assembly of the INES project 'International Education Indicators'. Lugano-Cadro. 16–18 September. Paris: OECD.

Bird, J. (1995) 'Multi-media brings life to bone-dry education', *The Times*.

Blanshard, B. (1974) *The Uses of a Liberal Education*. London: Alcove Press.

Bottery, M. (1993) 'The management of schools and citizenship', *Citizenship: The Journal of the Citizenship Foundation*, **3**(12), 6–7.

Boud, D., Cohen, R. and Walker, D. (1993) 'Introduction: understanding learning from experience' in D. Boud, R. Cohen and D. Walker (eds), *Using Experience for Learning*, pp. 1–17. Buckingham: The Society for Research into Higher Education and Open University Press.

Brandt, R. (1989) 'On parents and schools: a conversation with Joyce Epstein', *Educational Leadership*, October, 24–7.

Bridges, D. and McLaughlin, T.H. (eds) (1994) *Education and the Market Place*. London: Falmer Press.

Briscoe, D.B. (1990) 'Community education: a culturally responsive approach to learning' in J.M. Ross-Gordon, L.G. Martin and D.B. Briscoe (eds), *Serving Culturally Diverse Populations*. San Francisco: Jossey-Bass.

Broadfoot, P. (1991) 'Achievements of learning'. Paper presented at the General Assembly of the INES project 'International Education Indicators'. Lugano-Cadro, 16–18 September. Paris: OECD.

Bronowski, J. (1973) *The Ascent of Man*. London: BBC Publishing.

Brown, J. (1996) 'Religion in curriculum: a question of values', *The Age*, 2 April, Education 3.

Bruce, B., Kreefdt Payton, J. and Batson, T. (1993) *Network-Based Classrooms*. Cambridge: CUP.

Buffamanti, D.M. and Paulter, A.J. (1994) 'How we will learn in the year 2000: reengineering schools for the high performance economy', *Journal of Industrial Teacher Education*, **31**(4), 87–95.

Butcher, H., Glenn, A., Henderson, P. and Smith, J. (eds) (1993) *Community and Public Policy*. London: Pluto Press.

Campbell, D. (1992) 'Parents and schools working for student success', *NASSP Bulletin*, April, 1–9.

Campbell, D. (1995) 'The Socrates syndrome: questions that should never be asked', *Phi Delta Kappan*, **76**(6), 467–9.

Campoy, R. (1992) 'The role of technology in the school reform movement', *Educational Technology*, August, 17–22.

Candy, P.C. and Crebert, R.B. (1991) 'Lifelong learning: an enduring mandate for higher education', *Higher Education Research and Development*, **10**(1), 3–17.

Carr, D. (1991) 'Living on one's own horizon: cultural institutions, school libraries and lifelong learning', *School Library Media Quarterly*, **19**(4), 217–22.

Caruso, J. (1981) 'Collaboration of school, college and community: a bridge to progress', *Educational Leadership*, April, 558–62.

Chapman, J.D. (1990) *The Effectiveness of Schooling and of Educational Resource Management: The Analysis of Developments Across OECD Countries*. Paris: OECD.

Chapman, J.D. and Aspin, D.N. (1993) *Implications of the OECD Activity on the Effectiveness of Schooling and of Educational Resource Management for the Curriculum Re-Defined*. Paper given at OECD Conference on 'The Curriculum Re-Defined'. April. Paris: OECD.

Chapman, J.D. and Aspin, D.N. (1995a) *Securing the Future*. Paris: OECD.

Chapman, J.D. and Aspin, D.N. (1995b) *Realising a Lifelong Approach to Learning for All: A Review of OECD Work 1990–95*. Paris: OECD.

Charner, I. and Rolinski, C.A. (1987) 'Critical questions and issues for integrating education and work' in I. Charner and C.A. Rolinski (eds), *Responding to the Educational Needs of Today's Workplace*, pp. 87–91. San Francisco: Jossey-Bass.

Chase, R.A. and Durden, W.G. (1992) 'Linking a city's culture to students' learning', *Educational Leadership*, **50**(1), September, 66–8.

Chubb, J.E. and Moe, T. (1990) *Politics, Markets and American Schools*. Washington, DC: The Brookings Institute.

Cohen, B. (1981) *Education and the Individual*. London: Allen & Unwin.

Cohen, D.K. and Spillane, J. (1991) 'National education indicators and traditions of accountability'. Paper presented at the General Assembly of the INES project 'International Education Indicators'. Lugano-Cadro. 16–18 September. Paris: OECD.

Coleman, J.C. and Warren-Adamson, C. (eds) (1992) *Youth Policy in the 1990s*. London: Routledge.

Coles, B. (1995) *Youth and Social Policy*. London: UCL Press.

Collinge, L. and Coleman, P. (1992) 'Home–school collaboration: teacher practices and parent attitudes'. Paper presented at the Annual Meeting of AERA. San Francisco. April.

Commission on Non-Traditional Study (1973) *Diversity by Design*. San Francisco: Jossey-Bass.

Courtny, B. (1990) 'Community education for older adults' in M.W. Galbraith (ed.), *Education Through Community Organizations*. San Francisco: Jossey-Bass.

Cropley, A.J. (ed.) (1979) *Lifelong Education: A Stocktaking*. Hamburg: VIE Monograph, No. 8.

Cropley, A.J. and Knapper, C.K. (1983) 'Higher education and the promotion of lifelong learning', *Studies in Higher Education*, **8**(1), 15–21.

Cross, K.P. (1991) 'The renaissance in adult learning', *Community Services Catalyst*, **21**(4), 6–11.

Crowson, R., Boyd, W.L. and Mawhinney, H.B. (eds) (1996) *The Politics of Education and the New Institutionalism*. London: Falmer Press.

Cupitt, D. (1985) *The Sea of Faith*. London: BBC Publishing.

Darling-Hammond, L. (1991) 'Policy uses and indicators'. Paper presented at the General Assembly of the INES project 'International Education Indicators'. Lugano-Cadro. 16–18 September. Paris: OECD.

Dave, R.H. (1975) *Reflections on Lifelong Education and the School*. Hamburg: UIE Monograph.

Dave, R.H. (ed.) (1976) *Foundations of Lifelong Education*. Oxford: Pergamon Press.

Davis, B.C. (1989) 'A successful parent-involvement program', *Educational Leadership*, October, 21–3.

Davis, E., Wood, J.M. and Smith, B.W. (1986) *Recurrent Education: A Revived Agenda*. Sydney: Croom Helm.

Deem, R. and Brehony, K.J. (1994) 'The school, the parent, the banker and the local politician: what can we learn from the English experience in involving lay people in the site based management of schools?' Paper presented at AERA Annual Meeting. New Orleans.

Delors, J. (ed.) (1996) *Learning: The Treasure Within*. Paris: UNESCO.

Dewey, J. (1938) *Experience and Education*. New York: Macmillan.

Dewey, J. (1966) *Democracy and Education*. New York: Free Press.

Dryfoos, J. (1994) *Full-Service Schools*. San Francisco: Jossey-Bass.

Duncan, C.P. (1992) 'Parental support in schools and the changing family structure', *NASSP Bulletin*, April, 10–14.

Edelson, P.J. (1992) 'Leadership and the future of adult and continuing education' in P.J. Edelson (ed.), *Rethinking Leadership in Adult and Continuing Education*. San Francisco: Jossey-Bass.

Edwards Tufte, R. (1991) *Envisioning Information* (2nd revised edn). Cheshire, Conn.: Graphics Press.

Ehrenzweig, A. (1976) *The Hidden Order of Art: A Study in the Psychology of Imagination*. San Francisco: University of California Press.

Elliott, B.J. and Richards, M.P.M. (1991) 'Parental divorce and the life chances of children', *Family Law*, November, 481–4.

Elvin, L. (1975) 'Learning to be … ', *Education News*, No. 15.

Etzioni, A. (1995) *The Spirit of Community*. London: Fontana Press.

European Parliament (1995) Amended Proposal for a European Parliament and Council Decision establishing a European Year of Lifelong Learning. Brussels.

Evans, K. (1994) 'Change and prospects in education for young adults', *Comparative Education*, **30**(1), 39–47.

Evans, N. (1985) *Post-Education Society: Recognising Adults as Learners*. London: Croom Helm.

Evans, N. (1995) *Our Children at Risk*. Paris: OECD.

Evers, C.W. and Lakomski, G. (1991) *Knowing Educational Administration*. Oxford: Pergamon.

Evers, C.W. and Walker, J.C. (1983) 'Knowledge, partitioned sets and extensionality', *Journal of Philosophy of Education*, **17**(2), 55–70.

Fasano, C. (1991) 'Knowledge, ignorance and epistemic utility: issues in constructing and organising indicator systems'. Paper presented at the General Assembly of the INES Project 'International Education Indicators'. Lugano-Cadro. 16–18 September. Paris: OECD.

Faure, E. *et al.* (1972) *Learning to Be: The World of Education Today and Tomorrow*. Paris: UNESCO.

Feller, R. (1991) 'Employment and career development in a world of change: what is ahead for the next twenty-five years?', *Journal of Employment Counselling*, **28**, 13–20.

Fields, J. (1994) 'European action programmes and lifelong learning: a guide to recent developments', *Adult Learning*, **6**(3), 87–8.

Fittoussi, J. and Luna, F. (1996) 'Wage distribution, social cohesion and the knowledge-based economy' in *Employment and Growth in the Knowledge-Based Economy*. Paris: OECD.

Foray, D. and Lundvall, B. (1996) 'The knowledge-based economy: from the economics of knowledge to the learning economy' in *Employment and Growth in the Knowledge-based Economy*. Paris: OECD.

Forlizzi, L.A., Askov, E.N. and Carmen, P.S. (1994) 'Supporting lifelong learning: accumulated wisdom in the field', *Adult Basic Education*, **4**(2), 81–3.

Fragnière, G. (ed.) (1976) *Education without Frontiers: A Study of the Future of Education from the European Cultural Foundations 'Plan Europe 2000'*. London: Gerald Duckworth.

Friedman, B.M. (1988) 'Intergenerational Celebrations', *Educational Leadership*, May, 52–5.

Fullick, P. (1992) 'Links with industry and employers' in N. Foskett (ed.), *Managing External Relations in Schools: A Practical Guide*. London: Routledge.

Galbraith, M.W. (1990) 'Community education for older adults' in M.W. Galbraith (ed.), *Education through Community Organisations*. San Francisco: Jossey-Bass.

Gallie, W.B. (1956) 'Essentially contested concepts', *Proceedings of the Aristotelian Society*, **LVI**.

Gallie, W.B. (1964) *Philosophy and the Historical Understanding*. London: Chatto & Windus.

Gardner, H. (1985) *Frames of Mind: The Theory of Multiple Intelligences*. New York: Basic Books.

Gardner, H. (1987) *The Mind's New Science: A History of the Cognitive Revolution*. New York: Basic Books.

Gardner, H. (1991) *The Unschooled Mind: How Children Think and How Schools Should Teach*. New York: Basic Books.

Gelpi, E. (1984) 'Lifelong education: opportunities and obstacles', *International Journal of Lifelong Education*, **3**(2), 79–87.

Gelpi, R.E. (1985) 'Lifelong education and international relations' in K. Wain (ed.), *Lifelong Education and Participation*. Malta: University of Malta Press.

Giaquinta, J.B., Bauer, J.A. and Levin, J. (1993) *Beyond Technology's Promise*. Cambridge: CUP.

Goldring, E.B. (1986) 'The school community: its effects on principals' perceptions of parents', *Educational Administration Quarterly*, **22**(3), Spring, 115–32.

Grace, G.R. (1994) 'Education is a public good: on the need to resist the domination of economic science' in D. Bridges and T.H. McLaughlin (eds), *Education and the Market Place*. London: Falmer Press.

Greenberg, K.H., Coleman, L. and Wakefield Rankin, W. (1993) 'The cognitive enrichment network program: goodness of fit with at-risk gifted children', *Roeper Review*, **16**(2), 91–5.

Greger, S.I. (1972) 'Aesthetic meaning', *Proceedings of the Philosophy of Education Society of Great Britain*, **VI**(2), 137–63.

Gross, R. (1992) 'Lifelong learning in the learning society of the twenty-first century' in C. Collins and N.D. Mangieri (eds), *Teaching Thinking: An Agenda for the Twenty-First Century*. Hillsdale, NJ: Lawrence Erlbaum Associates Inc.

Guttman, A. (1987) *A Democratic Education*. Princeton, NJ: Princeton University Press.

Habermas, J. (1972) *Knowledge and Human Interests*. London: Heinemann.

Harris, C.K. (1979) *Education and Knowledge*. London: Routledge & Kegan Paul.

Harris and Associates (1987) 'Strengthening links between home and school'. *Metropolitan Life Survey of the American Teacher*. New York.

Hartnett, A. and Naish, M. (eds) (1976) *Theory and the Practice of Education* (2 vols). London: Heinemann.

Hayes, E.R. and Darkenwald, G.C. (1990) 'Attitudes towards adult education: an empirically based conceptualization', *Adult Education Quarterly*, **40**(3), 158–68.

Heath, S.B. and McLaughlin, M.W. (1994) 'The best of both worlds: connecting schools and community youth organisations for all-day, all-year learning', *Educational Administration Quarterly*, **30**(3), 278–300.

Hebenstreit, J. (1994) 'The future of technology in post-secondary education'. Paper presented at the International Conference on 'Learning Beyond Schooling'. December. Paris: OECD.

Hester, H. (1989) 'Start to improve home–school relations', *NASSP Bulletin*, January, 23–7.

Hiatt, D.B. (1994) 'No limits to the possibilities', *Phi Delta Kappan*, **75**(10), 786–9.

Hindess, E.F. (1972) 'Forms of knowledge', *Proceedings of the Philosophy of Education Society of Great Britain*, **VI**(2), 164–75.

Hirsch, D. (1992) *'Schools and Business: A New Partnership'*. Paris: OECD.

Hirst, P.H. (1965) 'Liberal education and the nature of knowledge' in R.D. Archambault (ed.), *Philosophical Analysis and Education*. London: Routledge & Kegan Paul.

Hirst, P.H. (1973) *Knowledge and the Curriculum*. London: Routledge & Kegan Paul.

Holmberg, B. (1986) *Growth and Structure of Distance Education*. London: Croom Helm.

Holmes, M. and Wynne, E.A. (1989) *Making the School an Effective Community: Belief, Practice and Theory in School Administration*. Philadelphia: Falmer Press.

Hornby, G. (1989) 'A model for parent participation', *British Journal for Parent Participation*, **16**(4), December, 161–2.

Hornby, G. (1990) 'The organization of parent involvement', *School Organization*, **10**(2 and 3), 247–51.

Hughes, P. (1993) *The Curriculum Re-defined: Implications from OECD Associated Projects*. Paris: OECD.

Hunter, M. (1989) 'Join the "Par-aide" in education', *Educational Leadership*, October, 36–41.

Huston, E. (1994) *Children in Poverty*. Cambridge: CUP.

Hyde, D. (1992) 'School–parent collaboration results in academic achievement', *NASSP Bulletin*, April, 39–42.

Illich, I. (1973) *De-Schooling Society*. Harmondsworth: Penguin Press.

Illich, I. and Verne, E. (1976) *Imprisoned in the Global Classroom*. London: Writers and Readers Publishing Co-operative.

Inman, S. and Buck, M. (1995) *Adding Value*. London: Trentham Books.

Ireland, T.D. (1978) *Gelpi's View of Lifelong Education*. Manchester: MUP.

Jackson, B.L. and Cooper, B.S. (1992) 'Involving parents in improving urban schools', *NASSP Bulletin*, April, 30–38.

Jacobs, G. (1993) 'The greening of the language classroom: using learner-generated materials for environmental education', *Guidelines*, **15**(2), 8–17.

James, M. and Mentz, M. (1994) *Lessons Learned about Forging Partnerships with Business, Industry and Community Groups*. Presentation given at the University of Western Australia, Perth, 6 November.

Jennings, J.M. (1992) 'Parent involvement strategies for inner-city schools', *NASSP Bulletin*, December, 61–8.

Jennings, W.B. (1989) 'How to organize successful parent advisory committees', *Educational Leadership*, October, 42–5.

Jonathan, R. (1989) 'Choice and control in education: parental rights, individual liberties and social justice', *British Journal of Educational Studies*, **XXXVII**(4), November, 321–38.

Kallen, D. (1979) 'Recurrent education and lifelong learning: definitions and distinctions' in *World Yearbook of Education 1979: Recurrent Education and Lifelong Learning* (ed. T. Schuller and J. Megary). London: Kogan Page.

Kant, I. (1964) *The Metaphysical Principles of Virtue* (trans. James Ellington). Indianapolis: Bobbs-Merrill Library of Liberal Arts.

Kirby, P.C., Paradise, L.V. and King, M.L. (1992) 'Extraordinary leaders in education: understanding transformational leadership', *Journal of Educational Research*, **85**(2), 303–11.

Kleinig, J. (1973) 'R.S. Peters' use of transcendental arguments', *Proceedings of the Philosophy of Education Society of Great Britain*, **VII**(2), July.

Knowles, J.L. and Scattergood, S.P. (1989) 'Education for parenting', *Educational Leadership*, October, 67.

Knowles, M.S. (1984) 'New roles for teachers as empowerers of lifelong learners', *Journal of Children in Contemporary Society*, **16**(3–4), 85–94.

Knowles, M.S. and Associates (1984) *Andragogy in Action: Applying Modern Principles of Adult Learning*. San Francisco: Jossey-Bass.

Knox, A.B. (1977) *Adult Development and Learning*. San Francisco: Jossey-Bass.

Kovesi, J. (1967) *Moral Notions*. London: Routledge & Kegan Paul.

Kuh, D. and Maclean, M. (1990) 'Women's childhood experience of parental separation and their subsequent health and status in adulthood', *Journal of Biological Science*, **22**, 121–35.

Kuhn, T.S. (1973) *The Structure of Scientific Revolutions*. Chicago: Chicago University Press.

Kulich, J. (1982) 'Lifelong education and the universities: a Canadian perspective', *International Journal of Lifelong Education*, **1**(2), 123–42.

Lakatos, I. (1976) 'Falsification and the methodology of scientific research programs' in I. Lakatos and A.W. Musgrave, *Criticism and the Growth of Knowledge*. Cambridge: CUP.

Lakatos, I. (1978) *The Methodology of Scientific Research Programmes*. Cambridge: CUP.

Langford, G. (1973) 'The concept of education' in D.J. O'Connor and G. Langford (eds), *New Essays in Philosophy of Education*. London: Routledge & Kegan Paul.

Lawson, K.H. (1979) *Philosophical Concepts and Values in Adult Education* (revised edn). Milton Keynes: Open University Press.

Lawson, K. (1982) 'Lifelong education: concept or policy?', *International Journal of Lifelong Education*, **1**(2).

Lengrand, P. (1975) *An Introduction to Lifelong Education*. London: Croom Helm.

Lengrand, P. (1979) 'Prospects of lifelong education' in A.J. Cropley (ed.), *Lifelong Education: A Stocktaking*. Hamburg: VIE Monograph, No. 8.

Lenk, H. (1994) 'Value changes and the achieving society' in OECD, *Societies in Transition: The Future of Work and Leisure*. Paris: OECD.

Lieberman, A. (ed.) (1990) *Schools as Collaborative Culture: Creating the Future Now*. London: Falmer Press.

Likona, T. (1988) 'How parents and schools can work together to raise moral children', *Educational Leadership*, May, 36–8.

Lindle, J.C. (1989) 'What do parents want from principals and teachers?', *Educational Leadership*, October, 12–14.

Livneh, C. (1988) 'Characteristics of lifelong learners in the human service professions', *Adult Education Quarterly*, **38**(3), 149–59.

Livneh, C. and Livneh, H. (1988) 'Factors differentiating high and low participants in lifelong learning', *Educational and Psychological Measurement*, **48**, 637–46.

Long, H.B. (1983) *Adult and Continuing Education: Responding to Change*. New York: Teachers College Press.

Loucks, H. (1992) 'Increasing parent/family involvement', *NASSP Bulletin*, April, 19–23.

Lutz, C. (1994) 'Prospects of social cohesion in OECD countries' in OECD, *Societies in Transition: The Future of Work and Leisure*. Paris: OECD.

MacDowell, M.A. (1989) 'Partnerships: getting a return on the investment', *Educational Leadership*, October, 8–11.

Mackay, H. (1993) *Re-Inventing Australia*. Sydney: Collins Angus & Robertson.

Maclean, M. and Wadsworth, M.E.J. (1988) 'The interests of children after parental divorce: a long-term perspective', *International Journal of Law and Family*, **2**, 155–66.

Manning, M.L. (1995) 'Addressing young adolescents' cognitive development', *The High School Journal*, **78**(2), 98–104.

Marsick, V.J. (1990) 'Human service organizations as communities of learning' in M.W. Galbraith (ed.), *Education Through Community Organizations*. San Francisco: Jossey-Bass.

Maudsley, E. and Dee, L. (eds) (1994) *Redefining the Future*. London: The Institute of Education Press.

McCombs, B.L. (1991) 'Motivation and lifelong learning', *Educational Psychologist*, **26**(2), 117–27.

McCook, K. and Geist, P. (1993) *Toward a Just and Productive Society: An Analysis of the Recommendations of the White House Conference on Library and Information Services*. Washington, DC: National Commission on Libraries and Information Science.

McGaughey, J.L. (1992) 'Symbolic leadership: redefining relations with the host organisation', *New Directions for Adult and Continuing Education*, **56**, 39–50.

McGuire, F.A., Dottavio, F.D. and O'Leary, J.T. (1987) 'The relationship of early life experiences to later life leisure involvement', *Leisure Sciences*, **9**(4), 251–7.

McLaughlin, T.H. (1994) 'Politics, markets and schools: the central issues' in D. Bridges and T.H. McLaughlin (eds), *Education and the Market Place*. London: Falmer Press.

Mendus, S. (ed.) (1988) *Justifying Toleration: Conceptual and Historical Perspectives*. Cambridge: CUP.

Merenda, D.W. (1989) 'Partners in education: an old tradition renamed', *Educational Leadership*, October, 4–7.

Meyeroff, M.K. and White, B.L. (1986) 'New parents as teachers', *Educational Leadership*, November, 42–6.

Miller, K. (1993) 'Assisting our communities: critical awareness and self-direction', *Community Services Catalyst*, **23**(1), 13–15.

Miranda, S. and Giovkos, D. (1994) 'Relations with members of the community involved in culture, the arts and ethnic communities and other school welfare agencies with a responsibility in education'. Unpublished paper. University of Western Australia, Perth, 11 November.

Montandon, C. (1992) 'Parent–teacher relations in Genevan primary schools: some reasons for their mutual misunderstanding'. Paper presented at the Annual Meeting of AERA. April. San Francisco.

Moody, H.R. (1987–88) 'Introduction: late-life learning', *Generations*, **12**(2), 5–9.

Moon, B. and Shelton Mays, A. (1994) *Teaching and Learning in Secondary School*. London: Routledge.

Morgan, T.D. (1993) 'Technology: an essential tool for gifted and talented education', *Journal for the Education of the Gifted*, **16**(1), 358–71.

Morris, L. (1994) *Dangerous Classes: The Underclass and Social Citizenship*. London: Routledge.

National Art Education Association (1993) *Creating a Visual Arts Research Agenda Toward the 21st Century*. Reston, Va: Commission on Research in Art Education.

Neurath, O. (1932) 'Protokollsätze' *Erkenntnis*, **3**, 204–14.

Nixon, J., Martin, J., McKeown, P. and Ranson, S. (1996) *Encouraging Learning: Towards a Theory of the Learning School*. Buckingham: Open University Press.

Nordic Council of Ministers (1995) *The Golden Riches in the Grass – Lifelong Learning for All*.

Nuckolls, M.E. (1991) 'Expanding students' potential through family literacy', *Educational Leadership*, September, 45–6.

Oddi, L.F., Ellis, A.J. and Altman Robertson, J.E. (1990) 'Construct validity of the Oddi continuing learning inventory', *Adult Education Quarterly*, **40**(3), 139–45.

OECD (1989) *International Educational Indicators: An Overview of Conceptual Issues*. Paris: OECD.

OECD (1989) *Schools and Quality: An International Report*. Paris: OECD.

OECD (1991) *Learning to Think: Thinking to Learn*. Paris: OECD.

OECD (1992) *High Quality Education and Training for All*. Paris: OECD.

OECD (1993) *An Introduction to Learning: Re-Defining the Curriculum in a Life-long Perspective*. Paris: OECD/CERI Study (A5).

OECD (1993) *The Curriculum Re-Defined: Background Document*. March. Paris: OECD.

OECD (1993) 'Investment knowledge and knowledge investment'. Paper presented as part of the Education Committee's activity on *Further Education and Training as Investment*. Paris: OECD.

OECD/CERI (1993) *Learning Beyond Schooling*. (An expert meeting held in Tokyo, October.) Paris. OECD.

OECD (1994) *The Context of the Conference – Learning Beyond Schooling*. December. Paris: OECD.

OECD (1994) *The Curriculum Re-Defined: Education for the Twenty-First Century*. Paris: OECD.

OECD (1994) *Distance Education and the Internationalisation of Higher Education*. December. Paris: OECD.

OECD (1994) *The Effectiveness of Schooling and of Educational Resource Management*. Paris: OECD.

OECD (1994) 'The future of post-secondary education and the role of information and communication technology: a clarifying report'. Presented at the International Conference on 'Learning Beyond Schooling'. December. Paris: OECD.

OECD/CERI (1994) *Investment in Education and Economic Growth*. Paris: OECD/CERI.

OECD (1994) *Jobs Study: Facts, Analysis, Strategies*. Paris: OECD.

OECD (1994) *Learning Beyond Schooling: Clarifying Report*. December. Paris: OECD.

OECD (1994) *Learning Beyond Schooling–New Forms of Supply and Demand: Background Report*. December. Paris: OECD.

OECD (1994) 'Lifelong learning: from ideal to reality'. Paper presented at the International Conference on 'Learning Beyond Schooling'. December. Paris: OECD.

OECD (1994) 'Markets for learning and educational services: a micro-explanation of the role of education and development of competence in macro-economic growth'. Paper prepared as part of the OECD/CERI activity on 'Investment in Education and Economic Growth'. Paris: OECD.

OECD (1994) *Societies in Transition: The Future of Work and Leisure*. Paris: OECD.

OECD (1994) *Quality in Teaching*. Paris: OECD.

OECD (1994) 'The views and activities of stakeholders in the internationalisation of higher education'. Paper presented at the International Conference on 'Learning Beyond Schooling'. OECD/CERI. Part of the CERI Study *Education in the New International Setting*. December. Paris: OECD.

OECD (1994) *Vocational Education and Training for Youth: Towards a Coherent Policy and Practice*. Paris: OECD.

OECD/CERI (1994) *What Works in Innovation: The Assessment of School Performance*. Paris: OECD/CERI.

OECD (1994) *Women and Structural Change*. Paris: OECD.

OECD (1995) *Environmental Learning for the Twenty-First Century*. Paris: OECD.

OECD (1995) *Issues Paper and Background Report for the 1996 Ministerial Meeting*. Paris: OECD.

OECD (1995) *Literacy, Economy and Society*. Paris: OECD.

OECD (1995) *Schools for Cities*. Paris: OECD.

OECD (1996) *Education and Training: Learning and Working in a Society in Flux*. Paris: OECD.

OECD (1996) *Employment and Growth in the Knowledge-Based Economy*. Paris: OECD.

OECD (1996) *Lifelong Learning for All*. Meeting of the Education Committee at Ministerial Meeting, 16–17 January. Paris: OECD.

Oran, G.M. (1993) 'Meeting the challenge', *Preventing School Failure*, **38**(1), 5–6.

Orstein, A.C. (1994) 'Curriculum trends revisited', *Peabody Journal of Education*, **69**(4), 4–20.

Osborne, R.J. and Freyberg, P. (1985) *Learning in Science: The Implications of Children's Science*. London: Heinemann.

Packer, A.H. (1994) 'Meeting the arts standards and preparing for work in the 21st century', a pre-conference paper prepared for the 'Arts Education for the 21st Century American Economy' Conference, September 1994, Louisville, Ky.

Papadopoulos, G. (1994) 'Linkages: a new vision of vocational and technical education' in OECD *Vocational Education and Training for Youth: Towards a Coherent Policy of Practice*. Paris: OECD.

Passmore, J.P. (1967) 'On teaching to be critical' in R.S. Peters (ed.), *The Concept of Education*. London: Routledge & Kegan Paul.

Paterson, R.W.K. (1979) *Values, Education and the Adult*. London: Routledge & Kegan Paul.

Paterson, R.W.K. (1984) 'Objectivity as an educational imperative', *International Journal of Lifelong Education*, **3**(1), 17–29.

Pauly, E., Kopp, H. and Haimson, J. (1995) *Homegrown Lessons: Innovative Programs Linking School and Work*. New York: Jossey-Bass.

Peirce, C.S. (1955) *The Philosophical Writings of Peirce* (ed. J. Buckler). New York: Dover Publications.

Pelavin Associates (1993) *Educational Standards in OECD Countries: A Compilation of Survey Standards*. Washington, DC: US Department of Education.

Peña-Borrero, M. (1984) 'Lifelong educational and social change', *International Journal of Lifelong Education*, **3**(1), 1–15.

Peters, M. and Marshall, J.D. (1996) *Individualism and Community*. London: Falmer Press.

Peters, R.S. (1965) 'Education as initiation'. Inaugural lecture in the University of London 1963, repr. in *Authority, Responsibility and Education*. London: Allen & Unwin revised edn, 1973; also in R.D. Archambault (ed.), *Philosophical Analysis and Education*. London: Routledge & Kegan Paul, 1965.

Peters, R.S. (1966a) *Ethics and Education*. London: G. Allen & Unwin.

Peters, R.S. (1966b) 'The philosophy of education', Chapter 3 in W. Tibble (ed.), *The Study of Education*. London: Routledge & Kegan Paul.

Peters, R.S. (1967) 'What is an educational process?' in Peters (ed.), *The Concept of Education*. London: Routledge & Kegan Paul.

Peters, R.S. (1979) 'Democratic values and educational aims' in Peters, *Essays on Educators*. London: Allen & Unwin.

Phillips, D.C. (1971) 'The distinguishing features of forms of knowledge', *Educational Philosophy and Theory*, **3**(2), 27–35.

Popper, K.R. (1943) *The Open Society and its Enemies*. Vol. I: Plato, Vol. II: Hegel and Marx. London: Routledge & Kegan Paul.

Popper, K.R. (1949) *The Logic of Scientific Discovery*. London: Hutchinson.

Popper, K.R. (1960) *The Poverty of Historicism*. London: Routledge & Kegan Paul (2nd edn).

Popper, K.R. (1972) *Objective Knowledge*. Oxford: Clarendon Press.

Popper, K.R. (1989) *Conjectures and Refutations: The Growth of Scientific Knowledge*. London: Routledge (5th revised edn).

Powell, J.P. (1965) 'The idea of liberal education', *Australian University*, **3**, 1–18.

Powell, J.P. (1970) 'On justifying a broad educational curriculum', *Educational Philosophy and Theory*, **2**(1), 53–61.

Quine, W.V. (1951) 'Two dogmas of empiricism', *Philosophical Review*, **60**, 20–45.

Quine, W.V. (1953) *From a Logical Point of View*. Cambridge, Mass.: Harvard University Press.

Quine, W.V. (1974) *The Roots of Reference*. LaSalle: Open Court.

Quine, W.V. and Ullian, J.S. (1970) *The Web of Belief*. New York: Random House.

Raggatt, P., Edwards, R. and Small, N. (eds) (1996) *The Learning Society*. London: Routledge.

Raizen, S. (1994) 'Learning and work: the research base' in OECD, *Vocational Education and Training for Youth*. Paris: OECD.

Ranson, S. (1993) 'Markets or democracy for education', *British Journal of Educational Studies*, **XXXXI**(4), December, 333–52.

Ranson, S. (1994) *Towards the Learning Society*. London: Cassell.

Ratz, J. (1986) *The Morality of Freedom*. Oxford: Clarendon Press.

Rawls, J. (1972) *A Theory of Justice*. Oxford: Clarendon Press.

Renwick, W.L. (1994) 'The future of face-to-face and distance teaching in post-secondary teaching'. Paper presented at the International Conference on 'Learning Beyond Schooling'. December. Paris: OECD.

Rich, D. (1984) 'Helping parents help their children to learn', *Educational Leadership*, **80**.

Richardson, M.D. and Prickett, R.L. (1994) 'Recognizing how adults learn: implications for principals', *NASSP Bulletin*, January, 85–9.

Richmond, R.K. (1979) 'The concept of continuous education' in A.J. Cropley (ed.), *Lifelong Education: A Stocktaking*. Hamburg: VIE Monograph, No. 8.

Rigsby, L., Reynolds, M. and Wang, M. (eds) (1995) *School–Community Connections*. San Francisco: Jossey-Bass.

Rorty, R. (1979) *Philosophy and the Mirror of Nature*. Princeton, NJ: Princeton University Press.

Ross-Gordon, J.M. (1990) 'Serving culturally diverse populations: a social imperative for adult and continuing education' in J.M. Ross-Gordon, L.G. Martin and D.B. Briscoe (eds), *Serving Culturally Diverse Populations*. San Francisco: Jossey-Bass.

Rumberger, R. (1991) 'Labour market outcomes as indicators of educational performance'. Paper presented at General Assembly of the INES project 'International Education Indicators'. Lugano-Cadro. 16–18 September. Paris: OECD.

Saterlie, M.E. (1988) 'Developing a community consensus for teaching values', *Educational Leadership*, May, 44–7.

Schmidt, D. (1986) 'Parents and schools as partners in preschool education', *Educational Leadership*, November, 40–4.

Schuller, T. (1992) 'Age, gender and learning in the lifespan' in A. Tuijnman and M. Van Der Kamp (eds), *Learning Across the Lifespan: Theories, Research, Policies*. Oxford: Pergamon Press.

Schuller, T. and Bostyn, A.M. (1993) 'Learners of the future: preparing a policy for the third age', *Journal of Education Policy*, **8**(4), 365–79.

Schwebel, M., Maher, C.A. and Fagley, N.S. (1990) 'The social role in promoting cognitive growth over the life-span', *Prospects*, **20**(3), 263–75.

Scottish Education Office (1991) *Country Report*. Submitted to a meeting of country representatives on 'The effectiveness of schooling and of educational resource management'. Paris: OECD.

Seeley, D. (1989) 'A new paradigm for parent involvement', *Educational Leadership*, October, 46–8.

Sergiovanni, T.J. (1994) *Building Community in Schools*. San Francisco: Jossey-Bass.

Simons, P. (1992) 'Theories and principles of learning to learn' in A. Tuijnman and M. Van Der Kamp (eds), *Learning Across the Lifespan: Theories, Research, Policies*. Oxford: Pergamon Press.

Slaughter, R. (1996) *New Thinking for a New Millennium*. London: Routledge.

Smethurst, R. (1995) 'Education: a public or private good?', *RSA Journal*, **CXLIII**(5465), December, 33–45.

Smith, R.M. (1992) 'Implementing the learning to learn concept' in A. Tuijnman and M. Van Der Kamp (eds), *Learning Across the Lifespan: Theories, Research, Policies*. Oxford: Pergamon Press.

Smith, R.M. (1994) 'Learning to learn: adult education' in *Encyclopaedia of Educational Research*. Oxford: Pergamon Press.

Soren, B.J. (1993) 'Nurturing mind, spirit and a love of the arts and sciences: schools and cultural organisations as educators', *Studies in Art Education*, **34**(3), 149–57.

Stern, D., Finkelstein, N., Stone, J., Latting, J. and Dornsife, C. (1995) *School to Work*. London: Falmer Press.

Stevens, A.D. (1993) *Learning for Life Through Universal Themes. Literacy*

Improvement Series for Elementary Educators. Portland: Northwest Regional Education Lab.

Stevens, B. and Michalski, W. (1994) 'Long term prospects for work and social cohesion in OECD countries: An overview of the issues' in OECD, *Societies in Transition*. Paris: OECD.

Stewart, D. (1994) Introductory address at the First Global Conference on 'Life-long Learning'. December. Rome.

Stock, A.K. (1979) 'Developing lifelong education: developing post-school perspectives' in A.J. Cropley (ed.), *Lifelong Education: A Stocktaking*. Hamburg: VIE Monograph, No. 8.

Stock, A. (1993) *Lifelong Learning: Thirty Years of Educational Change*. Nottingham: Association for Lifelong Learning.

Strike, K.A. (1982) *Liberty and Learning*. Oxford: Martin Robertson.

Stuebing, S. (1995) *Re-defining the Place to Learn: A Study of Technology and the Design of Learning Environments*. Draft Document. Paris: OECD.

Suchodolski, B. (1979) 'Lifelong education at the cross-roads' in A.J. Cropley (ed.), *Lifelong Education: A Stocktaking*. Hamburg: VIE Monograph, No. 8.

Swain, J., Finkelstein, B., French, S. and Oliver, M. (1996) (eds) *Disabling Barriers: Enabling Environments*. London: Sage.

Swedish Report (1993) *A School for Life*. Paris: OECD.

Szymanski, E.M. (1994) 'Transition: life-span and life space consideration for empowerment', *Exceptional Children*, **60**(5), 402–10.

Tawney, R.H. (1938) *Equality* (3rd revised edn). London: Allen & Unwin.

Thorkildsen, T.A. (1995) 'Is there a right way to collaborate?' in J.G. Nicholls, and T.A. Thorkildsen (eds), *Reasons for Learning: Expanding the Conversation on Student–Teacher Collaboration*. New York: Teachers College Press.

Titmus, C.J. (ed.) (1989) *Lifelong Education for Adults: An International Handbook*. Oxford: Pergamon.

Trigg, R. (1973) *Reason and Commitment*. Cambridge: CUP.

Tuijnman, A. and Van Der Kamp, M. (1992) 'Learning for life: new ideas, new significance' in Tuijnman and Van Der Kamp (eds), *Learning Across the Lifespan: Theories, Research, Policies*. Oxford: Pergamon Press.

UNESCO (1996) *Learning: The Treasure Within*. Paris: UNESCO.

Vandegrift, J.A. and Greene A.L. (1992) 'Re-thinking parent involvement', *Educational Leadership*, September, 57–9.

Vermilye, D.W. (ed.) (1977) *Relating Work and Education*. San Francisco: Jossey-Bass.

Villa, R.A., Thousand, J.S., Stainback, W. and Stainback, S. (eds) (1992) *Restructuring for Caring and Effective Education: An Administrative Guide for Creating Heterogeneous Schools*. Baltimore: Paul H. Brookes Publishing.

Vincent, C. (1993) 'Education for the community?', *British Journal of Educational Studies* **XXXXI**(4), December, 361–79.

Wagner, T. (1995) 'What's school really for, anyway? And who should decide?', *Phi Delta Kappan*, **76**(5), 393–8.

Wain, K. (1984) 'Lifelong education: a Deweyan challenge', *Journal of Philosophy of Education*, **18**(2), 257–63.

Wain, K. (1985a) 'Lifelong education and philosophy of education', *International Journal of Lifelong Education*, **4**(2).

Wain, K. (1987) *Philosophy of Lifelong Education*. London: Croom Helm.

Wain, K. (1993a) 'Lifelong education: illiberal and repressive?', *Educational Philosophy and Theory*, **25**(1), 58–70.

Wain, K. (1993b) 'Lifelong education and adult education – the state of the theory', *International Journal of Lifelong Education*, **12**(2), 85–95.

Wain, K. (ed.) (1985b) *Lifelong Education and Participation*. Malta: University of Malta Press.

Walker, J.C. and Evers, C.W. (1982) 'Epistemology and justifying the curriculum of educational studies', *British Journal of Educational Studies*, **30**(2), 213–29.

Wanat, C.L. (1992) 'Meeting the needs of single-parent children: school and parent views differ', *NASSP Bulletin*, 43–8.

Warnock, M. (1978) *Schools of Thought*. London: Faber & Faber.

Watson, B. and Ashton, E. (1995) *Education, Assumptions and Values*. London: David Fulton Publishers.

Watt, A.J. (1975) 'Transcendental arguments and moral principles', *Philosophical Quarterly*, **XXV**, 40–57.

Wedermeyer, C.A. (1981) *Learning at the Back Door: Reflections on Non-Traditional Learning in the Lifespan*. Madison, Wis.: University of Wisconsin Press.

Weil, S.W. (1986) 'Non-traditional learners within traditional higher education institutions: discovery and disappointment', *Studies in Higher Education*, **11**(3), 219–35.

West, P. (1994) 'The learning organization: losing the luggage in transit?', *Journal of European Industrial Training*, **18**(11), 30–8.

Wheeler, P. (1992) 'Promoting parent involvement in secondary schools', *NASSP Bulletin*, October, 28–35.

Whitaker, P. (1995) *Managing to Learn*. London: Cassell.

White, J.P. (1973) *Towards a Compulsory Curriculum*. London: Routledge & Kegan Paul.

White, J.P. (1982) *The Aims of Education Re-Stated*. London: Routledge & Kegan Paul.

White, P.A. (1979) 'Work-place democracy and political education', *Journal of Philosophy of Education*, **13**, 5–20.

Williams, C.P. and Savickas, M.L. (1990) 'Developmental tasks of career maintenance', *Journal of Vocational Behaviour*, **36**(2), 166–75.

Williams, D.L. and Chavkin, N.F. (1989) 'Essential elements of strong parent involvement programs', *Educational Leadership*, October, 18–20.

Willis, P. (1991) 'Community education in Australia: reflections on an expanding field of practice', *Australian Journal of Adult and Community Education*, **31**(2), July, 71–87.

Wills, D. (1993) 'Learning and assessment: exposing the inconsistencies of theory and practice', *Oxford Review of Education*, **18**(3), 383–402.

Winch, P.G. (1972) *Ethics and Action*. London: Routledge & Kegan Paul.

Wisniewski, E.J. (1995) 'Prior knowledge and functionally relevant features in concept learning', *Journal of Experimental Psychology: Learning, Memory and Cognition*, **21**(2), 449–68.

Wittgenstein, L. (1953) *Philosophical Investigations* (trans. G.E.M. Anscombe). Oxford: Basil Blackwell.

Wittgenstein, L. (1968) *Preliminary Studies for the Philosophical Investigations* (also known as *The Blue and Brown Books*) Oxford: Blackwell.

Wolf, J.S. and Stephens, T.M. (1989) 'Parent/teacher conferences: finding common ground', *Educational Leadership*, October, 28–31.

Woods, P. (1988) 'A strategic view of parent participation', *Journal of Education Policy*, **3**(4), 323–34.

Wringe, C. (1984) *Democracy, Schooling and Political Education*. London: Routledge & Kegan Paul.

Wringe, C.A. (1994) 'Markets, values and education' in D. Bridges and T.H McLaughlin (eds), *Education and the Market Place*. London: Falmer Press.

Za'rour, G.I. (1984) 'Continuing education: a challenge and a commitment', *International Journal of Lifelong Education*, **3**(1), 31–9.

Index